Photography and Writing in Latin America

PHOTOGRAPHY and WRITING in LATIN AMERICA

Double Exposures

Edited by

MARCY E. SCHWARTZ

and

MARY BETH TIERNEY-TELLO

UNIVERSITY OF NEW MEXICO PRESS

ALBUQUERQUE

Printed in the United States of America
10 09 08 07 06   1 2 3 4 5

Library of Congress Cataloging-in-Publication Data

Photography and writing in Latin America : double exposures /
[edited by] Marcy E. Schwartz and Mary Beth Tierney-Tello.
p. cm.
Includes bibliographical references and index.
ISBN-13: 978-0-8263-3808-2 (pbk. : alk. paper) ISBN-10: 0-8263-3808-9 (pbk. : alk. paper)
1. Literature and photography—Latin America—History. 2. Photography—Latin America—Influence. 3. Photography—Latin America—History. 4. Latin American literature—History and criticism. I. Schwartz, Marcy E., 1958– II. Tierney-Tello, Mary Beth, 1961–
TR183.P485 2006
770.98—dc22
2005025892

COVER ILLUSTRATION:
Eugenio Dittborn Chilean b.1943
The 7th History of the Human Face (the Scenery of the Sky), Airmail Painting No. 78, 1989
paint, fluorescent paint, metallic paint, screenprint, chalk,
thread on spunbonded polyester fabric; 214.0 x 141.0 cm each.
Art Gallery of Ontario, Toronto; Gift from the Volunteer Committee Fund, 1997

ITINERARY
1. Eugenio Dittborn, Santiago, Chile, March 1990
2. Transcontinental, Ikon Gallery, Birmingham, England, March–April 1990
3. Instituto de Cooperación Iberoamericano, I.C.I., Buenos Aires, Argentina, Nov.–Dec. 1991
4. Latin American Artists of the XXth Century, (MOMA), Estación Plaza de Armas, Seville, Spain, Aug.–Oct. 1992
5. Latin American Artists of the XXth Century, (MOMA), Hôtel des Arts, Paris, France, Dec.–Jan. 1992–93
6. Latin American Artist of the XXth Century, (MOMA), Ludwig Museum, Cologne, Germany, March–April 1993
7. La Casa de Erasmo de Rotterdam, Witte de Wiyh, Rotterdam, Holland, Dec.–Jan. 1993–94
8. Alexander and Bonin, New York, USA, Oct.–Nov. 1996
9. Art Gallery of Ontario, Ontario, Canada, July 1997

DESIGN AND COMPOSITION: Mina Yamashita

Contents

Illustrations

Acknowledgments

We gratefully acknowledge Wheaton College and Rutgers University for their support for photographs in several chapters.

We gratefully acknowledge Hiram College, and the Michael Dively Faculty Publication Fund, for their support for the photographs in chapter 3.

We would like to express our appreciation to the Wheaton College Art Department and especially to Christin Ronolder for her help with the reproduction of many of the photographs.

Our deepest gratitude goes to our families for their support during the course of this project. Special thanks to Rick, Sam, Abbie, Guillermo, Nicolas, and Liam.

Introduction

Marcy E. Schwartz and Mary Beth Tierney-Tello

> *Out of language, one can make scientific discourse, bureaucratic memoranda, love letters, grocery lists, and Balzac's Paris. Out of photography, one can make passport pictures, weather photographs, pornographic pictures, X-rays, wedding pictures, and Atget's Paris.*
>
> —Susan Sontag, *On Photography*

Despite the opposition and tension that critics such as Sontag note between writing and photography, the two modes of expression have a long history of partnership, particularly in Latin America. While Sontag's Parisian-oriented comment may seem an odd beginning for a book on Latin America, in fact her consideration of visual and verbal products in the context of urban modernity resonates on both sides of the Atlantic. As an Anglo-American cultural critic who takes on photography as an anthropological as well as an aesthetic phenomenon of contemporary culture, she is highly aware of the continuing colonialism of the European gaze. If Balzac and Atget evoke the historical and geographical beginnings of verbal and visual modernity, *Photography and Writing in Latin America* moves south to celebrate manifestations of words and images as they join forces in Latin America in ways that directly problematize the region's post-colonial, violent, and conflicted relationship with Europe and the United States. Yet *Photography and Writing in Latin America* examines Latin America's relationship with cultural and political powers abroad only as a point of departure, shifting focus to autonomous literary and artistic production that emerges from local and regional photographic currents.

This is the first book to document the extensive collaboration between writers and photographers in Latin America from the Mexican Revolution through the twentieth century. Some of these projects are explicitly collaborative exhibits with their catalogues, others involve writing that champions photography, and still others address photographers who have visually documented writers. Rather than mechanistic captioning and nostalgic visual biographies, the collaborations documented here represent dialogues, often friendships, from shared political and aesthetic positions. These powerful interartistic exchanges include collaborative books, catalogues, exhibits, demonstrations, and graphic art installations. *Photography and Writing in*

Latin America uncovers the charged encounters and aesthetic tensions between text and image in the context of these collaborations, bringing into focus the distinct artistic and ethical properties of verbal and visual representation. These projects offer sites for considering the ways in which relationships between visual and verbal representations have become so important in our visually saturated culture.

The contributors to this volume offer new perspectives from cultural, literary, and historical studies of verbal and visual exchange in Latin America in the twentieth century. These collaborations of photography and writing go beyond responding to and documenting contemporary multimedia realities. In fact they are the legacy of European New World exoticism, expansion, and colonization and reflect the consequent policies of racist discrimination and social marginalization that independence in the nineteenth century institutionalized within a discourse of otherness. A reliance on both the verbal and the visual became and remains one of the representational strategies in the continuing quest for autonomous cultural identification in a postcolonial context.

This introduction aims to provide a brief historical and cultural frame for understanding the persistent conjugation of the visual and the verbal in Latin American cultural expression. In his book *Picture Theory*, W. J. T. Mitchell examines the "pictorial turn" in contemporary culture, noting that it entails the "realization that *spectatorship* (the look, the gaze, the glance, the practices of observation, surveillance, and visual pleasure) may be as deep a problem as various forms of *reading* (decipherment, decoding, interpretation, etc.)" (16). Because most of the contributors to the present volume approach this topic from literature and cultural studies, we recognize and seek to account for the pictorial turn in our own work and the writing we study. We assume a broad spectrum of readers, some accustomed to the analysis of verbal representation, others specialized in the visual. We address the pictorial first, beginning with an exploration of the presence of the photographic image in Latin America, particularly the sociopolitical and aesthetic conditions that have determined and shaped photographic practice in the region. We then take up writing and the relationship between the visual and the verbal, surveying some of the hybrid works that combine both forms of representation from colonial times to the present. Overall, as we explore in the final section of the introduction, our objective is not to attempt to present an exhaustive analysis of the vast field of verbal-visual relations in Latin American culture, but rather to map out the historical and discursive conditions that have produced and sustained their dynamic interaction.

Photography and the Legacy of the Visual

Photography came to Latin America early in its technological development, and has been an essential tool for documenting the region's physical spaces and encounters among varied cultures. The exhibition and catalogue *Image and Memory: Photography from Latin America 1966–1994*, documents Latin America's charged relationship with the medium, highlighting recent photographic work together with histories of visual documentation across the vast region. As *Image and Memory* makes clear in its photographs and essays, during the nineteenth century numerous European experimenters with the new visual medium traveled and tested their techniques in Latin America, particularly in Brazil, which hosted several early naturalist photographers. Indeed in his essay in the volume, Latin American photohistorian Boris Kossoy traces photography's "multiple paternities" through French artist Antoine Hércules Romuald Florence, who settled in the province of São Paulo in the 1830s. He reproduced images on glass plates before Daguerre, and coined the term "photographie" (23).

Fascination with the region's visual uniqueness on the part of colonial explorers, European surrealists, ethnographic transcribers, and testimonial documentarists has contributed to the representation of Latin America as "other." Not only have foreign photographers pictured Latin America from the outside, but local photographers have also documented their own views, often drawing attention to the encounters and clashes of multiple cultural practices in a colonial or post-colonial context (Zamora 299–301).

As Nelly Richard mentions in her interview for this volume, photography began in Latin America as a technical resource but soon became a "theoretical figure," that is to say, a rhetorical and ideological strategy. Transformed into a medium with potent ideological capacities, photography projects the desire for otherness from abroad, captures the struggles of political independence and revolution, and records the progression toward cultural autonomy through both journalistic and artistic expression. Clearly photography has been manipulated as an instrument of the state while it has also served as a strategy of resistance. The use of photography in relation to the state and citizenship in Latin America falls into three general functional categories: recording ethnography, imposing surveillance, and documenting human rights abuses. In each category the critical dynamics of racism and marginality reveal how the manipulation of the photographic medium intersects with political power and resistance.

Since photography's inception, European ethnographers have turned their eye to the New World in order to document their "others," mostly for the purposes of European self-definition and to satisfy a hunger for the "exotic." As Kossoy points out, the *costumbrista* photography by Europeans of indigenous populations and those of African descent reveals the "idealized, caricatured, preconceived" notions that not only exoticized Latin America's cultural diversity but also justified and perpetuated the region's economic system of slave labor and oppression (41). The importation and establishment of photographic conventions from Europe therefore presented challenges as Latin Americans made efforts to reappropriate the medium and develop their own visual discourses for aesthetic, historiographic, commercial, and political ends. According to Kossoy, by the second half of the nineteenth century, photography had become the "mandatory medium" not only for landscape documentation and rural ethnography, but also for visually capturing urban modernization (such as the growth of the rail system and architecture) in order to project a new image abroad (37). Photography was also relied upon to document war and social conflict.

With a growing middle class, portrait photography in nineteenth- and twentieth -century Latin America became not only a mode of self-representation but also a way to tout a family's prosperity and fulfill class aspirations. In his book *Images of History: Nineteenth and Early Twentieth Century Latin American Photographs as Documents*, Robert Levine discusses the inherited conventions of portrait posing in early Latin American photography. In particular, he laments the lack of candid or spontaneous photos (even questioning how candid or spontaneous they might be when they seem less posed):

> The posed world created by photographers in nineteenth- and early twentieth-century Latin America consisted of subjects framed according to conventionally accepted ways of seeing. Studio poses provided the sitter a special space . . . a *picture*, that approximates his own as well as his society's ideal. (147)

Kossoy concurs, tracing the success of the *carte de visite* and noting that Latin Americans chose European attire and poses for their portraits (35). The Andeanist anthropologist Deborah Poole points out, however, that while the appropriation of such conventions on the part of the middle classes in the Andes became a vehicle to distinguish themselves from what they saw as the uncultured, racially "inferior" Indian masses, portraits of peasant families "seem to dismantle and subvert the framing devices inherent in studio photography" (213). In her book *Vision, Race and Modernity: A Visual Economy of the Andean Image World*, Poole reassesses the visual cultures and racial politics in the Andes from a critical perspective. Portraits of working-class and peasant subjects, she argues, "reroute and resist" the imposed conventions of framing and the pose (213).

Throughout the twentieth century and into the twenty-first, the legacy of the foreignizing ethnographic gaze remains, and the work of contemporary photographers continues to register resistance and contestation in forging a new visual language for the region. The paradox of ethnographic photography, even by photographers within Latin America, and even when these projects are not oriented directly by a

European gaze, is that it involves inherent racism and repressive politics, aspects discussed by many analysts. As Marina Pérez de Mendiola explains in a recent article on photography, ethnicity, and citizenship in Mexico,

> [t]he paradox lies, on the one hand, in the glorification of indigenous culture, and on the other, in the pathologization and erasure from civil society of the bodies producing this culture. (128)

Esther Gabara, in her chapter here, calls this process of idealizing the indigenous population "monumentalizing." She contends that rather than achieving any political or economic gain, this photographic monumentalization "freezes the indigenous communities in an inactive past, denying them political representation, human rights, and active benefits of citizenship." Nevertheless, in the context of such highly politicized productions, Deborah Poole's work on the Andean visual economy shows that pleasure and the aesthetics of looking make the workings of imperial or colonial power unpredictable and highly complex (17–20).

In the twentieth century, many Latin American states began using a different type of "portrait," the photo-ID card (*carnet*), to catalogue and identify their citizens for purposes of surveillance and social control. As Nelly Richard describes in her interview here, Chilean artists in the *avanzada* movement, such as Eugenio Dittborn, worked with these identity-card photos in various projects that denounce "the repressive grammar of the pose." She elaborates that "[u]nder dictatorship, the procedures for capturing and detaining a self in the prison of ID cards were analogous to the daily violations of identity undergone by Chilean citizens." Even as the state strove to document and control its populace, in part through the photography of identification cards, some citizens, in the face of human rights abuses and civil strife, sought to leverage photography's "truth value" as proof and evidence in a quest to document, denounce, or rectify such violence and trauma. In marches and demonstrations against this political violence, the same identity photos reappear enlarged on placards carried by mothers, grandmothers, wives, and sisters of the disappeared, particularly in Chile and Argentina. As Nelly Richard and Mary Beth Tierney-Tello mention in their contributions to this volume, the surveillance of the state through identity photographs is undermined when citizens fight back, using those very documents to counter dictatorship's dehumanizing tactics, through what Richard calls "the disidentification of signs."

Finally, art photography, while certainly not as prevalent as in European countries or in the United States, became increasingly important in Latin America in the twentieth century. Even then, however, experimental and art photography was displaced by the politically resonant, documentary photography that, through curatorial choices and official sponsorship, came to define Latin American photography in general (Fernando Castro 69). Anita Brenner's work, as Elissa Rashkin discusses in her chapter here, helped launch photography in Mexico as an art form, at the same time that her work used photography in the service of indigenous cultural survival. As documentation that is simultaneously an art form, Brenner's project repositioned the status of the photograph and of visual ethnography. Nevertheless, as Castro points out, recognition of aesthetically preoccupied photography increased in the 1980s; indeed, in the latter part of the twentieth century, photographic experimentation flourished among Latin American visual artists. The acceptance of such photography, that is, work that eschewed a strictly documentary, politically charged style, has been crucial in widening restrictive notions regarding what is distinctive about Latin American photography. As Castro concludes,

> [o]ne of the challenges for some Latin American photographers has been to adequately depict the vestiges of ancient indigenous cultures without falling prey to exoticism. Another challenge is its converse: how to capture the modern and postmodern urban culture of Latin America. (85)

The work of Jack and Pablo Delano in Puerto Rico and the United States is exemplary in this regard, straddling the divide between documentary and aesthetic vision.

The influence of photography on other art forms has also been substantial, from the Mexican muralists who relied on archival photographs for some of their images, to more contemporary self-portraiture (Poniatowska "Some Women Photographers" 48). Contemporary visual artists, such as New York-based Argentine Liliana Porter, combine photography with video work and silk-screen printing, in order to question the ontological status of the object represented as cultural icon as well as semiotic signifier. Eugenio Dittborn sums up the impact of photography in one of his artist books, recently exhibited at the Museum of Modern Art in New York:

> El pintor debe sus trabajos al cuerpo de la fotografía, embalsamado en y por la fotocopia, depósito de los despojos fotográficos. Debe sus trabajos a la intervención de la fotocopia, sobre la fotografía, intervención que automáticamente empalidece, calcina, perfora, yoda, drena, congestiona, fragiliza, deshidrata, reviene . . . y erosiona la corteza del cuerpo fotográfico preservándolo destruido. (n.p.)
>
> (The painter owes his works to the body of photography, embalmed in and by the photocopy, repository of photography's cast-offs. He owes his works to the intervention of the photocopy

> overtaking the photograph, intervention that automatically pales, calcinates, perforates, iodizes, drains, clogs, weakens, dehydrates, shrinks . . . and erodes the shell of the photographic body preserving it destroyed.)

While Benjamin reconceptualizes history through the technological advancements and reproductive nature of photography, Dittborn identifies photography as the aesthetic machine motivating contemporary art.

Writing and its Dialogue with the Visual

To more fully understand verbal-visual interactions in the context of Latin American culture in the twentieth century, it is useful to return to prephotographic word and image expression, such as the Mesoamerican codices and Guamán Poma de Ayala's *Nueva corónica y buen gobierno* (1615). These texts capture the encounter between European and indigenous cultures in striking combinations of verbal and visual signs. As Mesoamerican languages did not employ phonetic alphabets, the intersecting sign systems of indigenous logographs, Christian emblems, and Spanish chronicling created their own hybrid discourse. Guamán Poma's verbal account of Incan life is supported by drawings depicting the everyday customs of indigenous people and their mode of governance. A colonial view of Andean life, but from the other, colonized side, Poma de Ayala writes as a *criollo* striving to bridge his two cultures and world views (biblical Christian on his father's side, ruling-class Incan on his mother's). The reliance on both visual and verbal registers is one of the hallmarks of his work. Announcing the complexity of semiotic negotiation in Latin America, Guamán Poma became a precursor of the varied projects considered in this volume, long before the technological possibilities of photography.

Hybrid texts of words and images continue to emerge in Latin America and provide further insight into the intensity of verbal-visual culture. In nineteenth-century Mexico, for example, the artistic production of José Guadalupe Posada (1852–1913) consistently combined text and image in popular graphic prints and broadsides. Best known for his *calavera* (skeleton) figures, Posada enjoyed only modest fame during his lifetime but was rediscovered by the muralists in the 1920s and is considered the precursor of the famous Taller de Gráfica Popular (Popular Graphics Workshop), founded in 1937. Posada defined and established a style of popular illustration with verbal narrative that affected Mexican popular graphic art for the rest of the twentieth century.

Where Posada's work stems from popular political satire and the folkloric, other examples of such hybrid works draw on the religious and the propagandistic realms in their artistic expression. The popular Mexican *retablos* (ex-votos), small religious paintings on tin, incorporated both text and image in order to make the religious sentiments they represent accessible to all. More recently, Puerto Rican graphic artist Lorenzo Homar (1913–) has produced posters, illustrations of *plena* lyrics, and linoleum prints in order to advertise artistic events, reproduce regional legends, and offer political critique. An introduction to one of his books of political caricatures, *Aquí en la lucha, caricaturas*, quotes him exclaiming, "¡Si yo pudiera escribir!" (If only I could write!) (n.p.).[1] Homar consciously engages with language in his visual practice, as a recent exhibition and catalogue of his poster art confirms with its title, *Abrapalabra: la letra mágica: carteles, 1951–1999*. Such combinations of the visual and the verbal in popular cultural products underscore questions of literacy and representation, which have been consistent challenges as Latin American countries have attempted to construct a national identity and culture from the nineteenth century onward.

Such popular art forms necessarily arise from the clash and meshing of cultures that quite uniquely characterizes "Latin America." Manifestations of hybridity have become the focus of recent analyses of Latin American culture, such as Néstor García Canclini's now canonical *Culturas híbridas: estrategias para entrar y salir de la modernidad* (1989) and many reconsiderations of the colonial period. García Canclini's theory of hybridity proposes more fluid and less dichotomized notions of the "modern" and the "traditional," "local" and "cosmopolitan," "high" and "popular" culture as the basis for understanding Latin American cultural production and consumerism. His examples of verbal-visual images include, for example, the superimposing message of neon signs and nationalistic monuments in public space or the intersection of print and television culture when writers are interviewed on the screen. He celebrates the "impure art" of visual artists who consciously draw on and mix together images and conventions from art history, popular culture, and mass media. In these contemporary examples of hybridity, the combination of the visual and the verbal demonstrates the highly functional and persistent role of visual culture in Latin America

While hybrid cultural products certainly give us benchmarks for understanding a genealogy of Latin American visual-verbal culture, photography infiltrated the Latin American literary imagination very early on. Photography as a theme has played a significant role in Latin American fiction beginning in the early twentieth century, in texts that do not reproduce images but evoke them for a variety of purposes. Serving as a sign of modernity, a catalyst for the fantastic, or documentary evidence, allusion to photographs forms the narrative axis in fiction by Leopoldo Lugones, Adolfo Bioy Casares, Jorge Luis Borges, Angélica Gorodischer, Julio Cortázar, and Mario Vargas Llosa. Although the reader never *sees* the photographs, their presence motivates conflict and mystery and provides insight into some of the dilemmas provided by a medium that is at once a representation of reality and a part of that reality as well (Sontag 4). Ursula K. Le Guin's introduction to the English version of *Antología de la literatura fantástica (The Book of Fantasy)*, the anthology of fantastic short stories edited by Borges, Silvina Ocampo, and Bioy Casares (first published in Spanish in 1940), reminds us that the term *fantasy* comes from the Greek and means "to make visible" and in English came to mean the imagination: "the result of forming mental representations of things not actually present" (9). Photographs enter the fantastic not only through the very "magical" process of shooting and developing but also, as Barthes eloquently relates in *La chambre claire (Camera Lucida)*, through making present people who have died. At the beginning of Borges's famous story "The Aleph," the narrator evokes numerous photographs of Beatriz, a nostalgic reminiscence after her death that provides a prelude to the fantastic experience of visualizing the Aleph in the family's basement. Photographic phenomena play a similarly haunting role in Lugones's story "Hipalia," where a photograph-like image gradually appears on a basement wall and sucks the life out of a beautiful young girl. The description of photographs points out absence due not only to death. The family portrait in Gorodischer's story "Cámara oscura" ("Camera obscura") is at the center of the conflict between husband and wife, as the narrator retells the saga of his grandmother running away with an itinerant photographer.

Lugones, Borges, and Bioy Casares share a fascination with the scientific processes of photography, from capturing images with the lens to fixing them on a surface. In their fantastic narratives they link "modern" photography to ancient, magical quasi-religious rites or even the occult. Lugones's stories "Un fenómeno inexplicable" ("An Inexplicable Phenomenon") and "Los ojos de la reina" ("The Queen's Eyes") reveal the anxieties of mechanical reproduction. In Borges's "La otra muerte" ("The Other Death"), the photograph of a ghost unleashes a contest of competing representations. Visual reproduction as a means of accessing immortality becomes a paradox in Adolfo Bioy Casares's *La invención de Morel* (*The Invention of Morel*). In order to live for eternity in the presence of his imaginary lover, the protagonist eventually has himself photographed by a fantastical holographic "machine," even though it will mean his own demise, thus dramatizing the ambiguous status of a photographic image as intimately tied with death yet simultaneously promising immortality.

Short stories are analogous to photographs for Cortázar, as circumscribed vestiges of captured reality, "lo siempre asombroso de los cuentos contra el reloj" ("the always astonishing nature of antitemporal stories") ("Del cuento breve" 61).[2] His story "Las babas del diablo" ("Blow-Up") is probably the best-known Latin American text where photography has a protagonistic role. In this story, on which Antonioni based his film *Blow-Up*, an enlargement of a candid photograph in a Paris square causes the photographer to reinterpret the scene before him and realize how his shooting the picture has become part of the drama. In a later story by Cortázar, "Apocalipsis de Solentiname," slides taken on a trip to Nicaragua of naif-style indigenous paintings surprise the protagonist with scenes of torture and violence once they are projected on a screen and viewed back in Europe. Photography similarly plays a pivotal role in Mario Vargas Llosa's *El hablador*. The narrative is set in motion when the protagonist comes upon an exhibit of photographs of an indigenous community living in a remote part of the Peruvian jungle.

It should come as no surprise, given the imaginative territory of the photographic in Latin America and the rich panorama of fictional elaborations just outlined, that collaborative endeavors between photographers and writers in the region have been so frequent and fruitful. Projects of exchange between Latin American writers and photographers throughout the twentieth century have produced testimonials, documentaries, historical commentaries, ethnographies, poetic texts, and fiction. These cooperative ventures comment on mourning and memory, document revolution, redefine *indigenismo*, and characterize the explosion of urban space in their specific Latin American contexts. In such collaborative works, combining text with photographs causes the reader, the photographer, and the writer to reflect more critically on both the visual and the verbal as means of representation, contributing to wider debates on the underlying politics of representation. The relationship between verbal and visual representation in these projects dramatizes the particular ethical and political properties of each mode while they reflect their historical and social context. As our analysis demonstrates, whether a response to violence and loss or a reaffirmation of forgotten members of society, these projects choose to integrate the visual and the verbal rather than privilege one over the other.

Most of the projects *Photography and Writing in Latin America* discusses involve narrative rather than verse. While decorative, biographical books whose purpose is largely referential and nostalgic and collections of "illustrated" poetry do not enter into our consideration in this volume, examples of dialogue between poetry and photography abound. Pablo Neruda is perhaps the poet best known in Latin America for his fascination with photography. Argentine photographer Sara Facio has included him in many portraiture endeavors, most recently producing the exhibition and book *Geografía*. Guillermo Tejeda's book *Los disfraces de Neruda* (Neruda's disguises) takes the poet's experimentation with the visual mode even further, documenting a performed self through the (dis)play of disguises and costumes that contests the poetic and political biography most associated with the celebrated poet.[3]

Contemporary visual artists from Latin America exploit the verbal medium while experimental poets force their work to intersect with visual codes. Chilean poet Cecilia Vicuña incorporates photography into her poetry in order to question the process of representation and to deconstruct the very activity of writing. As Jill

Kuhnheim states in *Spanish American Poetry at the End of the 20th Century*, Vicuña expands her experimental aesthetic by "persistently shifting between literary and visual realms, defying preconceived categories, and questioning the authority of the word" (58). Uruguayan visual artist Luis Camnitzer manipulates photography with verbal messages in order to heighten the irony of his work. Kuhnheim comments on how he "brings together the verbal and the visual, not to illustrate or explain, but to create an interdependent context. . . . Neither image nor language make meaning explicit, but rather complicate any easy access to meaning" (64). The celebrated Chilean poet Raúl Zurita also incorporates visual elements in his poetry. Playing with authorial control, his intertextual experiments with self-portraits and visual inscriptions extend the boundaries of poetic space. His photos of desert writing, included in *La vida nueva*, and of sky writing, in the same collection as well as in *Anteparaíso*, are perhaps the best-known examples. Like Vicuña, Zurita intermixes the modern techniques of photographic reproduction with archaic writing practices in order to question the permanence of aesthetic productions such as books and to nurture the fragile hope of democracy after the dictatorship in Chile. His representations of writing through this variety of media "all draw attention to the material importance of signifiers, and remind us, in a world dominated by visible commodities, that neither word nor image is transparent" (Kuhnheim 79).

Among the prominent writers whose work has been especially affected by photography, Juan Rulfo stands out as a well-respected photographer in his own right. Rulfo's photography of Jalisco has been celebrated in exhibitions and catalogues. Often calling himself a photographer before a writer, his stunning landscapes and portraits indirectly illustrate his writing. Further enmeshing Rulfo's narrative with photographic images, a recent edition of the English translation of his novel *Pedro Páramo* has been published with a selection of photographs by Chicana photographer Josephine Sacabo, from her series "The Unreachable World of Susana San Juan: Homage to Juan Rulfo."

Fiction that involves photographs within the text itself, such as Belgrano Rawson's *Fuegia*, discussed here by Magdalena Perkowska-Álvarez, constitutes another genre of collaborative work that has been particularly inventive in recent years. Like the international best-seller W. G. Sebald, contemporary Latin American fiction writers exploit the visual within narrative genres to pursue issues of racism, problematize historical documentation, and highlight family trauma.[4] Peruvian writer Miguel Gutiérrez has published two novels with photographs by Julio Olavarría. The narrative of *La destrucción del reino* (1992), for example, revolves around a series of posed, black-and-white photographs taken in the ruins of an hacienda in Northern Peru of a young child whose face is covered with a veil. In *El mundo sin Xóchitl* (2001), Gutiérrez uses colored photographs by the same photographer as a point of departure for his narrative about an incestuous relationship between a brother and sister, representing the decaying Peruvian oligarchy. In the Mexican context, writer Margo Glantz published an autobiographical novel, *Las genealogías* (1981) as well as a book of criticism on Sor Juana Inés de la Cruz that both incorporate photographs. Diamela Eltit's novel *Lumpérica* includes photographs of the author with self-inflicted knife wounds, in order to underscore the pain and repression of the public and to lay bare society's inscriptions on the body.

The multimedia nature of these kinds of projects challenges the boundaries of each mode of expression. The motivation that brings together the verbal and the visual in such cases calls for an approach different from art history, an interpretation that is more interactive and intimate. Rather than accounting for the visual by writing about it, at a critical distance, from a historical or aesthetic position, these projects make demands not only on the reader-observer but also on each medium. Elissa Rashkin, in this volume, reveals in her discussion of the "fissures" in Anita Brenner's work how photography both documents art and is an art form of its own. Brenner relies on the anthropological method of notation for captioning images, but the shifting categories of "artist" versus "artisan" within the context of modernity complicate her stance. Esther Gabara, in her chapter here, calls attention to the "constant crossover" between photojournalism and art photography, as well as between "documentary" and artistic endeavors. Elena Poniatowska's career as both journalist and creative writer further confounds any rigid characterization. Her many collaborations with photographers and her hybrid fiction (Perkowska-Álvarez calls her novel *Tinísima* a biographical novel, and many critics consider *Hasta no verte Jesús mío* a testimonial novel) employ interviews, photography, personal correspondence, and fictitious invention. Photography is more than a technique or a documentary support for Poniatowska, who exploits it as yet another discursive strategy in her writing. As Leo Cabranes-Grant comments in this volume, the intersecting spaces of the visual and the verbal create "liminal areas where photos and words challenge each other."

The verbal texts in these projects are not accompaniments, captions, or explanations, but rather "serve to express the literary possibilities and limitations of the fixed image." Dan Russek makes this comment in his discussion of Tomás Eloy Martínez's *La novela de Perón*, a novel obsessed with photography but whose editions include no photographs.[5] Even when only an ekphrastic presence, according to Russek, photography exploits "the fuzzy limits between literary writing, journalistic research, and historical knowledge." Mary Beth Tierney-Tello, in chapter 4 of this volume, investigates marginalized and victimized communities in projects that reassert not only a testimonial voice but combat the facelessness of repression, isolation, forgetting, and violence. While the testimonial genre is known for its efforts in giving a voice to those who are silenced, the integration of photographs accents new aspects of this political move.[6] Tierney-Tello states that "[t]he testimonial, documentary impulse, the desire to provide a 'certificate of presence,' is at the heart of both text and photo." The testimonial inclusion of photographs functions as a strategy of consciousness raising and political urgency along with its more conventional, journalistic provision of evidence. Similarly, the inclusion or exclusion of captions with visual images affects the work's reception. Susan Meiselas's photodocumentary work, as Janis Breckenridge underscores in chapter 3 here, plays with captioning and silence in order to expose the origins and causes of political violence in Central America. Whether for testimonial immediacy, historical memory, narrative, or poetic intertextuality, photographs *encourage* verbalization, according to the contributors here, whereby they motivate narratives, problematize their stories, and defy the visual conventions of portraiture, documentary, and journalism.

While the hybrid qualities of these endeavors may seem to suggest a fusion or blending of discursive modes, in fact these projects are built around a disruptive tension that invigorates both their verbal and visual dimensions. As Perkowska-Álvarez asserts regarding Belgrano Rawson's *Fuegia*, the photographs in the novel *do not* serve as extratextual documents of authenticity or realism, but rather call into question the process of representation itself. The dissonance and even incompatibility between the visual and verbal texts generate arguments against interpretation and passive commentary and push the reader-observer to enter into new territories of expression. For example, Julio Cortázar, in the project Marcy Schwartz examines in chapter 5, scarcely mentions the Indian observatory that appears in each of the more than sixty photographs in his book, narrating a sort of competing and what at first appears disconnected essay on the migration of eels. While closer analysis reveals the associations between the images and the essay, the book toys with the reader's expectations in order to critique Western conventions of representation. The dissonance and tensions between text and image can often be integral to the representative strategies of such collaborative, hybrid works. As W. J. T. Mitchell explains, what resists a fluidity of exchange between text and photograph is often at the crux of how and what such combinations can signify (*Picture Theory* 285).

Double Exposure: Writing with the Visual

The book's four parts highlight political resistance, urban space, narrative experimentation with the visual, and interviews, respectively. In the first part, Writing and Picturing Revolution and Resistance, essays review the varied roles of photography in the context of revolution and violence in Latin America. Contributors examine the role of photographic documentation of the Mexican Revolution, early twentieth-century Mexican modernism, and the more recent state-sponsored violence in Central America and Chile. In each case, the authors examine the ways in which visual photographic representations have been key instruments of identification, interpretation, memory, and resistance. Part two, Refocusing the Urban, discusses how collaborative projects have redefined conceptions of urban space in Latin America. From projects that account for the urban explosion of Mexico City to Julio Cortázar's attack on the compromised position of the city in writing culture, these contributions engage the inextricable roles of visual expression and writing in rendering urban realities. Photography as a product of European urban industrialization established an aesthetic tradition practiced by photographers such as Atget. The chapters by Gabara and Schwartz trace the developments through the twentieth century of this urban mode. Cortázar questions the Europeanized intellectual hegemony of urban space, while recent Mexican projects "recycle" photographic urban clichés in the context of the megalopolis. Part three, Photographic and Narrative Confrontations, explores the integration of photographic images in novels, essays, and various forms of prose from Puerto Rico and Argentina. The essays in this section reveal the rich dialogues established between photographs and narratives in projects that focus on the gendered body, political figures, and marginalized groups.

All the critical essays in the volume strive to analyze Latin American writing and photography using both Latin American and European / Anglo-American critical tools. As we have pointed out, Western thinkers such as Barthes, Mitchell, Tagg, Berger, and Sontag have certainly helped frame photography studies in an international context.[7] The contributors to *Photography and Writing in Latin America* reveal their debt to Benjamin, Mitchell, and Barthes, whose contributions to the field have been particularly pivotal. For example, Mitchell's consideration of the "pictorial turn" defies the reduction of images to words just as it resists the absorption of words into pictures. Beyond a conflict between the visual and the verbal, he convincingly demonstrates that the contemporary interplay between the two modes is "even more volatile, intricate, and pervasive" than ever before in history ("Word and Image" 50). While often relying on the works of these thinkers, the essays included in this volume also identify theories of the visual and verbal within the collaborative texts themselves, revealing how these word/image products advance the intersection between these parallel modes of expression.

We further extend this dialogue with Latin American artists and theorists in part four, The Voice of the Image, which offers exclusive interviews with participants in such collaborative work. This section features specialists, among the most active in recent collaborations, commenting on their aesthetic vision, the challenges of combining verbal and visual media, their goals, and the impact of these verbal-visual projects on the local cultural scene. Photographers Sara Facio and Sebastião Salgado discuss their international photographic work and how their contact and collaboration with writers have enriched their visual enterprises. Cultural critic

Nelly Richard reflects on the role of visual work, photography in particular, in Chilean artistic movements as strategies of resistance to the repressive dictatorship of Augusto Pinochet (1973–90). Elena Poniatowska comments on her many projects with photographers, which have elaborated on her fiction as well her journalistic production. Having collaborated with photographers such as Graciela Iturbide, Poniatowska takes on women's domestic work, religious processions, the massacre in Tlatelolco, and Mexico's regional culture and poverty. Focusing on the close connection that Poniatowska's work maintains with photography, Amy Conger, in *Compañeras de México*, notes that her novel *Hasta no verte Jesús mío* describes the protagonist Jesusa Palancares "[a]lmost as if she had a hidden camera" (34), and considers the oral testimonial discourse of *La noche de Tlatelolco* "like a series of photographs" (35). This section of the text thus helps frame photography studies from a uniquely Latin American perspective. These interviews highlight that in Latin America cultural theory is often produced by the very practitioners of culture, blurring the theory-practice divide that seems to hold sway in cultural studies in Europe and the United States. A crucial goal of the present volume is to showcase such theoretical reflection by Latin American practitioners, who think theoretically *through* and *about* Latin America's visual and verbal cultural production.

Many of the essays here illuminate the transformation of "literature" into a powerful voice animating visual work. The artists and writers they discuss, through their books, novels, installations, and political and cultural activism, demonstrate the myriad ways in which verbal-visual collaboration charts new territory both aesthetically and politically. Their projects communicate photographically and verbally the urgency of human rights violations, the consequences of a discourse of the "other," and the social and aesthetic construction of gender. When John Berger commented on Susan Sontag's *On Photography*, he concluded that there is no single approach to such a visual medium as the photograph and called on language to help make sense of this revolutionary representational development:

> Words, comparisons, signs need to create a context for a printed photograph. . . . they must mark and leave open diverse approaches . . . around the photograph so that it may be seen in terms which are simultaneously personal, political, economic, dramatic, everyday and historic. (63)

Photography and Writing in Latin America aims to contribute to this expansive gesture, opening Latin America's visual and verbal dialogues to a wider audience by considering them as an expressive cultural phenomenon with regional and historical particularities. Beyond the individual collections studied in the following pages, within their local and regional traditions and historical urgency, the essays collected here dramatize the mutual reliance of verbal and visual practices in Latin America. While this interdependence of the visual and the verbal in mass media (journalism, advertising, electronic media, etc.) has become a commonplace, active collaboration between writers and photographers continues to interrogate this hybrid field. These projects assertively enter the arena of cultural production by launching new languages—in pictures and words—for exploring the dilemmas and challenges of Latin American social conditions, historical memory, and aesthetic experimentation.

Notes

1. José Antonio Torres Martino, in his introduction to the book of caricatures, continues, "Pero no necesita Homar saber escribir. Valen por centenares de palabras sus dibujos y ninguna elocuencia les aventaja en eficacia" (However, Homar doesn't need to know how to write. His drawings are worth hundreds of words, and there is no eloquence more effective) (n.p.).

2. This essay appears in *Ultimo round* with photographs by Rick Levy, Joe Kirkish, Douglass Kneedker, and Richard Zaris (acknowledgments on 293). His analogy between photographs and short stories is mentioned in his essay "Algunos aspectos del cuento."

3. The most recent example is the 2004 collection, edited by Tatelboim and Canseco-Jerez, *Pablo Neruda en noir et blanc (Images d'une vie et d'une oeuvre)*, published to commemorate Neruda's hundredth birthday.

4. Sebald's work has been translated extensively, and its enthusiastic reception outside of German letters, particularly in other European countries and in North America, has been studied along with the work itself.

5. The novel initially appeared as a *folletín* in the newspaper *El Periodista de Buenos Aires*, beginning in 1984, with photographs alongside it, but subsequent editions of the complete novel do not include photographs. See chapter 7 in this volume.

6. Other projects that draw on the testimonial mode and incorporate photographs as textual "voices" include Elena Poniatowska's *La noche de Tlatelolco* and the collection *Chile from Within* (by Ariel Dorfman and others).

7. Indeed, Hughes and Nobel, in their recent volume *Phototextualities*, suggest that works by Barthes, Benjamin, and Berger are "pretexts" to photography studies as a discipline.

References

Barthes, Roland. *Camera Lucida: Reflections on Photography.* 1980. Trans. Richard Howard. New York: Hill and Wang, 1981.

Berger, John. "Uses of Photography." In *About Looking*. New York: Pantheon, 1980, 48–63.

Bioy Casares, Adolfo. *La invención de Morel*. Buenos Aires: Emecé, 1953.

______. "The Invention of Morel and Other Stories" from *La trama celeste.* Trans. Ruth L. C. Simms. Illus. Norah Borges de Torre. Prol. Jorge Luis Borges. Austin: University of Texas Press, 1985.

Borges, Jorge Luis. *Obras completas*. 2 vols. Buenos Aires: Emecé, 1989.

Borges, Jorge Luis, Silvina Ocampo, and Adolfo Bioy Casares, eds. *Antología de la literatura fantástica*. Buenos Aires: Sudamericana, 1940.

______. Intro. Ursula K. Le Guin. *The Book of Fantasy*. New York: Viking, 1988.

Castro, Fernando. "Crossover Dreams: Remarks on Contemporary Latin American Photography." In *Image and Memory: Photography from Latin America 1966–1994*. Eds. Wendy Watriss and Lois Parkinson Zamora. Austin: University of Texas Press, 1998, 57–94.

Conger, Amy. *Compañeras de México: Women Photograph Women*. Riverside, CA: Regents of the University of California, 1990.

Cortázar, Julio. "Algunos aspectos del cuento." *Casa de las Américas* 61.15–16 (1963).

______. *Cuentos completos*. 2 vols. Madrid: Alfaguara, 1994.

______. "Del cuento breve y sus alrededores." *Ultimo round*. Vol. 1. Mexico City: Siglo XXI, 59–82.

Delano, Jack. *Puerto Rico Mío: cuatro décadas de cambio; four decades of change*. Washington, D.C.: Smithsonian, 1990.

Delano, Pablo. *Faces of America: Photographs*. Intro. Robert Coles. Washington, D.C.: Smithsonian, 1992.

Dittborn, Eugenio. *The Present Work Is a Re-Edition of Two Earlier Publications*. Franklin Furnace Artists' Books Collection, 1981.

Dorfman, Ariel, et al. *Chile from Within 1973–1988*. Photos Paz Errázuriz. New York: Norton, 1990.

Eltit, Diamela. *Lumpérica*. Santiago, Chile: Seix Barral, 1998.

Facio, Sara. *Geografía de Pablo Neruda*. Photos Sara Facio and Alicia D'Amico. Text Pablo Neruda. Barcelona: Ayma, 1974.

García Canclini, Néstor. *Culturas híbridas: estrategias para entrar y salir de la modernidad*. Mexico City: Grijalbo, 1989.

Glantz, Margo. *Genealogías*. 1981. Mexico City: Alfaguara, 1998.

______. *Sor Juana: la comparación y la hipérbole*. Mexico City: CONACULTA, 2000.

Gorodischer, Angélica. "La camara oscura." In *12 mujeres cuentan. . . .* Buenos Aires: La Campana, 1983, 157–74.

Gutiérrez, Miguel. *La destrucción del reino*. Photos Julio Olavarría. Lima: Milla Batres Editorial, 1992.

______. *El mundo sin Xóchitl*. Photos Julio Olavarría. Lima: Fondo de Cultura Económica, 2001.

Homar, Lorenzo. *Abrapalabra: la letra mágica: carteles, 1951–1999*. Rio Piedras: Museo de Historia, Antropología y Arte, Universidad de Puerto Rico, 2000.

______. *Aquí en la lucha, caricaturas*. Intro. J. A. Torres Martino. San Juan, Puerto Rico: La Escalera, 1970.

Hughes, Alex, and Andrea Noble, eds. *Phototextualities*. Albuquerque: University of New Mexico Press, 2003.

Kossoy, "Photography in Nineteenth-Century Latin America: The European Experience and the Exotic Experience." In *Image and Memory: Photography from Latin America 1966–1994*. Eds. Wendy Watriss and Lois Parkinson Zamora. Austin: University of Texas Press, 1998, 19–54.

Kuhnheim, Jill S. *Spanish American Poetry at the End of the 20th Century: Textual Disruptions*. Austin: University of Texas Press, 2005.

Levine, Robert M. *Images of History: Nineteenth and Early Twentieth Century Latin American Photographs as Documents*. Durham: Duke University Press, 1989.

Mitchell, W. J. T. *Picture Theory: Essays on Verbal and Visual Representation*. Chicago: University of Chicago Press, 1994.

______. "Word and Image." In *Critical Terms for Art History*. Eds. Robert S. Nelson and Richard Shiff. Chicago: University of Chicago Press, 1996, 47–57.

Pérez de Mendiola, Marina. "Mexican Contemporary Photography: Staging Ethnicity and Citizenship." *boundary* 2 31,3 (2004): 125–53.

Perkowska-Álvarez, Magdalena. "La negociación del espacio de la mujer en la historia en *Tinísima* de Elena Poniatowska." *Estudios* 5,10 (1997): 193–215.

Poma de Ayala, Felipe Guaman. *El primer nueva corónica y buen gobierno*. Eds. John Murra and Rolena Adorno. 3 vols. Mexico: Siglo XXI, 1980.

Poniatowska, Elena. *Hasta no verte Jesús mío*. Mexico City: Era, 1969.

______. *La noche de Tlatelolco*. Mexico City: Era, 1971.

______. "Some Women Photographers of Mexico/Algunas Fotógrafas de México." In Conger 43–55.

______. *Tinísima*. Mexico City: Era, 1992.

Poole, Deborah. *Vision, Race, and Modernity: A Visual Economy of the Andean Image World*. Princeton: Princeton University Press, 1997.

Rulfo, Juan. *Pedro Páramo*. Trans. Margaret Sayers Peden. Photography Josephine Sacabo. Austin: University of Texas Press, 2002.

______. Carlos Fuentes (text). *Mexico: Juan Rulfo: Fotógrafo*. Barcelona: Lunwerg, 2001.

______. *Juan Rulfo's Mexico*. Text, Carlos Fuentes. Washington, D.C.: Smithsonian, 2002.

Sontag, Susan. *On Photography*. New York: Farrar, Straus and Giroux, 1973.

Teitelboim, Volodia, and Alejandro Canseco-Jerez. *Pablo Neruda en Noir et Blanc. (Images d'une vie et d'une oeuvre)*. Paris: Maison d'Amérique Latine, 2004.

Tejeda, Guillermo. *Los disfraces de Neruda*. Santiago, Chile: Planeta Chilena–La Máquina del Arte, 1995.

Vargas Llosa, Mario. *El hablador*. Barcelona: Seix Barral, 1987.

Vicuña, Cecilia. *Precario/Precarious*. Trans. Anne Twitty. New York: Tanam, 1983.

Zamora, Lois Parkinson. "Quetzalcóatl's Mirror: Reflections on the Photographic Image in Latin America." In *Image and Memory: Photography from Latin America* Eds. Wendy Watriss and Lois Parkinson Zamora. Austin: University of Texas Press, 1998, 293–375.

Zurita, Raúl. *Anteparaíso*. Santiago, Chile: Editores Asociados, 1982.

______. *La vida nueva*. Santiago, Chile: Universitaria, 1997.

Part I

Writing and Picturing Revolution and Resistance

Chapter One

Representing the Mexican Revolution

Bending Photographs to the Will of *Historia Gráfica*

John Mraz

Like myths, photographs leave us on the surface. In order to encounter the wealth of information available in pictures, research must be carried out in the contexts within and for which they were produced, as well as in those within and for which they have been reproduced. By itself, a photograph only offers the opportunity to signify, the possibility of meaning. A photograph's connotation is given to it by the concrete discourse within which it is situated. Hence, a photograph must be "historicized" in order to know what it "means," because its "meaning" is, finally, the accumulation of significances that have been fixed to it in the different situations within which it has appeared.[1]

Visual history is ubiquitous in Mexico: photographs, postcards, calendars, T-shirts, coffee mugs, ashtrays, and other bric-a-brac are a quotidian experience, although the images are rarely accompanied by words to describe the scenes represented. Hence, *historia gráfica* (pictorial history) is the medium that most explicitly assigns meaning to historical photographs. Picture histories occupy a significant niche in a country with high levels of semi-literacy, and this genre has a long trajectory in Mexico, most apparently in the large-format, multi-volume series that reproduce thousands of photographs, accompanied by a wide assortment of texts. Since the 1920s, the story of Mexico's past has often been told through picture histories, and they continue to be an important forum in which leading historians have participated, including scholars with the prestige of Lorenzo Meyer, Enrique Florescano, Luis González y González, Javier Garciadiego, and Álvaro Matute, among many others.

The historias gráficas that have been produced in Mexico vary considerably in terms of image research and reproduction, as well as in the quality of their written texts. However, with some exceptions, they share a tendency common to the genre throughout the world: they usually show little respect for what photos could tell us about the past.[2] The graphic investigations, and the research carried out for the written texts, are like two parallel rails that give the appearance of meeting on the horizon but never really work together. The historians who pen the essays and cutlines have generally had nothing whatsoever to do with the visual investigation, which is commonly assigned to student assistants. Hence, the pictures essentially illustrate texts that have been written completely apart from any questions or clues that could have arisen from searching among old photographs. Moreover, the image research has been limited largely to simply finding pictures, rather than recovering the information that, as we shall see below, enables us to recount marvelous stories about the past. On those few happy occasions when visual and written research have somehow functioned together, the mutual benefits are evidence that photography ought to be situated in a dialectic relationship with text, stimulating and orienting research, rather than reduced to being attractive filler sought in a process unrelated to what many historians consider to be the real investigation, that carried out in words.[3]

Most historias gráficas are produced without any significant research into the images—who made them, for what reason, when and where they were taken, or what is occurring in the pictures; the easy way out is "illustrationism." John Berger has commented about photography that, "[u]nless the viewer is already familiar with the subject, everything which is photographed takes the indefinite article *a*. *The* pair of boots becomes *a* pair of boots" (60). The cutlines usually employed in historias gráficas rely on this tendency, often spouting generalities that are at odds with the specificity of photography itself; they use historical photos to represent generalizations instead of presenting the particularities they depict. Verbal concepts are conventional symbols for similarities: the word *tree*, for example, describes a woody perennial plant with one main stem that develops many branches. The difference between the media is illustrated in the fact that you cannot photograph the concept *tree*, you can only photograph a particular tree. Thus, a photo is by its nature a document of a specific moment, a particular fraction of a second, a unique history. For Barthes, a photograph "is the absolute Particular, the sovereign Contingency, matte and somehow stupid, the *This* (this photograph, and not Photography), in short, what Lacan calls the *Tuché*, the Occasion, the Encounter, the Real, in its indefatigable expression" (4). However, while the generalities created by illustrationist cutlines are at odds with the very specificity of the photographic medium, a photograph's particularity can only be developed and revealed through identifying with verbal captions that which appears in it.

Perhaps more importantly, the cutlines sometimes fabricate histories that are blatant falsifications of that which appears in the picture. A photo of a worker preparing *nixtamal* (ground corn meal used for tortillas) provides a trenchant example of "Revolutionary" obfuscation (fig. 1.1). When this picture was published in the series *Así fue la Revolución Mexicana* (Florescano 1207), the accompanying cutline stated, "[d]ebts contracted by workers would not affect their families." The image appeared within a discussion of "[t]he problem of the workers," and was placed next to a text reproducing the provisions of Article 123, the section of the 1917 Constitution that "constituted the most enlightened statement of labor protective principles in the world to that date" (Knight 470–71). No doubt the picture appeared to offer a convenient illustration of the Article's stipulation that a worker's indebtedness could not be passed on to his family members. Presumably taken before the Revolution that would cure social ills such as usury, the photo evidently presents us with a middle-aged woman who had been forced to work at menial labor, because she had apparently inherited her husband's obligations at his death. Eliminating any reference to the date when the photo was made enabled the series editors to give the impression that the woman suffered from the vulnerability of workers during the Porfiriato (1876–1910).

Nevertheless, this photo was taken in 1919, and the good intentions of Article 123, printed around the photo and on the facing page, stand in shocking juxtaposition to the reality of this woman's (and her colleagues') situation. For example, though the Article contained far-reaching reforms related to women and childbirth, the woman in this photo, Luz Duani (a widow with six children), asserted that the company "didn't give them anything," when interviewed by Juan de Bereza (an investigator from the Secretariat of Industry, Commerce, and Labor).[4] Article 123 legislated an eight-hour workday and forbade women to work overtime, but the women de Bereza talked to usually labored "from 4:00 a.m. until seven or eight at night." Article 123 stipulated that indemnification be paid for accidents or work-related illness; the women told de Bereza that, not only did they receive no aid or compensation, but, moreover, they were immediately replaced. The women were virtual prisoners in the nixtamal mills: they practically never left them, because their bosses insisted that they sleep there to guard the machinery, with neither toilet facilities nor ventilation, and only a thin, flea-ridden mat between them and the cold, damp, cement floor (not exactly the sort of housing Article 123 contemplated in its clause that "all businesses must provide comfortable and hygienic habitations for their workers"). De Bereza summed up the women's situation: they were treated "like slaves."

The basic tasks of "photohistory" (the representation of history in photographs) are essentially the same as historiography (the representation of history in words): research and documentation.[5] Had the authors of *Así fue la Revolución Mexicana* dedicated themselves to this discipline, they would have been able to recount a story about the past far richer than that which they attempted to counterfeit through illustrationism. Instead, they ripped this picture out of its real situation

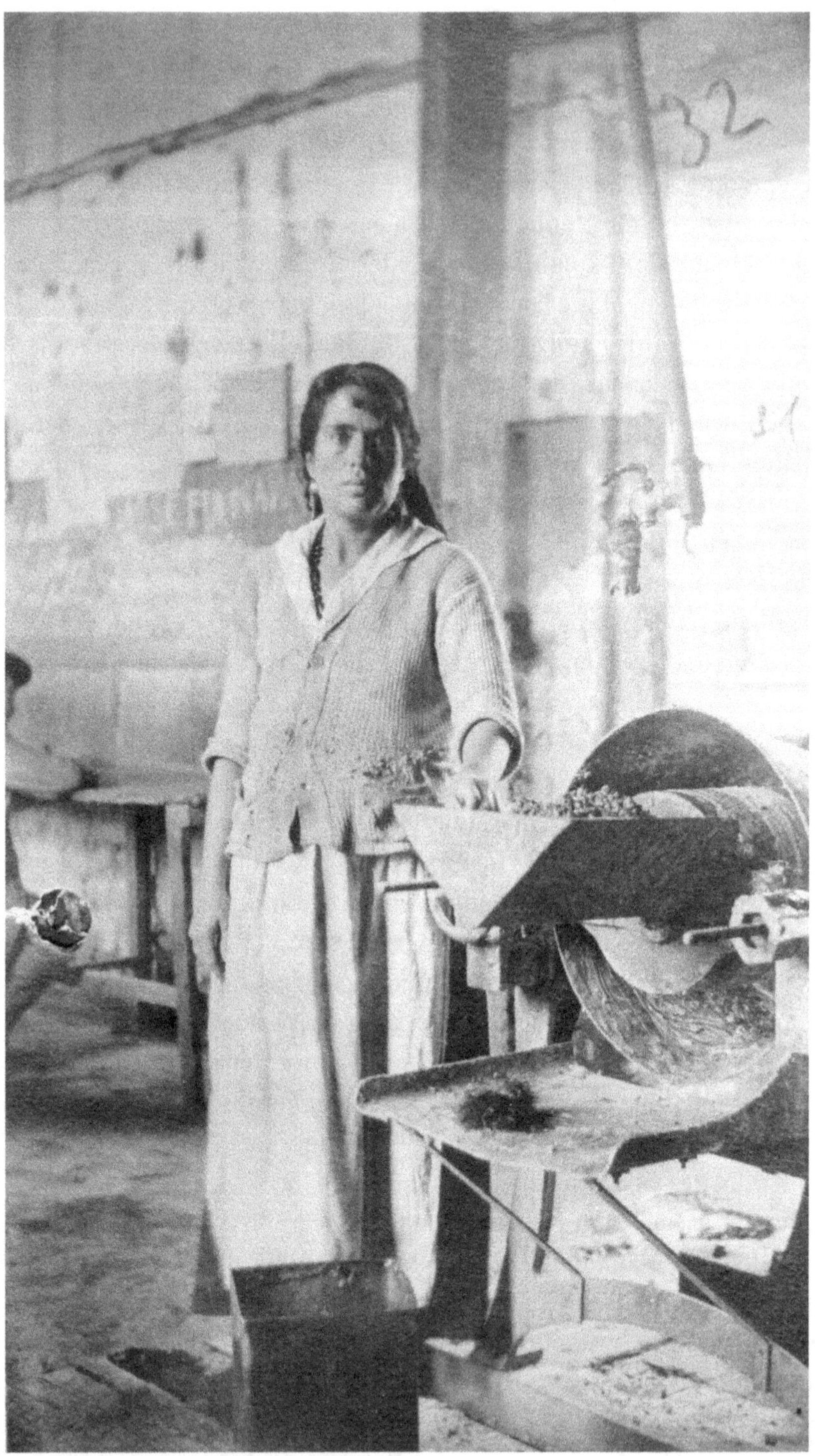

Fig. 1.1. Photographer unknown, Luz Duani viuda de Guzmán, worker in *nixtamal* mill, Mexico City, December 1919. Archivo General de la Nación, Ramo del Trabajo, 173–12.

and misappropriated it for purposes far removed from its original intention, that of documenting the gap between law and reality in post-revolutionary Mexico. The photo was recontextualized so as to legitimate the New Order wrought by the 1917 Constitution—a regime embodied most immediately in those who inherited the Revolution: the Partido Revolucionario Institucional (PRI) and President Miguel de la Madrid, whose remarks introduce the series.

In Mexico, most recent historias gráficas have been produced with public monies, but private initiative was crucial to the genre's beginnings. Agustín Víctor Casasola founded a newsphoto agency (Agencia Mexicana de Información Gráfica) during 1912, in order to compete with photographers who streamed into Mexico to cover the Revolution that was a magnet for journalists from all over the world, the first such conflagration accessible to modern communications media. Casasola was both a photojournalist and an entrepreneur (much like Mathew Brady during the U.S. Civil War); he contracted men to work for him or purchased images that had already been taken.[6] In 1921 he began to produce visual histories with his archive, editing an *Álbum histórico gráfico*. It must have been a profitable enterprise, for his son, Gustavo, took the family business to new heights from 1942 on, publishing and steadily reprinting many picture books, the most important of which are the two series *Historia gráfica de la Revolución Mexicana* and *Seis siglos de historia gráfica de México*.[7]

Although the Casasolas were the first to systematically explore the public's thirst for pictured history, their works leave much to be desired as models for how to use photographs. The poor reproduction and large grain leaves imperceptible elements that are visible in works of higher quality.[8] A more serious problem is created by the fact that we do not know who took the pictures: one researcher has found the work of almost five hundred photographers in the Casasola Archive (Gutiérrez Ruvalcaba). This leads to difficulties in determining what is really occurring in the images, above all because Gustavo Casasola used photographs by whim, turning them into whatever was convenient for the theme at hand. One participant in the Revolution complained of inaccuracies: "That was the truth and not what Casasola wrote in the second volume of his *Historia gráfica*" (López de Nava Camarena 92). The fact that the photo identifications in the Casasola series cannot be trusted makes them problematic even as a catalogue, for we would have to find the original publications of the pictures in order to be able to use them with any rigor.[9]

The officialism of the Casasola historias gráficas is demonstrated convincingly in their alignment with the PRI's self-representation as the heir of the Revolution. In his enduring production of the *Historia gráfica de la Revolución Mexicana*, Casasola steadfastly extended the Revolutionary era to include the most recent photographs, implying that this process was continuing and that the PRI was therefore a Revolutionary political force. Hence, the last pages of the latest edition of *Historia gráfica de la Revolución Mexicana* document the appointment of President Luis Echeverría's cabinet, presenting functionaries—gray men in dark suits—as if they constituted some sort of "Revolutionary" government.

The fact that all Echeverría's cabinet members are male is expressive of a major meta-text in this and later series of historia gráfica, that is even more pernicious: "great men" made the Revolution, and they continue to make it. Some 65 percent of all the photographs published in the *Historia gráfica de la Revolución Mexicana* are of political leaders: the presidents and their ministers; the warlords, caudillos, and caciques that people the early volumes; the suits—bankers, entrepreneurs, labor bosses, and governors—that come to predominate.[10] "Great men" are a familiar focus in picture histories, as can be observed in the percentage of photographs dedicated to them in other Mexican historias gráficas: *Biografía del poder* (74 percent), *Así fue la Revolución Mexicana* (62 percent), and *Historia gráfica de México* (47 percent).[11] The utilization of so many portraits makes me ask what we really learn from photographs of politicians, for their physiognomy tells us little about the past.[12] Instead, the real object of such imagery is to situate male chieftains as if they were history incarnate, the sum total of past struggles encapsulated in a leader's representation.

The golden age of subsidized historia gráfica was the reign of Miguel de la Madrid (1982–88). This is somehow appropriate, for his rule was the last gasp of "Revolutionary Nationalism," the PRI's strategy for co-opting cultural expression, as *La Revolución* began to be replaced by the neoliberal ideology of privatization. His regime paid for the writing, visual research, and massive printings of several voluminous series: *Memoria y olvido*, a collection of assigned "monographs" by various authors (Martínez Assad); *Así fue la Revolución Mexicana*, a sumptuously produced paean to the cataclysm of 1910–17 (Florescano); *Biografía del poder*, gossipy hagiographies of the New Order's heroes (Krauze); and *Historia gráfica de México*, the obligatorily titled series hurriedly thrown together to take advantage of funds remaining in the final year of the *sexenio*, the six-year presidential term (Aguilar Camín et al. 1988). The history recounted in the texts of these works is markedly better than that of the Casasola albums, because it was usually farmed out to specialists. However, although the quality of the visual research varies, the series are alike in that the images are almost invariably divorced entirely from the texts. Hence, they are little more than illustrated histories, in which the essays have been constructed completely apart from the investigations undertaken for the imagery. At the end of de la Madrid's rule, a "spin-off" of the new historias gráficas proposed an alternative: *Veracruz, imágenes de su historia* was produced by the Veracruz state government, focusing on regional history; it may well represent the most rigorous effort so far to incorporate photography in studies of Mexican history (Delgado).[13]

The series *Memoria y olvido: imágenes de México* (Martínez Assad, ed.) was produced in 1982–83 by the Martín Casillas press, in conjunction with the Secretary of Public Education, and consists of twenty volumes. Six thousand copies of each book were printed, a significant output for Mexico, where between five hundred and a thousand is a normal print run. All the images come from the Archivo General de la Nación, so their general source is acknowledged and, in a few of the books, specific photographers or collections are identified. The image research and selection is very good, thanks to the collaboration of Alfonso Morales, a leading scholar of Mexican visual culture. However, the texts are uneven, and only two volumes make any explicit reference to the imagery. Further, the printing is extremely poor, resulting in grainy, high-contrast, washed-out images; for that reason, these books are much less useful as history than they would have been with decent reproductions.

One book in this series demonstrates how crucial it is to identify photographers in order to unmask the intentions behind the making of a photograph: Andrea Martínez's *La intervención norteamericana: Veracruz, 1914*. This volume is a good example of what we can learn from this information, for almost all the pictures are attributed to one of two photographers: P. Flores Pérez or Melhado. The vast majority of Melhado's photos are of the invading forces: a group of four heroically posed marines fire their 45's toward the enemy, aiming through a gaping hole in a bombed-out building (fig. 1.2) (Martínez 35); U.S. naval police carry out an inspection (Martínez 59); marines relax in a plaza, drinking from large cups (Martínez 63); two marines sit behind a Remington typewriter, looking back at the photographer (Martínez 64). The camera of Flores Pérez (at least as it is presented in Martínez's book) was turned in the other direction. He did, of course, take pictures of the occupying intruders, often foregrounding Mexican dead, perhaps as a way of pointing to U.S. responsibility. Some such photos were candid: he captured a U.S. sailor with his rifle pointed down at bloodstained corpses shortly after intense street fighting (fig. 1.3) (Martínez 153).[14] However, a staged photo reminiscent of Melhado's "four marines" shows Flores Pérez's intention even more clearly. Here, although the two marines are posturing in firing position fully as gallantly as those in Melhado's composition, a "dead" Mexican has been placed in the foreground, providing an obvious victim of U.S. imperialism.[15]

Flores Pérez did not limit his work to denouncing the war against civilians; he also documented resistance to the invasion, as well as solidarity among the residents of the port. One photo documents Mexican soldiers lying flat in what appears to be street fighting (Martínez 26). The image is quite realistic, although the two men off to the side, who seem to be standing rather carelessly in conversation, might make one doubt whether it was made during combat. Photography of actual fighting in the Revolution is quite rare. The camera's weight and slow exposure times were factors so adverse that images of action may be limited largely to the pictures made

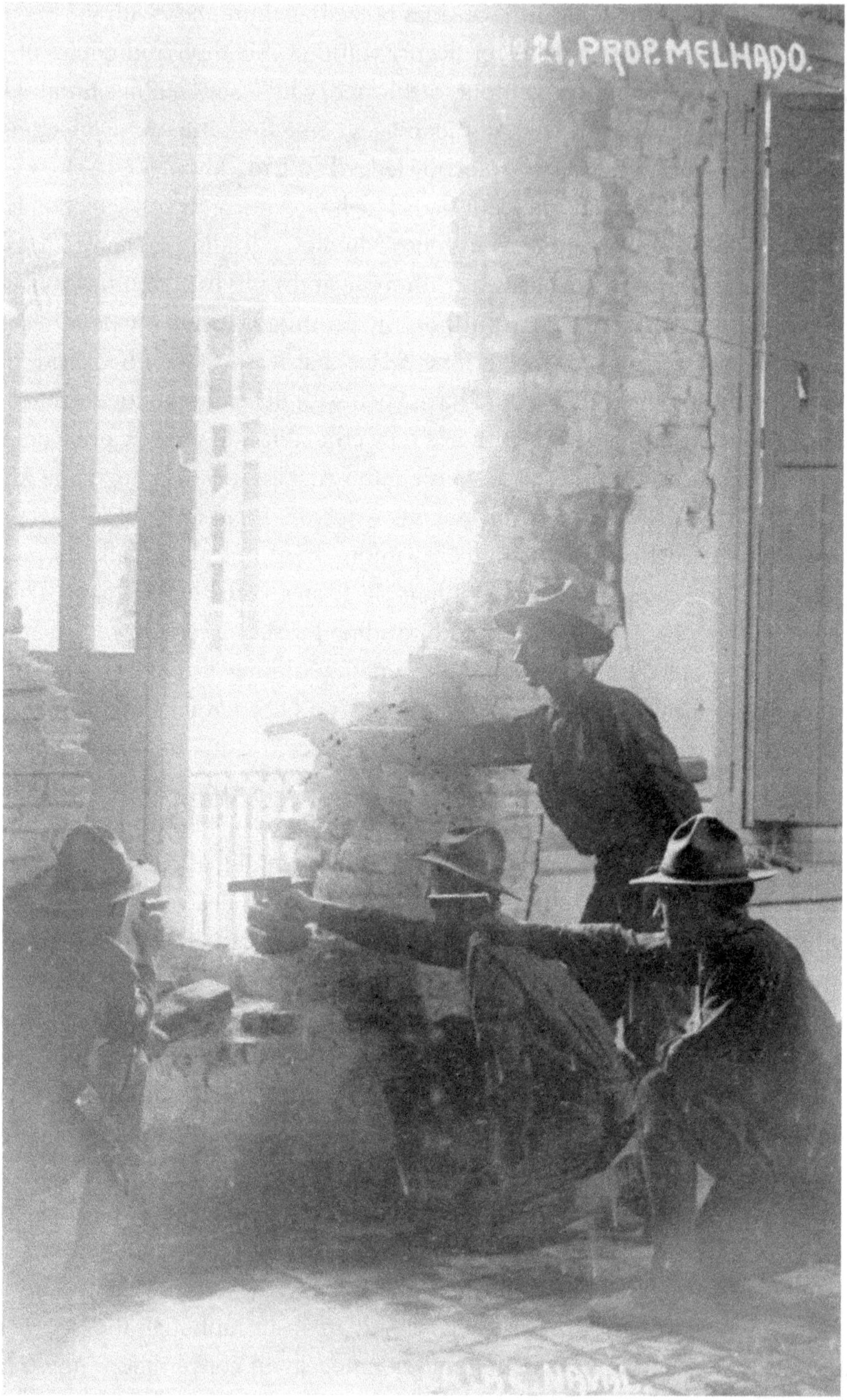

Fig. 1.2. U.S. Marines pose as if firing out of a ruin, Veracruz, 1914. Archivo General de la Nación, Fondo Propiedad Artística y Literaria, Melhado, Intervención norteamericana.

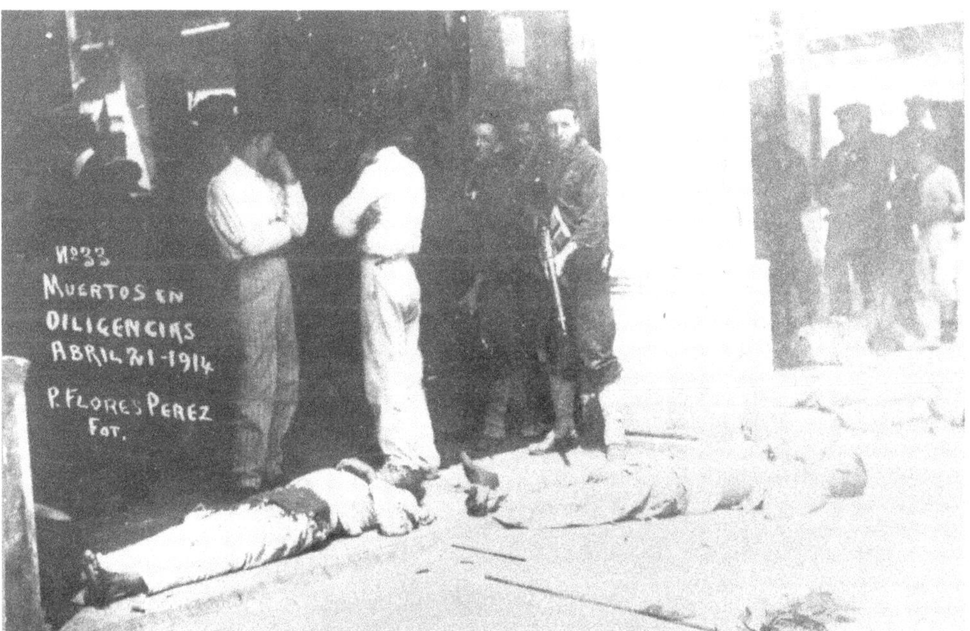

Fig. 1.3. P. Flores Pérez (?), U.S. sailor and Mexican dead, Veracruz, 1914. Archivo General de la Nación, Fondo Propiedad Artística y Literaria, Flores Pérez, Intervención norteamericana.

by Jimmy Hare, during the Maderista uprising on the northern frontier, or those that Manuel Ramos and the Casasola brothers (Agustín Víctor and Miguel), shot during the "Tragic Ten Days."[16] Another picture shows a crowd gathered in front of military headquarters, demanding weapons with which to resist (according to the legend written on the photo) (Martínez 27). And, in other images, Flores Pérez demonstrates solidarity among the people by photographing a stretcher crew carrying a wounded person (Martínez 36), as well as picturing the wholesale rejection of the invaders by Veracruz residents in the massive turnouts for the funerals of the heroes José Azueta (Martínez 66) and Benjamín Gutiérrez Ruiz (Martínez 67).

Flores Pérez's insistence on denouncing the invasion and attesting to resistance is demonstrated in photographs that were "directed" to provide visual records of opposition and civilian casualties. Photos show men firing into and out of houses in ruins, bodies scattered about, while children ostensibly peer at the action from behind a wall (Martínez 31–32). In one photo ("Effects of a machine-gunning"; fig. 1.4), we see a man pointing with a pistol, while the ground nearby is littered with three corpses (Martínez 33). In another picture taken from the same spot, titled "Destruction caused by a machine-gunning" (fig. 1.5), the man with the pistol seems to be leaving, while on the ground the three corpses have changed into other bodies, lying in different positions (Martínez 34)! Comparing these two images makes it clear that Flores Pérez reconstructed scenes. The fact that these photographs were

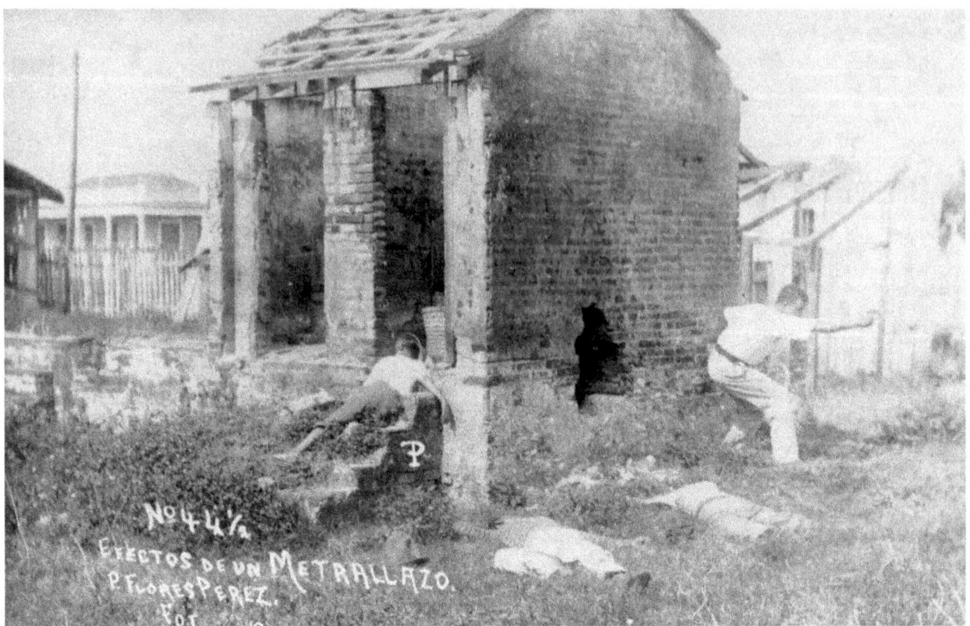

Fig. 1.4. P. Flores Pérez, Directed photos of resistance, Veracruz, 1914. Archivo General de la Nación, Fondo Propiedad Artística y Literaria, Flores Pérez, Intervención norteamericana.

staged in no way invalidates them as historical documents, and the famous "Case of the Rearranged Corpse" from the U.S. Civil War provides an antecedent to Flores Pérez's activities.[17] The resistance that this photographer pictured, whether in real combat imagery or post facto re-creation, represented opposition to the invasion on both the part of the populace and Flores Pérez.

In 1985, the Senate joined with the Secretary of Public Education to publish the series *Así fue la Revolución Mexicana,* as part of the celebrations for the 175th anniversary of independence and the 75th anniversary of the Revolution. It consists of eight volumes, with essays by a significant number of established scholars who obviously had nothing to do with the visual research; as is typical in these historias gráficas, the texts and the images are essentially irrelevant to one another. Moreover, the graphic investigation (coordinated by Gloria Villegas) is mediocre; for example, the series relies heavily on the Salvat Archive, from which they have reprinted poor reproductions of photographs, rather than undertaking research in Mexican archives. A particularly striking example is the very first image of the series: the picture of the "Red Battalions" has obviously been rephotographed from a published reproduction rather than printed from a negative, something apparent in the enormous grain left by the screen of its previous publication. With minimal effort, they could have had a superb copy made from the negative in the INAH Fototeca. While the series does identify the general source of the imagery—Salvat Archive, the Hemeroteca Nacional,

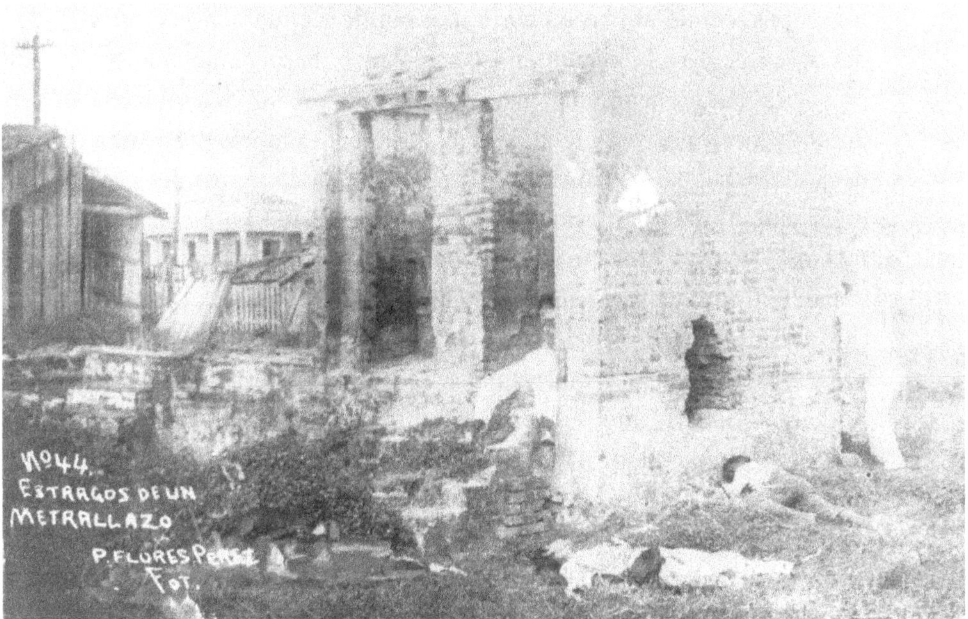

Fig. 1.5. P. Flores Pérez, Directed photos of resistance, Veracruz, 1914. Archivo General de la Nación, Fondo Propiedad Artística y Literaria, Flores Pérez, Intervención norteamericana.

the INAH Fototeca—no information is provided about the photographers.

The government spared no expense for this series. Around forty thousand copies of each volume were published (a very large print run in Mexico, especially for hardbound volumes), on expensive paper. Although much money was invested in the project, above all in paying for materials and the numerous authors, it appears that there were either few funds for, or little interest in, graphic research and reproduction, because the expenditures were wasted by curiously deficient printing, including the use of sepia tone for many photographs, further reducing their detail. The officialism of the series was made clear immediately in the introduction provided by then-president Miguel de la Madrid:

> En los momentos de incertidumbre, los mexicanos hacemos una reflexión reiterada acerca de los principios, los ideales y los logros del proyecto que nos dio vida como nación independiente. Para el pueblo de México la historia, más que una imagen inerte del pasado, es el fundamento de la construcción nacional y una guía para la acción futura. Uno de los acontecimientos que más ha transformado la vida de nuestro país es la Revolución de 1910; el gran movimiento social que le dio una nueva orientación al desarrollo histórico de México. Este gran vuelco histórico, en el que participaron todos

> los grupos sociales, todas las corrientes políticas y todas las regiones del país, integró a la nación en un sólo cauce de preocupaciones y proyectos. Paradójicamente, al mismo tiempo que fue una lucha de grupos y facciones, esa lucha en que participaron tantos mexicanos decantó los problemas principales del país y señaló los ideales y las metas que unificaron los esfuerzos de los mexicanos para construir una nación más libre, justa y democrática, integrada geográfica, social, cultural y políticamente, en un sólo proyecto nacional. (Florescano 5–6)
>
> (In moments of uncertainty we Mexicans reflect on the principles, ideals, and successes of the project that brought us life as an independent nation. For the Mexican people, history is more than an inert image of the past; it is fundamental to national construction, and a guide for future action. One of the events that has most transformed our country's life is the 1910 Revolution, the great social movement that gave a new orientation to Mexico's historical development. This great historical upheaval, in which all social groups, all political currents, and all the country's regions participated, brought the nation together into one channel of concerns and projects. Paradoxically, at the same time that it was a battle of groups and factions, this struggle unified the efforts of Mexicans to construct a nation . . . integrated geographically, socially, culturally, and politically, in a single national project.) (my translation)

What a magnificent distillation of official history; and it comes as no surprise that the "national integration" is effected fundamentally through the preponderance of the images of the "great men" who made the Revolution. That is, in this framing, the leaders who actually fought to the death against one another were instead shown to be somehow constructing a unity: Zapata together with Madero (who betrayed Zapata) and Carranza (who had Zapata killed), Villa together with Obregón (who probably ordered Villa's death). If this were true, it would indeed be the paradox of which de la Madrid spoke. However, the "single national project" did not result from the armed struggle but, rather, is a concoction of the party dictatorship that controlled the post-revolutionary state.

Although *Historia gráfica de México* appears to have a lower percentage of photographs dedicated to history's "great men" than the other series, they nonetheless remain a visual core. For example, volume 8 opens with photographs of Adolfo de la Huerta, Woodrow Wilson, and Albert Fall. The insistence with which this series visually features political leaders is illustrated in the repetition of the same photographs of Lázaro Cárdenas (Aguilar Camín 1988, 8: 82, 154), and Plutarco Elías Calles (70, 151). Volume 9 provides another take on presidentialism: the inauguration of Luis Echeverría is shown in two different photographs, both of which are equally empty of historical information, because the only thing to appear in the images are Echeverría and out-going president Gustavo Díaz Ordaz (1964–70) in suits, one of them wearing the presidential sash (Aguilar Camín 9: 125, 154).

As is apparent in the reliance on such imagery, *Historia gráfica de México* demonstrates little respect for what the visual might contribute to history, a lack of esteem that is exemplified in the photo of "Adelita." Without identifications that anchor photographs to their reality, their aesthetic force can sometimes generate myths, decontextualized symbols that disfigure our understanding of the past. The famous photograph of "Adelita" offers one example, for the woman hanging out of the train has become "[t]he paradigmatic image of the *soldadera*, the Mexican soldier's faithful companion" (Rodríguez Lapuente 74). *Historia gráfica de México* provided the following cutline for this image: "Adelita-the-*soldadera*, a photo taken by Agustín V. Casasola in 1910, which would very soon become one of the emblems of the Revolution, just like the famous song with almost the same name, 'La Adelita.'"[18] This can only be described as a condensed comedy of errors. We do not know when the photo was taken, but it was surely not 1910, because there were few troop movements in that year. It is much more likely that the photo belongs to the same period as the famous farewells in the train station, the 1913–14 struggle of Victoriano Huerta to hold onto power. We do not know who took the photo; it could have been Agustín Víctor or Miguel Casasola, or it might have been José María Lupercio, or J. H. Gutiérrez, or Manuel Ramos, or Antonio Garduño, or any other photographer who covered the moving scenes staged between the Huertista soldiers and the women who went to bid them farewell (or join them in the war). Finally, it may well have been the very editors of *Historia gráfica de México* who first invented the title of "Adelita" for this photo, and it was almost certainly derived precisely from the song, "La Adelita," which is about a soldadera and trains.[19]

The editors of *Historia gráfica de México* followed the usual practice of cropping the negative in which "Adelita" appears, removing the right half of the original image. That half of the glass plate is broken, but we can still see a group of women standing on the platforms of the train cars. When we ask who Adelita was, her location in the train may provide an important clue. Soldaderas usually traveled on top of, or underneath, the cars. The women who traveled inside the cars were often the prostitutes of federal officers. Analyzed as a whole, the image could contribute to our historical knowledge about the Revolution, for it provides a "lead" about the living conditions of some women. The cropped version of "Adelita" only serves as another Revolutionary myth, because the vitality evinced by this woman makes her a repository for, and symbol of, all the attributes of the legendary soldaderas.

Enrique Krauze authored *Biografía del poder*, which was funded by the Secretary of Agriculture and published by the prestigious, government-owned Fondo de Cultura Económica in 1987, with a large print run: again, forty thousand copies were produced of each of the eight volumes that focus on Mexican leaders from Porfirio Díaz to Lázaro Cárdenas. The graphic investigation is good, probably due to Aurelio de los Reyes, and the archival source of each image is acknowledged. However, individual photographers are not identified, the reproduction is poor, the paper is of a low quality, and the relationship between the text and the photographs is merely illustrative. Nonetheless, the main problem with *Biografía del poder* is that the vast majority of the photographs are of "great men"; the series was advertised as presenting "history's human face," but the only visages in sight are those of "history's makers." One contribution photography can make to history writing is that of "personalizing the past": on seeing individual human beings, we remember that it is people who really forge history, for as Sartre declared, "I believe that a man can always make something out of what is made of him." Utilizing photographs as a way of "personifying" the history of ordinary beings—bringing into view individuals from below who are usually excluded from dominant historiography—is of course quite a different matter from employing images of heroes to feed into the celebrity culture that is itself largely a product of modern visual media.

Biografía del poder embodies the transformation of Mexican culture under Miguel de la Madrid. The relation with the government that Krauze developed to produce this series enabled him to accumulate an enormous corpus of Mexican images: the Secretary of Agriculture opened the doors to the national archives, and the pictures were paid for with public monies. Krauze has used this mass of images to produce books (for his press, Clío) and television programs (for Televisa), which are so far from the rigor one expects of history—even historia gráfica—as not to merit comment here. The process by which he acquired the cultural clout he wields today was articulately analyzed by Claudio Lomnitz: "Krauze's power was amassed in a moment in which the government turned its back on public education and research and subsidized a process of cultural privatization that had similar characteristics to other privatizations: enormous concentration of power in very few hands, and the formation of a new elite" (220).

The ascension of Carlos Salinas (1988–94) to the presidency marked the moment at which culture was definitively privatized. The mask of Revolution was discarded, and the participation of the state in cultural production was questioned, as the U.S. model of private initiative became increasingly dominant.[20] Within this climate, historia gráfica has diminished, as institutions publish single volumes rather than series. Nonetheless, one of the most important investigations into the photography of the Mexican Revolution came to fruition in 1998: *Los Salmerón*, a study by Blanca Jiménez and Samuel Villela of the Salmerón family members who dedicated themselves to photography in Guerrero throughout the twentieth century. The dynasty's founder, Protasio Salmerón, began taking pictures around 1900, and his son, Amando Salmerón, became Emiliano Zapata's photographer. Later Salmeróns covered social activities, political meetings, and the 1960 university movement with a sharp eye for the inequalities of class in Mexico. Both a photohistory and a history of photography, this book interrogates images in order to analyze them as documentary sources for social history, as well as placing this family of photographers within a historical context.[21]

In sum, the Mexican Revolution spawned the many historias gráficas that have been nourished by photographs of "Adelita" peering intensely from the train, of Villa lolling in the presidential chair, and of Zapata seated firmly on horseback. Visual history is a quotidian experience in Mexico: postcards, calendars, T-shirts, coffee mugs, ashtrays, and other bric-a-brac transmit images from the past, although they are rarely accompanied by words to describe the scenes represented. The multifarious picture histories produced by this culture have been the medium most adept in assigning meanings to historical photographs. Hence, they offer a vision of Mexican history that is at least two-fold: on the one hand, we find the surface of yesterday embalmed in these paper-thin slices of time past; on the other, we discover the *machista* and *officialista* discourse promoted by image selection and verbal texts that bend photographs to the will of historia gráfica.

Notes

1. Of course, although verbal texts are the single most important element in determining photographic meaning, they are not the only factor. The physical context of an exhibition apportions meaning to images, as does the overall message constructed by pictures in a book. Consider, for example, the significance of picture editing in Sebastião Salgado's *Other Americas*, where the absence of verbal text and the minimal titles create a situation in which the meaning of the images is determined entirely by their accumulated effect. Because many of the photos are of people with somber, even distressed expressions, often in the presence of some form of death—as well as divided from one another by formal structures—mystery, anguish, and estrangement are the sensations they evoke. I compare this situation to Salgado's later works, where text is much more important (Mraz "Sebastião Salgado").

2. Rafael Samuels noted a curious situation in Britain, where he asserted that secondary schools "were far more hospitable to the reception of photography—and far more critical and self-aware in their use of it—than university historians who lent their dignity and authority to coffee-table books and Sunday colour supplement articles, but showed no sign of incorporating old photographs into their teaching materials or primary research" (Samuels 321).

3. For an example of how photographs can be used in social history, see my articles "Mexican History in Photography," "De la fotografía histórica," and "Más allá de la decoración," and my book *Imágenes ferrocarrileras. . . .*

4. I have analyzed this case in my article "'En calidad de esclavas.' . . ."

5. The concept *photohistory* seems to be one option for describing attempts to prepare reasonably serious histories with photographs. At any rate, I prefer it to *historiophoty*, which is what Hayden White (1193) offers as a "relatively adequate" way of characterizing "the representation of history and our thought about it in visual images and filmic discourse." White's formulation seems unnecessarily complicated, and while it may be useful for talking about history done with photographs, I have my doubts about its adequacy in talking about media that employ audio components, such as film or video.

6. The Casasola Archive was acquired by the Instituto Nacional de Antropología e Historia in 1976 and consists of some half million images (Arroyo 11).

7. A publishing history of the Casasolas would be a formidable task. *Historia gráfica de la Revolución* was evidently first published in 1942 and covered the period 1900–40. See the interview with Gustavo Casasola ("Gustavo Casasola"). In the credits for *Historia gráfica de la Revolución*, Gustavo Casasola attributes the collecting of materials and the photography to his father, noting that he (Gustavo) directed and finished it; a version of this work was republished in the 1950s. In the 1960s, the series became *Historia gráfica de la Revolución Mexicana*, with a five-volume collection published by Editorial Trillas that extended the period covered to 1960. In 1973, Trillas expanded this to a ten-volume set, which it republished in 1992; this series takes the Revolution up to 1970. *Seis siglos de historia gráfica de México* seems to have appeared first in 1962, and has always been published by Gustavo Casasola. The second set was published in 1967–69; the third series appeared in 1971; the fourth version was published in 1978; the latest version appeared in 1989, and was published by the Editorial Gustavo Casasola in conjunction with the Consejo Nacional para la Cultura y las Artes.

8. For good reproductions of Casasola imagery, see Arroyo as well as Lara Klahr and Hernández, Maawad, and Ortiz Monasterio.

9. Perhaps the definitive example of the Casasola penchant for erasing the authorship of photos and transforming their meaning can be found in the appropriation of Paco Mayo's award-winning photograph of a literacy campaign, one of the best-known of the five million images in the Hermanos Mayo archive. See my discussion of this tendency in Mraz, "Picturing Mexico's Past." The only scholar to have undertaken an analysis of Revolutionary photography in its contexts of publication is Ariel Arnal Lorenzo.

10. This number was arrived at by counting the photographs in Gustavo Casasola 1973. Of the 980 total photographs, 637 were of "great men," that is, the male "makers of history." This category does not include nameless soldiers, *campesinos*, or workers, nor does it identify men who are not in a leadership capacity—for example, the individuals who are being executed for forgery or desertion. Later volumes appear to contain an even higher percentage of "great men."

11. This is no exhaustive survey. I analyzed one volume from each series, comparing the total number of photos to those that pictured "great men" in some way. A few exceptions to the rule have recently appeared; see the photographs in Lau and Ramos, as well as those in Poniatowska.

12. One possible use would be to employ those pictures to open up questions about racial attitudes—for example, comparing photos of Porfirio Díaz taken in 1876 with those made in 1910, in order to determine whether he was whitening his skin over that period.

13. I have analyzed this series in Mraz, "Picturing Mexico."

14. This photograph offers an interesting lesson in the difficulties of determining authorship. It was published in the classic picture history by Anita Brenner (no. 97), where it is credited to Brown Bros., and the left-hand side of the picture is cropped. In the Martínez book, the left side

of the photo is occupied by the annotation of Flores Pérez: "Muertos in Diligencias [Dead in Diligencias]. Abril 21, 1914. P. Flores Perez, Fot." (Martínez 53). According to historian Bernardo García Díaz, Diligencias was an area "where one of the strongest nuclei against the invader was concentrated" (García Díaz 157, my translation). The complexity of this case can be seen in the fact that García Díaz reproduces the same photo, but with the following inscription written on it: "Hadsell. Killed in Front of Hotel Diligencias." The screw has yet another turn: both the Hadsell image and the Flores Pérez picture are housed in the AGN.

15. Martínez did not include this photo in *La intervención norteamericana*, perhaps because she could not locate it in the AGN (a problem I faced as well). It can be seen in García Díaz (154). Martínez seems unaware of the difference between the photographers she employs merely to illustrate a straight history of the invasion.

16. The authors of a groundbreaking study on "Zapata's photographer" remarked that, "[i]t is strange that there is not a single combat photo among those made by Amando Salmerón" (Jiménez and Villela 50).

17. I have discussed the question of direction in photojournalism at some length, as well as the specific case of the "Rearranged Corpse," in my book on Nacho López (169–85). See also my article "What's Documentary about Photography?"

18. This was the caption used in the original fascicle; in the series published the next year, it was changed to read, "In the lens of Agustín V. Casasola, women were incorporated in the revolutionary disorder" (Aguilar Camín et al. 7: 100–101).

19. No reference is made to the name "Adelita" in any other historia gráfica, although this photo is invariably reproduced.

20. A recent study shows that the U.S. government has expended enormous funds to finance reactionary culture through the CIA; see Frances Stonor Saunders, *The Cultural Cold War*.

21. See Jiménez and Villela. I have reviewed this and other books on Mexican photography in my article "Photographing Mexico."

References

Aguilar Camín, Héctor, et al. *Historia gráfica de México*, Fascículo 7. Mexico City: Editorial Patria-INAH, 1987

Historia gráfica de México, 10 vols. Mexico City: Editorial Patria-INAH, 1988.

Arnal Lorenzo, Ariel. Fotografía del zapatismo en la prensa de la Ciudad de México, 1910–1915. M.A. thesis., Universidad Iberoamericana, 2002.

Arroyo, Sergio Raúl. "El Fondo Casasola en la Fototeca Nacional del INAH." In *Mirada y memoria: Archivo fotográfico Casasola. México: 1900–1940*. Mexico City: Secretaría de Relaciones Exteriores, 2002, 11.

Barthes, Roland. *Camera Lucida*. Trans. Richard Howard. New York: Hill and Wang, 1981.

Berger, John. "Another Way of Telling." *Journal of Social Reconstruction* 1.1 (1980): 57–75.

Brenner, Anita. *The Wind That Swept Mexico: The History of the Mexican Revolution 1910–1942*. New York: Harper & Brothers, 1943.

Casasola, Agustín Víctor. *Álbum histórico gráfico: contiene los principales sucesos acaecidos durante las épocas de Díaz, de la Barra, Madero, Huerta y Obregón*. Mexico City: Agustín V. Casasola, 1921.

Casasola, Gustavo. "Gustavo Casasola: todos nuestros ayeres." In Cristina Pacheco, *La luz de México. Entrevistas con pintores y fotógrafos*. Mexico City: Fondo de Cultura Económica, 1988, 116–25.

______. *Historia gráfica de la Revolución Mexicana, vol.* 3. Mexico City: Trillas, 1973.

______. *Seis siglos de historia gráfica de México.* Mexico City: Gustavo Casasola, 1962, 1967–69, 1971, 1978; Gustavo Casasola and Consejo Nacional para la Cultura y las Artes, 1989.

Delgado, Ana Laura, coord. *Veracruz, imágenes de su historia.* 8 vols. Veracruz: Archivo General del Estado de Veracruz, 1989–92.

Florescano, Enrique, ed. *Así fue la Revolución Mexicana.* 8 vols. Mexico City: Senado de la República–SEP, 1985–86.

García Díaz, Bernardo. *Puerto de Veracruz.* Vol. 8, *Veracruz: imágenes de su historia.* Veracruz: Archivo General del Estado de Veracruz, 1992.

Gutiérrez Ruvalcaba, Ignacio. "A Fresh Look at the Casasola Archive." Special issue: *Mexican Photography. History of Photography* 20.3 (1996): 191–95.

Jiménez, Blanca, and Samuel Villela. *Los Salmerón. Un siglo de fotografía en Guerrero.* Mexico City: INAH, 1998.

Knight, Alan. *The Mexican Revolution*, vol. 2. *Counter-Revolution and Reconstruction.* Cambridge: Cambridge University Press, 1986.

Krauze, Enrique. *Biografía del poder.* 8 vols. Mexico City: Fondo de Cultura Económica, 1987.

Lara Klahr, Flora, and Marco Antonio Hernández. *El poder de la imagen y la imagen del poder: fotografías de prensa del porfiriato a la época actual.* Chapingo: Universidad Autónoma Chapingo, 1985.

Lau, Ana, and Carmen Ramos. *Mujeres y Revolución, 1900–1907.* Mexico City: Instituto Nacional de Estudios Históricos de la Revolución Mexicana, 1993.

Lomnitz, Claudio. "An Intellectual's Stock in the Factory of Mexico's Ruins: Enrique Krauze's *Mexico: Biography of Power.*" In *Deep Mexico, Silent Mexico.* Minneapolis: University of Minnesota Press, 2001, 212–27.

López de Nava Camarena, Rodolfo. *Mis hechos de campaña.* Mexico City: Instituto Nacional de Estudios Históricos de la Revolución Mexicana, 1995.

Maawad, David, ed. *Los inicios del México contemporáneo: Fotografías Fondo Casasola.* Mexico City: CNCA–FONCA–Casa de las imágenes–INAH, 1997.

Martínez, Andrea. *La intervención norteamericana: Veracruz, 1914.* Vol. 11, *Memoria y olvido: imágenes de México.* Ed. Martínez Assad. Mexico City: Martín Casillas–SEP, 1982.

Martínez Assad, Carlos, ed. *Memoria y olvido: imágenes de México.* 20 vols. Mexico City: Martín Casillas–SEP, 1982–83.

Mraz, John. "De la fotografia histórica: particularidad y nostalgia." *Nexos* 91 (July 1985): 9–12.

______"'En calidad de esclavas': obreras en los molinos de nixtamal, México, diciembre, 1919." *Historia obrera* 24 (March 1982): 2–14.

______. *Imágenes ferrocarrileras: una visión poblana.* Vol. 59, *Lecturas Históricas de Puebla.* Puebla: Gobierno del Estado de Puebla, 1991.

______. "Más allá de la decoración: hacía una historia gráfica de las mujeres en México." *Política y cultura* 1 (1992): 155–89.

______. "Mexican History in Photographs." In *The Mexico Reader: History, Culture, Politics.* Ed., Gilbert Joseph and Timothy Henderson. Durham, NC: Duke University Press, 2002, 116–57.

______. *Nacho López, Mexican Photographer.* Minneapolis: University of Minnesota Press, 2003.

______. "Photographing Mexico." *Mexican Studies / Estudios Mexicanos* 17.1 (2001): 193–211.

______. "Picturing Mexico's Past: Photography and *Historia Gráfica.*" Special issue: *Memory and Nation in Contemporary Mexico, South Central Review*, forthcoming.

______."Sebastião Salgado: Ways of Seeing Latin America." *Third Text 16.1 (2002):* 15–30.

______. "What's Documentary about Photography? From Directed to Digital Photojournalism." *Zonezero Magazine*, www.zonezero.com, 2002.

Ortiz Monasterio, Pablo, ed. *Jefes, héroes y caudillos: Archivo Casasola*. Mexico City: Fondo de Cultura Económica, 1985.

Poniatowska, Elena. *Las soldaderas*. Mexico City: Era, 1999.

Rodríguez Lapuente, Manuel. *Breve historia gráfica de la Revolución Mexicana*. Mexico City: G.Gili, 1987.

Salgado, Sebastião. *Other Americas*. New York: Pantheon, 1986.

Samuels, Rafael. *Theatres of Memory*. London: Verso, 1994.

Saunders, Frances Stonor. *The Cultural Cold War: The CIA and the World of Arts and Letters*. New York: The Free Press, 1999.

White, Hayden. "*Historiography and Historiophoty*." *American Historical Review* 95.5 (1988): 1193.

Chapter Two

Idols Behind Altars

Art, Authorship, and Authority in the Mexican Cultural Renaissance

Elissa J. Rashkin

Mexico cannot be measured by standards other than its own, which are like those of a picture . . . only as artists can Mexicans be intelligible.
—Anita Brenner, *Idols behind Altars*

In 1926, the young journalist and writer Anita Brenner invited photographer Edward Weston to collaborate with her on what would become an ambitious work tracing the historical, cultural and spiritual roots of Mexican modern art. Departing in June, Weston, his partner and apprentice Tina Modotti, and Weston's teenage son Brett spent months visiting the states of Oaxaca, Puebla, Michoacán, Jalisco, Guanajuato, and Querétaro, as well as working in Mexico City and surrounding communities. At that time, the cultural renaissance involving muralists and other artists was in full swing; during the same period, conflict between the church and the post-revolutionary central state was escalating into civil war, and uncertainty prevailed in the countryside. Braving the reticence of provincial priests and the suspicions of indigenous villagers, the team photographed religious icons and traditional pottery, masks and toys, church facades, pulquerías, and murals. The end result was *Idols behind Altars*, published in 1929. The book contained over 350 pages of text and 72 photographic plates, presenting a persuasive new view of Mexican indigenous culture: not as fading relic of a vanquished past, nor as colorful object of tourist curiosity, but rather as a strong, vibrant, culture of resistance and vital source of inspiration for the artists of post-revolutionary Mexico.

Brenner's book emerged out of a context that Helen Delpar has described in *The Enormous Vogue of Things Mexican: Cultural Relations between the United States and Mexico, 1920–1935*. In the wake of the Revolution, explains Delpar, diplomatic relations between the United States and Mexico were uneasy, and the images of

Mexico that predominated in the U.S. mass media were racist stereotypes, infused with a political edge. Some people in the United States, however, were drawn to the dynamism of the reborn nation and to the cultural and political experiments it had generated. Many Americans—leftist intellectuals, writers, artists—turned to Mexico as an alternative to a war-exhausted Europe and their own country, which they saw as increasingly mechanized, repressive, and sterile. Brenner became one of the most active promoters of Mexican arts and culture, while Weston and Modotti would create striking photographs that helped define Mexico's essence for a public hungry for imagery of a mythic country at once timeless and in the process of profound change.

Written for this public, *Idols behind Altars* offered English-speaking readers an overview of issues surrounding contemporary cultural production in Mexico. It also brought together two complementary ideological projects that flourished in the 1920s: on the one hand, the quest of many in the United States to find cultural alternatives south of the border, and on the other, the quest of Mexican intellectuals to forge a post-revolutionary cultural identity that would unite and uplift the nation. Unsurprisingly, these projects were fraught with contradiction, and the interpretations of Mexico that they produced have since been contested and often rejected as propagandistic and naïve.[1] In this essay, I argue that the issues that arise in a work like *Idols behind Altars* are productive for our understanding of the politics of representation, in the 1920s as well as today. In particular, points of tension found in the text concerning the issue of authorship—and consequently, cultural authority—become fruitful points of departure for a renewed discussion of the role of indigenous peoples and traditions in the construction of Mexican national identity, as well as in the practical life of the nation. These issues, I will argue, emerge with special complexity around the Weston and Modotti photographs and their role in the project. However, it is necessary first to develop a general context by looking at the substance of Brenner's text, which the photos and other illustrations are used to support.

Conquest, Creativity, and Resistance

In 1926 Anita Brenner was twenty-one years old and beginning what would be a distinguished career as an interpreter of Mexican history and culture. The daughter of Jewish immigrants, born in Mexico but raised partly in the United States, Brenner was uniquely positioned to observe Mexican culture from within and without. Upon her arrival in Mexico City in 1923, she joined the important intellectual circles of the day, working with scholars such as Manuel Gamio and Ernest Gruening and socializing with the artists and cultural figures whose work she would energetically promote, not only in her writing but also to galleries and collectors when she relocated to New York, in 1927. Her book is based on knowledge gained through her work as a reporter and researcher as well as on personal experience and perceptive observation of Mexican society and culture. Some parts are openly autobiographical while others rely on sources that she as often as not leaves unidentified. The work as a whole transcends generic boundaries, moving fluidly between historical reportage, anthropological observation, philosophical speculation, art criticism, and storytelling.

In the book's first chapter, Brenner presents a vision of Mexico as an integrated totality whose land, people, culture, architecture, and art are deeply interrelated.

> Mexico resolves itself harmoniously and powerfully as a great symphony or a great mural painting, consistent with itself, not as a nation in progress, but as a picture, with certain dominant themes, certain endlessly repeated forms and values in constantly different relationships, and always in the present, like the Aztec history-scrolls that were also calendars and books of creed. (15)

This description aptly characterizes Brenner's own text; for although *Idols* generally proceeds from past to present, it does not narrate a chronological history, but rather seeks to describe elements existent in 1926 upon which history has acted in specific ways with particular results, artistic as well as sociopolitical. For Brenner, the past in Mexico returns to shape the present to such a degree that the terms *past* and *present* lose their meaning. This is particularly true with regard to Mexican art, where "the same elements produce similar results, demonstrably, a hundred years apart, and since these are elements that have nothing to do with date, three hundred years later" (92). The elements she refers to are indigenous and Spanish, and it is the diverse processes of adaptation and syncretism, of cultural survival, assimilation, and resistance, that must be studied if one is to understand contemporary Mexican culture.

In her ironically titled chapter "The White Redeemers," Brenner depicts with unusual acuity the violence inflicted upon the indigenous population after Cortés's arrival on the coast of Veracruz, in 1519. Based on historical accounts, her presentation implicitly challenges the views of prominent Mexican thinkers such as José Vasconcelos, who considered the Spanish invasion to have had a "civilizing" influence on Mexico.[2] The next chapter outlines the structures of exploitation that developed under colonial rule and shows the direct relationship between the sumptuous churches and mansions built by the colonizers and the brutal exploitation of the mass of the Mexican people. As the chapter title "Churrigueresque" suggests, Brenner here begins to focus on the relationship between the social and the aesthetic, postulating artistic expression as a potent form of struggle. A pair of apocryphal anecdotes about victims of the Inquisition who escaped death through the sheer power of their art sets the stage for the exploration in subsequent chapters of the post-conquest transformation of the Mexican imaginary, focusing on the survival of the indigenous worldview, its expression under colonialism and in contemporary popular forms such as retablos and pulquería paintings, and its apparent rebirth following the 1910–20 Revolution.

The book's title encapsulates the history of indigenous survival that Brenner wishes to emphasize. Faced with the catastrophe of European conquest and domination, native Mexicans found ways to maintain their traditions by masking them under an apparent conversion to Christianity. Crucifixes and saint statues made by indigenous artisans often concealed objects (idols) that represented the older beliefs, while churches built by local laborers were similarly adorned with motifs whose decorative appearance belied a symbolic significance readily legible to native viewers. To the extent that Mexicans did accept the teachings of the Catholic priests, they transformed them to meet their own spiritual needs, creating a native faith whose underlying paganism very often transgressed the boundaries set by the Inquisition.

Idols behind Altars in some ways anticipates concerns taken up more recently by cultural historian Serge Gruzinski, who in *The Conquest of Mexico* uses maps, records of the Inquisition, and other evidence to trace the subtle effects of colonization on the indigenous imaginary. Brenner's emphasis, however, is less on the transformation of the native worldview than on its stubborn survival: "through the four muffled centuries since Cortez, the nation, disintegrated, lived as a unit still. You find it flowing like a river, dissolving its bewilderments and griefs, emerging" (128). One of these moments of emergence is the Revolution, which becomes the book's point of transition from folk art and culture in the broad sense to the cultural renaissance of the 1920s and its individual participants. If art was an integral part of native life and a means of covert resistance across four centuries, the post-revolutionary government gave art a place in its nation-building project. Artists of all backgrounds found in Mexico a rich source of thematic and formal inspiration; with the mural movement, the walls of public buildings began to display images of the workers and peasants that earlier regimes had abhorred and excluded from their centers of power. "In the span of one generation," wrote Brenner, "Mexico has come to herself. Her first and definitive gesture is artistic" (314).

This artistic gesture, however, is no longer the work of anonymous artisans, but rather of the artists whose work is considered in the second half of her book: David Alfaro Siqueiros, José Clemente Orozco, Diego Rivera, Francisco Goitia, and Jean Charlot, as well as others treated in less detail. Although some of these artists viewed themselves as craftsmen (forming the Revolutionary Syndicate of Technical Workers, Painters, and Sculptors to assert their solidarity and equal status with other workers), their break with the European art tradition was ultimately limited. For while they did take part in public art projects, leftist organizations, and other

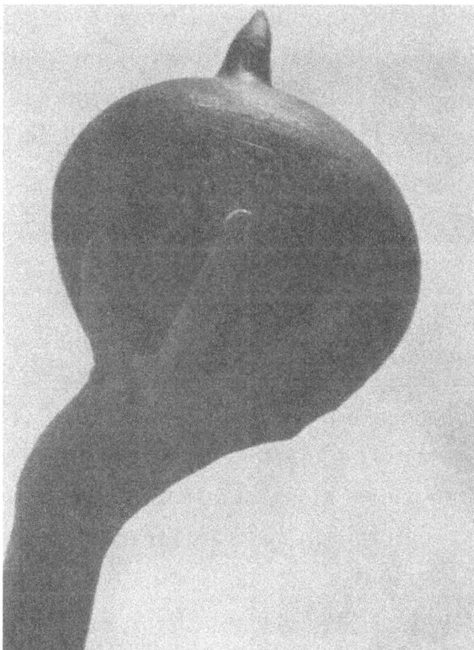

Fig 2.1. Edward Weston, *Hand of the Potter Amado Galván*, from *Idols behind Altars*, 1929.

nontraditional activities, it was not these acts but rather the marketing of their work through commissions, exhibitions, and gallery sales that would win them renown as modern masters. In the 1920s, reviews, articles, and exhibitions tended to equate these painters with the country itself, and to an extent, that is the interpretation presented in *Idols*: "her first and definitive gesture is artistic." But if these individuals now represented Mexico, what of the native craftspeople whose "innate" aesthetic sensibility and creative drive is exalted in the first part of the text?

Brenner's own notion of culture as a terrain of struggle invites engagement with a problem that her book does not directly address: that of authorship as a sign of cultural authority. The remainder of this essay examines this complex issue as it presents itself in three ways: the hierarchical positioning of "artists" and "artisans" within the text; the role of the two photographers as contract workers, artists, and participants in the production of *Idols behind Altars* as a collaborative text; and the role of photography itself in creating meaning. Each of these issues, when examined closely, reveals fissures and divisions that challenge the book's unifying vision: dissonant notes that undermine the unity of Brenner's harmonious "symphony."

Artists vs. Artisans

The frontispiece of *Idols* is a photo that stands as a symbol of the book as a whole. (fig. 2.1) A potter's hand raises a wet, semi-formed clay vessel into the air; both hand and vessel are partially silhouetted against a bright sky, with the effect that the hand

and clay are joined. This dramatic image reinforces Brenner's contention about the harmonious relation of man to his natural surroundings and man's creativity as an extension of this relationship. The hand as a traditional symbol of the human capacity for creation is also a synecdoche for indigenous man and his place in the universe: here, flesh, earth, and sky are one.

At the same time, *Hand of the Potter Amado Galván*, with its subcaption "Photograph by Edward Weston," is the only photo in the book directly attributed to a particular photographer, and also refers to the book's only named traditional artisan. The double signature Weston-Galván distances the photo and its content from artisanal tradition and relocates it in the realm of art in the occidental sense, in which the signature authenticates a unique individual creation. The photo is thus the symbolic culmination of two parallel efforts: one, the project of Brenner's book, being the vindication of indigenous Mexican art forms as equal to or greater in value than those derived from the European tradition; the other, peripheral to the text but not to Weston's participation in its production, being the effort to recognize photography not only as a means of reproducing images but also as an art in itself.

Idols behind Altars contains 118 illustrations, 72 of which are photographic plates. Of the photos, 37 are reproductions of artworks whose creators are identified in the captions, while 30 are photographs of antiquities, colonial religious art, or contemporary folk and popular art objects, the majority of whose producers are anonymous. A small number depict other subjects: *Pyramid of the Sun at San Juan Teotihuacan, Maguey, Interior of Native House, Painters and Masons at Work*. The bulk of the photos, however, depict either the art of known individuals working in the present or that of unknown craftspeople from various eras of Mexico's history.

In her "Notes on Illustrations," Brenner combines these two categories, noting that:

> Photographs and other illustrations were chosen in all cases for their artistic value, bearing in mind the typical, and the best expressions of Mexican art. The pleasant amazement which no doubt they will cause to artists and collectors will be amazement only because the ancient and modern art of this continent, as strong and as unique as that of any people in the history of humanity, has been so little examined. (333)

This statement reflects a widespread tendency of the era to regard Mexican art as both national and part of a cultural patrimony proper to artists throughout the Americas (Delpar 128–33). It also ignores a major division that the rest of the text creates and reinforces, namely that between artists and artisans.

This division goes beyond the presence or absence of authorial identification attached to the works, for in the case of both ancient and modern craft production, the identity of individual producers is often impossible to discern; at best, certain styles and genres may be linked to a particular village or region. In cases where a creative agent can be identified, Brenner does so; nevertheless, in discussing traditional art pieces, she uses conventions of anthropological documentation, presenting data such as size and function and privileging the typical rather than unique elements of each piece. In the notes on the works of named artists, on the other hand, her approach is that of a journalist, with emphasis on the personal history and vision of the individual. No longer "typical," the modern works are described in terms of their specificity, albeit within a clearly delineated sociopolitical context. While the craftsmen are objects of ethnographic study, the artists are subjects whose work is produced and judged according to modern aesthetic and intellectual standards.

The barrier between "craft" and "art," reflective of class and race prejudice, was a barrier that the Revolutionary artists and their supporters, such as Brenner, sought to overcome. The hierarchical separation that nevertheless seeps into *Idols* is symptomatic of their failure to do so. Two illustrations that seem to blur the line between the anonymity of the artisan and recognition of the individual artist ultimately attest to the resilience of that barrier. The first is *Hand of the Potter Amado Galván*, whose annotation describes the potter as "one of the most gifted of contemporary Mexican craftsmen" (333), whose style distinguishes him from other artisans in the same village of Tonalá (339). His association in the caption with the distinguished photographer Edward Weston further enhances Galván's status as an artist. In addition, the painted Galván vase shown in *Idols* fig. 30 is photographed in such a way as to emphasize its aesthetic rather than use value; the form of the vase is eliminated, so that the painted decoration appears flat, like a painting, giving the impression of "pure" rather than "decorative" art. However, Galván's genius is ultimately found to be intuitive, hence primitive: he is described as "remarkably uninfluenced in technique," he "holds his brush in the ancient native manner, which is surprisingly like the Chinese way" (339). His vase, though aesthetically rendered, is explained in Brenner's notes as illustrating the capacity of native pottery to incorporate novel content while retaining traditional form and techniques.

The second illustration, *Christ in the Garden of Olives* (*Idols* fig. 24), a woodcarving by Manuel Martínez Pintao, appears in the book amidst a discussion of religious syncretism and colonial art. A contemporary figure whose friends and admirers included Rivera, Charlot, and Weston, Pintao is presented in the book as an artisan deeply occupied with craft, whose work springs intuitively from the same hybrid sources as the baroque art of the colonial period. But in this case the carver is not an anonymous Indian laborer but rather a Spaniard, and his work is discussed individually and related to his biography. Although Brenner theorizes that Pintao's work might well have been produced by other craftspeople at other moments in Mexican history, in practice she grants Pintao the authorial status that the native artisans do not have and links him to the modern artists whose work is explored in the second half of the book. Galván's pottery, however masterful, remains typical, while Pintao's carving, though evocative of the colonial baroque, is associated only with Pintao, the artist.

That the categories "artist" and "artisan" indicate a hierarchy of value would probably have been denied by Brenner, who was certainly aware of the lack of importance that traditional craftspeople attached to the authorial signature. It is not the book's failure to transform "artisans" into "artists" that is at issue, but rather its inadvertent displacement of "artisans" once "artists" emerge to carry the torch of Mexican cultural identity in the post-revolutionary period. In her biography of Brenner, Susannah Glusker notes that *Idols behind Altars* was originally intended as two separate volumes: one on Mexican decorative arts, the other on the role of art in the Revolution. Because of the high cost of reproducing photographs, Brenner was forced by publishers to combine the two into one volume (89–90). Thus her attempt to link indigenous creative expressions with modern art, placing them on a continuum yet differentiating them discursively, is at least in part a result of production constraints. Nevertheless, the notion that modern artists represented the culmination of centuries of tradition and transformation was a popular one during the 1920s and 1930s, when the "vogue" for Mexican art in the United States led to exhibitions that included not only modern artists such as Rivera and Orozco but also traditional and contemporary folk art and art by schoolchildren.[3]

This juxtaposition, as is easy to perceive with hindsight, ignores the social and economic disparities affecting the thousands of anonymous artisans whose "innate" genius became the wellsprings from which the few recognized artists drank. The former, belonging to the subterranean stratum of what Guillermo Bonfil Batalla famously calls "México profundo" (deep Mexico), in fact disappear from the text at the very moment when their cultural and aesthetic contribution is recognized and incorporated into the hegemonic art of "México imaginario" (imaginary Mexico). The native artisans fail to become subjects in their own right and instead are used to validate the work of the urban modernists—and both of these, as Delpar shows, become a compelling attraction for international tourism.[4] Given that assimilation (often described as "civilization") of Mexico's large indigenous population was the policy advocated by most public officials and their advisors in the 1920s, the negation of indigenous subjectivity has political implications. Brenner's book, in its depth and complexity, gives greater weight to indigenous values than many other texts of its time, and in fact has recently been depicted as "reverently Indianist" (Albers,

"Tina Modotti" 17) and "messianic" (Cordero Reiman 25). Nevertheless, through its (perhaps forced) adoption of an evolutionary trajectory in which the traditional gives way to the modern, *Idols behind Altars* participates in the post-revolutionary project that Bonfil Batalla called "La redención del indio por la vía de su desaparición" (170) (the redemption of the Indian through his disappearance).

Creative Authority and the Collaborative Text

The issue of authorship in *Idols behind Altars* emerges in other forms besides the categorization of artistic production discussed above. Although the modern artists studied in the book are accorded the authorial signature that authenticates their authority as creative subjects, those who participated directly in the book's production occupy a more complex position. In fact, besides the commissioned photographers, many other artists contributed to Brenner's project. Some of the chapters are based on earlier essays that Brenner coauthored with Jean Charlot; according to Glusker, these were published sometimes under one name, sometimes under the other, or both (89). Charlot's contribution to the book is uncredited, perhaps by mutual agreement, and it is surely this loose attitude toward signature in her own writing that allows Brenner to include a large number of graphics without crediting their producers. In the heady atmosphere of the 1920s, copyright—the authorial signature as market commodity—was far less important than the spirit of collective purpose.

The photographers, on the other hand, are clearly named in the text, yet closer examination of their participation undercuts the apparent authority of this naming. At issue, first of all, is Tina Modotti's role in the project. The contract that Weston signed with the project's sponsor, the Universidad Nacional de México, specified work to be done by Weston and an "assistant"; Weston's assistant, Modotti, was by then a photographer in her own right, and as the two had long enjoyed a professional as well as personal partnership, her role in the *Idols* project was never formalized in writing. The photographs from the expedition were rarely signed, giving rise to a debate over their authorship that, though irresolvable, reinforces the importance of signature as authenticator of value.

Brenner herself, in the book's acknowledgments, refers to the "two photographers who shared this commission, Edward Weston and Tina Modotti" (7). Recent scholarship, particularly feminist scholarship, has taken up this characterization of the project as part of its effort to validate Modotti's work as a photographer. Olivier Debroise writes that the work that Modotti did for *Idols behind Altars* "opened doors to her in Mexico" (214). In fact, after the *Idols* project, Modotti became the principal photographer for the magazine *Mexican Folkways* and was sought after for her skillful documentation of mural projects. Yet Weston scholar Amy Conger argues that there is no compelling proof of Modotti's authorship of any of the photos other than one made at an earlier date (*Head of Christ, Idols* fig. 18). An entry in Weston's journal that has been used to minimize Modotti's photographic contribution reads: "if a woman had not been in our party, especially Tina, with her tact and sympathy for the Indians, a woman which made the group seem less aggressive, Brett and I would never have finished the work" (Weston 175). In this entry, the author's son seems to replace Modotti as Weston's cophotographer, yet Brett Weston recalled that neither he nor Modotti contributed photographs to the project (Conger 49).

Interestingly, recent research by Patricia Albers has uncovered photographs taken by Modotti during the *Idols* trip and mailed to her ex-mother-in-law in the United States. Unlike the still lifes required by the book, these photographs depict people and landscapes and reflect Modotti's interest in the rhythms of Mexican life. Based on the available evidence, it seems plausible that on the expedition Modotti primarily served as interpreter, negotiator, and technical assistant to Weston, while taking photographs for her own use and pleasure. However, the exact authorship of the *Idols* photos will probably never be known, and the debate that the question has generated is symptomatic of the power—and market value—that our society grants to the authorial signature, whether deployed to uphold the reputation of a recognized "master" or to validate the contribution of a talented artist unfairly neglected on the basis of her gender.

To further complicate the question, Conger points out that technical details of some of the photographs suggest that they were taken by neither Weston nor Modotti—again indicating the lack of concern for authorial signature in the process of developing the project. Indeed, *Tortillera* (*Idols* fig. 29) seems to cast doubt on the very existence of an "author." This illustration shows an artist's rendering of a terra cotta figure that depicts a woman making tortillas, characterized by Brenner as a clay portrait. The *tortillera* is interpreted by three artists in succession: the potter working from life, the artist sketching the figurine, and the photographer reproducing the drawing. Brenner, however, speaks only of the figurine, not the successive layers of representation (fig. 2.2).

The figure is described as a type produced mainly by the Panduro family in Tlaquepaque, Jalisco; the maker of this particular piece, however, is not identified. The authorship of the drawing is even less clear, for even though the artist—Jean Charlot, who would depict this same clay figure in paintings as late as 1967—warrants a full chapter elsewhere in the book, here he is not named. Yet comparison with Weston's original photo of the Tlaquepaque piece reveals the uniqueness of Charlot's style.[5] The original piece and Charlot's rendition clearly reflect the visions of two different artists, yet they are superimposed in such a way as to hide the second artist's role in creating meaning. Similarly, the photographer's intervention (in this case minimal) is not addressed, for like all of the book's illustrations, its purpose is simply

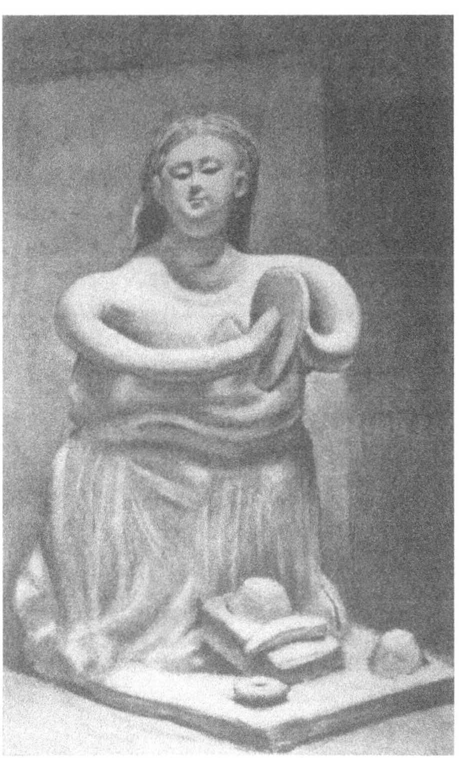

Fig 2.2. *Tortillera*, from *Idols behind Altars*, 1929.

to present its subject matter. Thus, unlike that of *Hand of the Potter Amado Galván*, Brenner's framing of *Tortillera* discards the importance of authorship altogether. It is an interesting paradox that in a book about art and artists, not only is the authority of individual creators frequently undermined, but the power of representation, especially photographic representation, is ignored.

The Photographic Intervention

To what extent did *Idols* bring into play the cultural authority of what I will continue to refer to as Weston and Modotti's photographs? It is safe to state that Brenner herself was a sincere admirer of both photographers, having known them socially, written favorable articles on Weston for *Revista de Revistas* and the *Brooklyn Eagle*, and been photographed by both. However, the images published in *Idols* did not always preserve the artists' vision. Conger—who judges the whole project rather harshly—cites alterations, such as those made to the photo of the *pulquería El Charrito* (*Idols* fig. 48), which originally included a man looking out of a window above the bar, but which in the book is cropped just above the pulquería's name, eliminating the building's second story (Conger 46, 51). The original framing plays the deep space suggested by the open window against the flatness of the painted exterior, and also uses the two incidental human figures (one at sidewalk level in the bottom left, the

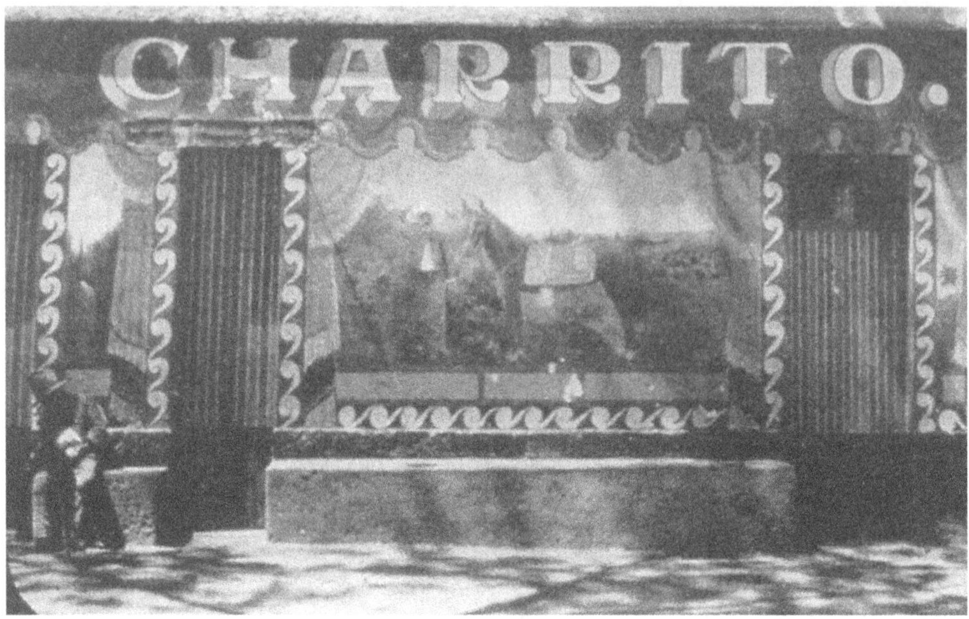

Fig 2.3. Edward Weston, *Pulquería El Charrito*, from *Idols behind Altars*, 1929.

other in the upper right) to create a dynamic diagonal across the main rectangular plane and to highlight the role of the pulquería in the social life of the neighborhood. The book's cropped version eliminates these aspects, thus fulfilling its purpose as illustration but downplaying the interest of the photograph as art (fig. 2.3).

Weston, for his part, viewed the commission primarily as a job, poorly paid but carrying the benefit of allowing him to leave the city and travel through the Mexican countryside. Constraints on subject matter and the pressure to work quickly prevented him from taking full ownership of the project as a creative opportunity; however, he wrote in his daybook that the "four hundred negatives to be done appear at present as a herculean task—for each one must be exceptional in interest, technically fine, and must be finished within a few months" (163). His journals show that the task was indeed an arduous one, but most of the resulting photographs met his rigorous standards. Weston at this time was developing and refining his ideas regarding photography as presentation rather than interpretation; rejecting the prevailing model of "artistic" photography, based on artificially evocative compositions and effects, his goal was to render "the thing itself," not by effacing the photographic medium, but rather by utilizing it as effectively as possible. Evaluating his own work in his journal, he often proclaimed the success of a photo by noting that he had "seen correctly."

The images included in the book break not only with the conventions of photographic pictorialism, but also with the picturesque depiction of ethnic and

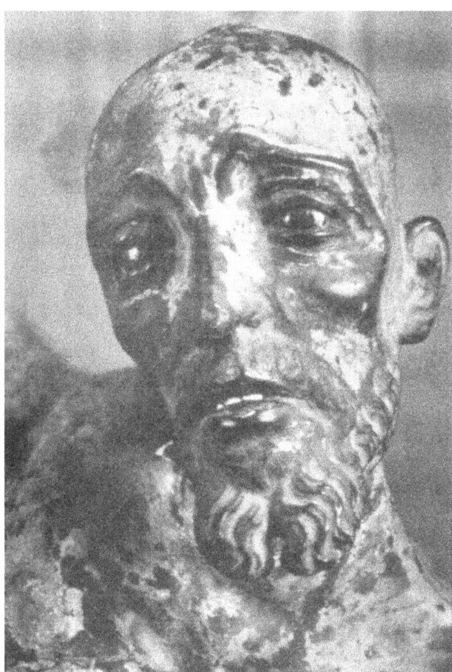

Fig 2.4. Tina Modotti, *Head of Christ*, from *Idols behind Altars*, 1929.

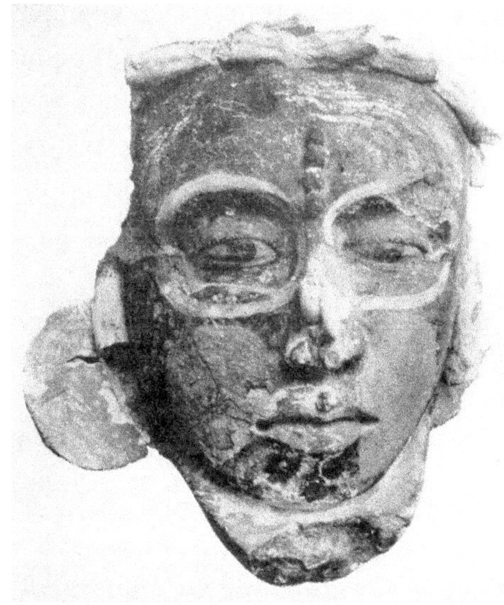

Fig 2.5. *Polychrome Maya sculpture*, from *Idols behind Altars*, 1929.

regional "types" exemplified in contemporaneous works such as Hugo Brehme's *México pintoresco* (1923) and the photography magazine *Helios* (Mraz 10). Instead, they remove single objects from their everyday context, emphasizing their expressive power. Although only a few shots include actual people, many depict artistic renditions of the human form and are framed much like portraits. This is significant insofar as the photographic art, especially in Mexico, developed and gained legitimacy through portraiture (Debroise 26). Photography, wrote Roland Barthes, "began, historically, as an art of the Person: of identity, of civil status, of what we might call, in all senses of the term, the body's *formality*" (79). Although the *Idols* project is normally discussed in relation to Weston's and Modotti's work with still life, it is interesting to find that its photographs do for their stone, wood, and painted subjects what portraits did (and still do) for their human ones: affirm—or transform—their social status, valorize their existence by fixing it in time and space for posterity. But unlike portraits of the bourgeoisie, the faces that look out of the pages of *Idols* are indigenous faces, faces depicted according to an indigenous vision, or a modernist vision intent on reclaiming indigenous origins. The eerie humanity of the *Head of Christ*, with its luminous features, expresses the suffering of his makers and worshippers (fig. 2.4); a Totonac mask (*Idols* fig. 9) smiles across the centuries, its irrepressible humor challenging stereotypes of Indians as somber and impassive; a Mayan sculpture from the Yucatan (*Idols* fig. 10) gazes back at the camera as if to defy its worn and damaged condition and assert its presence as a living subject despite years of colonial domination and repression (fig. 2.5). If, as Barthes suggests, every photograph implies "the return of the dead" (9), in this case the return has political consequences. For the "dead" in this case are Mexico's indigenous multitudes whom, as Bonfil Batalla shows, almost every government from 1521 on has sought to repress, eliminate, or render invisible. In the *Idols* photographs these dead are resurrected, arising to demonstrate their continued existence and claim their place at the center of the modern Mexican nation.

Considered as a narrative in themselves, the photographs constitute a strong argument for the artistic and spiritual value of the Mexican art tradition, somewhat different from the one made by Brenner in the written text—for Weston's indifference to the social context of his subject matter has the effect of placing all of his subjects on equal footing. For Weston, it was the characteristics of each object photographed that counted, not necessarily their "typical" features. Although well aware of the debates taking place around him regarding the role of the artist in society, Weston had little interest in contributing to revolutionary change, promoting *indigenismo*, or supporting any cause other than that of his own creative development. Therese Mulligan points out that a photograph like his *El Charrito* "denotes not only Weston's preoccupation with native art, but his concern to minimize the physical and psychological distance between the subject and the viewer" (78). His attraction to popular art was visceral and aesthetic; the playfulness and integration of form and function he found in Mexican crafts was an antidote to the pretentious self-importance he associated with the art world in the United States. Moreover, his understanding of photography as a material process as well as a creative act led him to feel a kinship with the artisan tradition. His *Hand of the Potter Amado Galván* is, in a sense, a self-portrait.

This affinity between photographer and traditional artisan was, of course, limited. Although Weston and Modotti frequently lacked the financial freedom to operate as full-time artists and sold commissioned portraits to make ends meet, their world was far removed from that of rural craft producers, who by 1926 were finding their art increasingly dependent upon and subject to the needs of the capitalist marketplace. During the course of his travels for the *Idols* expedition, Weston noted a decline in artistic quality in many regions and attributed it to the lamentable impact of outside influences. Truly fine indigenous art, he believed, was "unspoiled," and in confrontation with modernity, its rapid extinction was inevitable. Unlike Brenner, who in *Idols* expressed optimism about the Mexican people's ability to adapt and change while retaining their essential character, Weston could not conceive of a positive indigenous response to modernity. His delight in Mexican popular art contains a seed of sadness—perhaps, the sadness of impending death that, for Barthes, is the condition of photography itself (96).

Conclusion: Toward a Non-Hierarchical Cultural Pluralism

Mexico proved decisive in both Weston's and Modotti's professional careers. For Modotti, whose Mexican work constitutes the bulk of her comparatively small oeuvre, her engagement with Mexican subjects is seen as key in the development of a social commitment inseparable from her art.[6] She continued to work in Mexico until early 1930, documenting mural projects, contributing to *Mexican Folkways* and other magazines, and creating increasingly politicized imagery that nevertheless adhered to the rigorous formal criteria developed during her years with Weston. In 1930 she was deported under slim pretexts in retaliation for her Communist activities. Before leaving Mexico, she wrote to Weston, "I almost owe it to the country to show, not so much what I have done here, but especially what *can be done*, without recurring to colonial churches and charros and chinas poblanas, and the similar trash most fotographers [sic] have indulged in" (Albers, *Shadows, Fire, Snow* 228).

Weston returned to the United States in 1926, after completing the *Idols* project, and gradually his images of natural forms (shells, peppers, the California coast) eclipsed his Mexican work. Yet his few years in Mexico marked a crucial turning point in his development. His experimentation with Mexican popular art objects initiated his trajectory as a master of the still life, and it was in Mexico that he attained the level of skill and confidence that would guide his work from then on. In an often-quoted journal entry, Weston wrote,

> These several years in Mexico have influenced my thought and life. Not so much the contact with my artist friends as the less direct proximity of a primitive race. Before Mexico I had been surrounded by the usual mass of American burgess—sprinkled with a few sophisticated friends. Of simple peasant people I knew nothing. And I have been refreshed by their elemental expression,—I have felt the soil. (190)

The "primitive race" did not benefit nearly so much from the attention bestowed on its artistic expression by Weston, Modotti, Brenner, and countless tourists, museum-goers, scholars, and artists during the 1920s and 1930s. As Néstor García Canclini shows in *Transforming Modernity*, artisanal production did not die out in the twentieth century as a consequence of Mexico's capitalist modernization; rather, as traditional communities lost the ability to meet their needs in a self-sufficient manner, craft manufacturing emerged as an economic alternative. Today, crafts, rather than being industrialized, preserve "authenticity" as a selling point; however, most objects of everyday use are now factory-produced, while "authentic" forms of production are employed to create souvenirs for tourists and objects to decorate foreign and upper-class homes.[7] Since the producers' economic circumstances lead them to sell their work very cheaply, the commercial craft economy both assuages and perpetuates poverty.

The inequality that is frankly and grotesquely illustrated in the anecdotes from Weston's *Daybooks* that depict Modotti and Weston persuading villagers to sell their few treasured belongings or even the shirts off their backs for the artists' sheer aesthetic pleasure has not changed since the 1920s. For the post-revolutionary governments did not incorporate Mexico's indigenous communities into their national project; on the contrary, the inclusion of indigenous images and symbols in nationalist discourse belied their exclusion, as the Zapatista rebellion that broke out in 1994 (and other indigenous interventions before and since) have made painfully clear. To acknowledge this is not to discount the pioneering efforts of Brenner, Weston, and Modotti, each of whom, in *Idols* and elsewhere, worked hard and often brilliantly to counteract the entrenched disdain for native culture produced by colonialism, racism, and class division. Over seven decades later, the limitations in their ideas are more readily apparent, but to critique them is to recognize the greater understanding of social processes available to us today, an understanding produced by the failures of the past.

In the 1920s, influential thinkers formulated programs on behalf of an indigenous other: well-intentioned efforts that were crippled by their apparently inevitable replication of existing power relations and social divisions. Similarly patronizing policy making continues to this day, but the persistence and strength of indigenous organizing and self-representation has forced the politically committed nonindigenous intellectual of today to realize that it is not enough to appreciate or appropriate native cultural traditions, or to incorporate multicultural elements and/or participants into existing institutions, without substantially transforming the latter. Rather, we must take seriously the calls being issued by indigenous communities and organizations for economic reform and political self-determination.

To this end, we may conclude by echoing García Canclini's bold call for "a systematic change of all means of cultural production, circulation, and consumption":

> We must reorganize institutions devoted to artistic and artisanal promotion and distribution, construct an alternative history of art and an alternative theory of culture, alternative schools, and alternative mass media . . . However, this reorganization of the cultural realm will be fully accomplished only in a society that is not based on the commercial exploitation of men and women and their work, or at least where people fight to build such a society. (114)

In such a pluralistic and democratic society, where the integrity of all subjects is fully recognized and respected, perhaps the harmony envisioned by Brenner may finally be realized.

Notes

The author wishes to thank Susannah Glusker for her comments on drafts of this chapter, and Peter Rashkin for technical assistance.

1. See Pérez Montfort for a useful critique of the "deber ser" implicit in post-revolutionary nationalist discourse.

2. Marentes (*José Vasconcelos*) argues that Vasconcelos's idealization of Spanish "civilization" and corresponding view of indigenous Americans as backward was not a later development (as some scholars claim), but one fully present in his writings of the 1920s. As minister of education (1920–24), Vasconcelos founded the Misiones Culturales (cultural missions) in order to bring modernity to the Mexican countryside; his Departamento de Educación y Cultura Indígena (department of indigenous culture and education) published biographies of Spanish missionaries as examples to its teachers and hung their portraits in its offices (Morales Mora 83–84).

3. While Rivera seems to have benefited from this type of publicity, Orozco resented it bitterly. Writing to Jean Charlot about an ill-fated exhibit at New York's Art Center in February 1928, he complained that "el único objeto de la exhibición es vender cháchara de 'arte' (?) 'popular mexicano,' un negocio comercial, para el cual nuestros cuadros sólo han servido de carteles de propaganda" (54) (the only point of the exhibition is to sell knick-knacks of "popular Mexican" "art" (?), a commercial business, for which our paintings have only served as advertising posters).

4. Brenner's next book, *Your Mexican Holiday*, was in fact a tourist guide.

5. Weston's photo of the figurine is reproduced in *México en la obra de Jean Charlot* (60).

6. The literature on Modotti is extensive. Studies focusing on her work in Mexico include: Albers's and Cordero Reiman's essays in *Tina Modotti and the Mexican Renaissance*; Figarella, *Edward Weston y Tina Modotti en México*; González Cruz Manjarrez, *Tina Modotti y el muralismo mexicano*; Lowe, *Tina Modotti and Edward Weston: The Mexican Years*; and Noble, *Tina Modotti: Image, Texture, Photography*.

7. Interestingly, agencies acting as brokers for craft producers have encouraged the use of signature to raise the monetary value of artisanal work, attracting collectors and creating a place for traditional artisans within the art marketplace. An alternative form of marketing is that proposed by fair-trade advocates, who often support production cooperatives and emphasize social and ecological concerns.

References

Albers, Patricia. *Shadows, Fire, Snow: The Life of Tina Modotti*. New York: Clarkson Potter, 1999.

______. "Tina Modotti and the Mexican Renaissance." In *Tina Modotti and the Mexican Renaissance*. Paris: Jean-Michel Place, 2000, 11–23.

Barthes, Roland. *Camera Lucida: Reflections on Photography*. 1980. Trans. Richard Howard. New York: Farrar, Straus and Giroux, 1981.

Bonfil Batalla, Guillermo. *México profundo: una civilización negada.* Mexico City: Grijalbo, 1990.

Brehme, Hugo. *México pintoresco.* 1923. Mexico City: Porrúa and INAH, 1990.

Brenner, Anita. *Idols behind Altars.* New York: Payson and Clarke, 1929.

______. *Your Mexican Holiday.* New York: GB Putnam Sons, 1932.

Conger, Amy. *Edward Weston in Mexico, 1923–1926.* Albuquerque: University of New Mexico Press, 1983.

Cordero Reiman, Karen. "Cloaks of Innocence and Ideology: Constructing a Modern Mexican Art, 1920–1929." In *Tina Modotti and the Mexican Renaissance.* Paris: Jean-Michel Place, 2000, 25–35.

Debroise, Olivier. *Mexican Suite: A History of Photography in Mexico.* Austin: University of Texas Press, 2001.

Delpar, Helen. *The Enormous Vogue of Things Mexican: Cultural Relations between the United States and Mexico, 1920–1935.* Tuscaloosa and London: University of Alabama Press, 1992.

Figarella, Mariana. *Edward Weston y Tina Modotti en México.* Mexico City: Universidad Nacional Autónoma de México, 2002.

García Canclini, Néstor. *Transforming Modernity: Popular Culture in Mexico.* Trans. Lidia Lozano. Austin: University of Texas Press, 1993.

Glusker, Susannah Joel. *Anita Brenner: A Mind of Her Own.* Austin: University of Texas Press, 1998.

González Cruz Manjarrez, Maricela. *Tina Modotti y el muralismo mexicano.* Mexico City: Universidad Nacional Autónoma de México, 1999.

Gruzinski, Serge. *The Conquest of Mexico: The Incorporation of Indian Societies into the Western World, Sixteenth–Eighteenth Centuries.* Trans. Eileen Corrigan. Cambridge: Polity, 1993.

Lowe, Sara. *Tina Modotti and Edward Weston: The Mexico Years.* London: Merrell Holberton, 2004.

Marentes, Luis A. *José Vasconcelos and the Writing of the Mexican Revolution.* New York: Twayne, 2000.

México en la obra de Jean Charlot. Mexico City: Instituto Nacional de Bellas Artes, 1994.

Morales Mora, Mario. "Y la utopía se hizo luz." *Misiones Culturales: los años utópicos 1920–1938.* Mexico City: Instituto Nacional de Bellas Artes, 1999, 69–131.

Mraz, John. "Envisioning Mexico: Photography and National Identity." Duke University–University of North Carolina Program in Latin American Studies, Working Paper Series, Working Paper 32. Durham, NC: Duke University, 2001.

Mulligan, Therese. Introduction. *Modotti y Weston: Mexicanidad.* A Coruña and Madrid: Fundación Pedro Barrié de la Maza, 1999.

Noble, Andrea. *Tina Modotti: Image, Texture, Photography.* Albuquerque: University of New Mexico Press, 2001.

Orozco, José Clemente. *El artista en Nueva York (Cartas a Jean Charlot y textos inéditos, 1925–1929).* Mexico City: Siglo XXI, 1971.

Pérez Montfort, Ricardo. *Avatares del nacionalismo cultural: cinco ensayos.* Mexico City: CIESAS, 2000.

Weston, Edward. *The Daybooks of Edward Weston.* Vol. 1: *Mexico.* Ed. Nancy Newhall. Millerton, NY: Aperture, 1961.

Chapter Three

Narrative Imag(in)ing

Susan Meiselas Documents the Sandinista Revolution in Nicaragua

Janis Breckenridge

It was with a sense of urgency that Susan Meiselas's award-winning photographic documentation of human suffering and armed conflict proliferated among the world's leading newspapers and newsmagazines in the late 1970s and early 80s. Although a young and relatively unknown freelance photographer only recently affiliated with Magnum, she rapidly became the foremost photojournalist to cover the Sandinista revolution in Nicaragua and was the first photographer to record the El Mozote massacre in El Salvador. As Laurence Shames eloquently observed at the time, "[w]hen Latin American revolutions hold the news, she often holds the negatives" (42), for Meiselas's images of insurrection throughout Central America dominated respected publications including the *New York Times*, the London *Times*, *Time* magazine, *Geo*, and *Paris Match*.

Meiselas quickly gained international recognition as a war photographer offering an unconventional approach. Drawing upon her background in anthropology, the young photographer recorded the peoples' standard of living and harsh working conditions together with their experience of physical violence and armed combat. In this way, her coverage incorporated the broad social context behind popular insurrection. In Nicaragua, and later in El Salvador, Meiselas strove to portray the individual civilian's experience of civil war and thus capture the complexity of violent social revolution. It is for this reason that in his insightful review of *Nicaragua*, Harvey Kaye lavishes praise upon these images. In light of John Berger's notions regarding historical consciousness (understood as celebrating the personal experience of history), Kaye insists that "this work of Meiselas is the best contemporary example I have seen of the alternative photography Berger is calling for" (90).[1] In Kaye's estimation, by self-consciously employing unconventional practices (that is, by creating a testimonial to a people, place, and time rather than merely reporting "sensationalist" news events), the committed photographer becomes a storyteller engaged in the construction of collective memory. Accordingly, throughout this essay, I analyze the narrative dimension of *Nicaragua*. In addition to photographic content (the story), I pay particular attention to narrative structure, especially the placement of sequenced images, the controlled use of blank space, and the incorporation of testimonial voices.

As indicated in articles, reviews, and interviews, Meiselas became increasingly preoccupied with the official treatment of her in-depth coverage.[2] The exigency of making events known gradually gave way to Meiselas's developing awareness and growing disillusionment with the media's superficial treatment of her carefully selected and captioned images. Concern with the appropriation of her photographic record replaced the photographer's initial satisfaction concerning the efficiency and speed with which these pictures were viewed around the world. A few years later, Meiselas would reflect upon the process of distributing her images and express dismay that "getting a story out to a particular market may lead to the diminishing and distortion of their intended meanings" ("Some Thoughts" 12). Not only did she maintain interest in tracing the individual and independent history of these popular images—many of which came to have a life of their own, even appearing in stenciled form together with pro-Sandinista graffiti throughout Nicaragua—she further sought out the protagonists who appear in her photographs. Her aim, in part, was to evaluate the effect of the revolution upon their individual lives. But of particular interest, according to Meiselas, was "how the people there saw themselves in the photographs" (Coleman 29). This project resulted in the creation of *Pictures from a Revolution* (1991), a documentary film that appeared ten years after the Sandinista victory.[3]

Dissatisfaction with the interpretation of her visual record, which in her opinion had not only been decontextualized but also made incomprehensible, led Meiselas to assume direct editorial control and "create a book that would link otherwise isolated images together to make them understandable" ("Some Thoughts" 11). The resulting visual narrative, *Nicaragua: June 1978–July 1979* (1981) features seventy-one uninterrupted, full-page, color photographs documenting the successful Sandinista revolution. Supplementary textual material—including historical documents, testimonial accounts, and poetry—follows the photo-essay. In a somewhat paradoxical fashion, considering her concern with the co-option of her images, the body of the text provides the reader with few clues for decoding the photographs. This remains particularly surprising, given that the appendix presupposes a reader unfamiliar with this small country. Literally placing Nicaragua on a map and then presenting factual information in the form of encyclopedic statistics and a chronological timeline, this textual account supplements the visual narrative with a wide range of testimonial voices. Furthermore, this final section reproduces each photograph as a black and white contact image now explicated through detailed captioning. In this way, the appendix offers an array of textual references that foster a contextualized rereading of the sequenced images.

Unlike the standard newspaper or magazine format, where photographs complement written text, Meiselas incorporates an extensive register of cultural documents and oral testimony without overshadowing the visual imagery. With *Nicaragua*, the photographic essay offers a sustained narrative reading through sequenced visual images: verbal registers serve as subtexts (or postscripts) that augment the visual narrative. Thus it is through her photographs that Meiselas, as storyteller, narrates how prolonged conditions of extreme poverty and brutal oppression lead to the emergence and escalation of armed revolt.

The book format not only grants permanency to images that would otherwise receive limited exposure, but further permits a contextualized reading whereby the photographs are understood and interpreted in relation to each other. For this reason, I conceive of and study *Nicaragua* as a narrative unit, rather than a series of isolated images. Close readings of individual photographs are performed within the context of the overall narrative, with a particular focus on the interplay between pictorial images and written text. The isolation of text from image, the mutually informing and mutually dependent components that comprise the photographic essay, produces an unresolved tension that underlies *Nicaragua*.

Imaging/Voicing: A Retrospective

The integration of pictorial narrative and individual voices is a consistent attribute of Susan Meiselas's work. Her first project, a documentation of the lives of women performing in traveling strip shows, combines photographic representation with sound recordings. A gallery installation at the Whitney Museum exposed the viewer not only to visual images but also to the experience of aural immersion—conversations in which the women reflect upon their own lives were juxtaposed with live recordings from actual shows. In its original printed format, *Carnival Strippers* (1976) retains this verbal dimension by converting the audio into written text that is strategically placed among the photographs. A recent reprint (2003) offers a revised selection and ordering of the photographic images together with an audio CD featuring an assemblage of the subjects' voices.

The effort to facilitate her subjects' self-representation becomes increasingly vital in Meiselas's later works. *Nicaragua* exclusively features her own images and isolates the verbal component of the narrative. Only a decade later, with *Pictures from a Revolution*, would the photographs serve as a catalyst for the subjects to comment directly on the images as well as reflect upon the impact of recent historical events on their own lives. In contrast, the collaborative *El Salvador: Work of Thirty Photographers* (1983) inserts Meiselas's visual documentation into a text featuring the work of both foreign and local photographers in direct dialogue with the voices of local participants (as reproduced by Carolyn Forché, a self-proclaimed "poet of witness" whose 1982 volume *The Country Between Us* details El Salvador's civil war). Simultaneously chronicling popular struggle through photographic imagery and textual material, *El Salvador* features captioned black-and-white images frequently "interrupted" by transcriptions from conversations and interviews with local residents. Thus it provides a verbal dimension to the photographs that remains absent, or at least separated and distanced, in *Nicaragua*.

With subsequent projects Meiselas moved from a position of contributor and coeditor to place herself solely in an editing role. *Chile from Within: 1973–1988* (1990), which documents life under the Pinochet regime, exhibits images and texts by resident and exiled Chileans and in this way attempts to facilitate self-expression. Meiselas explains that the aim was to "let the world see Chile through *Chilean* eyes" (Harris 24, emphasis in original). However, the reader cannot fail to notice that the book privileges the voices of well-known literary figures, especially the coeditors Marco de la Parra and Ariel Dorfman (whose words originally appeared as op-ed pieces in the *New York Times*). A more recent effort, *Kurdistan: In the Shadow of History* (1997), originated with the documentation of physical evidence of human rights violations uncovered by forensic experts. The final version of this extensive project, which examines the encounter between East and West, traces the history of a displaced people through a collection of images and oral accounts. Documenting the recent "discovery" and subsequent contact with a native culture, *Encounters with the Dani* (2003), Meiselas's latest publication, likewise addresses the inherent dangers of representing the "exotic other."

In creating visual testimonies, Meiselas conscientiously strives to let her subjects speak—often placing their own voices and images in dialogue with her photographic record. This alternative practice of photojournalism, in contrast with the more cursory treatment offered by press publications, allows the viewer to perform an interactive reading that links sequenced visual imagery with testimonial narrative and cultural material, including historical documents and literature. Yet, as the artist herself has suggested, "the problem for the photographer remains: how to create images and a sequence that's sustaining and engaging, but asks people to wait, to not think they know, but to be suspended and uncertain along with those pictured whose lives are unpredictable and unraveling" (Ritchin 41).

Visualizing Violence

Meiselas's first Latin American project, *Nicaragua*, resolves this "problem" by offering the reader a suspenseful visual narrative that follows the conventional format of a well-constructed plot. Turning the pages, the viewer becomes a witness to escalating social tensions that climax in armed revolt. Plot resolution takes the form of the happy ending: the denouement consists of victorious celebrations. Nevertheless, until a more complete picture is revealed in the appendix, the reader remains in suspense, uncertain of the specific details and political machinations that motivate the narrative action.

Although framed with verbal texts, the photographs that capture history in *Nicaragua: June 1978–July 1979* bear few initial textual clues to guide the viewer toward a single or "correct" interpretation of the visual argument. Rather, the story of a people who embrace armed revolt is rendered through pictorial representation alone; as Meiselas insists, "the pictures should speak for themselves" (Taylor 1350).[4] Only a few brief quotes, a title page (specifying the location, the time period, and the photographer), a "table of contents" (outlining the main events covered) and an epigraph (pointing to the silenced sociopolitical context under which these events transpired) aid the reader in "unraveling" or deciphering the visual narrative.[5] Nonetheless, as more than one critic has observed, the narrative flow produced by the scrupulously selected and carefully sequenced photographs is not difficult to follow. "The political message is a relatively simple, linear one, easily read off the sequence of images: poverty and exploitation beget repression, which leads to resistance and finally, revolution" (Binford n.p.). In fact, the plot has been aptly summarized in even more reductive terms: "resignation gives way to defiance, defiance to assault" (Imrie 1202). Yet these synopses focus exclusively upon historic causality or the story, neglecting to consider the structural devices that generate this coherent, narrative reading.

The content of the images comprising *Nicaragua* represents historic events, as the aforementioned reviewers make apparent. Nonetheless, in addition to following the plot or storyline of this gradually unfolding chronicle, an appreciation of textual layout is crucial to interpreting the progression of images. Complementing the development of narrative action, the repetition of key thematic elements (including masks, fire, and graffiti) as well as recurring visual stimuli (especially the use of intense color) further link the photographs and thereby reinforce the escalating sequence of images.

Scenes depicting the harsh quotidian reality of peasant life—in particular the stark living conditions and the arduous labor performed by both men and women—introduce the reader to Nicaragua. One immediately enters a desolate rural village comprised of a few meager dwellings, where a solitary pig roams free and rain muddies the otherwise empty street. We later discover (through the caption in the appendix) that this is in fact the main street of town. Subsequent images include a woman hand-washing laundry in a dirty puddle and a sweat-drenched man shouldering a large burlap sack. He struggles to climb a steep plank, while an overweight overseer, comfortably perched on a stool, casually looks on.[6] Once again,

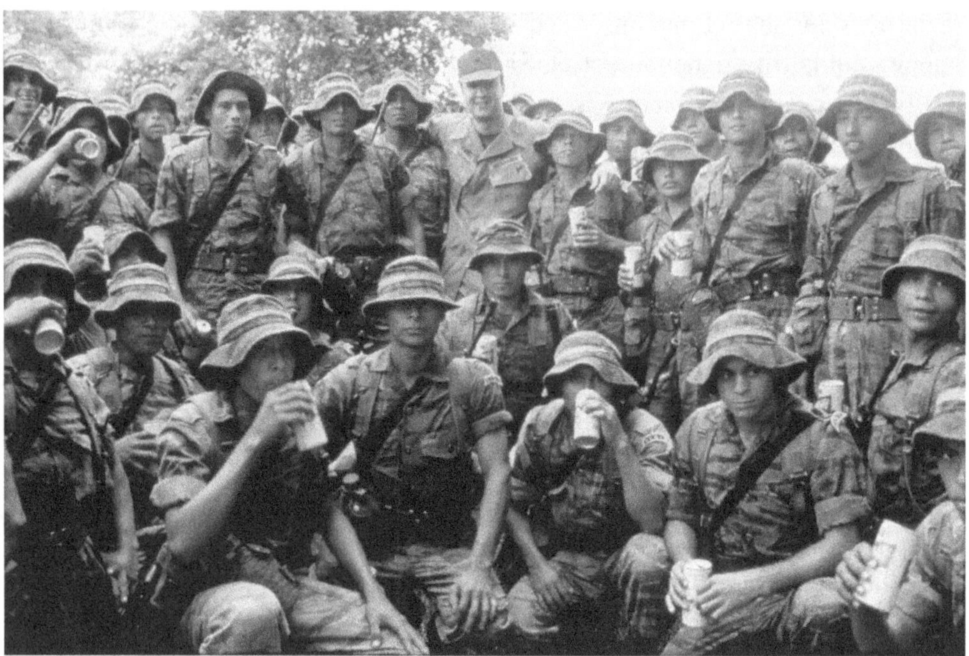

Fig. 3.1. Susan Meiselas/Magnum Photos. Anastasio Somoza Portocarrero, 27-year-old son of the president and head of the elite infantry training school (EEBI). Following a tradition of the United States Army, the recruits celebrate graduation with Schlitz beer. From *Nicaragua*, 1979.

the captions supplement our initial reading by providing additional information—we find that the first image portrays a "[w]oman washing laundry in sewer of downtown Managua," while the second documents a man "[l]oading one hundred pound sacks of grain, Granada." The separation of word and image, that is, the distancing of the visual text from the following contextualized rereading of the same images, made possible with the addition of captioning, produces differing responses. While poverty and harsh working conditions are not lost upon the viewer during a primary reading, the addition of statistical data and factual information increases our knowledge of daily hardship beyond the initial aesthetic or sensual experience.

Given the isolation of text and image, *Nicaragua* must rely upon a detailed linkage between successive photographs in order to create and sustain the narrative progression. This is accomplished in a variety of ways: the gradual unfolding of a recognizable plot, thematic unity, and visual clues that connect images. The continual advancement of the story, achieved through both content and form, reinforces the reader's recognition of the photographs as a visual text. For example, a blue sky marked with soft, billowing clouds links the images of the woman washing clothes with that of a field worker. Were it not for the sharp contrast between the urban and rural backgrounds that clearly distinguish the settings, the opposing pages could easily be mistaken for a panoramic shot.

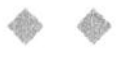

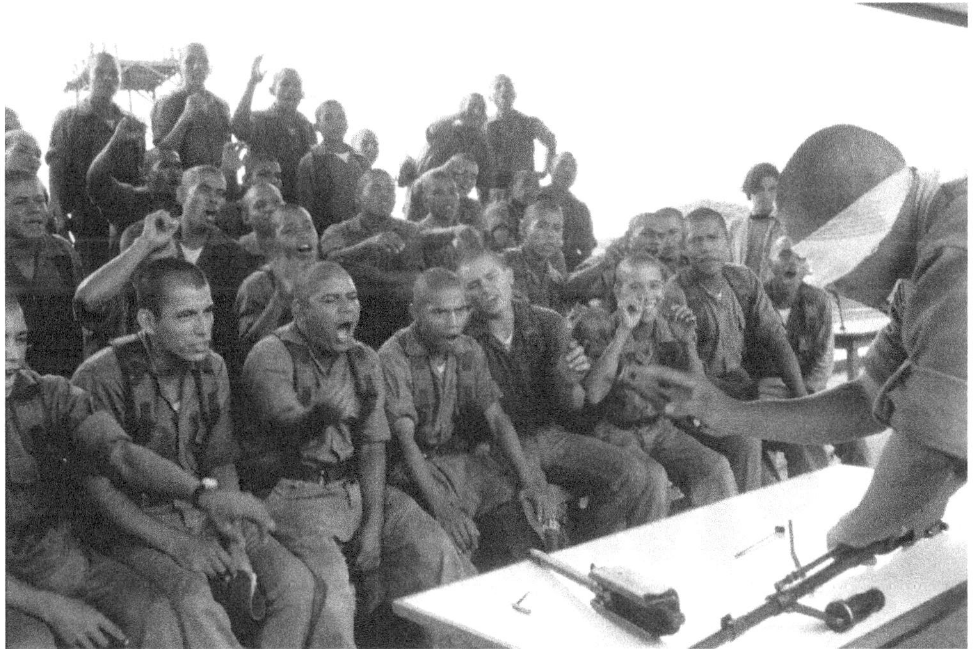

Fig. 3.2. Susan Meiselas/Magnum Photos. New recruits to National Guard practice blindfolded dismantling of a gun. From *Nicaragua*, 1979.

Likewise aiding narrative progression, the depiction of a dark-skinned maid serving a white family in a country club setting (information which must, of course, be gleaned from the appendix) serves as a transitional image and clearly marks a shift in thematic content. On the one hand, we are made aware of the sharp division between classes characteristic of Central American nations. At the same time, the reader is carefully led from representations of the working poor to depictions of those with affluence and power; subsequent images depict the dictator and his military men.

An additional visual clue demarcates this radical change in the story line and further prepares the reader for a sudden shift in narrative content. The meticulous textual layout incorporates only a few blank pages—underscoring the significance whenever this technique is employed. The use of blank space in *Nicaragua* serves two fundamental purposes: to effectively isolate images of particular weight (Binford notes that this strategy prevents graphic images from detracting from adjoining photographs) or, alternatively, to signal changes in narrative sequence.

In addition to calling the reader's attention to changing directions in plot, the empty page introducing the first depiction of Somoza accentuates the starched whiteness that characterizes the official dress not only of the dictator, but of his entire entourage. Unnecessarily identifying President Anastasio Somoza Debayle—who clearly wears the presidential sash—the caption at first seems merely redundant,

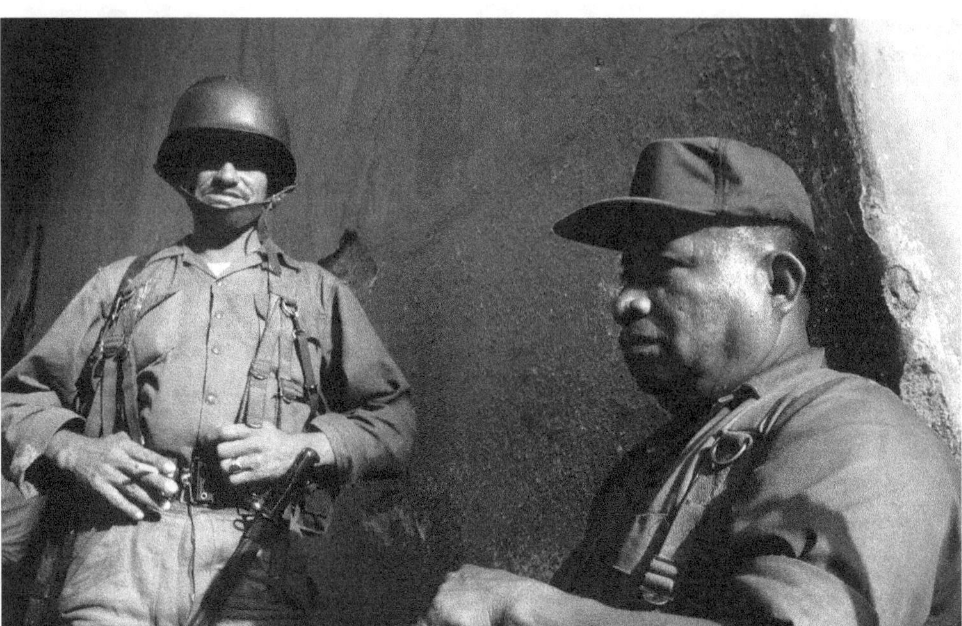

Fig. 3.3. Susan Meiselas/Magnum Photos. National Guard on Duty. From *Nicaragua*, 1979.

with the possible exception of locating this image in time, namely June of 1978. However, the text further indicates that the president is opening a new session in congress: thus, in narrative terms, the story shifts from poverty (the peasant workers) to wealth (the country club) to political power.

The following series of images confirms that in Nicaragua political power entails the control of both congress and the military. Much in keeping with the function of the near-perfect sky uniting adjoining images of peasant workers, the opaque horizon and similarly uniformed figures allow separate images of soldiers to blend together (figs. 3.1 and 3.2). Yet subtle indicators differentiate the two groups. The first company poses calmly around their leader and gazes obediently at the photographer. Their controlled, orderly conduct, as well as their careful, symmetrical arrangement, suggests official, well-disciplined troops. In contrast, an off-center grouping of men displaying chaotic behavior—the soldiers yell and raise their fists as they cheer on a comrade who assembles a weapon while nothing less than a bandana serves as a blindfold—leads the reader to speculate that they represent rebel forces. Although united by identical backdrops, the juxtaposed photographs reveal the soldiers' markedly contrasting temperaments. The uncertain reader must turn to the appendix for guidance. In this case, the captions clarify any ambiguity (and correct a possible misreading), clearly identifying both armies as extensions of the state: the elite infantry led by Somoza's son and new recruits to the national

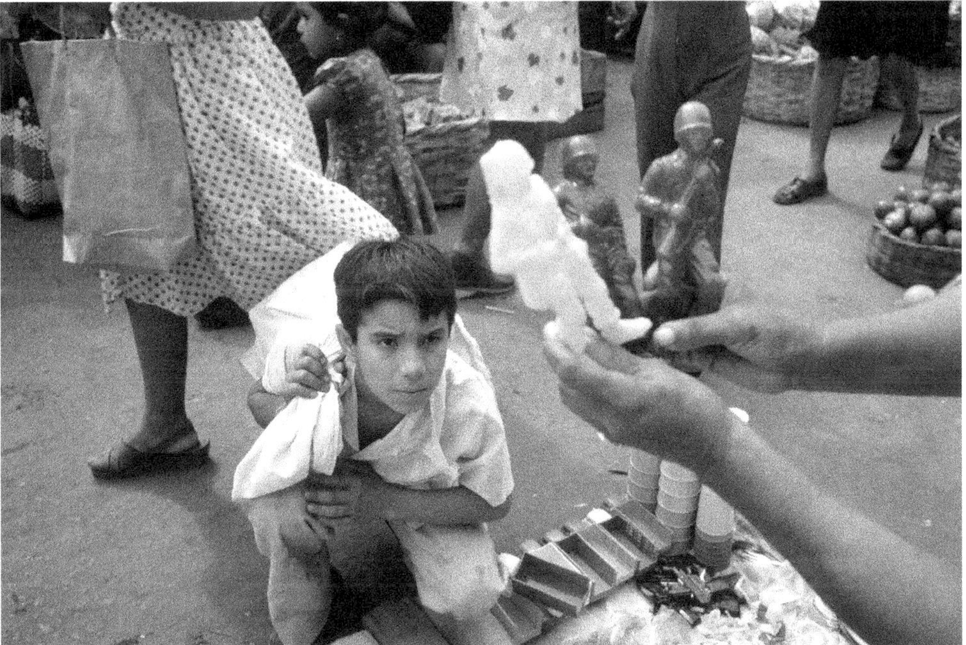

Fig. 3.4. Susan Meiselas/Magnum Photos. Diriamba. Market Place. From *Nicaragua*, 1979.

guard (often composed of peasants and the working class).

More significantly, the captions further inform the viewer of otherwise invisible connections between these armed forces and the United States—the national guard is reported to carry U.S.-made rifles, and the elite troops carry out traditions typical of the U.S. Army. The textual material at the book's conclusion maintains a sustained emphasis on United States military involvement in Nicaragua, yet its inimical presence, though pervasive, remains virtually unseen in the photographs. The visual narrative fosters broad reader interpretation (at the risk of creating an incomplete or erroneous picture), while the captions refine or even transform one's initial impression.

In much the same way as it was introduced, this section of *Nicaragua* concludes with images that reinforce the dichotomy between social sectors, while serving as a transition for the scenes that follow. A striking image of a young boy in a marketplace contemplating colorful toy soldiers mirrors the reader's own position—we likewise contemplate members of the national guard who are depicted on the opposing page (figs. 3.3 and 3.4). The hesitant adolescent assumes a submissive, kneeling pose and looks up at the plastic figures (evident symbols of authority) with a quizzical expression. Although we view the juvenile from above (a position of power and superiority), a child's perspective on the background is maintained. Rendered as if from his eye level, only the legs and feet of passersby are visible (in fact, the only

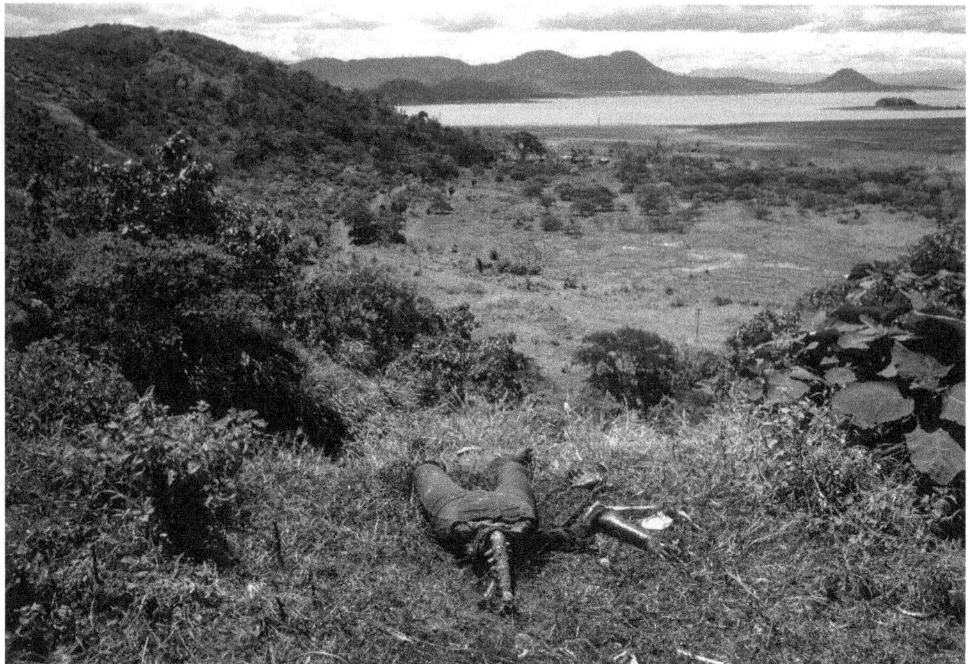

Fig. 3.5. Susan Meiselas/Magnum Photos. Cuesta del Plomo, hillside outside Managua. From *Nicaragua*, 1979.

person fully visible is another child). In contrast, the real soldiers' upper bodies dominate the frame. One of the guards looks down at the camera in the same way that we peer at the boy. However, his demeanor carries a latent threat. The triangular play of gazes (from military personnel to outside reader, from us to the boy) parallels the positioning of the three soldiers in the vendor's hands. In this way, the stage has been set and the characters introduced, such that the viewer is led to sympathize, if not identify, with the subjects being photographed.[7]

What follows is perhaps the most disturbing image of the collection (fig. 3.5). The narrative departs from representations of latent violence to more graphic depictions of brutality. As the text chronicles increasing social unrest and confrontation, this particular image captures the horrific reality of threats being carried out. A beautiful landscape with lush vegetation, serene lake, gentle mountains, and rolling clouds remains punctuated by the chilling presence of a dismembered corpse prominently displayed in the foreground. Appropriately set apart by a blank page, this pivotal image—which for Meiselas served as "evidence" verifying the stories she was hearing ("Some Thoughts" 29)—signals that the people not only suffer inequality and economic exploitation, but also endure extreme physical violence carried out directly on civilian bodies. After identifying the location as a well-known site for assassinations by the national guard, the caption simply states, "People searched here daily for missing persons" (14). The reader's initial shock, resulting from the horror of the scene, is magnified by the matter-of-fact textual explanation regarding the everyday nature of such atrocities.

Meiselas has commented on the difficulty for an outside audience to assimilate this scene: "the American public could not relate their reality to this image. They simply could not account for what they saw" ("Some Thoughts" 11). It is the photographer's contention that contextualizing graphic representations of violence and brutality within a narrative sequence renders such images comprehensible. I would add that this photograph, in addition to revealing the difficulty of comprehending Nicaragua's quotidian violence, exposes the reader's apprehension when a representation of extreme violence disrupts an ordinary aesthetic. This image represents a typical landscape photograph marred by the unbearable presence of the abject. The viewer tends to separate the distinct components of the image—to isolate the graphic horror of the mutilated corpse from the natural beauty of the surroundings. In fact, readers struggle to incorporate the anomalous messages contained in this unsettling image much in the same way as they must learn to assimilate and accurately interpret the diverse scenes and narrative sequencing presented throughout the entire photo-essay.

Continuing with its precise placement of images, *Nicaragua* documents increasing forms of resistance coupled with mounting repression. Through deliberate narrative sequencing, Meiselas leads us to understand that protest marches and funeral processions quickly lead to preparations for armed resistance. At the same time, we are shown that heavily armed soldiers, military tanks, and air strikes are the government's response to protest and popular uprising. Tensions escalate and suspense builds as scenes of insurrection climax in full-scale civil war.

Demonstrators who shout, shake their fists, and raise placards characterize three successive shots of protest marches (figs. 3.6, 3.7, and 3.8). At first the similar content of these repeated depictions seems merely redundant. But, as with the overall layout of *Nicaragua*, the meticulous textual arrangement highlights escalating tensions: from the intensity of individual anguish to the communal anger of the multitude, from personal grief to collective unrest. With each image, the camera angle widens to allow more and more of the subject matter to be revealed within the frame. A close-up focuses upon the anguished reactions of particular individuals, even as it permits the viewer to gaze voyeuristically into an open casket. Shot from a slightly elevated position, its perspective produces a dizzying and almost claustrophobic effect. The viewer, positioned just above the pallbearers, remains caught up among the dense throng. In contrast, a second, frontal shot captures advancing demonstrators head on. Their protestations (as well as the arresting gaze of a martyr whose photograph leads the procession) are aimed directly at the viewer, who now remains set apart from the crowd. Finally, a wide-angle shot effectively conveys the extensive participation in

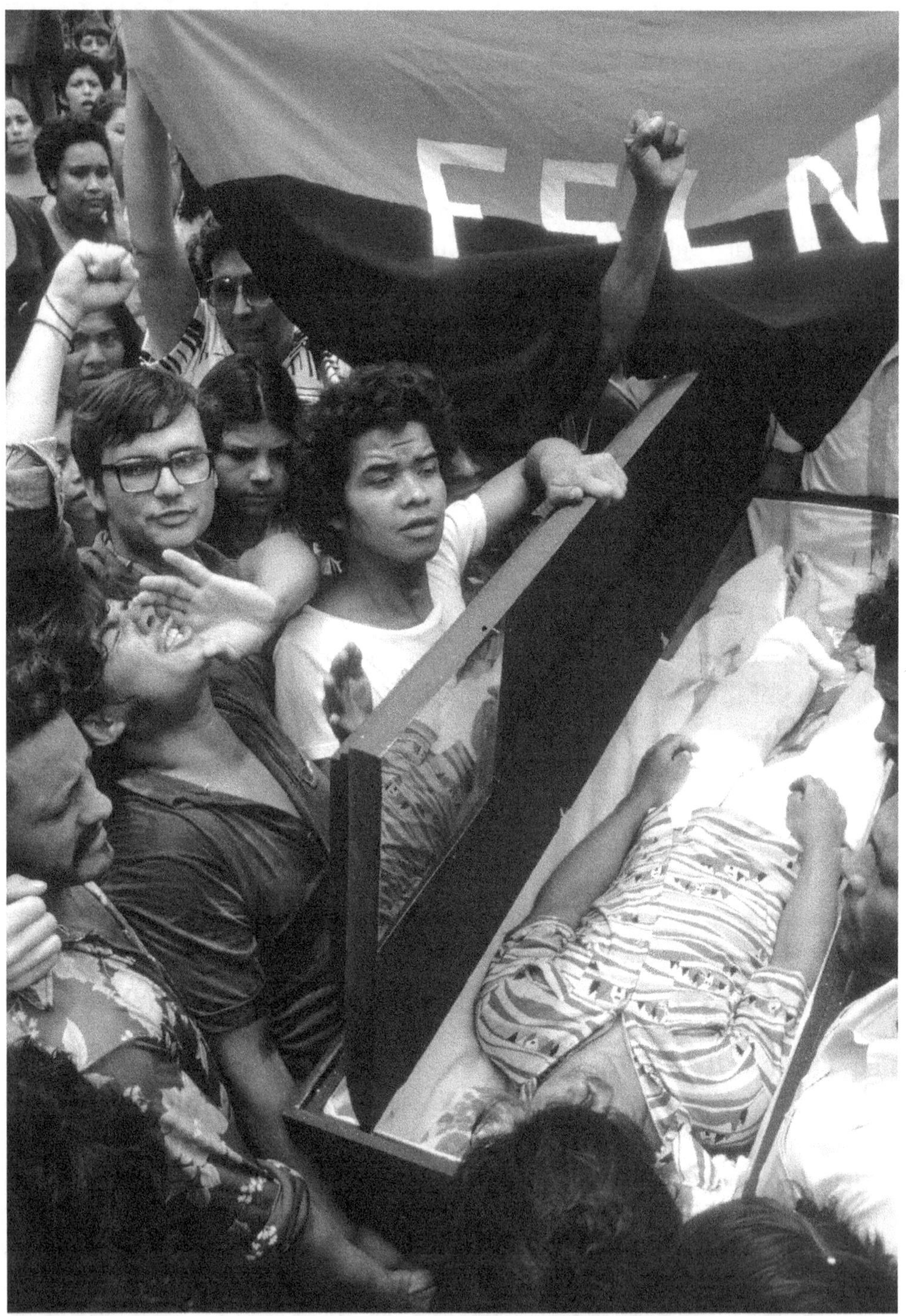

Fig. 3.6. Susan Meiselas/Magnum Photos. Diriamba. Burial of Worker. From *Nicaragua*, 1979.

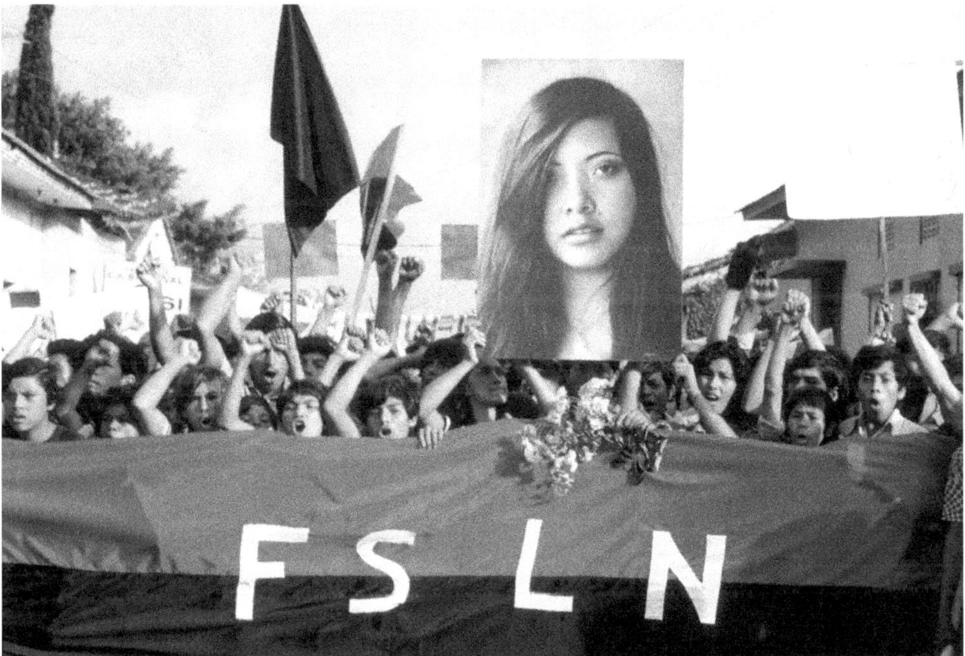

Fig. 3.7. Susan Meiselas/Magnum Photos. Jonotepe. A Funeral Procession. From *Nicaragua*, 1979.

these collective protests. Although this gradual panning out creates the illusion that these scenes originated from a single march, the captions indicate otherwise. In this way, we are shown that countless people participated in such demonstrations and that these events occurred throughout the country.

Again, it is not merely narrative content that links these photographs of collective protest. The images are primarily connected by means of formal composition, color, and internal text. Specifically, the banner of the Frente Sandinista de Liberación Nacional (FSLN)—where a red-and-black background sports large white lettering that clearly identifies the opposition group—serves both as a historical marker and a visual stimulus uniting successive photos. As Binford indicates, with these photographs Meiselas's layout achieves impeccable "aesthetic balance." Precisely inverse images appear on opposing pages. The signature banner floats over the open casket and effectively closes off the upper edge of the photograph on the left. In contrast, the vibrant banner—now held just below the front line of demonstrators—frames the lower portion of the photograph on the right, even as the martyr's enlarged portrait hovers overhead. The FSLN capitalized on the symbolic import of this imposing image—her eternally youthful presence seems to have literally arisen from the dead. The reader discerns that, ironically, her portrait remains far more captivating than the actual corpse openly displayed in the funeral procession (see figs. 3.6 and 3.7). As will be discussed shortly, photographs within photographs throughout *Nicaragua*

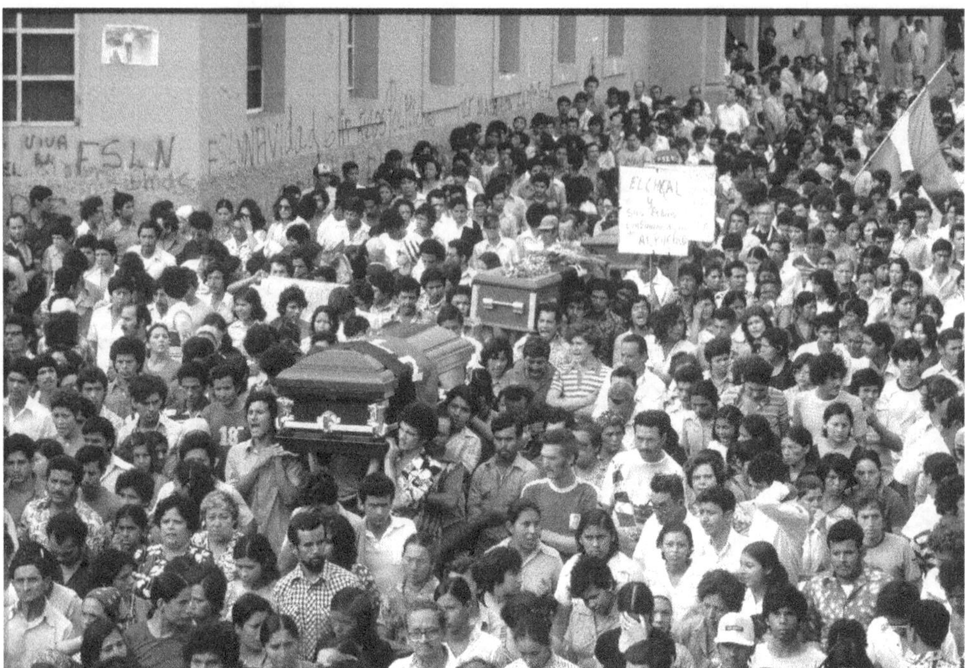

Fig. 3.8. Susan Meiselas/Magnum Photos. Jonotepe. Coffins of students being carried in the streets. From *Nicaragua*, 1979.

speak to the ability of visual images to condense meaning even as they instruct the viewer on the critical skills necessary for interpreting a visual narrative.

Once again a blank white page indicates a transition in narrative content. At the same time, a faint arrow etched in pale blue graffiti directs our gaze to an unlikely revolutionary, a man who is not only heavy-set but clad in blue jeans and a bandana. Only his rifle reveals his identity. While the caption clearly announces that "popular forces begin final offensive," the writing on the wall more subtly indicates the protagonistic role played by ordinary citizens. This unmasked fighter earnestly directs our attention to the pages that follow. He not only aims his weapon at the military troops invading town on the next pages (the caption verifies that this is indeed the same town), but literally beckons or points his finger, anxiously signaling the beginning of the final offensive. His obvious excitement and enthusiasm anticipate the narrative's climax. The reader, positioned as a comrade in arms (furthering the identification process), is invited to directly engage the narrative's rapidly unfolding events. We are encouraged not only to observe the conflict, but also to participate in the ensuing combat, where an impromptu civilian militia faced uniformed, well-trained, and heavily equipped military personnel (fig. 3.9).

Representations of combat climax when an iconic Che Guevara–like rebel launches a Molotov cocktail. Each individual and every weapon that appear on the

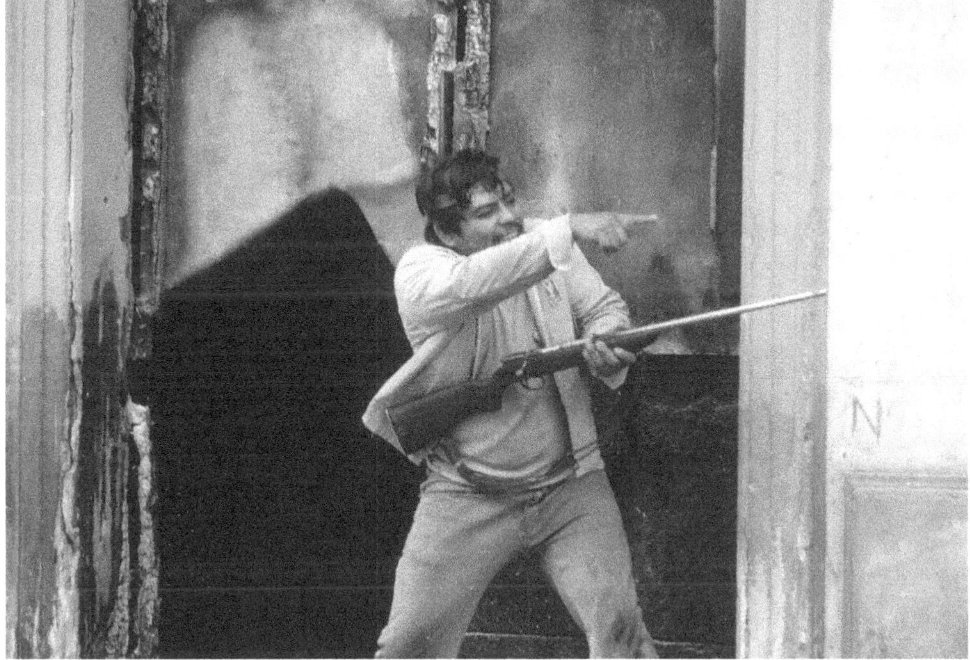

Fig. 3.9. Susan Meiselas/Magnum Photos. Jonotepe. Masaya. June 8, 1979. Popular Forces begin final offensive. From *Nicaragua*, 1979.

facing pages literally point to this central figure, whose motion (parallel to that of the previous combatant) accelerates the forward momentum of the narrative. As we turn the page, the movement of our eyes traces the path of the fiery projectile which seems to ignite an image of Somoza. A clear symbol of defeat, the flaming image of the dictator suggests victory for the popular forces. The reader need not rely on captions to confirm that the regime has been overthrown, for ensuing images of jubilant celebrations verify triumph.

However, the final page layout, which stands as a visual epilogue to the pictorial narrative, graphically illustrates the identification and recovery of victims for burial, as well as the process of urban renewal (figs. 3.11 and 3.12). An unsettling image of a father retrieving the unrecognizable remains of his charred son (identified by his nearby shoe, according to the caption) warns of the ongoing cost of civil war. At the same time, the emergence of political artwork in public spaces reminds the reader that history remains to be recorded. As a muralist paints a mythically proportioned Sandinista fighter, significantly detailing the gun he carries, the reader comprehends that propaganda will be the new weapon of the FSLN. The larger-than-life proportions and intensely bright colors hint at an overly optimistic interpretation of recent history. Not only do the closing photographs stand as a "bleak portent of the arduous task of rebuilding a nation," as one critic has suggested (Polemis 358); even

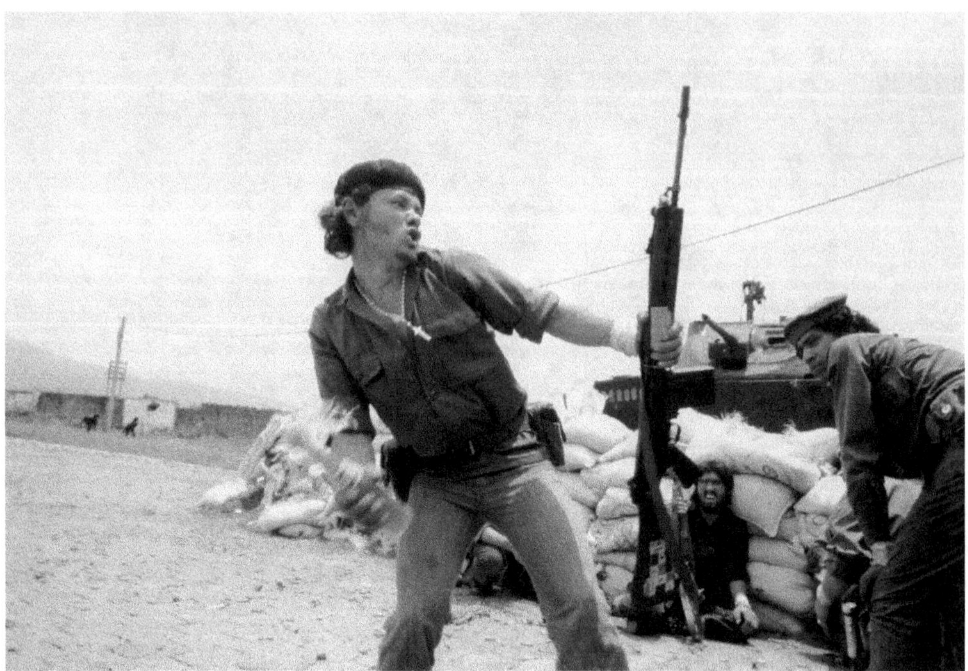

Fig. 3.10. Susan Meiselas/Magnum Photos. Estelí. Sandanistas at the walls of the Estelí National Guard Headquarters. From *Nicaragua*, 1979.

more importantly, they signal the task of constructing public memory. Although the caption (which merely states "Wall, Managua") downplays its symbolic import, the final image can be read as a self-conscious gesture on the part of Susan Meiselas. Just as the committed art piece celebrates the victory of the popular forces, *Nicaragua* commemorates the civilian experience of civil war through visual representation.

Narrating Images: Interpreting Recurring Themes

Throughout the text, we have witnessed the growing independence of Meiselas's photographic images, although the captions provide relevant information such as the date and location, as well as the translation of textual messages (graffiti and placards, for example). Initially, the captions supply additional, highly specific information not readily discernable in the photograph. These particular details augment elements within the photo, make apparent otherwise invisible connections to other images, or clarify textual ambiguity and thus correct possible misreadings. However, as readers become immersed in the visual narrative, they are less and less likely to turn to the appendix. Especially on encountering images of combat, viewers become engrossed in the mounting tension and the rapid textual momentum. At the same time, familiarity with narrative content fosters growing confidence in one's ability to accurately interpret the photographs, thus rendering the captions less crucial to narrative comprehension.

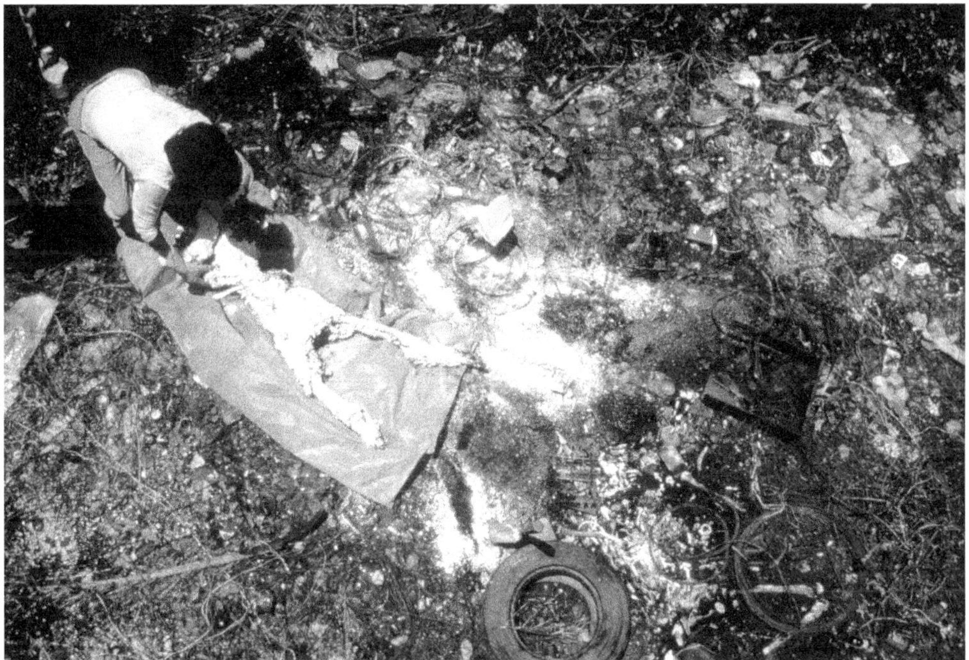

Fig. 3.11. Susan Meiselas/Magnum Photos. Father collecting remains of assassinated son, identified by a shoe nearby. From *Nicaragua*, 1979.

Not coincidentally, the written text now offers less auxiliary information, often only locating battle scenes and victorious celebrations in time and space. Together with this decreasing reliance on captions, the sequenced photographs increasingly make visible the many thematic elements that recur throughout *Nicaragua*.

Such leitmotifs include the repetition with difference of both masks and fire, elements closely tied to the escalating plot. The reader witnesses the gradual unmasking of the protagonists participating in the revolutionary struggle (Emerson 174). Opposite the title page, a masked face peers over barbed wire and looks directly at the reader, as if longing for liberation. The beautiful, expressionless mask obscures any underlying tension and contributes to the atmosphere of suspense and uncertainty that Meiselas deems indispensable. The caption explains that rebels in Monimbo adopted traditional Indian dance masks in order to conceal individual identity.[8] As rebellion became more widespread, however, these traditional masks gave way to ski masks and bandanas and were eventually discarded altogether. For this reader at least, it is not coincidental that the first undisguised fighter to be prominently photographed in a public setting is in fact the revolutionary who signals the final offensive and points the way to victory. In sharp contrast, throughout the narrative, no uniformed guardsmen or paramilitary forces make any such effort to disguise themselves; rather, they flaunt their impunity.

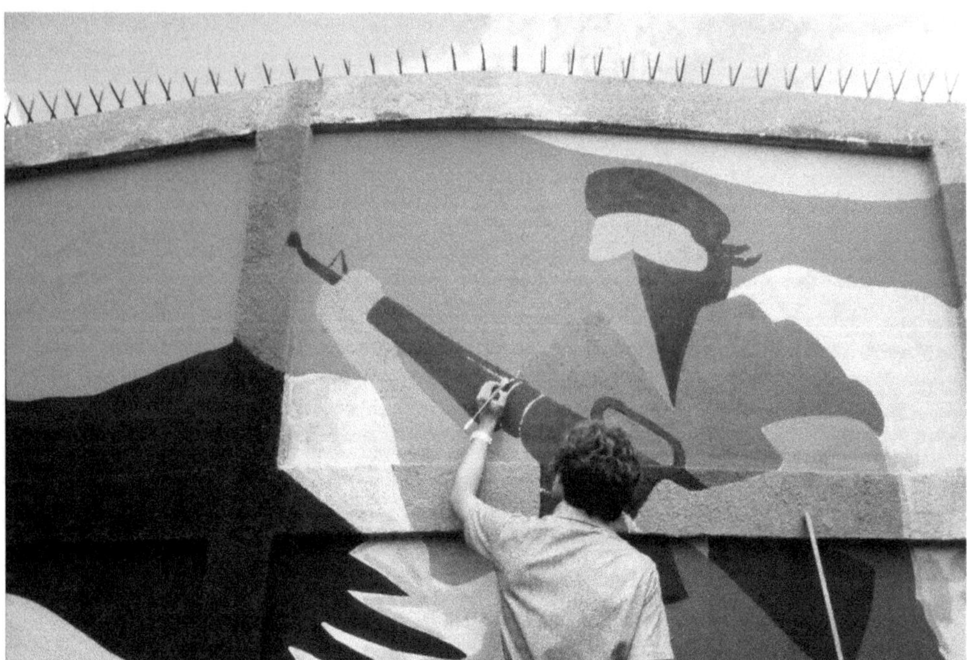

Fig. 3.12. Susan Meiselas/Magnum Photos. Managua. Wall. From *Nicaragua*, 1979.

Likewise, recurring images of fire parallel the escalating tension of the narrative plot. Bonfires deliberately set on street corners not only attest to the people's unrest, but also, as the text explains, indicate that the guard was losing control. Images of the flaming car of an informer, as well as the use of tear gas to disperse a student demonstration, testify to the increasing use of violence. Bodies burned for purposes of sanitation (the text makes clear that the Red Cross operated in this way as an attempt to control rampant disease) indicate the toll that poverty and civil war took upon the civilian populace.[9] Finally, the flaming Molotov cocktail, which seemingly ignites an image of Somoza together with the body of a fallen member of the national guard, heralds the defeat of the existing power structure.

As with the photographs of masks and fire, the carefully sequenced images in which photographs appear within the frame likewise reflect the overall narrative progression, in that they graphically illustrate Somoza's fall. Early in the text, a portrait of the dictator, which prominently features the numerous medals decorating his uniform, towers over new recruits who must file beneath. The image clearly symbolizes the dictator's omnipresence and absolute authority. In contrast, toward the book's conclusion, flames destroy his stately image, and there can be no doubt that the dictator has suffered defeat. Photographs within photographs in *Nicaragua* do not involve self-conscious commentary on the process of image making, nor do they stand as a critique of the role of the photographer. With careful consideration, however, these meta-photographs can be understood to point toward the act of reading photographic images. More specifically, they ask us to consider the ways in which photographs can be used and, even as we hold *Nicaragua* in our hands, remind us that we must be critical readers of visual imagery. Each of the internal photographs captured by Meiselas has clearly been utilized to deliver a political message; that is, each serves purposes of propaganda. Whether the intention is to represent the absolute and unquestionable authority of the state, or, conversely, to illustrate the repression and victimization suffered under its rule (as with the portrait of the beautiful, young female student leader that leads the funeral procession–protest march in fig. 3.7), photographs condense meaning. We witness the efficacy of symbolic images to convey ideological positions and sway public opinion—by either commanding respect or evoking sympathy.

Another significant recurring theme—the appearance of written text within the photographic frame—remains tied to narrative development, in that internal messages chronicle changing attitudes, especially mounting anger and resentment. In fact, one can literally read how "resignation gives way to defiance, defiance to assault" (Imrie 1202), through the progression of graffiti.[10] The strong presence of graffiti in these images draws our attention to the pervasive though more subdued presence of such visualized text in numerous other photographs. Interestingly, Meiselas did not speak Spanish when she arrived in Nicaragua. However, as she revealed to Liba Taylor, she felt that she could easily interpret "the very expressive graffiti—although I could not read the language I could figure out what they were saying" (1348). It is not an insignificant detail that the photographer had to visualize language in order to understand it. This experience runs parallel to our reading of *Nicaragua*—we likewise rely on the use of color and imagery in a visual narrative in order to interpret the author's message.

Immediately following the photograph of the mutilated corpse on the ridge, a public inscription directly addressed to the dictatorship demands information from the regime regarding disappearance: "Donde esta Norman Gonzáles que conteste la dictadura JRN" (JRN is an opposition group that Meiselas fails to identify) (Where is Norman González? The dictatorship must answer—JRN). This highly accusatory entreaty evolves into even more direct repudiation and condemnation of the dictator. A later message demands the removal of the national guard: "Fuera la GN de Monimbó. El pueblo se estan muriendo por culpa de Somoza" (National guard get out of Monimbo. The people are dying because of Somoza). Scrawled in large red letters, the text has seemingly been penned in the blood of a youth whose corpse lies just below these caustic and confrontational words. Situated in close proximity to victims of physical violence, both defiant declarations testify to extreme repression, even as they speak to rising indignation and increasingly open rebellion. A final, more politically motivated and elaborately artistic inscription (also painted in hues of red) reflects societal ideology along party lines. The call for a popular democratic government, in particular the MPU, or "United People's Movement," signals the goal and eventual achievement of the revolution, that is, the need for a radical change in the basic power structure, so that the people might represent themselves.

Readers, especially if unfamiliar with the Spanish language, may be drawn to the captions due to the language barrier. But on turning to the appendix, they discover that the captions offer more than a mere translation of these public inscriptions; they also reveal otherwise invisible links to other images in the narrative sequence. For example, we discover that the angry lettering demanding information for locating Norman González appears on the burned house of a Somoza sympathizer. This information ties the photograph more directly to subsequent images of protest, especially the burning car of a Somoza informer. Thus these aggressive acts of violence remain justified as having been carried out in retaliation for the very situations of exploitation, repression, and disappearance that we have witnessed throughout *Nicaragua*.

Despite the importance of layered textual markers, the contact image reprinted in the appendix ironically conceals a second inscription on this very same wall. In this way, the supplementary text can be seen to impart *less* information. Upon close examination of the full-page, uncaptioned photograph, one can literally read between the lines to discover an additional message, one that is completely erased in the appendix: "Monimbo nunca se rendirá FSLN" (Monimbo will never surrender—FSLN), subtly referencing the protest banners so prominently displayed before. In fact, all three of the photographs featuring graffiti in *Nicaragua* reveal a complex layering of texts masking prior inscriptions. Thick patches of paint as well as the artistically rendered hand calling for popular government overtly efface previously inscribed proclamations.

The traces of these earlier texts remind the viewer that emphasizing a particular reading necessarily involves silencing other possible meanings. Although multiple voices compete for attention on the walls of *Nicaragua*, subordinated exchange remains silenced or literally cut off with the framing of the photograph. This palimpsest renders visible the structural underpinnings of the book. The graffiti itself resists heteroglossia, even as it gives voice to popular expression. In much the same way, the photographs, especially as augmented by the textual material, allow the protagonists to speak. Critics have not failed to observe that Meiselas's narrative favors the opposition.[11] As we shall see, the visual narrative, together with the testimonial voices and historical material compiled in the appendix, openly advances the cause of the Sandinistas.

Verbalizing Violence

The visual narrative examined thus far comprises only part of *Nicaragua*. Meiselas anticipated the response of critics, such as Tim Imrie, who have noted that "it is difficult to appreciate the meaning of the photographs fully without knowing something about the history of the country and the state of its people at the start of the revolution" (1201). The photographic record aptly portrays economic exploitation, violent repression, and armed revolt. Nonetheless, the appendix, appropriately entitled "Captions, Texts, Chronology," offers a radically different approach to the same story. Following the visual narrative produced primarily through photographs in dialogue, the appendix places text and image side by side, allowing a more immediate and direct interaction between word and image.

Black-and-white contact images supplemented with captions repeat the full-page color photographs but remain secondary to a variety of textual registers. Precise data in the form of maps, statistical reports, treaties, and communiqués effectively anchor the visual narrative in Nicaragua's specific sociopolitical reality. This concrete, factual reporting also stands as evidence to substantiate the selections that follow, validating the credibility of persuasive documents and personal accounts. The photographs also depend upon less objective sources, including letters, oral testimony, and poems, whose function is to foster a contextualized rereading of the photo-essay. Personal anecdotes, precisely positioned in relation to particular images from the narrative sequence, detail individual experiences of historical events and thus animate the still photographs. Memories, as recounted by participants, enhance (or perhaps alter) the viewer's previous understanding of the now subordinate images, while simultaneously eliciting empathy and encouraging reader identification.

Meiselas chose this format, whereby the textual is distanced from the visual narrative, in response to a publishing dilemma. *Nicaragua* appeared simultaneously in multiple languages (English, Spanish, and French). Separating the material that required translation kept the cost down, which was of utmost importance to the author. Nonetheless, critics remain in disagreement as to the efficacy of this strategy. It has been argued that the images would be better understood if directly accompanied by explanatory text: "it would more effectively reach the reader were visual and written materials interpolated rather than grouped and distanced from one another" (Binford n.p.). Instead of outright condemnation, other critics have offered hesitant approbation. While acknowledging the awkwardness of constantly turning to the appendix for explanations, Imrie recognizes the ability of a purely aesthetic reading to subjectively render popular insurrection. In his view, inserting textual material would have detracted from the accelerating rhythm and mounting tension expressed visually. "This segregation of all textual information has irritated a number of people, but because the flow of the photographs is crucial to their ability to convey the feeling and pace of the events, captions would in fact have been a distraction" (1202). I do not wish to engage in a comparative assessment of these strategies, but instead will address the relationship between the appendix and the visual narrative in terms of content, temporal positioning, and audience.

The appendix opens with a map that not only indicates the precise geographic location of the specific towns photographed, but further places Nicaragua within Central America. An inlay then situates these nations in relation to Mexico, thereby stressing a regional dimension to the conflict as well as providing a point of reference readily identifiable to a North American audience. In somewhat contradictory fashion, the final section thus assumes a reader unfamiliar with the region—a sharp contrast to the ideal viewer of the visual narrative, who, as Imrie reasons, requires a basic familiarity with the sociohistorical context to accurately assess the uncaptioned photographic images.

Following this visual orientation, the reader is confronted with a dramatic juxtaposition of clashing ideologies. By means of textual layout, the voice of Sandino (who led a peasant army and was assassinated by Anastasio Somoza in 1934) is made to confront representatives of the American government. Even as the state department obtains exclusive and perpetual rights to Nicaraguan territory, whose possessor shall reportedly "control the destiny of the Western Hemisphere," the idealized revolutionary (in whose honor the Sandinistas identify themselves) vows to resist "the Yankee empire" (n.p.). These passages, dating from the turn of the century, not only affirm the cyclical nature of history, but also document the fact that longstanding U.S. domination of Nicaragua has consistently met with popular resentment. In addition, these excerpts foreshadow a shift in narrative content. Whereas the visual narrative chronicles popular insurrection against the Nicaraguan dictator, the appendix recasts this national conflict in terms of North American imperialism.

For this reason, the "problem" of the appendix is not merely how to sustain interest, build narrative climax, and maintain uncertainty. To be sure, Meiselas aims to resolve initial doubt and ignorance with the presentation of factual evidence that does not diminish the reader's interest in the subject. However, given the specific content of the appendix, the author must further negotiate a way to implicate the audience of its complicity without alienating her readership. To this end, Meiselas appeals to the reader's sympathy, personalizing the conflict and humanizing the struggle in an attempt to foster an identification process. The appendix presents readers with a cast of characters, ordinary citizens presumably like themselves, who recount their experiences and justify armed combat as a necessary response to prolonged exploitation and brutal repression. As eloquently summarized by Sandino, "We are not military, we are armed citizens" (n.p.).

Critics of both documentary photography and literary *testimonio* would agree that such an identification process remains an uneasy if not an altogether impossible proposition. Arguing that testimony is a militant speech act delivered from an interpersonal class or ethnic position aiming to raise the (politically distanced) reader's consciousness, Doris Sommer emphatically denies that the differences between testimony's subjects and the consumers of testimonial literature can be overcome in order for identification to occur. In fact, the literary critic sternly warns that readers should "proceed with caution" and acknowledge not merely their incapacity but also the undesirability of such intimacy.[12] Similar concerns are voiced throughout Martha Rosler's seminal article "in, around, and afterthoughts (on documentary photography)." Likewise describing documentary as carrying "information about a group of powerless people to another group addressed as socially powerful" (306), Rosler criticizes liberal documentary's tendency to intentionally elicit pity from the ascendant classes, who are then called upon to "rescue" the oppressed (325). In her view, the supposed charitable impulse behind reformist documentary (understood as social-work propagandizing) functions precisely to preserve class distinction. *Nicaragua*, in depicting agency and militancy rather than victimhood, escapes such condemnation. Nevertheless, readers find themselves confronted with the same competing emotional responses of empathy coupled with shameful accountability.

Throughout the appendix, words spoken or written by those actively involved in the revolution retell the story rendered visually through Meiselas's photographic record. Given their particular placement, certain texts appear to directly address the photographed subjects. For example, a telegram to Somoza—ironically identified by the numerous exaggerated epithets with which the government-sponsored newspaper, *Novedades*, hails the national leader—accompanies the photograph of the president opening a session of congress. This excessive nomenclature contrasts sharply with the quietly unassuming signature, "your humble servants." The overtly mocking tone of the telegram, published in an opposition newspaper, seriously undermines the self-imposed dignity, authority, and stately presence of the accompanying photograph.[13] Similarly, a letter sent to members of the national guard (identified as poor citizens who enlisted solely to overcome poverty) asks the soldiers to appeal to their conscience when commanded to kill peasants and workers. The entreaty accompanies an image of new recruits, followed by a depiction of hardened veterans. Nonetheless, as with the graffiti, Meiselas does not provide space for their response. The text deliberately silences those in power, so that the marginalized citizenry can speak.

In fact, the majority of the texts give voice to the otherwise silent protagonists of the images. Eyewitness accounts and anecdotes shared by members of the FSLN, neighborhood organizers, and ordinary citizens (including laborers, professionals, clergy, housewives, students, and adolescents) augment the visual record by relating personal experiences of the events depicted. These voices complete the accompanying pictures. In much the same way as the visual narrative relied on the sequencing of photographs to construct a suspenseful story, the appendix operates through the careful arrangement of text and image. Testimony about fleeing from the national guard explicates an image of a woman running with her naked son in her arms. The words of a housewife who recalls sharing coffee and crackers with the troops are placed beside images of civilians serving food to the revolutionary forces. A poignant description of air raids accompanies the photograph of a bomb strike, while a passage recounting the construction and use of a homemade bomb shelter supplements the image of a similar structure. Likewise, a thumbnail image of youths practicing throwing contact bombs is accompanied by a father's testimony relating how the contact bomb originated with children's firecrackers, while a mother tells how chlorate was obtained without arousing suspicion. These testimonials affirm that the revolution affected everyone and consistently emphasize an imbalance of power. The resistance, they insist, possessed few weapons and was mainly composed of inexperienced fighters, that is, ordinary citizens.

The appendix also gives voice to the clergy (including nuns, priests, and bishops), who would otherwise remain absent from the visual narrative. As might be expected, these representatives of the Church (who undoubtedly espouse liberation theology) condemn social injustice and human-rights violations. More surprisingly, they actively condone armed resistance and demonstrate ecclesiastical support for the revolution; a priest recounts why he entered combat, while the archbishop explains that the exhaustion of nonviolent resistance justifies armed revolt. Thus the textual material, together with the photographs, portrays a victimized citizenry with no viable alternatives.

Whereas the visual narrative emphasizes the military repression carried out by Somoza, the appendix highlights U.S. involvement. As mentioned previously, the captions identify the artillery of the national guard as U.S. weaponry and further document the adoption of U.S. traditions by the elite troops, while Sandino opposes the Chamorro-Bryan treaty granting the United States unlimited control of Nicaraguan territory. However, the most damning indictment comes from an FSLN commander who denounces U.S. support for the Nicaraguan dictator:

> it is with the weapons that the gringos sell the Somoza government that our people are being murdered . . . the bombs dropped on Matagalpa as well as the planes are made in the U.S. The tear gas, the M-16 rifles, the equipment used by the Nicaraguan army is produced in the United States. It is the military aid of the U.S. to Somoza which continues to maintain Somoza in power. (appendix n.p.)

This accusation, which questions the moral authority of the United States to mediate in the internal Nicaraguan conflict, further challenges North American readers to confront their own complicity. Thus, the empathy evoked by the photographic essay, in combination with the testimonial accounts, contends with the emerging realization of U.S. responsibility. The unresolved tension between word and image that underpins *Nicaragua* directly parallels the North American reader's conflicting emotions of empathetic identification coupled with guilt.

Together with the transformation in narrative content, an important temporal shift occurs between the visual and the textual sections of *Nicaragua*. The photographs capture events as they unfold, and in this way Meiselas's dramatic visual narrative successfully creates suspense and maintains uncertainty. The appendix, in contrast, presents a more complex temporal positioning. Although the popular insurrection of 1978–79 stands as a permanent reference point, the texts establish a direct link between the current Sandinista revolt and the peasant uprising that took place approximately fifty years earlier. In fact, the textual registers illuminate details across the span of nearly a century, nuancing and considerably extending the account provided by the images. Historical documents predating the revolution alternate with passages contemporaneous with the events chronicled. Nevertheless, the majority of the testimonies reflect upon the uprising as an event of the past. These retrospective commentaries confer a nostalgic tone upon circumstances only recently experienced. Having vicariously participated in these events by viewing the visual narrative, the reader, together with the speakers, is led to reexamine the significance of the revolution. Initially immersed in historical events as they literally play out before one's eyes, the viewer experiences a visceral reaction with respect to the visual narrative. The appendix, in turn, adds a new layer of understanding to support and extend this emotional response and further provides the context to allow for a more analytical reevaluation of the aesthetic documentation in light of the textual material.

As we have seen, the final two images form an epilogue to the visual narrative, emphasizing not only the ongoing costs of war, but also the need to record events. To accompany this visual postscript, the final textual insert (positioned opposite the chronology with which *Nicaragua* closes) offers a literary reflection on the meaning of the revolution. "The Parrots," a poem written by Nicaraguan author Ernesto Cardenal (identified earlier in the appendix simply as "poet and priest," but who went on to become the minister of culture after the revolution), unites *Nicaragua*'s many threads. Using the analogy of contraband parrots forcefully removed from their mountain refuge in order to be exported to the United States, "where they would learn to speak English," Cardenal paints a romanticized portrait of the *compas*, or revolutionary heroes. In keeping with Meiselas's depiction of the Sandinistas, this vision presents an innocent, oppressed community, who, guided by the ideals of liberty and the love of one's homeland, resist U.S. imperialism. At the same time, ending on the tragic note that "forty-seven had died," this poetic interpretation acknowledges the loss suffered in order to peacefully return to routine existence.

Likewise, Meiselas's narrative goes beyond documentation and offers an aesthetic interpretation of historic events. This analysis of the interaction between text and image reenacts the way in which a reader comes to know *Nicaragua*. To overcome the isolation of the visual and the textual, the viewer must perform an interactive reading that integrates all these narrative components. Captioning grounds the viewer's subjective, visceral response to the visual aesthetics. Furthermore, the pairing of the visual narrative with historical documents and testimonial accounts allows for an expansion of time (a retrospective approach relates the revolution to long-standing socioeconomic conditions) as well as narrative content (the appendix recasts Nicaragua's internal conflict in terms of North American imperialism). In creating a decidedly pro-Sandinista "emotive documentary" (as Imrie defines Meiselas's project, 1202), the photographer, as committed storyteller, overcomes the reductionist tendencies of the media and renders violence intelligible through broad contextualization.

Notes

1. Tim Imrie also situates his study of Meiselas's work within this contextual framework and likewise concludes that *Nicaragua* "precisely corresponds to Berger's definition of an alternative photography" (1203).

2. One can trace Meiselas's increasing consciousness regarding the media's application of her images. In 1982, when asked if her photographs had been misused, she defended the press as sympathetic to the Sandinista cause: "At that period, no . . . fundamentally the pictures weren't misrepresented" (Taylor 1350). However, by 1991 she would indicate otherwise: "When my pictures are published in magazines they are seen as illustrations of news stories, as fragments of an event, and, as such, remain isolated from the histories from which they came" (*British Journal of Photography* 12). Don Snyder's article "Mixing Media" offers an insightful analysis of two exhibitions in which Meiselas explores how "shifting contexts of representation" (36) affect the (mis)interpretation of her images. These installations revealed the media's use of her images together with the process of creating *Nicaragua*.

3. Unlike the "rephotographic project" condemned by Martha Rosler (318) for exposing the continued shame of poverty and oppression, Meiselas's subjects reflect on the euphoria and optimism that characterized the Sandinista revolution. Nonetheless, a sense of post-revolution disillusionment pervades the film.

4. This approach precisely inverts the representational strategy employed throughout *La noche de Tlatelolco*, a testimonial that likewise draws on both verbal and visual evidence to document governmental repression of popular protest in Mexico. In her text, renowned journalist, author, and critic Elena Poniatowska intricately fuses numerous testimonial voices in order to heighten

tension and gradually achieve narrative climax. A series of black-and-white photographs serves as a visual preface or prologue and provides supplementary documentation to this oral collage.

5. The "table of contents" announces the division of *Nicaragua* into three unique parts, corresponding to the chronological development of the narrative. Sections entitled "The Somoza Regime," "Insurrection," and "The Final Offensive" bear the precise dates of June 1978, September 1978, and June 1979–July 1979, respectively. Yet these distinct "chapters" remain obscure within the text, thus questioning the tendency to create sharp boundaries or artificial delineating dates for the gradual unfolding of historical events.

6. The appearance of an elbow just at the edge of frame marks the presence of another manual laborer. The probable assembly line of such workers magnifies the import of this photograph as documenting a more general social problem.

7. The captions offer no information, with the exception of the precise location, that is not readily apparent in the images themselves. The result may be to encourage the viewer to perform a closer reading of the photographs, as I have, in an effort to ascertain their meaning.

8. A parallel effort to protect her subjects was made on the part of the photographer: "I insisted that only those photos that showed people wearing masks be used since the mask was a very critical element of disguise for those people participating in the insurrection" ("Some Thoughts" 12). When *Time* failed to honor this request, Meiselas felt that lives were endangered. As she explains here, this lack of editorial concern precipitated Meiselas's unease with the media.

9. These images further signal photography's limitations. The stench of burning bodies, indicated by passersby who hold handkerchiefs to their mouths and noses, can only be conveyed to the viewer through visual clues. Likewise, images of the final offensive are accompanied in the appendix by the voice of a civilian, who relates that "the smell of gunpowder was in the air, the smell of war" (n.p.), reminding the reader that pictures cannot convey the complete sensory experience of armed combat. Similarly, while the viewer often witnesses screaming, especially at demonstrations, these protests remain unheard in much the same way that Somoza is shown to have remained deaf to the Nicaraguan people.

10. Graffiti remains especially relevant as a direct representation of the voice of the people. Also significant are advertisements. A reminder of the ubiquitous presence of imperialism, such signs point to the root cause of Nicaragua's social strife. One prominent and somewhat expected example is the repeated reference to Coca-Cola.

11. In Binford's view, *Nicaragua* is "clearly sympathetic to the Sandinista cause," and Kozloff points out that the text is "unquestionably on the side of those who resist" (unpaginated catalogue essay).

12. See Doris Sommer's article "Not Just a Personal Story: Women's Testimonios and the Plural Self" and her later book *Proceed with Caution when Engaged by Minority Writing in the Americas*.

13. Later in the appendix, Meiselas's text further derides Somoza, when he insists that he will not leave the country because he has the support of his people. Not coincidentally, this statement immediately follows an FSLN communiqué detailing recent operations and remains directly linked to thumbnail images of a Sandinista training camp.

References

Binford, Leigh. "Revolution: The Central American War Photography of Susan Meiselas and Adam Kufeld." *Estudios Interdisciplinarios de América Latina y el Caribe*, 9.1, (enero–junio 1998), n.p. <http://www.tau.ac.il/eial/IX_1/binford/html>.

Coleman, Sarah. Interview with Susan Meiselas. *PhotoMetro* 17.17 (1999): 26–31.

Emerson, Gloria. "Susan Meiselas at War." *Esquire* 102.6 (1984): 165–74.

Forché, Carolyn. *The Country between Us*. Cambridge and New York: Harper and Row, 1981.

Harris, Melissa. "*Susan Meiselas.*" *Aperture* 133 (fall 1993): 24-33.

Imrie, Tim. Review, *Nicaragua: June 1978–July 1979*, by Susan Meiselas. *The British Journal of Photography*, 20 Nov 1981: 1201–3.

Kaye, Harvey J. Review, *Nicaragua: June 1978–July 1979*, by Susan Meiselas. *Studies in Visual Communication* 8.3 (1982): 90–93.

Kozloff, Max. "Photojournalism and Malaise." Catalogue essay in *Photojournalism in the 80s*. University Art Gallery, University of Massachusetts, October 1985, n.p.

Meiselas, Susan. *Carnival Strippers*. New York: Farrar, Straus and Giroux, 1976.

______. *Encounters with the Dani: Stories from the Baliem Valley*. New York: International Center of Photography; Göttingen, Germany: Steidl, 2003.

______. *Kurdistan: In the Shadow of History*. New York: Random House, 1997.

______. *Nicaragua: June 1978–July 1979*. New York: Pantheon Books, 1981.

______. "Some Thoughts on Appropriation and Use of Documentary Photographs." *Exposure* (1989): 11–15.

______. ed. *Chile from Within, 1973–1988*. Photographs by Paz Errázuriz et al. Texts by Marco Antonio de la Parra and Ariel Dorfman. New York: W.W. Norton, 1990.

______. ed. *El Salvador: Work of Thirty Photographers*. New York: Writers and Reader, 1983.

Meiselas, Susan, Richard P. Rogers, and Alfred Guzzetti, eds. *Pictures from a Revolution*. New York: Kino on Video, 1991.

Polemis, Cindy. "The Colour of War." *Creative Camera* (1982): 356–58.

Poniatowska, Elena. *La noche de Tlatelolco*. Mexico City: Era, 1971.

Ritchin, Fred. "Susan Meiselas: The Frailty of Frame, Work in Progress." *Aperture* 108 (Fall 1987): 32–41.

Rosler, Martha. "in, around, and afterthoughts (on documentary photography)." In *The Contest of Meaning: Critical Histories of Photography*. Ed. Richard Bolton. Cambridge, MA: MIT Press, 1989, 303–40.

Shames, Laurence. "Susan Meiselas." *American Photographer* 6 (March 1981): 42–55.

Snyder, Don. "Mixing Media." *Photo Communique* (Spring 1987): 28–36.

Sommer, Doris. "Not Just a Personal Story: Women's Testimonios and the Plural Self."
In *Life-Lines: Theorizing Women's Autobiography*. Eds. Bella Brodzki and Celeste Schenck. Ithaca: Cornell UP, 1988, 107–30.

______. *Proceed with Caution When Engaged by Minority Writing in the Americas*. Cambridge, MA: Harvard University Press, 1999.

Taylor, Liba. Interview with Susan Meiselas. *The British Journal of Photography* 17 (1982): 1348–50.

CHAPTER FOUR

On Making Images Speak

Writing and Photography in Three Texts from Chile

MARY BETH TIERNEY-TELLO

Writers are often called upon to provide a context for photographs, to attempt to explain and determine the meaning of the images that alone seem to provide a testament to truth, but one that can only be partially discerned. Several collaborative projects from Chile form part of the tradition of the written essay that accompanies, explains, or speaks for a set of photographs. Photo-essays such as *La manzana de Adán / Adam's Apple* (Paz Errázurriz and Claudia Donoso, 1990), *El infarto del alma* (Paz Errázuriz and Diamela Eltit, 1994), and *Flores en el desierto / Flowers in the Desert* (Paula Allen, with prologue by Isabel Allende, 1999) provide a privileged site for examining the complex exchanges between word and image inherent in such hybrid works.[1] More specifically, these three works combine photography and writing in order to reclaim a marginal reality, that is, to "make present" individuals or groups that have been semi-obliterated by official culture. Published in the wake of Pinochet's dictatorship, these books necessarily address questions of representation and memory in the aftermath of political violence and disappearance. The combination of writing and photography in these projects, furthermore, performs a defiant "memory work" that undoes the practices of forgetting that have accompanied Chile's Transition to democratic rule.[2]

Memory has received extended attention recently, particularly from scholars focusing on the Holocaust and other traumatic events, as evidenced in works by Mieke Bal, Cathy Caruth, Marianne Hirsh, Annette Kuhn, and Dominick LaCapra. In the Latin American context, memory studies have moved to center stage in the aftermath of dictatorships, as evidenced in recent works by Andreas Huyssen and Elizabeth Jelin, among others. Debates emerge about the "past," about the place of memory and forgetting, as countries such as Argentina, Chile, and Brazil make the transition to democratic rule. As Elizabeth Jelin points out in her book *State Repression and the Labors of Memory*, the struggle is not simply one between remembering and oblivion, but between competing memories, such that "the space of memory is thus an arena of political struggle . . . not only over the naming of what took place in the past but over the meaning of memory itself" (xviii).

Many of the thinkers engaged in what Annette Kuhn (*Family Secrets*) terms "memory work" acknowledge that documentary photography and testimonial literature perform valuable cultural functions as acts of memory and witnessing.[3] As Mieke Bal suggests:

> Art—and other cultural artifacts such as photographs or published texts of all kinds—can mediate between the parties to the traumatizing scene and between these and the reader or viewer. The recipients of the account perform an act of memory that is potentially healing, as it calls for political and cultural solidarity in recognizing the traumatized party's predicament. (x)

Such "healing," however, predicated on empathy and identification, can be dubious when it entails a seemingly easy appropriation of another's pain. Recent criticism makes clear that both writing and photography can "use" others' lives in ways that turn these others into objects and usurp their subjectivity.[4] As Marianne Hirsch points out, "the challenge for the postmemorial artist is precisely to find the balance that allows the spectator to enter the image, to imagine the disaster, but that disallows an overappropriative identification that makes the distances disappear, creating too available, too easy an access to this particular past" ("Projected Memory"10). I will argue that the three texts analyzed here achieve such a balance to varying degrees, and that this balance is facilitated by the combination of photography and writing. By combining the visual and the verbal, these projects can perform the politically urgent task of "making present," while also simultaneously calling into question representational practices of appropriation. In this way, they bring into relief the aesthetic and ethical effects of combining the verbal and the visual in such collaborative, contestatory works.

Testimonio and documentary photography are, perhaps even more pointedly than other types of cultural production, a product of their sociopolitical context. The military dictatorship of Augusto Pinochet that governed Chile between 1973 and 1990 used violent repression to paralyze the political and civil life of the country, thus assuring the obedience and complicity of the majority of the population. The regime aspired to be the source of all authority, employing a univocal discourse that purported to be the origin of all meaning and attempted to eliminate dissonance of any kind.[5] As several critics have pointed out, testimonial literature in many ways forms a counterdiscourse to that of authoritarianism.[6] Testimony could bring to the fore the voices of subjects who formed the margins not only of the "gran familia chilena" (the great Chilean family), espoused by the regime's rhetoric, but also of the new national family, promoted during the Transition to democratic rule.[7]

In the aftermath of the authoritarian regime, photography also has taken on a variety of significant functions.[8] As a tool of social control, photography was used by the state to identify citizens as well as to catalogue the activities of those deemed "subversive" by the secret police. As a tool of the opposition to authoritarian control, on the other hand, photography had the power to document abuses of the regime and to serve as proof of the existence of the disappeared. Following Roland Barthes's assertion that every photograph is, in some way, a "certificate of presence," critic Nelly Richard points out that: "La propiedad que tiene el documento fotográfico de ser un certificado de presencia que atestigua de lo que *fue*, lo convierte en *guardián del recuerdo*" ("The photographic document certifies a presence that is witness to what it *was*, converted into a *guardian of memory*").[9] Richard explains that since collective memory was repressed by authoritarian practices, photography could—and did—take on the function of critical tool.[10] In the Chile of the Transition to democratic rule, photography can also provide an antidote to what Richard describes as "operaciones de borradura" (*Resíduos* 15) (operations of erasure). As Richard explains, such erasure is not only political or institutional, but cultural: a seductive, television-driven consumer culture can effectively work to erase and render "borroso" (blurred) the history and painful experiences of the dictatorship (*Residuos* 15–16). The photograph, particularly the black-and-white documentary portrait, can "make present" those quite literally disappeared, or at the very least "made absent," from the official, full-color representations of Chile.

Reframing Memory: Photography as Subject in *Flores en el desierto*

In defiance of such erasure, documentary photographer Paula Allen's *Flores en el desierto / Flowers in the Desert* features a series of photographs of a group of women searching the northern Chilean desert for their loved ones. These women's husbands, lovers, or brothers had been detained, then brutally murdered, by a military regiment on a mission later dubbed "the caravan of death," which arrived in their city of Calama in October of 1973. The wrenching photographs picture these women as they search for the remains of their disappeared, as they hold candlelight vigils and memorials, as they witness the uncovering of a mass grave in the desert. The photos are accompanied by a side-by-side bilingual text in Spanish and English, including a literary prologue by Isabel Allende, a historical presentation by Patricia Verdugo, an introduction by Paula Allen, and the testimonies of the women themselves, which form the bulk of the written text. The photographs and texts thus attempt to provide a "certificate of presence," a document, a memorial, of what happened to these men disappeared so many years ago, as well as of the relentless struggle of the women to find their bodies

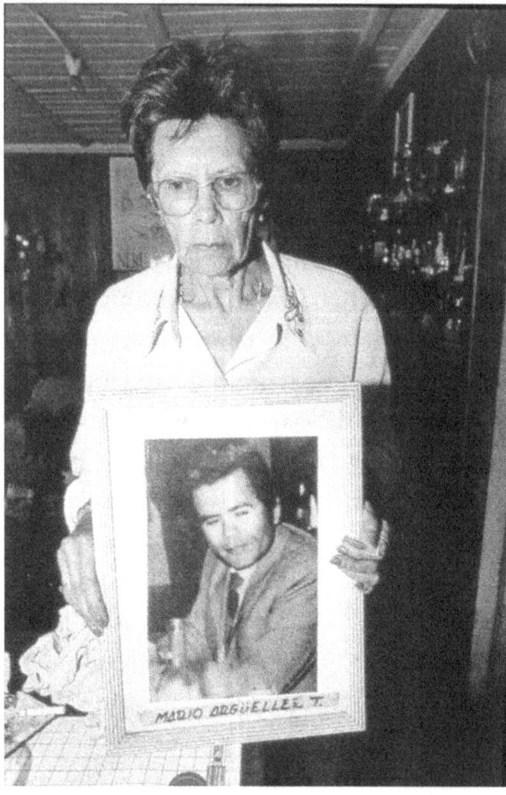

Fig. 4.1. Paula Allen. Violeta Berríos. From *Flores en el desierto / Flowers in the Desert*, 1999.

or some trace of their death. The project thus becomes a ritual of mourning and remembering the disappeared and also a documentation of the struggles of those left behind, bereft not only of their loved ones, but also of their bodies and the possibility of performing the more traditional rites of burial and mourning.

The lives that have been truncated, paralyzed, "captured" in these photos, are as much the lives of the survivors as the lives of those murdered. The words of the survivors in the written testimonies return again and again to the disappeared and the women's efforts to recover their bodies. The photographs likewise document both the survivors and the disappeared, who hauntingly appear in the form of old family photographs and portraits *within* Paula Allen's shots of the women of Calama. In one of the most compelling images (fig. 4.1), Violeta holds a picture of her *compañero*, executed twenty years earlier. The young, happy face of her now disappeared companion contrasts sharply, shockingly with the age and sadness of her own, lined by grief, anger, and resolve.[11] She averts her gaze from the camera as well as the picture of her lover, focusing on some other reality—perhaps on the task at hand of recovering his body and finding out the truth regarding his death.

The photographs of portraits of the disappeared detail, in a doubly referential way, the death, loss, and simultaneity of absence, always present in a photograph. As

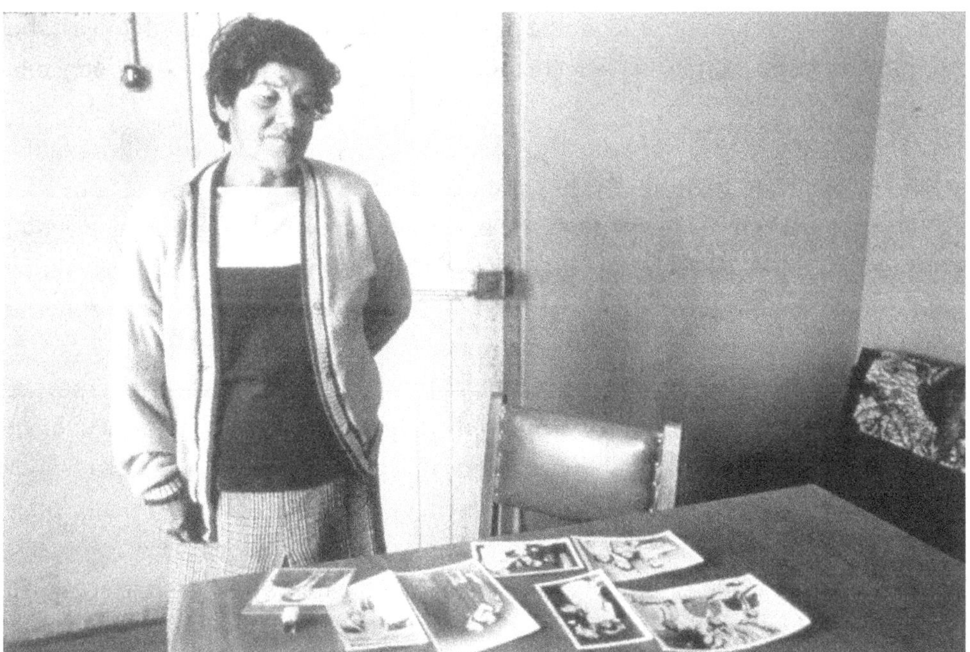

Fig. 4.2. Paula Allen. Brunilda Rodríguez. From *Flores en el desierto / Flowers in the Desert*, 1999.

Roland Barthes points out, the photograph is an emanation of the referent, but of a referent necessarily absent. This is why the photograph is ambiguously referential, according to Marianne Hirsch: it is "[the photograph]'s status as relic, or trace, or fetish—its 'direct' connection with the material presence of the photographed person—that at once intensifies its status as harbinger of death and, at the same time . . . its capacity to signify life" (*Family Frames* 19–20). Photography is thus capable of referring to lived reality like no other medium, but in its stillness, and in its existence independent of and in the absence of its referent, it also uniquely conjures death. This is, clearly, quite literally so in the photographs of the disappeared within the photographs in *Flores en el desierto*.[12]

In some of these shots, the women gaze at the photographs of the missing, immersed in their own mourning. For example, in one portrait (fig. 4.2), we see an older woman in her simple home, her face distant and sad, as she contemplates the family snapshots we assume to be of the typical milestones included in the family album. Yet these photographs are spread out not as a proud or nostalgic reminder of past happy times, but as the sole vestiges of a life cut short by a violent, politically motivated death. She stands apart from the photographs, the stance of her body reiterating her separation from her loved one. The woman does not show the viewer these photos, nor does she look at the camera. She gazes down at them herself, her posture and facial expression reflecting contemplation, resignation, and individual mourning.

These photographs reframe the memory of the disappeared within family relations, picturing them in a very particular form of the family album. But what is conventional about the portraits of the disappeared (school photos, wedding portraits) contrasts with the photographs of the survivors, which do not comply with the conventions of the family album, but rather with those of the journalistic photograph that seeks to record the experience or aftermath of a traumatic event. By picturing the disappeared as photographic objects of contemplation, of memory, of mourning, the book serves to testify not only to the disappearance of these subjects but also to the trauma, the emotional marks, that these disappearances have left on their survivors. This trauma is obviously based on a severing of family relationships. But by presenting this family trauma in a bilingual memorial book, the author also tries to make the reader-spectator share in this trauma, to become a witness, moving the women's personal pain into a wider public, cultural, and political realm.

The photographs within the photographs become, in the absence of the body, the feeble traces, the lone residue, of the lives cut short by violence. Indeed such photos in the end become more real than the bones and fragments finally discovered by the women, as the written text makes clear. One of the women says, upon confronting the remains of her loved one, "Cuando pensaba en sus fotos, casi todos sonriendo yo no podía dejar de llorar. Esto es lo que quedó de ellos: pedazos de cuerpos y un fuerte olor a podrido" ("I would think of their photographs, almost all of them smiling, and I couldn't stop crying. This was what remained of them—pieces of bodies and a strong smell of rotting") (76). Violeta meanwhile reports how such family photographs of her husband become necessary to reconstruct his skeletal remains for identification purposes. In turn, forensic photographs re-appear in another of Allen's photographs, spread out in all their gory impersonality on a family bed, the flowered bedspread serving to reframe the "evidence" within an intimate context. In this way, while the forensic photograph becomes *familiar*, the family photograph is called upon to perform the dual function of documentary memorial, serving both intimate memory and forensic evidence.

In some of Allen's photographs, the composition and content work to make the personal loss symbolize the wider social trauma of political violence. In several of the shots, the women pointedly show their photographs to the viewer and the world, making us witness to their loss, and thus broadening the effect of the trauma. In these cases, the photograph functions as political performance, becoming a political act, a *denuncia*, both a statement and a demand that refuses the "erasure" of these lives by the military. In one photo for example, the surviving woman shows the viewer two photographs—the original and a photocopy pinned to clothing during marches. The picture exemplifies the transformation of the photograph from document to performance, from showing what was, to enacting a political protest.

Parts of the written text likewise reflect the increasing sense of community, the politicization of the women's grief, and the shift from private to public expressions of pain. One woman, for example, describes her transformation:

> En esa época yo me compadecía mucho a mí misma. Pensaba que era la única que se sentía así. Luego, al comenzar a hablar con las demás mujeres, cada emoción que ellas expresaban me hacía sentir comprendida.
>
> During this time, I felt so sorry for myself. I thought I was the only one feeling this way. When I talked to the other women every emotion they expressed made me feel understood. (40)

Another points out: "Pertenecer a la Agrupación nos dio más valor y permitió que nuestras voces se escucharan en todas partes" ("Belonging to the Association gave us more courage and allowed our voices to be heard everywhere") (40). The testimonial narrative here is the connection, painful and insistent, between those murdered and the survivors who share in the trauma, between the photographs within the photographs and Allen's pictures of these women. The format itself—which transcribes the words of each of the women in turn, focusing on their searches in the desert and their daily struggles—complements the photographs, the writing serving as "snapshots" of their stages of grief and of the progress of their investigation.

The written texts, particularly the women's testimonials, thus complement the photographs in *Flores en el desierto*, functioning, in Roland Barthes's terms, to "anchor the images" ("Rhetoric of the Image" 38–40). With the inclusion of the testimonies and the historical explanations, the photographs cannot be reduced to free-floating images of strange, stark landscapes and unknown persons in pain. Text and image explain and enrich each other, becoming mutually more powerful and functional in both political and emotional terms.

Both the black-and-white photography and the transcription of the women's testimony utilize a seemingly "unadorned," simpler aesthetic in order to appeal to "truth." Black-and-white photography, in our age of the norm of color snaps, can seem more aesthetically preoccupied and complex, and clearly these photographs take great care with composition, framing, focus, and light—in short, with the aesthetic. Yet perhaps more importantly, black-and-white photography performs the idea of history, of what was, of what remains, bringing into sharper focus not only history, but loss.[13] Certainly, black-and-white, as opposed to color, photography involves deliberate

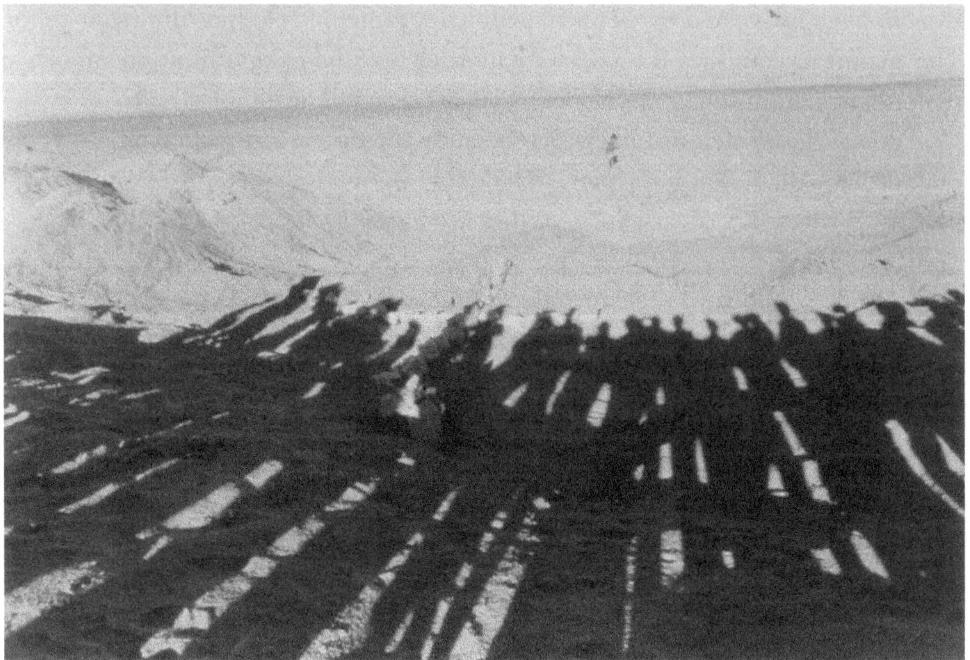

Fig. 4.3. Paula Allen. Fosa común / mass grave site. From *Flores en el desierto / Flowers in the Desert*, 1999.

aesthetic choices that have a particular impact on the viewer. Such photographs project a more "artesanal" mood, as opposed to one of commercial efficiency and mass production. One photograph (fig. 4.3) inscribes loss in a particularly powerful way, showing not only the mass grave of the executed in the desert, but the shadows of the survivors cast upon it. The stark landscape, the cross of stones, the grave, and the shadows together conjure Chile's violent past, inscribing such loss in the nation's imaginary and into the future, as evoked by the lone child on the other side of the grave. Such photographs provide a contrast to slicker, commercial, full-color views of the new Chile projected in television, advertising, and such productions as *El pabellón de Chile: huracanes y maravillas en una exposición universal*, the accompanying text to Chile's exhibit in the 1992 World's Fair in Seville, Spain. These visual images of the "new" Chile participate, as Nelly Richard explains, in an international graphic language "cuyos colores planos rechazaban la adherencia de texturas demasiado rugosas de la memoria y de la historia que debieron alisarse fotográficamente para la pose turístico-comercial del desarrollo modernizador" (*Residuos y metáforas* 166) (whose flat colors rejected the adherence of the overly rough textures of memory and history that had to be smoothed out photographically for the tourist-commercial pose of modernizing development). According to Richard, such photography elides pain and the past, focusing instead on the presence of the marketplace.[14]

Likewise, the women's testimonies evoke the past in a straightforward, spare style. Yet they are meticulously edited, shaped, and grouped into chapters, in order to form a linear, coherent narrative from the disappearance to the excavation of a mass grave. Furthermore, a few, selected lines of the women's words are occasionally set off alone on a page, in order to highlight particularly poignant turns of phrase, to increase their emotional impact, or to challenge the reader to think critically about the nation's past. For example, on one page these words appear alone: "'Estábamos en tiempo de guerra,' eso es lo que dicen para justificar sus mentiras. Y yo me pregunto: '¿Qué guerra?'" ("'We were in a state of war,' that is what they say to justify their lies. And I ask myself, 'What war?'") (72). Such words become, visually and conceptually, like epitaphs and also like linguistic and visual traces of the national trauma that stubbornly refuse to be erased.

Both the writing and the black-and-white photography clearly do have aesthetic or formal concerns. Yet both purport to use that aesthetic as a method of salvaging what has been left behind—the traces, the remains, the evidence—that defy and undo the Chile of the Transition, which would rather erase such vestiges of the violence of the dictatorship. The purported "transparency," or referentiality, of testimonial writing—which has, in turn, been problematized in some of the criticism of the genre—is not called into question here, but is rather leveraged to the maximum degree, perhaps because the text's objective of radicalizing, politicizing, and performing memory cannot afford to cast doubt on such referentiality.[15] In a similar way, although documentary photography is here doubly present, its political and ethical stature is never questioned, in order to convey in the most powerful way possible both the trauma perpetrated by the military and its refusal to be silenced by a culture of erasure and feel-good marketing ploys.[16]

Ironically, it is the more literary prologue by Isabel Allende that brings into focus some of the ethical dilemmas inherent in the reception of documentary works that strive to represent and salvage a marginal reality. There, Allende turns the women of Calama into virtual symbols for our consumption, poeticizing their struggles while seeming to allow the reader to appropriate their moral rectitude and courage by merely reading their words, viewing their small bodies facing the immense desert alone, and seeing their faces etched in pain. Allende stages the women of Calama as beyond reproach, mythic, calling them "símbolos eternos" ("eternal symbols"):

> Las mujeres de Calama son pobres de pobreza irremediable, son pacientes de paciencia absoluta, son fuertes y están solas. Por años nadie ha escuchado su clamor, por años la justicia ha ignorado su angustia. . . . Nada puede vencerlas, ni el tiempo, ni la indiferencia del mundo, ni la esperanza mil veces rota y vuelta a remendar.

> The women of Calama are the poor of unredeemed poverty, the patient of absolute patience, they are strong and they are alone. For years no one has listened to their cries; for years justice has ignored their anguish . . . Nothing can conquer them, not time, not the world's indifference, not their hope shattered a thousand times and a thousand times patched back together. (7)

> Ellas escriben en la arena del desierto la verdadera historia de Chile, la que los textos escolares omiten, la prensa calla, los gobiernos ocultan y los militares, impunes y arrogantes, niegan . . . Esas mujeres de Calama, lavadas por el sufrimiento, no olvidan. Ellas son nuestra conciencia.
>
> In the desert, they are writing the true story, the truth that textbooks omit, that the press does not print, that governments hide, and the military—unpunished and arrogant—deny . . . The women of Calama, purified by their suffering, do not forget. They are our conscience. (8)

Interestingly, "la verdadera historia de Chile" becomes "the true story" in English, to facilitate "our" identification with these truth seekers. The pain and struggle of these women is thereby more seamlessly called upon to perform, symbolically at least, the function of "our conscience," whomever that "our" may be construed to embody.

In this way, *Flores en el desierto* dramatizes the dilemmas of the documentary photo-essay in particularly poignant terms. On the one hand, it is impossible to argue with the need to counter an official erasure of these lives. And yet, as compelling as Allende's portrayal of these women's strength and refusal is, her reading of the women also raises questions: what desires are being served by this beautiful book, what guilt assuaged, and what difficult questions sidestepped? Converting the women's pain into images and symbols can allow the reader, particularly the international reader, to "enjoy" them, even to feel pleasantly virtuous while "commiserating" with them, all at a comfortable, privileged distance. By serving to represent a collective "conscience," these women can symbolically perform the "heavy lifting," the hard labor, of the refusal of what Nelly Richard calls "la sepultación oficial del recuerdo" (*Resíduos y metáforas* 30) (the official burial of memory). In spite of such reservations, *Flores en el desierto* is a necessary, militant book that stubbornly confronts the official erasure of the past. The book's photographs and testimonies effectively reframe the remains of the brutality of the dictatorship. By appearing in photographs alongside old snapshots of their smiling loved ones, as well as alongside boxes of their rotting and disfigured corpses, the women recast impersonalized violence as an assault on individual and intimate relationships, thereby repersonalizing political events and obliging history to take into account private experiences and memories of pain, love, and loss.

Documentary Testimony and the Art of the Other: *El infarto del alma* and *La manzana de Adán*

El infarto del alma and *La manzana de Adán*, both featuring photographs by Paz Errázuriz, self-consciously focus on the difficulties inherent in representation and identity, and on the act of photographing marginal subjects. Errázuriz's work has consistently and urgently focused on those most marginalized by the dictatorship, confronting the viewer with what has been omitted or blotted out of the collective memory or imaginary. For *El infarto del alma*, Errázuriz photographed patients of a state mental hospital who were lovers. Her thirty-eight black-and-white photographs feature shots of couples in various poses.[17] Many feature frontal shots, in which the subjects stare directly at the photographer and, in effect, at the viewers. Almost all embrace or hold hands, emphasizing their relationship and their status as couple. After seeing the photographs and visiting the hospital, Diamela Eltit wrote the accompanying text. This hybrid work combines sections of fictional narrative, meditations on love and insanity, and testimony—the transcribed testimony of one of the patients, the fictionalized testimonio of another, and a testimony of Eltit's own visits to the asylum.

In *La manzana de Adán*, the forty-three black and white photographs, taken between 1982 and 1987, are primarily of a group of homosexual, transvestite prostitutes. The majority of the photographs are, like those of *El infarto del alma*, posed portraits, in particular of two of the travestis, who are brothers, and their mother. Some of the photos are of the subjects dressed as men, but mostly they appear in drag. The accompanying text by Claudia Donoso combines testimony of the prostitutes, journalistic reportage, interviews, and letters. A translation of this text into English follows the photographs.

Both of these works oblige the reader and spectator to reflect on the use of photography in cases such as these, that is, in books for aesthetic consumption that also strive to make a contestatory political statement or provide some sort of vindication for the marginalized. The "others" photographed in these books are, furthermore, marginalized by virtue of their sheer identity. While the women of Calama are politically and economically "other," silenced with regard to the brutal fate of their spouses and brothers, the "others" photographed by Paz Errázuriz are objects of neglect, scorn, or revulsion by virtue of their homosexuality or insanity. The subjects Errázuriz has chosen are for this reason particularly precarious social outcasts and especially vulnerable to voyeuristic looking.

As Kerry Tremain notes in defense of documentary photography, "the gaze of the voyeur and that of the witness are not the same" (37). Yet in spite of the good intentions of any photographer of marginalized subjects, photography on some level is always a colonization, reflecting, as Susan Sontag puts it, "the urge to appropriate an alien reality" (63). Both *El infarto* and *La manzana* seem to respond to such an "otherness" and the desire to access it. If documentary photography in general can immobilize troubling subjects by turning them into images, projects like those of Errázuriz would seem to permit the viewer to observe and appropriate such "others," turning them into aesthetic objects and neutralizing their most disturbing aspects.[18]

It is perhaps this "otherness," and the voyeuristic desire to appropriate it, that Sontag finds most troubling about Diane Arbus's work (which bears a certain resemblance to Errázuriz's in terms of subject matter). For Sontag, Arbus was uninterested in ethical journalism or in history (42). Her images of mental patients and drag queens in New York become, for Sontag, a coy and sinister project, since it is one based "on distance, on privilege, on a feeling that what the viewer is asked to look at is really *other*" (34). While Errázuriz's work—with its prostitutes, boxers, circus people, and mental patients—also focuses on the marginalized, it responds in an explicit way to a historical reality. As Claudia Donoso points out in an article on photography under the military regime, "[s]i en Chile estaban desapareciendo a las personas, [Errázuriz] desplazó su respuesta al señalamiento de zonas perennemente amenazadas por la invisibilidad y la exclusión . . ." ("16 años de fotografía" 32) (If in Chile they were disappearing people, Errázuriz shifted her response, gesturing at zones perennially threatened with invisibility and exclusion). Errázuriz's photographs of forgotten, repressed subjects are a political response and a challenge, as well as a visual antidote to the social amnesia enacted in response to authoritarian practices.

But even allowing for a possible political reading, such photographs of subalterns can still be seen as appropriative—perhaps even more so *because of* their aesthetic quality. The subjects undoubtedly have less access to privilege and power than the photographer who "takes" their image. And, as Sontag observes, photography can turn even the most painful reality into an image for commercial consumption and aesthetic appreciation (108–12). Both *El infarto del alma* and *La manzana de Adán* take another's mental illness, suffering, or perceived "otherness" and turn it into art.[19] But combining text with photographs can cause the reader, the photographer, and the writer to reflect more critically on both the visual and the verbal as means of representation.[20] The potential tensions between words and images demand a more active, participatory reception by the viewer or reader. Such hybrid texts invite—or even require—a more reciprocal and dynamic interaction between photographer and subject, between photographs and viewers, between self and other.

At every turn, photographs seem to reinforce a concept of identity as individual

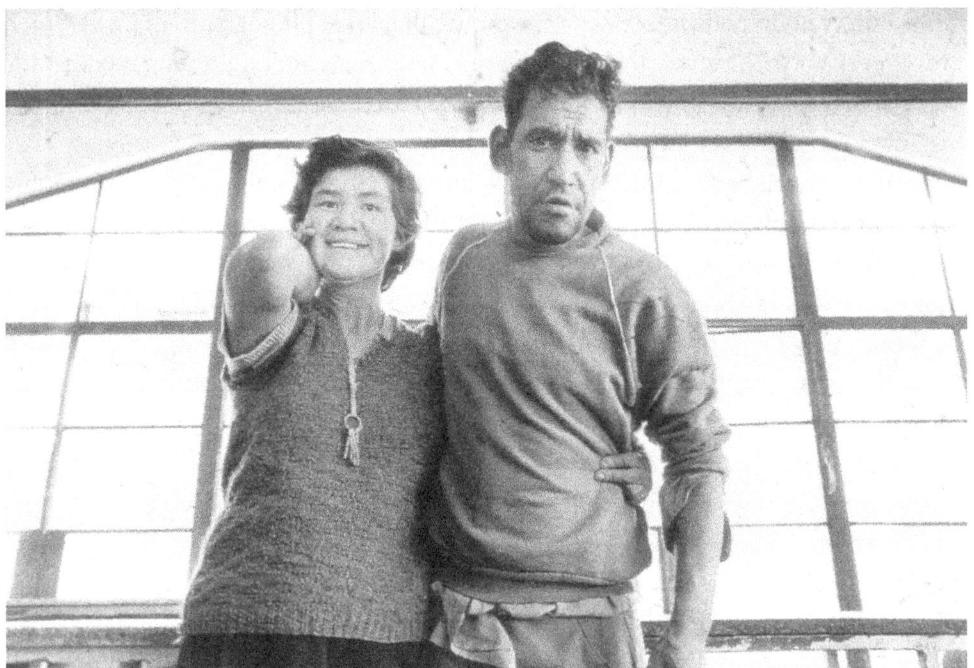

Fig. 4.4. Paz Errázuriz. Untitled. From *El infarto del alma*, 1994.

and unitary. The photograph began, as Roland Barthes observes, as "an art of the Person: of identity, of civil status" (*Camera Lucida* 79). In her essay on Latin American photography, Lois Parkinson Zamora reminds us that for the camera, "identity is a question of individual psychology"; the portrait, in particular, encodes, in her words, "the singular life, the idiosyncratic self" (303). Indeed, the beautiful, glossy portraits of *El infarto del alma* seem to work to consolidate these subjects' identities, providing at least an appearance of conforming to a comprehensible couplehood. In many of the photographs, the subjects stare directly, at times even defiantly, into the camera, as if to declare their worth and their pride in their partner, as if to affirm themselves as subjects. In one example, we can see such affirmation both through the expression on the subjects' faces and through the low-angle viewpoint of the photograph and the illuminated background (fig. 4.4).

There is a certain documentary, testimonial function to the photographs, and several components of the text reconfirm and complement this function.[21] To begin with, Eltit records the inmates' comments to her about their relationships: "El me da té y pan con mantequilla" (He gives me tea and bread with butter), or "La cuido yo" (I take care of her).[22] In the section of the text entitled "Diario de viaje" (travel journal), Eltit describes her own experiences in the hospital and observes the photographer's interaction with the patients. Errázuriz is, according to Eltit, "[l]a tía que les toma fotografías que prueban, aún frente a ellos mismos, que están vivos, que después de todo conservan un pedacito de ser" (the auntie that takes photographs of them which prove, even to themselves, that they are alive and that, after all, they retain a little piece of being). According to Eltit, "Paz Errázuriz convierte a su ojo en un don para los asilados. Les regala en su mirada fotográfica, la certeza de sus imágenes" (Paz Errázuriz converts her eye into a gift for the inmates. She gives them her photographic gaze, the certainty of her images).[23] Through Eltit's text, we come to see how both Errázuriz and Eltit have focused all their aesthetic, professional energies on these subjects, in order to confer a dignity and respect that defy their marginalized status.[24] In some ways, the written text of *El infarto del alma* functions like an extended caption, working, as Sontag puts it, to "firm up the political associations and moral meaning of a photograph" (108).

Yet even as the written text of *El infarto del alma* attempts to "firm up" the meaning of the photographs, certain aspects of Eltit's text focus on resisting such consolidation.[25] She explicitly questions the adequacy of language to represent this reality: "¿Qué sería describir con palabras la visualidad muda de esas figuras . . . ?" (What would it be to describe with words the mute visuality of those figures . . . ?). Eltit's words do attempt to "speak" for these subjects, but in a way that does not gloss over the schisms, the ruptures, and the unspeakability of these subjects' lives. For example, the sections of the text titled "La Falta" (The Lack) are fragments of text that appear alone on a page: "Las horas suman 35 días, 200 noches. Ya no sé cuál esperanza sostiene a mi cuerpo en medio del hambre, del hambre, del hambre. Ah, otro minuto. 100 noches, 400 días" (The hours add up to 35 days, 200 nights. I no longer know which hope sustains my body in the midst of hunger, of hunger, of hunger. Ah, another minute. 100 nights, 400 days). On the most basic level, these segments testify to the patients' dehumanizing circumstances and their deprivation. However, in forgoing logic and straight testimony in favor of a poetics of fragmentation and delirium, the text resists and confounds any notion of an easy documentary.[26] In this sense, the fragmentation of the text serves to undo the photographic "consolidation" of these subjects. Furthermore, the text tells us that these portraits include individuals who in many cases do not even know their own names.

Eltit's text articulates a voice that allies us as spectators with the subjects of the photos. The fragments of the text entitled "El infarto del alma" (heart attack of the soul), are a first-person, fictional narrative from the perspective of a woman literally mad with desire for her now absent lover. Yet the first words of this narrative, which appear alone on the first page, seem to address the reader directly: "Te escribo: ¿Has visto mi rostro en algunos de tus sueños?" (I write to you: Have you seen my face in any of your dreams?) The picture on the facing page (fig. 4.5) is of a solid couple, staring seriously at the camera. Framed by the squareness of the tiles and the right angles of the surrounding walkway and building, the couple occupies the center

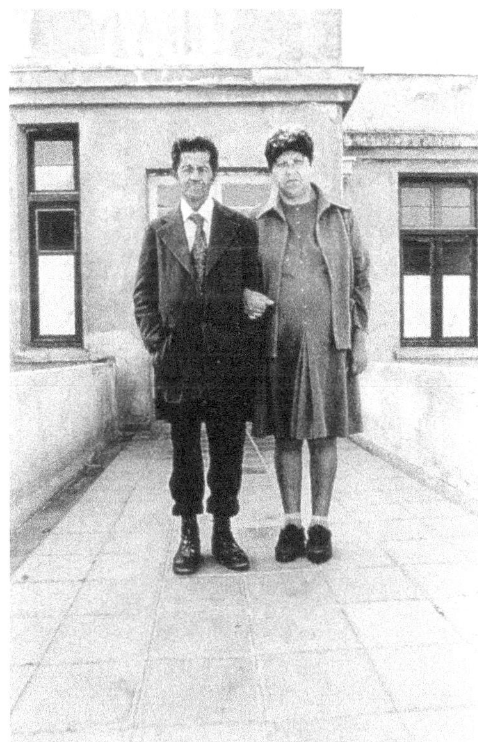

Fig. 4.5. Paz Errázuriz. Untitled. From *El infarto del alma*, 1994.

of the photograph, their arm-in-arm, straightforward stance connoting traditional gender roles. Rather than the hospital-issued sweatsuits, their attire is formal and traditional, the woman in a dress, the man in a suit and tie. The conventions here, both photographic and relational, would seem to lead readers to answer, yes, we have seen these figures before. Nonetheless, in looking at this picture, we must wonder, who asks the question, and of whom?[27]

On the next page, the text continues: "¿Aparezco en tus sueños serena o reprochándote por las abrumadoras faltas que contiene el pasado? . . . Ah, tú y yo habitamos en una tierra difusa, con grietas tan profundas que impiden el encuentro" (Do I appear in your dreams serene or reproaching you for the overwhelming faults that the past contains? . . . Ah, you and I inhabit a diffuse land, with cracks so deep they impede the encounter). This "tierra difusa," this ambiguous "tú y yo," urges Eltit's readers to glimpse a continuity, although significantly, with "grietas profundas," between the supposedly "other" world of the asylum documented in the photographs, and their own *historias de amor*. Such a textual strategy, together with the photograph, works to insert the reader into the scene of writing, making the relation of the spectator to the photographed subjects more dynamic and complex. And the use of the second person in the text enables the images to reflect back to us, in an even more compelling way, an image of ourselves.[28]

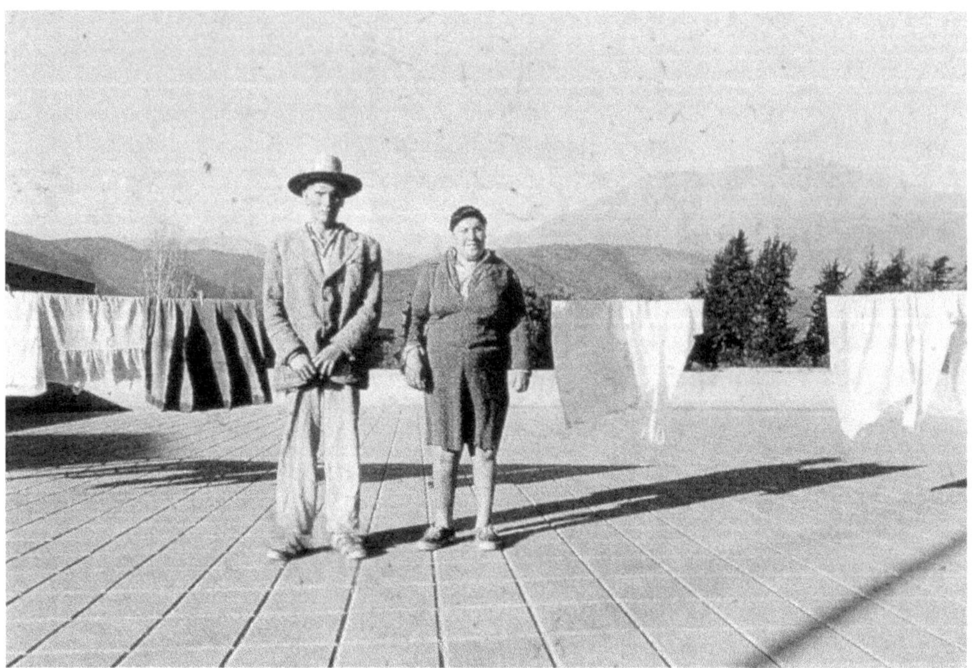

Fig. 4.6. Paz Errázuriz. Untitled. From *El infarto del alma*, 1994.

Such reflection back resonates with the hauntingly familiar poses observed in the pictures. We have seen these poses before, in their affectionate couplehood, their loving embraces, their domesticated familiarity.[29] In one photograph, for example, (fig. 4.6), the couple poses somewhat awkwardly, in front of laundry hung out to dry on what appears to be a rooftop patio. The mountainous landscape, the cast of sunlight and shadows, the laundry in the background, all seem reminiscent of a life in the countryside, of a couple standing in front of the site of their life and labor rather than two patients confined to a psychiatric hospital. The woman, with her conventional dress and solid stance, seems entirely, and unremarkably, matronly. On the other hand, the man's tentative, slightly frightened pose, the way he holds his hands, and the way his sneakers peek out from beneath too short trousers, all make him seem more like a child, providing the clue that this is not, ultimately, an ordinary *campesino* couple. While all the photos contain some similar clue that these are not "ordinary" couples, their poses nonetheless reiterate the conventions of couplehood. In another photo, for example, the couple's embrace, in spite of their physical appearance that does not conform to usual criteria of beauty and attractiveness, refers to any number of poses we have seen before in popular culture, with the man leaning coolly against the car, hands thrust in pockets like James Dean, and the woman suggestively turned toward her lover, while casting a flirtatious glance at the camera (fig. 4.7). Both the photographic conventions of the portrait

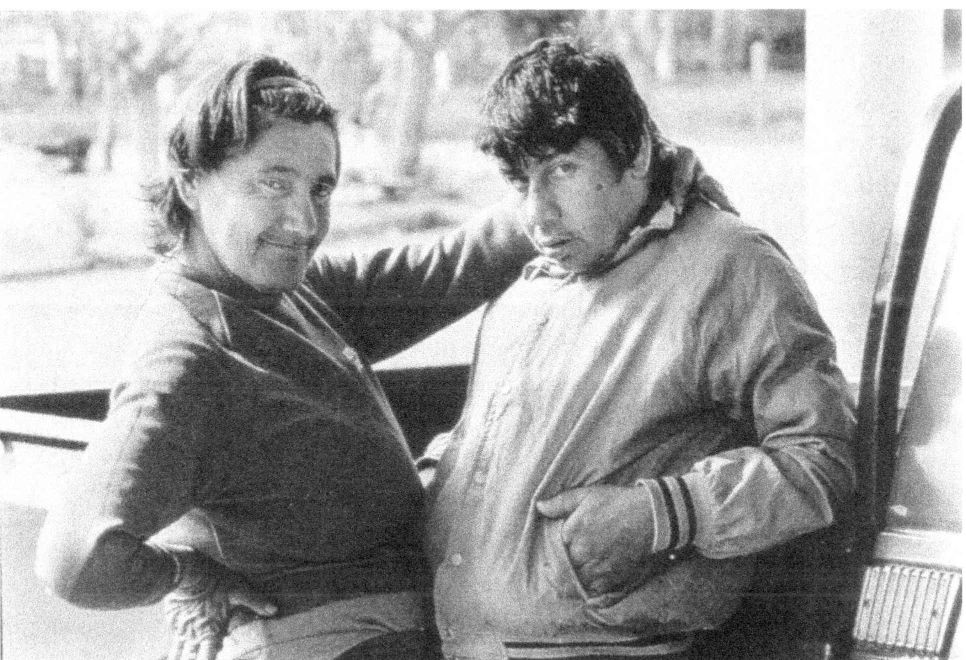

Fig. 4.7. Paz Errázuriz. Untitled. From *El infarto del alma*, 1994.

and the poses chosen reinforce a sensation of familiarity, of affiliation, of reflection of our own cultural norms.

The writing that accompanies the images both names and complicates this specularity. Eltit's text at points draws attention to the role of parody in the images. In her "Diario de viaje," she notes that their poses repeat an aesthetic, yet she wonders: "¿Cuál es el lenguaje de este amor? . . . ¿que estética amorosa los moviliza?" (What is the language of this love? . . . What aesthetic of love mobilizes them?). The couples engage in a parodic spectacle that, as Eltit puts it, works to contradict their mental illness: "La parodia amorosa se reitera entre los asilados como un espectáculo íntimo cuya única utilidad es contradecir su diagnosticada enfermedad" (The parody of love is reiterated among the inmates like an intimate spectacle whose only utility is to contradict their diagnosed illness). Certainly, if the love these couples enact is a defiant, parodic performance, they are not merely objects of photographic curiosity, but active subjects, social actors. Furthermore, by reading these poses as parody, Eltit causes the photographs to refer to the reader's own reality in a critical way, and forces us to confront received notions of couples, of identity, of self-representation.

The text thus questions the illusion of transparency and the myth of referential immediacy and self-identity perpetuated by both testimonial practice and photography.[30] Eltit writes that "la gran pregunta que recorre a los cuerpos que habitan en el reclusorio siquiátrico parece ser: '¿Quién soy?,' pregunta que se torna crucial e insoslayable cuando el yo está en franco estado de interdicción" (the great question that runs through the bodies that inhabit the psychiatric sanatorium appears to be: Who am I? A question that becomes crucial and inescapable when the "I" is in a marked state of interdiction). At the same time, the photographic subjects are portrayed by Eltit as eager to see themselves represented, to see their "self" documented for both others and themselves to "see," as real, as concrete, as *there* in defiance of their social erasure. *El infarto del alma* in this way manages to make the other "present," even while calling into question its own representational strategies.

La manzana de Adán / Adam's Apple similarly produces tensions and exchanges between text and image. A large portion of the thirty-six pages of text that precede the photographs is composed of fragmentary testimonies of several of the homosexual prostitutes working in a brothel in Talca in 1984. These brief sections seem to operate almost like verbal snapshots, capturing snippets of the prostitutes' experiences and personal lives. There are several fragments in this section that describe the dictatorship's violent repression and degradation of homosexuals. In the first segment, for example, Pilar explains what happened to her and other homosexuals when Pinochet came to power:

> Para el golpe estábamos con la Leila en Valparaíso y nos llevaron a todas a un barco que había arraigado en el puerto. Nos llevaron allá con los ojos vendados en una camioneta. Seis días estuve ahí amontonado, con los otros en un hoyo. Lo primero que hicieron los milicos fue cortarnos el pelo, que nos arrancaban de raíz y después nos orinaban encima. Nos pegaron tanto. . . . Eramos como treinta homosexuales arriba del barco. Nos fueron soltando de a poco. (11)
>
> We were with Leila in Valparaíso when the coup occurred and they took all of us to a ship moored in the port. They took us there blindfolded, in a van. For six days I was left there, piled up with the others, in the hole. The first thing the soldiers did was cut our hair; they pulled it out by the roots and afterwards they pissed on us. They kept hitting us . . . There were some thirty of us homosexuals on board. We were released one by one. (91)

Other testimonies relate the subjects' struggle to survive economically, their decision to dress as women, their sexual desire and hopes for love, and their fears of old age and dying. One of the subjects, for example, describes herself: "Yo me miro al espejo y sé que no paso por mujer . . . Pero me fascina echarme pintura, ponerme tacos y vestido. Yo te salgo con las uñas pintadas a todas partes. Vestida de mujer me siento más realizada, más segura. La vida me la he ganado pintándome" (17)

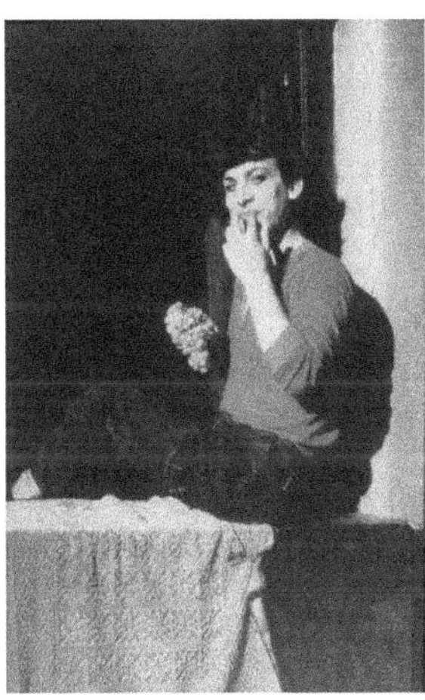

Fig. 4.8. Paz Errázuriz. Andrea Polpaico. From *Manzana de Adán/Adam's Apple*, 1990.

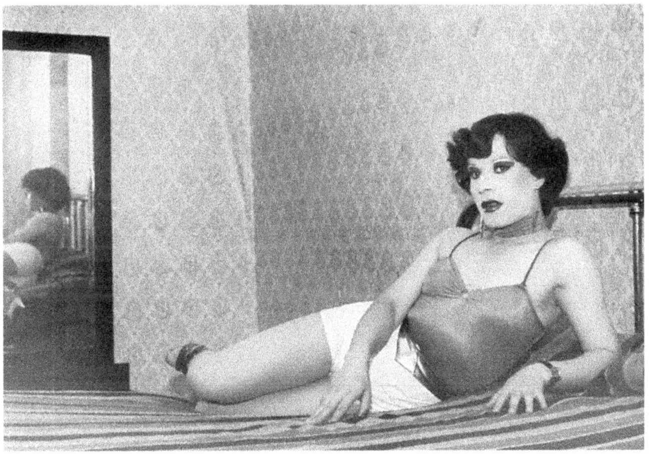

Fig. 4.9. Paz Errázuriz. Evelyn. From *Manzana de Adán/Adam's Apple*, 1990.

("I look at myself in a mirror and I know that I don't pass for a woman . . . But I am fascinated by putting on make-up, wearing high heels and a dress. I go everywhere with my painted nails. When I'm dressed as a woman I feel more fulfilled, more secure. I've earned my living painting myself" 97). The verbal description of the process and implications of cross-dressing is reflected quite literally in several of the photographs showing the subjects dressing as women. In other sections of the text, Donoso describes her collaboration with Errázuriz—for example, their stay in the brothel and their friendship with Mercedes Sierra and her two sons, Pilar (or Keko) and Evelyn (or Leo). The author reflects on the project itself, showing the effect these encounters have had on her, in this way refusing an uncritical appropriation of these subjects' stories, from the outside.

What we see in the photographs that follow the text is a physical response to the dictatorship's attempt to dehumanize these subjects and make them seem completely "other." The photographs use the conventions of portrait photography, working to reaffirm the individual as individual and certify the presence of the person in a humanizing, aesthetically pleasing form. The sociopolitical context of the testimonies is not directly documented in the photographs. That is, the photographs include no snapshots of the police raids, the beatings, or the general harassment of homosexuals described in the written text. These portraits do not picture the subjects as victims, but rather present them as producers of culture, not only documenting their difficulties and pain, but relishing their pleasures and triumphs as well. In a photograph of Andrea, sitting in a window, eating grapes, the angle of the light, the

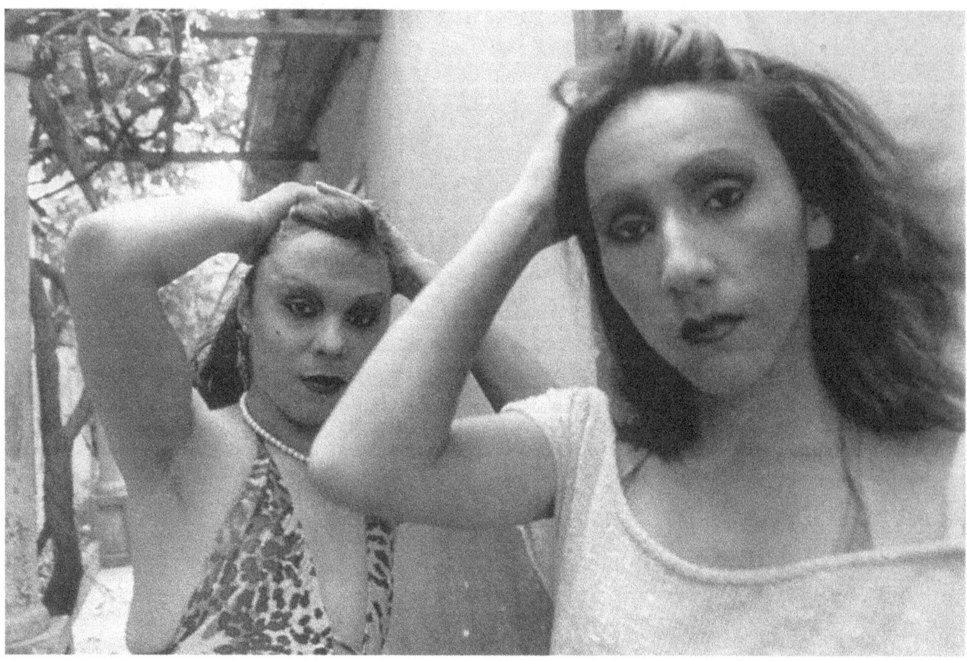

Fig. 4.10. Paz Errázuriz. Coral, Macarena. From *Manzana de Adán/Adam's Apple*, 1990.

framing of the body by the window, the placement of the tablecloth draped over the windowsill, all point to a self-consciously posed photograph, one that suggests pleasure, beauty, and abundance (fig. 4.8).

Perhaps most importantly, the aesthetic criteria that guide this pose, with a resounding resemblance to certain renaissance paintings, could be either Andrea's or the photographer's. Although the photographs do provide a glimpse of the subjects' precarious living conditions, they are frequently posed shots of individual subjects, often dressed as women, in the provocative poses drawn from the aesthetic of glamour magazines or conventional pictorial representations of the female nude or woman as sexual object. In one photograph of Evelyn, she lies odalisk-style on the bed, her carefully made up face and sexually provocative attire reflecting the "finished product" of the process of cross-dressing that gives her so much pleasure (fig. 4.9).

The testimonial, documentary impulse, the desire to provide a "certificate of presence," is at the heart of both text and photo. The subjects in both seem to declare their presence to the reader, viewer, photographer, and writer: In spite of everything, I am here. Even more importantly, the attitude of these photographic subjects reflects not sheer survival alone, but the desire for beauty and the pleasure of looking beautiful and sexually desirable, humanizing them even further.

Another way the photographs and the text resonate is in their ambiguities regarding gender. The photographs often embody such gender ambivalence, since

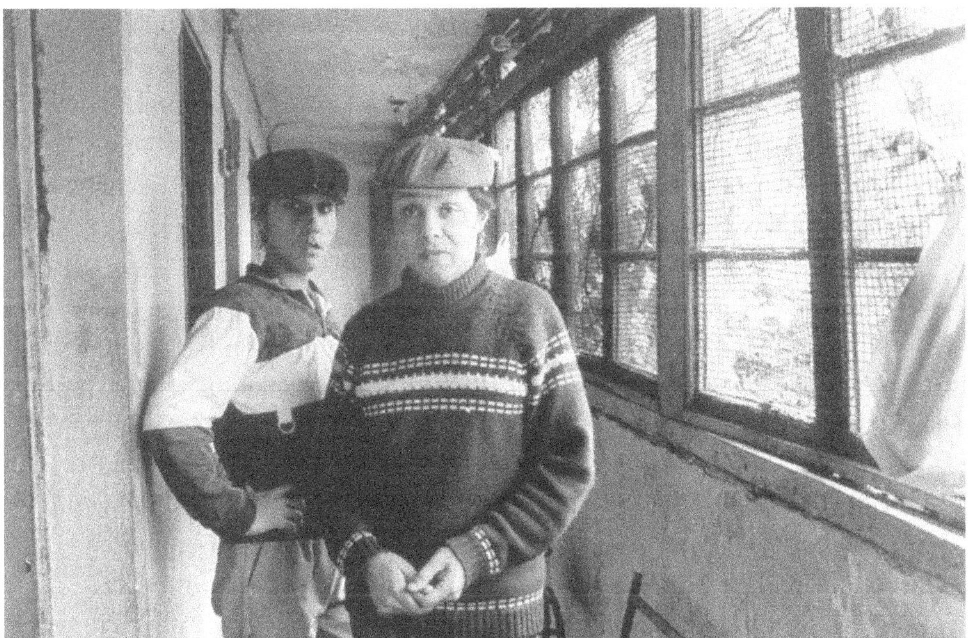

Fig. 4.11. Paz Errázuriz. Macarena, Coral. From *Manzana de Adán/Adam's Apple*, 1990.

the subjects themselves frequently display both feminine and masculine attributes. Sometimes this uncertainty is located in the space between contrasting shots of an individual as different genders (figs. 4.10 and 4.11). At certain points, the captions provide a dissonance with the image, such as in the photos of the subjects dressed as men but identified by their female names. Language itself is also the site of gender ambivalence within the text. Here, for example, Andrea refers to herself alternately in the masculine and the feminine, an ambiguity not captured by the English version: "Uno piensa en el futuro y es eso lo que la aterra . . . Como a una le fascinan los hombres, cuando llega a viejo se siente rechazada" (17–18) ("It's frightening to think of the future . . . If you're fascinated by men, when you get old you feel rejected" 97–98). In this way, text and image both reinforce and undo each other. Identities, in the spaces between word and image, name, and pose, seem less stable, more fluid and far more complex as we read and then look at the photographs. Furthermore, the effect of the photographs of the subjects in drag—or in various stages of dressing in drag—is to destabilize and parody gender identity, to show it as discontinuous with anatomical sex.[31] Such gender ambiguities ultimately must revert to the reader and viewer, since they show—as Judith Butler and others have demonstrated—that all gender is performative.[32]

While the layout of *La manzana de Adán* separates text from image more than that of *El infarto del alma*, the distance only underscores the resonance between words and image. If the reader proceeds in order, the subject's written stories appear before the photographs of their bodies. Nonetheless, there is an inevitable tendency to flip back and forth, as readers and viewers actively seek to understand the images, to copaginate the various figures with the testimonies. Neither text nor image is complete or self-sufficient. Indeed, it is as if the presence of both in this way points to the insufficiency of each representational system.[33]

In both *El infarto del alma* and *La manzana de Adán*, the parodying poses, the interaction of text and image, and the multiple voices of the written text all work to disrupt an easy appropriation of the subjects. A more dynamic relation between self and other seems to emerge in these encounters between photographer, author, subject, and reader. This could be the type of creative exploration critic and filmmaker Trinh Minh-ha describes when she argues for a more dynamic and fluid conception of difference and what she calls the "work of differentiation"(140). As she puts it, "[e]xploring oneself and one's culture in its interaction with other selves and other cultures remains a vital process when *understanding is creating—is creation*" (140). Both texts attempt to represent others, but they continuously reflect on the means or possibilities of doing so. They indeed work to "make present" others who have been erased from official discourse and who reside in the most precarious and vulnerable social spaces imaginable. However, these books resist a representation of the other based on distance, or based on their conceptualization as essentially different and apart from ourselves. It is as if these texts take as a premise another point made by Minh-ha: "one can never point to the other without pointing to oneself" (148). In this way, both texts ultimately draw the reader, the author, the photographer, and the subjects of the photographs into a relationship that is at once critical and collaborative.

Notes

1. See W. J. T. Mitchell, especially 285–86.
2. I take the term *memory work* from Annette Kuhn (cited in Nancy K. Miller 52).
3. See Bal, et al., for several essays that address the issue of art and literature as "acts" of cultural memory.
4. See, for example, Gareth Williams's essay on *testimonio* and Martha Rosler's article ("in, around, and afterthoughts") on documentary photography.
5. As Mary Louise Pratt explains, "Esta implacable letanía monoglósica tenía como objetivo no sólo descartar, sino *prohibir* un concepto de la cultura y de lo social como espacios de legítimo conflicto, heterogeneidad y negociación de diferencias" (19–20) (This implacable monoglossic litany had as its object not only to reject, but to *prohibit* a concept of culture and the social as spaces of legitimate conflict, heterogeneity, and negotiation of differences).
6. Indeed, Ariel Dorfman has examined the proliferation of testimonial texts during and after the dictatorship. On this issue, see also Mary Louise Pratt 20.

7. See Munizaga and Ochensius for an analysis on the use of the family metaphor in Pinochet's discourse. See Nelly Richard *Resíduos* (199–218) for an analysis of the remobilization of traditional gender roles by the church and the state during the period of the Transition. As she puts it: "el gobierno de la Transición democrática necesitó hiperbolizar el discurso de la Familia para fundar nuevos vínculos de estabilidad comunitaria que se encargaran de naturalizar el reencuentro del país consigo mismo" (200–201) (the government of the democratic Transition needed to exaggerate the discourse of the Family in order to form new ties of community stability that would take charge of naturalizing the country's reencounter with itself).

8. Claudia Donoso, "16 años de fotografía" 30. Yet even official photographs, such as those used for national identity cards, could be put to diverse uses. As Donoso points out in her essay on photography in Chile at the time, family members of the disappeared marched through the streets waving placards with enlarged copies of these photographs as testimony to their loved ones' existence.

9. *Margins and Institutions/Márgenes e instituciones* (131, 41). See Barthes 87, where he refers to photography as embodying a certain "certificate of presence."

10. See Richard's "The Photographic Condition" in *Margins and Institutions/Márgenes e instituciones* and Donoso's "16 años de fotografía."

11. As Nelly Richard remarks with regard to the Agrupaciones de Derechos Humanos, such women are "los que encarnan el pasado, los que llevan sus estigmas en carne viva sin querer maquillarlos con las cosméticas del bienestar y sus modales de la entretención" (*Resíduos y metáforas* 43) (those who embody the past, those who wear their stigmas in the flesh without wanting to gloss them over with the cosmetics of well-being and its entertainment behavior).

12. It is as if, as Luis Cárcomo puts it with regard to another context involving photographs of photographs of the disappeared, "the *death* of the photographed becomes metaphorical and at the same time literal" (113).

13. Paula Allen has given several reasons for her use of black-and-white photography in this project. First, she states that she wanted to neutralize the desert, insisting that color did not add to the story and that the mood of the project was better reflected in black-and-white. She also relates black-and-white photography to long-term narrative, more emotional pieces, noting that *Flores* was a decade-long project for her. Finally, she insisted that at the time she began, color photography would have been so costly that it would have made it more difficult for her to share her photographs with her subjects, a key aspect of her work, which she views primarily as that of a human-rights activist who uses photography as her medium (pers. comm., August 2003; classroom lecture, March 2004).

14. See Richard's analysis of the photo-essay produced for the Chilean exhibition at the 1992 Expo in Seville, Spain ("El modelaje gráfico," in *Resíduos y metáforas,* particularly 163–66).

15. As Luis Cárcomo asks at the beginning of his excellent essay "Mediated Memory": "Why is it that discourses that approach questions of memory and representation tend to elide their conditions of technological (re)presentation?" (104).

16. The book itself, and its presence on the world market, perform an urgent and necessary counterpoint to slicker, commercial projections of the new Chile of the official discourse of the Transition (see n. 13, above). The entire book becomes an example of what Annette Kuhn calls "memory work": "an active practice of remembering which takes an inquiring attitude towards the past and the activity of its (re) construction through memory" ("A Journey through Memory" 186). As Kuhn describes it in her book *Family Secrets,* memory work is "a method and a practice

of unearthing and making public untold stories, stories of 'lives lived out on the borderlands,' lives for which the central interpretive devices of the culture don't quite work" (9). This "memory work" is doubly enacted here: performed, both visually and verbally, not only by the testimonial subjects themselves, but by the author and the reader as well.

17. Errázuriz has stated that she began the series of photographs on psychiatric hospitals in 1981 due to a rumor, which she later found out was unfounded, about the "disappeared" being held in these institutions (Hopkinson 32).

18. As Canadian critic and photographer Martha Rosler says about such photographic projects: "Documentary is a little like horror movies, putting a face on fear and transforming threat into fantasy, into imagery. One can handle imagery by leaving it behind. (*It is them, not us.*)" ("in, around, and afterthoughts" 306).

19. As Virginia Domínguez puts it in her essay: "Experimenting with form and pushing for semiotic self-determination will not by themselves lead us to transcend the salvage paradigm, but they might, in conjunction, be jarring enough to call attention to the problem. That in itself is a necessary condition for any possible transformation beyond the salvage paradigm" (137).

20. As Linda Hutcheon points out in her essay on postmodern photography, "What the *mixing* of the text and image often does is to underline, through the use of direct verbal address to a viewer, the fact that . . . pictures too represent both a scene and the look of a viewer, both an object and a subject" (135). In her essay on black women who use both photography and text in their work, Kellie Jones observes that adding text to photographs "changes the traditional relationship between the photographer and the subject, forcing the practitioner in some way to explain her voyeurism" (133).

21. Elsewhere I have analyzed *El infarto del alma* with regard to testimonial practice ("Testimony" 86–92), and my comments here build on that analysis.

22. All translations of this text are my own. The pages of the book are unnumbered.

23. As Eltit continues, "Cuando captura sus poses, les confirma la relevancia de sus figuras, cuando les sonríe, reconoce en ellos lo divinizado de sus conductas corporales. Cuando se inclina buscando el ángulo, les dedica todo su profesionalismo" (n.p.) (When she captures their poses, she confirms for them the relevance of their forms, when she smiles at them, she recognizes in them the deified nature of their physical behaviors. When she bends over, looking for the right angle, she dedicates to them all of her professionalism).

24. Regarding this aspect of the photographs and Errázuriz's dedication, Nelly Richard points out that: "[Errázuriz] trata estos cuerpos desgraciados con el mismo profesionalismo (precisión de ángulos, incisión de luz, decisión de encuadre) con el que la foto publicitaria cuida a sus más agraciados modelos" (*Resíduos y metáforas* 252) ([Errazuriz] treats these wretched bodies with the same professionalism (precise angles, incisive lighting, and decisive framing) with which the publicity photo takes care of its most attractive models).

25. In her essay on *El infarto*, Nelly Richard elaborates on this point, following Roland Barthes: "El enamorado parece loco porque lo gobierna la irracionalidad de una pasión que lo enajena y lo convierte en un poseído, en alguien invadido por un otro" (*Resíduos y metáforas* 260) (The lover seems mad because he is ruled by the irrationality of a passion that alienates him and converts him into someone possessed, invaded by another). *El infarto* complicates such "*locura*" even further by imagining/imaging the unimaginable: "el loco enamorado." (260) (the madman in love).

26. The text also here refuses the logic of interrogation that informs the testimonial genre (see Ramos).

27. I explore the range of possibilities regarding this question in my essay "Testimony, Ethics and Aesthetics in Diamela Eltit." The written text here interacts with the image to produce what Linda Hutcheon calls the riddling effect of postmodern photography (125), which demands an active participation on the part of the reader to try to decipher the verbal-visual meanings. With regard to the active participation required of the reader of such texts, Kellie Jones has observed that combining photography with text requires the viewer to spend more time with the work, necessarily engaging more actively as reader-participant.

28. Sandra Lorenzano has explored the way *El infarto del alma* becomes a mirror for ourselves, observing that: "[e]n esas miradas se encuentran nuestras miradas, esos rostros podrían ser los nuestros" (97) ([i]n those gazes can be found our own gazes, those faces could be our own).

29. Our recognition is perhaps not surprising given that, even as the portrait promises a manifestation of individual identity, it also, as Richard puts it, "moldea la expresión humana según los estereotipos visuales de la convención fotográfica del retrato" (*Resíduos* 107) (molds human expression according to the visual stereotypes of the photographic conventions of the portrait).

30. See Hirsch, *Family Frames*, 84.

31. Here I draw from Judith Butler. "The parodic replication and resignification of heterosexual constructs within non-heterosexual frames brings into relief the utterly constructed status of the so-called original, but it shows that heterosexuality only constitutes itself as the original through a convincing act of repetition. The more that 'act' is expropriated, the more the heterosexual claim to originality is exposed as illusory" (724).

32. As Butler further points out, gender performance is also compulsory, since "acting out of line with heterosexual norms brings with it ostracism, punishment, and violence" (725). We see the results of such compulsory acts—or the refusal to perform them—in the testimony.

33. See Martha Rosler's *3 works* and her critical essay "in, around, and afterthoughts" for an analysis of the inadequacy of both visual and verbal representational systems and of her photomontage on the Bowery, which points out this inadequacy.

References

Bal, Mieke, et al., eds. *Acts of Memory: Cultural Recall in the Present.* Hanover and London: University Press of New England, 1999.

Barthes, Roland. *Camera Lucida: Reflections on Photography.* 1980. Trans. Richard Howard. New York: Farrar, Straus and Giroux, 1981.

______. "Rhetoric of the Image." 1964. In *Image-Music-Text.* Trans. Stephen Heath. New York: Farrar, Straus and Giroux, 1977, 32–51.

Butler, Judith. "Imitation and Gender Insubordination." In *Literary Theory: An Anthology.* Eds. Julie Rivkin and Michael Ryan. London: Blackwell, 1998, 722–30.

Cárcomo Huechante, Luis. "MEDIAted Memory: Writing, Photography, and Performativity in the Age of the Image." In *Beyond the Lettered City: Latin American Literature and Mass Media.* Hispanic Issues 22. Eds. Edmundo Paz-Soldán and Debra A. Castillo. New York and London: Garland, 2000, 103–16.

Caruth, Cathy. *Trauma: Explorations in Memory.* Baltimore: Johns Hopkins University Press, 1995.

Domínguez, Virginia. "Of Other Peoples: Beyond the 'Salvage' Paradigm." *In Discussions in Contemporary Culture.* Ed. Hal Foster. Dia Art Foundation New York: The New Press, 1998.

Donoso, Claudia. "16 años de fotografía en Chile: memoria de un descontexto." *Revista de Crítica Cultural* 1.2 (1990): 28–32.

Donoso, Claudia, and Paz Errázuriz. *La manzana de Adán / Adam's Apple*. Santiago, Chile: Zona Editorial, 1990.

Dorfman, Ariel. *Some Write to the Future: Essays on Contemporary Latin American Fiction*. Durham and London: Duke University Press, 1991.

Eltit, Diamela, and Paz Errázuriz. *El infarto del alma*. Santiago, Chile: Francisco Zegers, 1994.

Ferrer, Rita. *Yo, fotografía / I am photography*. Santiago, Chile: Ediciones de La Hetera, 2002.

Hirsch, Marianne. *Family Frames: Photography, Narrative and Postmemory*. Cambridge and London: Harvard University Press, 1997.

______. "Projected Memory: Holocaust Photographs in Personal and Public Fantasy." In *Acts of Memory: Cultural Recall in the Present*. Ed., Mieke Bal, et al. Hanover and London, University Press of New England, 1999, 3–23.

Hirsch, Marianne, ed. *The Familial Gaze*. Hanover and London: University Press of New England, 1999.

Hopkinson, Amanda, ed. and trans. "Paz Errázuriz." In *Desires and Disguises: Five Latin American Photographers*. London: Serpent's Tail, 1992.

Hutcheon, Linda. *The Politics of Postmodernism*. London and New York: Routledge, 1989.

Huyssen, Andreas. *Present Pasts: Urban Palimpsests and the Politics of Memory*. Stanford, CA: Stanford University Press, 2003.

Jelin, Elizabeth. *State Repression and the Labors of Memory*. Trans. Judy Rein and Marcial Godoy-Anativia. Contradicions. 18. Minneapolis: University of Minnesota Press, 2003.

Jones, Kellie. "In Their Own Image (Black Women Artists Who Combine Text with Photography)." *Artforum* 29 (November 1990): 132–38.

Kuhn, Annette. "A Journey Through Memory." In *Memory and Methodology*. Ed. Susannah Radstone. Oxford and New York: Berg, 2000, 179–96.

______. *Family Secrets: Acts of Memory and Imagination*. London and New York: Verso, 2002.

LaCapra, Dominick. *History and Memory after Auschwitz*. Ithaca, NY: Cornell University Press, 1998.

Lorenzano, Sandra. "Cicatrices de la fuga." In *Creación y resistencia: la narrativa de Diamela Eltit, 1983–1998*. Ed. María Inés Lagos. Nomadías / Serie Monográfica Santiago, Chile: Cuarto Propio, 2000, 93–107.

Miller, Nancy K. "Putting Ourselves in the Picture: Memoirs and Mourning." In *The Familial Gaze*. Ed. Marianne Hirsch. Hanover and London: University Press of New England, 1999

Minh-ha, Trinh T. "Of Other Peoples: Beyond the 'Salvage' Paradigm." In *Discussions in Contemporary Culture*. 1987. Ed. Hal Foster. Dia Art Foundation New York: The New Press, 1998, 138–41.

Mitchell, W. J. T. "The Photographic Essay: Four Case Studies." In *Picture Theory: Essays on Verbal and Visual Representation*. Chicago: University of Chicago Press, 1994, 281–322.

Munizaga, Giselle, and Carlos Ochsensius. "El Discurso Público de Pinochet (1973–1976)." In *The Discourse of Power: Culture, Hegemony and the Authoritarian State in Latin America*. Ed. Neil Larsen. Minneapolis: Ideologies & Literature, 1983.

El pabellón de Chile, huracanes y maravillas en una exposición universal. Santiago, Chile: La Máquina del Arte, 1992.

Pratt, Mary Louise. "Des-escribir a Pinochet: desbaratando la cultura del miedo en Chile." In *Creación y resistencia: la narrativa de Diamela Eltit*, 1983–1998. Ed. María Inés Lagos. Nomadías / Serie Monográfica. Santiago, Chile: Cuarto Propio, 2000, 17–32.

Ramos, Julio. "Dispositivos del amor y la locura." In *Creación y resistencia: la narrativa de Diamela Eltit*, 1983–1998. Ed. María Inés Lagos. Nomadías / Serie Monográfica. Santiago, Chile: Cuarto Propio, 2000, 111–25.

Richard, Nelly. *Márgenes e instituciones: arte en Chile desde 1973/Margins and Institutions: Art in Chile Since 1973*. Melbourne, Australia: Art & Text, 1986.

______. *Residuos y metáforas (Ensayos de crítica cultural sobre el Chile de la Transición)*. Santiago, Chile: Cuarto Propio, 1998.

Rosler, Martha. *3 works*. Halifax: Nova Scotia College of Art and Design, 1981.

______. "in, around, and afterthoughts (on documentary photography)." In *The Contest of Meaning: Critical Histories of Photography*. Ed. Richard Bolton. Cambridge and London: MIT Press, 1992, 303–40.

Sontag, Susan. *On Photography*. 1973. New York: Doubleday, 1990.

Tierney-Tello, Mary Beth. "Testimony, Ethics, and the Aesthetic in Diamela Eltit." *PMLA* 114.1 (1999): 78–96.

Tremain, Kerry. "Introduction: Seeing and Believing." In *Witness in Our Time: Working Lives of Documentary Photographers*, by Ken Light. Washington and New York: Smithsonian Institution Press, 2000, 1–11.

Williams, Gareth. "The Fantasies of Cultural Exchange in Latin American Subaltern Studies." In *The Real Thing: Testimonial Discourse and Latin America*. Ed. Georg M. Gugelberger. Durham and London: Duke University Press, 1996, 225–53.

Zamora, Lois Parkinson. "Quezalcóatl's Mirror: Reflections on the Photographic Image in Latin America." In *Image and Memory: Photography from Latin America 1866–1994*. Eds. Wendy Watriss and Lois Parkinson Zamora. Austin: University of Texas Press, 1998, 292–375.

Part II

Refocusing the Urban

Chapter Five

Writing Against the City

Julio Cortázar's Photographic Take on India

Marcy E. Schwartz

Mirar fotos es siempre mirar en otra parte; tomarse fotos es estar yendo hacia el lugar en que van a mirarnos.

(Looking at pictures is always looking somewhere else; taking photographs of ourselves is to be going toward the place where they're going to be looking at us.)
—Néstor García Canclini

Photography's initial identification with urban worlds, where the flâneur's gaze transcribes Atget's Paris or Victorian London, persists in contemporary photographic projects. Susan Sontag insists that photographers began as "artists of the urban sensibility" (56), and traces the photographic aesthetic as intrinsic to the experience of city spaces. For Sontag, even documentary photography of rural poverty extends from urban habits of seeing. The architecture, artificial light, and interclass encounters of urban life make the association of photography with cities almost a commonplace. In fact, the world's first photograph, produced in 1826 by Nicéphore Niepce, is a view of urban rooftops (reproduced in Freund 32). Photography's evolution from upperclass daguerreotypes and portraiture, together with the mechanical and scientific advances of the industrial revolution, link its history to urban social and spatial configurations.[1]

European and American cities occupy so much photographic space historically that the urban foundation of photographic reproduction might appear at first to be an exclusive characteristic of the industrialized first world. However, even in Latin America photography cannot seem to escape this urban sensibility. Despite the colonial view (voyeurism?) that searches out the exotica of the jungle and rural plains and objectifies indigenous communities, the photographic enterprise in Latin America maintains an urban focus, often to the point of obsession.

The enduring link between an urban perspective and the Latin American photographic aesthetic is evident in Julio Cortázar's work. Visual images, often direct references and anecdotes regarding photography, pervade Cortázar's fiction and essays. His stories are almost always ensnared in the labyrinths of urban networks (highways, subway systems, arcades), and the plots of his novels are played out in the mappings and overlappings of Paris, Vienna, and Buenos Aires.[2] As Dan Russek has observed:

> Photography in general, and street photography in particular, is an endeavor particularly well suited to a man who railed against the boring habits of civilized life, who hailed the insights of intuition and spontaneity, who reveled in revealing surprising aspects of everyday things, and whose creative processes depended not on the development of predetermined plans, but in the flaneuristic, unexpected discoveries that those processes yield. ("Fixing Images" n.p.)

Photography serves his fictional plots in stories such as "Las babas del diablo" ("Blow-Up") and "Apocalipsis de Solentiname" ("Apocalypse in Solentiname"), where photographs or slides challenge conventional realism and become vehicles for the fantastic. The photographic process itself functions as an analogue to writing. Photograph albums emerge among Cortázar's preferred metafictional metaphors for the aesthetic of *Rayuela* (*Hopscotch*) (chapter 91), where snapshots are analogues of the episodic chapters as well as of the "Lado de allá" fragments in the novel. The novel's structure, complete with instructions to the reader, invites a reading strategy that resembles leafing through a photo album.

Cortázar's work directly incorporating the visual along with the verbal pushes generic limits to question the place of art and the values and politics of representation. *Libro de Manuel* (*A Manual for Manuel*) goes even further than *Rayuela* in directly metafictionalizing the album, this time as a scrapbook. The novel tells the story of the selection and accumulation of materials (articles, stories, advertisements, etc.) to be included in the scrapbook, while it also hints that it might *be* the very scrapbook that the novel recounts (thus the title). The verbal text makes room on the page for the reproduction of numerous newspaper clippings and photographs that create a hybrid visual-verbal novel.[3]

Alongside his fiction, Cortázar is known as the author of books that defy neat classification, such as those that María de Lourdes Dávila calls "almanaques literarios" (literary almanacs) (*Ultimo round* and *La vuelta al día en ochenta mundos*) and "catálogos" (*Territorios* and *Silvalandia*). What especially distinguishes these "catalogue" or collage projects, collaborations with visual artists, is a proposed interdependence resulting from a forced encounter between the visual and verbal texts. Dávila insists that in these books the visual images never occupy an inferior plane, nor do they simply serve as "adyacencia ornamental" (13) (ornamental adjacence). They incorporate popular culture and icons in order to question discursive practices. Their provocative dissonance relies on parallel narratives of words and images that challenge the boundaries between "art" and popular media.[4] Cortázar designs new spaces for visual images by making them into a language. Many critics consider books such as *Ultimo round* and *La vuelta al día en ochenta mundos* "architectural" works that offer parallel planes of signification, or "floors," with visual images (often photographs) that appear next to, above, or below the verbal text. Calling into question the primacy of both modes of representation, language and image conspire in the construction of new spatial territories.

Cortázar's well-known photographic collaborations occupy a special niche in his extensive engagement with the visual. These collaborations fall more easily into the category of albums or art books, what critics such as W. J. T. Mitchell call "the photographic essay." Cortázar's best known collections feature urban centers, such as Sara Facio and Alicia D'Amico's *Buenos Aires, Buenos Aires* or Alecio d'Andrade's *París, ritmos de una ciudad.* His essays in these projects explore city space in ways that parallel his fiction. The photographs and text, as accomplices in the *flâneurie* of rendering urban space elastic and malleable, together launch fantastic moves. Here the essays on and photographs of his two urban homes occupy the interstices of urban movement, travel, longing, and memory.[5]

The cosmopolitan imperative pervades his photographic collaborations whether or not the visual material documents urban surroundings. In the collaboration *Alto el Perú* (1984), a project seemingly removed from urban concerns, Cortázar frames photographs by Manja Offerhaus of the Peruvian altiplano in the context of viewing them from Paris. His essay intervenes in the ethnographic rural scenes with mentions of Parisian neighborhoods and European films, grappling with the ethics of ethnographic photography of Latin America with his self-referential critique of the urban intellectual, "ya tan ajeno a esto sobre una mesa de París" (25). The anxiety over the narrator's urban situatedness emerges throughout Cortázar's essay, where the European city emblematically absorbs the distance (geographical and ideological) between him and the scenes in the photographs. The first two images in the book, in fact, are of Cortázar himself being photographed by Offerhaus in his Parisian apartment (7, 9), taken by Carol Dunlop, Cortázar's wife (fig. 5.1).

The requirements of the photographic essay, as Mitchell outlines in *Picture Theory*, include "equality, independence and collaboration" between the verbal text and the photographic images (290). While Cortázar's projects mentioned thus far certainly

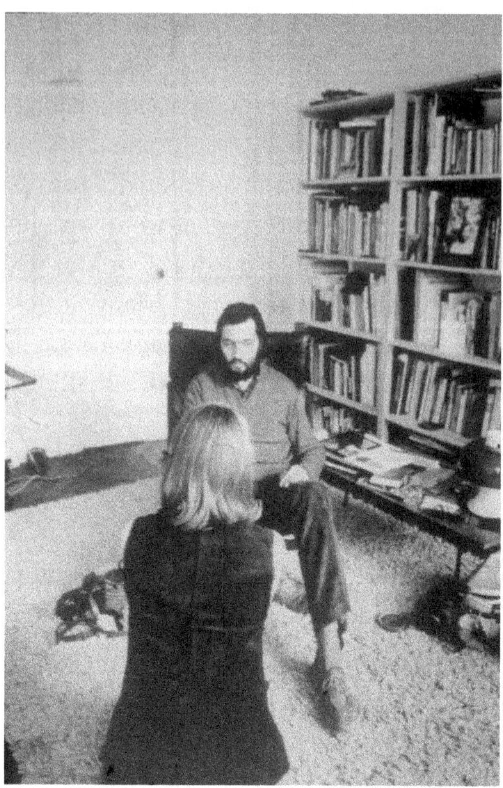

Fig. 5.1. Cortázar being photographed by Manja Offerhaus, taken by Carol Dunlop. Courtesy of Stéphane Hébert. From *Alto el Peni*.

abide by these "requirements," *Prosa del observatorio* (1972) pushes them to their limit. In this work, where Cortázar includes and comments on his own photographs, the visual and the verbal are even more intimately linked. The interdependence between the visual and the verbal is built around a different creative process here than in books such as *Territorios*, *Silvalandia*, and the photographic collaborations. In *Prosa*, "el viaje textual desembarca en el territorio artístico" (Dávila 179) (the textual voyage disembarks in artistic territory). Rather than a dialogue (and some of Cortázar's collaborative essays incorporate dialogue into the verbal discourse, recreating the collaboration or fictionalizing the interaction between the writer and visual artists), *Prosa* proposes a narrative that projects the verbal and the visual through a single focal point.[6] Lida Aronne-Amestoy calls the photographs and the essay in *Prosa* "co-texts" where "el ícono no es soporte, sino matriz de la palabra" (58) (the icon is not a support but rather the origin of the word). Cortázar exploits his position as both author and photographer to comment on each medium's limitations and possibilities.

One of Cortázar's least studied works, *Prosa* falls outside the strict category of collaboration, since in this case he is author of both photographs and text. Nor does it function as an art catalogue, as Cortázar avoids using this book to launch himself

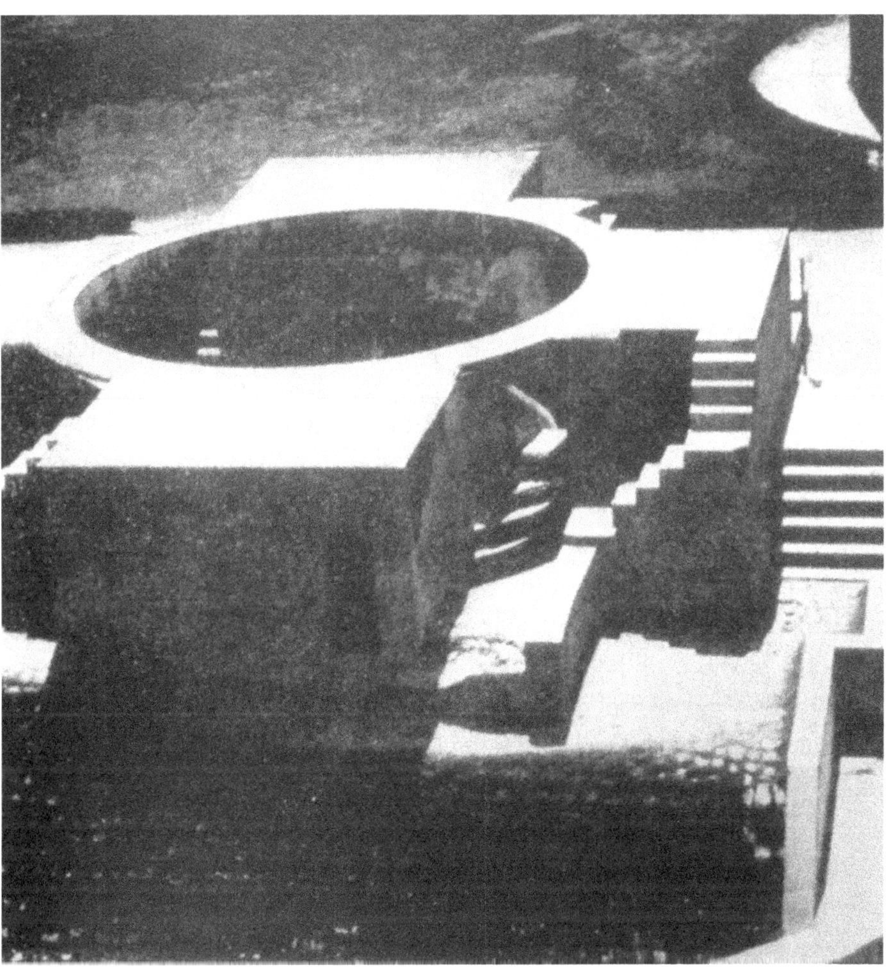

Fig. 5.2. Aerial view from *Prosa del observatorio* by Julio Cortázar. Authorization, Agencia Carmen Balcells.

as a photographer, but rather includes his photographs almost apologetically. I have chosen to highlight it here because it stands out as the only photographic project in which he is both author and photographer, and therefore it marks a significant, even culminating, moment in the evolution of his engagement with visual discourse.

In *Prosa*, Cortázar documents Jai Singh's eighteenth-century astronomical observatories through the lens and through language. The book includes nineteen photographs of stone stairways, ramps, archways, pillars, gardens, gongs, and observation platforms. As is his practice in many of the collaborative photography volumes, his essay does not appear as a preface or introduction *before* the visual images, but rather *surrounds* the photographs dispersed throughout the book. The verbal text adopts a snapshot-like fragmentation in its separation into twelve sections from three to ten pages long, including the photographs, distinguished by breaks on the page. Occasionally the breaks are accompanied by an aerial view, combining visual distance with a change in narrative style or point of view (fig.5.2).

Cortázar's essay shifts among an array of discursive practices—epistolary, scientific, poetic—as it surrounds the photographs. He includes some mention of the observatories, but most of the essay discusses freshwater eels and their migration to the ocean, with corollary discussions of the Milky Way, critiques of the scientific method, and meditations on the elasticity of time and space, using the Moebius strip as an emblem. The visual-verbal text resists a totalizing and unifying structure or vision. There are few panoramic photographs of the observatory sites, but instead an insistence on individual pieces, corners, angles, or curves. Aronne-Amestoy notes that the apparently random, fragmentary order of the photographs offers an "[e]ncuadre mutilado y ángulo de visión desplazado [que] contribuyen a destruir la transparencia referencial . . . y que presupone un visor . . . no convencional, descentrado y móvil" (59) (mutilated frame and displaced angle of vision that contributes to destroying referential transparency . . . and that presupposes an unconventional, decentered, and mobile viewpoint). The photographs and the essay together manipulate the synecdochal relationship between the parts and the whole in order to decenter the viewer. *Prosa* resists classical pictorial and compositional perspectivism by continual movement and shifting of both the camera and the text, destroying hegemonic unity. Cortázar in *Prosa* reconfigures urban design as he unseats the binary opposition between visual images and language.

Although *Prosa* suggests a veering away from urban concerns, with the book's decidedly non-metropolitan focus (tertiary cities in a developing country with a European colonial past), as a cultural product it seems unable to escape the weight of the city. The cosmopolitan imperative guides Cortázar's lens in Jaipur and Delhi to register the urbanness that both launches photography and sustains writing culture, from the founding institutional mechanisms of the Western *polis* to the spatial and spiritual imposition of imperial expansion and colonialism. While the verbal text in this project recalls many issues common to Cortázar's photographic collaborations, it targets the urban perspective as a politically compromised positionality. Anything but a celebration of that cosmopolitan imperative, Cortázar's essay interacts with his visual images under the burden of the urban.

Critics have debated the genre of this book since its publication. Rosario Ferré considers the essay a romantic prose poem and identifies its philosophical roots, with all the anxiety of influence, in Novalis, Poe, and Lugones. Andrew Bush suggests another set of associations, through a dialogue between *Prosa del observatorio* and Lezama Lima. Aronne-Amestoy details how *Prosa* parodies discursive practices such as the scientific essay, the epistle, didactic prose, historiography, and love poetry through a series of oppositions and a process of dissection into "subtipos discursivos"

(56) (discursive subtypes). The different discursive styles converge and overlap in a simultaneity of narrative forms.[7] Other critics concur that Cortázar's essay experiments in merging generic categories and, as his readers have come to expect, bending the rules of the game. Jaime Alazraki calls the text of *Prosa* both a poetic and political document that culminates as its author's ideogrammatic epiphany ("Tema y sistema" 93, 94). According to Alazraki, Cortázar combines the strategies of the prose poem, the essay, and fiction, "articulando narración y poesía para formular su credo poético-político" (104) (articulating narration and poetry in order to formulate his poetic-political credo). He even goes so far, toward the end of his essay on *Prosa*, as to call it a political manifesto (109).[8]

Cortázar himself avoids assigning this book any generic or narrational category, capitalizing on its plurisemic quality in order to provoke the readers' reactions. He sees photography as a revolutionary tool and manipulates the joining of the visual and the verbal for the purpose of "una disonancia que asume la posibilidad de renovación" (Dávila 43) (a dissonance that assumes the possibility of renovation). In keeping with that opening toward new possibilities of multimedia expression, he refuses to designate, determine, or assign any singular or primary narrative function, particularly in order to avoid all the readerly expectations that those kinds of labeling further restrict. I read *Prosa* as a special case of Cortazarian collaborative media, where the visual and the verbal reinvent spatial trajectories to critique and reinvent urban space.

While the generic challenges of *Prosa* are less the focus here than Cortázar's experiments with recreating a narrational city, the debates over the book's categorization and how it eludes any critical consensus in terms of genre are important indicators of its aggressive metadiscursivity. Cortázar attacks binarism at every turn, from the initial *apparent* opposition of words and images to the work's stylistic variance to the erasure or blurring of the distinction between natural realms such as the oceans and the sky. The narrative structure that winds among examples of discursive practices culminates as a metadiscourse. The book narrates its own referential and metaphorical process through a spatial destabilization that undermines the Western gaze by juxtaposing it with an Eastern model.

Few critics engage the verbal-visual interaction in their assessments of *Prosa*, relegating the photographic element to the referential or pictorial. However, as Aronne-Amestoy states, this project is Cortázar's "reivindicación de la imagen como discurso" (58) (revindication of the image as discourse). With Cortázar in the role of both author and photographer, *Prosa* needs to be considered as a major statement about how he intertwines the visual and the verbal. Cortázar's essay style in his other varied projects with visual artists avoids "explanation" and "illustration" of the visual material to offer a verbal accompaniment that interacts with the visual text. Even more intricately in *Prosa*, Cortázar suggests a simultaneity of discourses that invites a parallel reading strategy.

Rather than asserting his authority over both text and images, Cortázar incorporates into the book a tension around his dual authorship roles. His questioning of authority, verbal or visual, introduces an uneasiness around authoritative discourses (scientific, literary, photographic, philosophical) that is central to the project. Cortázar does not claim to be a visual artist and even discredits his photographs at the beginning of the book:

> Las fotos de los observatorios del sultán Jai Singh (Jaipur, Delhi) fueron tomadas en 1967, con una película de mala calidad; en París, Antonio Gálvez las convirtió en lo que aquí se muestra y que le agradezco. (7)
>
> (The photos of Sultan Jai Singh's observatories (Jaipur, Delhi) were taken in 1967, with poor quality film; in Paris, Antonio Gálvez transformed them into what is shown here, and for that I thank him.)

"Las fotos" and "París" frame the structure of this acknowledgment, which is organized chronologically according to the production of the visual images. The passive voice and word order lend agency to the photos rather than to the photographer; Paris introduces the second part of the acknowledgment to account for and situate the developing. He includes Paris unparenthetically as the site of developing and printing, marking it as the city of inscription. The book's final verbal message again situates the project in space, "París, Saignon, 1971" (78), the scenes of writing. These localizing phrases simultaneously situate and separate, distinguishing Jaipur from Paris, distancing the reader from the photos, and identifying Cortázar (and the scientists and philosophers he cites) apologetically in their Western and urban locatedness.[9]

The title of *Prosa* initiates this insistence on *place*. From the ambivalent preposition and article *del* emerge hints at travel narrative, one of the discursive forms many critics have associated with this book. The title seems to announce the narrator's voice coming *from* the observatory, while at the same time suggesting the narrative is *about* the observatory; in fact Cortázar ironically subverts both of those expectations. Jai Singh's structures serve as both origin and destination, point of departure and object of desire, for a trajectory that moves between the spatial realms of the seas and the sky. The image of the Moebius strip, mentioned several times in the text, encompasses the very conception of this project, where the outside and inside no longer can be distinguished from one another. The observatory, the product of Jai Singh's art and science and his vantage point for observing the skies, is both the subject of Cortázar's photographs and the point of departure for his discussion of the eels' migration. The verbal text says little about the observatory, since the architectural structures are narrated through the photographs, which in turn serve as the reader-viewer's perspective for Cortázar's projected undersea exploration. The photos and verbal text together become a sort of travel diary from and about India that propose their own itinerary, rooted in the urban. Similar to what Dávila notes in Cortázar's "Carta del viajero" (a chapter in *Territorios*), "se vuelve a un tiempo cartografía y movimiento en el espacio, descripción del viaje y el viaje mismo" (209) (it becomes simultaneously cartography and movement in space, description of the trip and the trip itself).[10]

Cortázar continually juxtaposes the realms he explores in *Prosa* with the city. The critique of the city gains momentum as the verbal text progresses. The narration encourages seeking out "encuentros fuera de la ley de la ciudad" (66) (contacts outside the law of the city). The eels in particular occupy a spatial zone far removed from the urban: "comprenderás que nada de eso puede decirse desde aceras o sillas o tablados de la ciudad" (13) (you will see that none of this could be said from sidewalks or chairs or city blocks). Cortázar's fascination with other species has been well documented in his short fiction; his first collection of stories entitled *Bestiario* and other stories, highlight his exploration of other life forms as a means of ontological experimentation. His fictionalization of lower life forms, such as fish, reptiles, and insects, in particular, underscores the juxtaposition he proposes vis à vis urban space. His story "Axolotl," the most obvious example, with its tale of interspecies metamorphosis, takes place in the Parisian scientific institution of the Jardin des Plantes.[11] Later stories, such as "Carta a una señorita en París," suggest that the inexplicable, surreal emergence and reproduction of rodents (the character vomits rabbits) is incompatible with, or perhaps a form of resistance against, the confines of urban space. In *Prosa* Cortázar attacks the scientific method of animal classification as compromised by the politics of urban bureaucracies (academic organization and discourse, lettered habits of analysis). He champions eels in *Prosa* for their chemically coded instincts, which seem to defy the natural laws of science, pushing them to escape their environment. They are the revolutionaries swimming against the urban current.

In *Prosa*, Cortázar celebrates Jaipur as an urban plan, whose observatory is one of the principal structures of Jai Singh's (1700–43) planning for the city that was founded in 1727. Differing from other Indian cities, which developed organically, Jaipur was planned on a geometric grid (Davies 371). The observatory is positioned in the center of the walled city, near the palace. Although he avoids verbal description of the city, Cortázar's essay, along with the focus and arrangement of the photographs, situate the structures in their urban plan. Singh's perfectionism and insistence on numerical precision are evident in the original design, which divides the city into seven sectors, rather than the traditional nine of a mandala plan. Aman Nath considers Singh's plan both innovative and progressive (58), noting that water supply and security were paramount in the design. The observatory, while perhaps foreign to Western notions of urban landscapes, occupies a significant urban position. Cortázar's book undercuts the conventional (and expected) binary opposition between the cosmopolis and the periphery through an ironic manipulation of the ethnographic gaze, as he asserts that Jaipur is an urban paradigm.[12] However, many architectural historians of India suggest that Jaipur was inspired by European cities:

> There is a striking rationality about the layout of Jaipur that puts us in mind of Europe—and makes us wonder if the town planning might not have been European-inspired after all. . . . (Sten Åke Nilsson, quoted in Nath 63)

> Jaipur was, quite clearly, conceived as a show piece capital, in a spirit somewhat similar to the Paris of Napoleon III. (Nath 72)

In *Prosa del observatorio*, Cortázar's essay detours around but cannot avoid his distrust of Western models and uses of the city, however they may have implicated Jaipur. Paradoxically, his alternative, Eastern model may share an uneasy sympathy with Paris.

Cortázar's cultural concept of the city inextricably links writing to the urban. The city is both a form of inscription and mapping, as well as a generator and source of written institutional discourse. While this idea of the lettered city is frequently evoked in Latin America (see Rama), Cortázar manipulates theories of urban inscription with some surprising results in this photographic project on India. *Prosa* relies on a synthesis of media where photography and architecture perform as inscription, along with the amalgam of discourses (scientific writing, prose poetry, epistle, etc.) incorporated into the verbal text. The observatory becomes an ideogram, its own "written" physical manifestation for and toward the stars, an institution for scientific thought and activity, a platform for phenomenological investigation. The city as a cultural construct serves the project as another subdiscourse, a spatial plane as well as a discursive category that produces writing and signs. Jai Singh's mathematical and astronomical advances, Cortázar's photography and writing all emerge from and are compromised within urban structures.

Both the observatory and Cortázar's essay (the physical and the linguistic) create links between water, earth, and sky. While water and the migration of eels seem to be the foreign element to the photographs as well as to the purpose of an observatory, demanding an elaborate analogy provided by the verbal text, in fact water was a preoccupation of Jai Singh's, along with the stars. He is believed to have designed in 1732 the Nahagarh cistern, located very near the Jaipur observatory. The cistern is one of some two thousand below-ground stepwells built between the seventh and ninth centuries in India. After periods of famine, Gujarat and Rajasthan saw surges in the building of stepwells and ponds. Part of a cult of water in an arid zone, stepwells were cut into the ground with a deep, narrow corridor that opens where the stairs meet the water. As architectural historian Morna Livingston explains, their function and design are interrelated:

> Continuous steps from ground level to the bottom of the structure lead to water, no matter how great the variation in the water table. During the monsoon, when the water table is high, water levels will reach the upper steps and only a short descent is required. As the water table drops slowly after the monsoon, a longer descent is necessary, but the water surface always laps against a step and can always be reached. (xix)

Livingston's study of Indian stepwells opens with a description that recalls Cortázar's fluid connections metamorphosing between animal and mineral, as well as between earthly, oceanic, and celestial realms:

> Wherever a stepwell links brilliant Indian sun to a clear pool of water, two separate worlds are joined. In the well's stone corridors people move between one realm and the other. . . . Excavation is balanced with construction–one pair of opposites in a series that includes sky and water, solid and liquid, empty and full. (1)

While the photographs of *Prosa* draw the viewer into the density of the observatory's physical structures, the text announces a yearning for a zone of conciliation: "quisiera asomar a un campo de contacto" (50) (I would like to come out on a field of contact) where the presence of water contributes to an enmeshing of natural elements. The substance of water, as a metaphor for the sky as well as a life force in a dry land, also provides the metaphor of thirst for knowledge in Cortázar's attack on Western scientific modes of investigation. "Jai Singh sabe que la sed que se sacia con el agua volverá a atormentarlo, Jai Singh sabe que solamente siendo el agua dejará de tener sed" (51) (Jai Singh knows that thirst if relieved with water will come back to torment him, Jai Singh knows that only by being the water will he no longer be thirsty). Jai Singh's participation in stepwell construction also justifies the essay's "migrating"

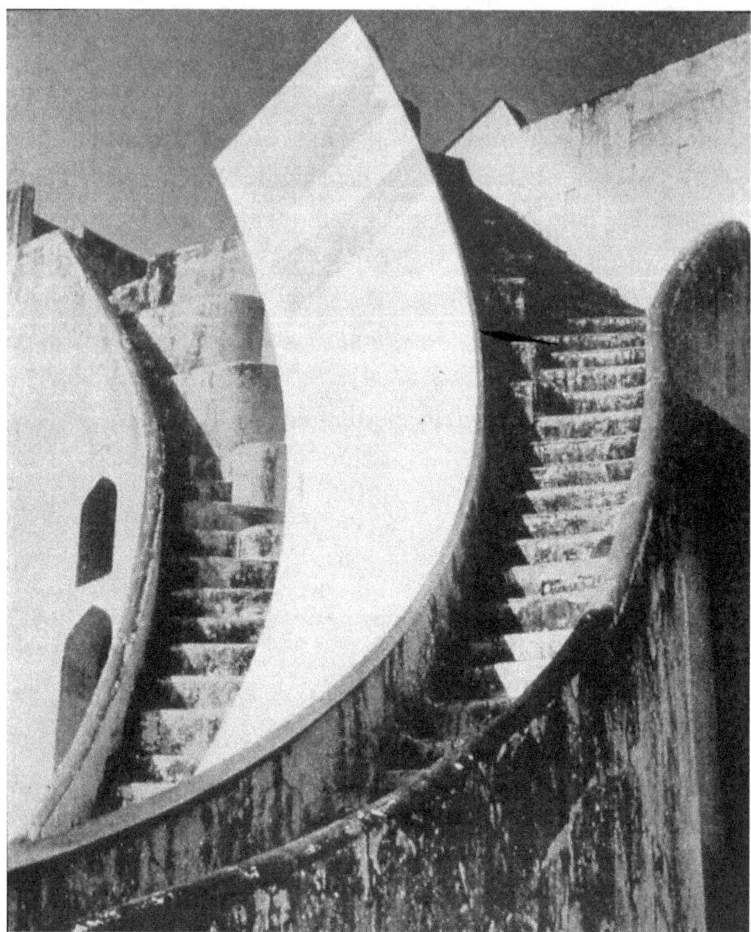

Fig. 5.3. Curving stairways and shadows from *Prosa del observatorio* by Julio Cortázar. Authorization, Agencia Carmen Balcells.

between elements and lends images that might appear banal ("thirst for knowledge") an unexpected force.

Cortázar incorporates the structure and function of stepwells, with their fluctuating water level that guarantees access to water in all seasons, into both the visual and verbal components of *Prosa*. His photographic insistence on stairways—including the book's opening image (5)—underscores the importance of connections that bridge physically distinct realms. The solidness of the stone and marble structures might seem to contrast with or counterbalance the fluidity of the Milky Way or the eels' migration; however, Cortázar's photographic and visual language emphasizes the stairways' curves, bends, and ramps. One photograph features parallel curving staircases with shadows that render the uppermost and lowermost steps indistinguishable (fig. 5.3).

The verbal description on the facing page focuses on the curves that in turn render the solid structure more fluid:

> [L]a lenta curva de las máquinas de mármol o la cinta negra hirviente nocturna al asalto de los estuarios . . . que eso que fluye o converge o busca sea lo que es y no lo que se dice: perro aristotélico, que lo binario que te afila los colmillos sepa de alguna manera su innecesidad cuando otra esclusa empieza a abrirse en mármol y en peces, cuando Jai Singh con un cristal entre los dedos es ese pescador que extrae de la red, estremecida de dientes y de rabia, una anguila que es una estrella que es una anguila que es una estrella que es una anguila. (14–16)
>
> ([T]he slow curve of the marble machines or the nocturnal boiling black ribbon at the assault of the estuaries. . . . let whatever flows or converges or searches be what it is and not what people call it: Artistotelian dog, may the binary that sharpens your fangs somehow learn of its obsolescence when another scaled creature starts to emerge in marble and fish, when Jai Singh, with a crystal between his fingers, is that fisherman who removes from the net, trembling from teeth and from fear, an eel that is a star that is an eel that is a star that is an eel.)

Perhaps the most cited passage of the text, this back-and-forth equivalency between the eels and the stars creates a sort of medieval emblem together with the shadowed stairs. Cortázar highlights visually and verbally in Jai Singh's structures a physical fluidity that he exploits as an image for ontological metamorphosis and revolution.

In *Prosa*, stairways create vertical connections through the visual images, while they suggest conceptual connections narratively. One description of stairs in the essay evokes the descent to water but synesthetically shifts toward the sky at the end: "esas interminables teorías de peldaños que Jai Singh escalaba en una lenta caída hacia el cielo" (50) (those interminable theories of steps that Jai Singh climbed in a slow fall toward the sky). Another passage introduces the eels' "revolución" in their challenge of the depth and cold of the sea to migrate. Accessing this revolution

> es también serpiente negra de ida, lentos peldaños hacia la plataforma que reta el musgo astral, serpiente plateada de regreso. (63)
>
> (is also a black serpent on the way out, slow steps toward the platform that challenges the astral moss, a silver serpent on the way back.)

The essay associates the eels' mercury with the skies, elides liquid and solid realms, climbs the steps toward a revolutionary ethos:

> Todavía es tiempo de sargazos, de guerrillas parciales que despejan el monte sin que el combatiente alcance a ver una totalidad de cielo y mar y tierra. (64)
>
> (It is still the time of gulf-weeds, of partial guerrillas that clear the forest without any combatant getting close enough to see any totality of sky, sea, and earth.)

> [U]n dibujo de la realidad trepa por las escaleras de Jaipur, ondula sobre sí mismo en el anillo de Moebius de las anguilas, anverso y reverso conciliados, cinta de la concordia en la noche pelirroja de hombres y astros y peces. (70)
>
> ([A] drawing of reality climbs up the stairs of Jaipur, winds around itself in the Moebius strip of eels, front and back reconciled, ribbon of concord in the red-haired night of men and stars and fish.)

Stairways as avenues of connection also serve the metaphysical militancy of Cortázar's fantastical convergences, which rely on urban constructions while at the same time defying them.

Prosa establishes a convergence among photography, astronomy, and architecture as methods of writing that all coincide in Cortázar's concept of the urban. The most obvious level of these scriptural mappings is Cortázar's narration. As the verbal bridge between the water and the sky, the essay is his linguistic tightrope for crossing borders and accessing other realms.[13] However, *Prosa* pushes these analogies and convergences of writing far beyond the metanarrative turns that readers have come to expect in Cortázar. Each form of writing overlaps with another in this book, creating interdependent discourses that map space at the same time that they critique and even defy conventional conceptions of space. The relationship between the photographs and the verbal essay parallels the associations between other realms in this volume, whereby they facilitate contact with one another in order to refashion conceptions of spatial accessibility. Jai Singh's architectural structures ("máquinas de mármol," marble machines) help access the stars, and urban planning generates the maps that configure the city and support the very framework for institutions such as observatories.

Jai Singh's stairways connect him to the stars, serving as inscriptions of urban space as well as vehicles for transcending that space. The astral domain as a form of inscription in *Prosa* recalls Walter Benjamin's association between stars and photographic language, whereby constellations suggest the possibility of mimesis and the origins of reading. Eduardo Cadava elaborates on the implications of the stars in Benjamin's theory of visual representation:

> Like photography, stars are therefore another name for what makes similarity possible, for the process of mimetic reproduction. They are the models on which Benjamin bases the theory of likeness that underlies his reflections on language. (27)

Benjamin frequently relied on astrological metaphors for his theory of knowledge (ideas are compared to constellations) and for theories of time (viewing a star implies travel through many light-years, "an illumination in which the present bears within it the most distant past and where the distant past suddenly traverses the present moment" Cadava 28).[14] Cortázar's narration in *Prosa* frequently jumps from the seas to the skies where the stars function as an indecipherable alphabet:

> Retornar al fragor silencioso de las corrientes submarinos . . . también el cielo es así en las noches despejadas cuando las estrellas se amalgaman en una misma presión, conjuradas y hostiles, negándose al recuento, a las nomenclaturas, oponiendo una aterciopelada inalcanzabilidad a la lente que las circunda y abstrae, metiéndose de a diez, de a cien en un mismo campo visual . . . enraizadas en los mitos del cielo. (32–34)
>
> (Returning to the silent clamour of the undersea currents . . . the sky is also like this on clear nights when the stars collect all pressed together, under a spell and hostile, refusing to be counted, named, opposing the lens that surrounds them and abstracts them with an unreachable velvet, positioning themselves ten at a time, a hundred at a time in the same visual field . . . rooted in the myths of the sky.)

The photograph that this passage surrounds features a wall darkened by a long shadow where the open sky fills in nearly half the frame (fig. 5.4). Aerial views (see fig. 5.2) and shots such as this one that feature or angle toward the sky (39, 51, 61, 69) often accompany breaks on the written page, helping to delineate the sections or fragments of the verbal text. In this example, a small cupola perches on the uppermost point of the wall, suggesting the comparably minuscule dimensions of the stellar observer in relation to the rest of the structure. Cortázar makes reference to celestial bodies in other photographic projects where the play of light is always a central concern. In his essay accompanying photographs of the Peruvian altiplano, he narratively reconstructs the shadows and tones in an image of a young mother with her baby, mapping the mother's breasts onto a metaphorical night sky: "*astro* diminuto en torno al cual se diría que las dos cabezas giraban armoniosas hasta que

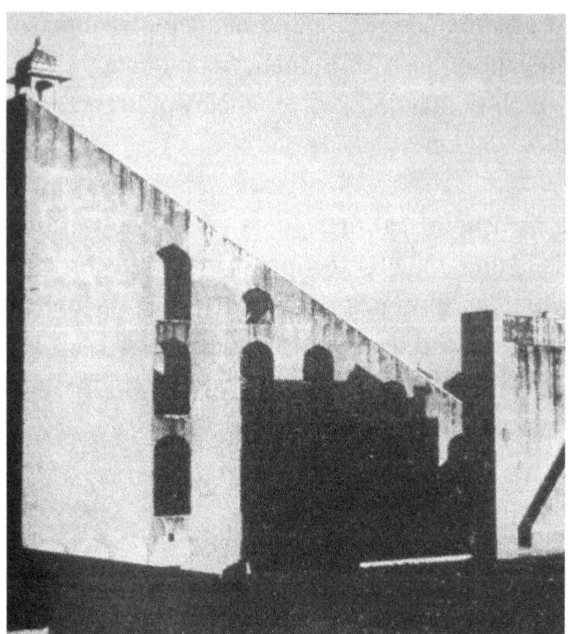

Fig. 5.4. View angling toward the sky from *Prosa del observatorio* by Julio Cortázar. Authorization, Agencia Carmen Balcells.

mi llegada las fijó en lo alto y lo bajo, sueño y vigilia como grandes *lunas* en torno al pequeño *sol* atezado" (*Alto el Perú* 21, emphasis added) (tiny star around which one could say that two heads rotated harmoniously until my arrival fixed them above and below, dream and vigil like big moons around the little blackened sun). The fluid movement between earthly and celestial realms breaks through spatial boundaries, challenging conventional metaphysical limitations.

In Cortázar's essays and collaborative work such as *Prosa*, photography provides a provocative analogue to the fantastic in his fiction. Where his narrative structures and plots insist on linking discontiguous historical moments and distanced locations in space, photography offers a concrete way to physically manifest other places and other times. The celestial metaphors underscore how for Cortázar the photographic medium erases temporal and spatial limitations, and confirms the interconnectedness between time and space that his work, particularly his fiction, celebrates. In another photographic essay, Cortázar highlights how photographs not only bring the viewer and the photographed subject closer but also distance them from one another: "una distancia que nadie podría medir en kilómetros, en años luz" (*Alto el Perú* 23) (a distance that no one could measure in kilometers, in light years). That he uses light years as an impossible measure links the photographic process to stars. Photography, according to Cortázar, "no congela el tiempo como suele decirse; muy al contrario, lo libera de su versión primaria" (*Alto el Perú* 49) (does not freeze time as the saying goes; quite to the contrary, it liberates it from its first version). Photography serves his continual effort to confound and surpass the conventionally conceived boundaries of time and space, as do Jai Singh's observatories.

Writing is both an essential tool and a restrictive system of conventions in *Prosa*. On the one hand, Cortázar capitalizes on writing and therefore reading on which humans depend for observing the stars and navigating the seas. These faculties serve as avenues for connecting otherwise distinct and mutually exclusive domains. Photography also becomes a mode of reading and writing (focusing a camera, producing images). On the other hand, *Prosa* problematizes writing for its often politically compromised and philosophically limiting role. The narration targets writing for perpetuating dominant discursive structures through its products such as dictionaries, parchments, doctoral theses, and personal diaries. The institutions and disciplines (libraries, academic science, news/press agencies) that produce, store and justify these objects of writing are attacked for restricting modes of discourse and therefore controlling perception and human experience. In one passage of *Prosa*, Cortázar directly challenges scientists "profesor Fontaine" and "señora Callamand" for "la sórdida paradoja de un empobrecimiento correlativo con la multiplicación de bibliotecas, microfilms y ediciones de bolsillo, una culturización a lo jíbaro" (52–54) (the sordid paradox of an impoverishment that correlates with the multiplication of libraries, microfilms, and paperbacks, a country bumpkin culturization). In the epistolary passage that follows, a letter to the scientist Madame Bauchot, he continues to enumerate the written specimens of urban culture. He criticizes a dependence on the "vendaje de la ciencia" (bandaging of science) on the part of readers such as "ese hombre que lee el diario y compra libros y quiere saber, entonces la enumeración la clasificación de las anguilas y el fichero de estrellas nebulosas galaxias" (58–59) (that man who reads the newspaper and buys books and wants then to know, the enumeration the classification of the eels and the file cabinet of stars nebulous galaxies). The flow of words here seems to lack punctuation, drawing attention to the forced fluidity of the enumeration, pointing out the flaws in writing and language. Throughout these passages, references to urban space interrupt the text's underwater odyssey and intersect with Jai Singh's observatories. The Parisian café, the Latin Quarter and a few particular street names evoke the edifice of French academic disciplines in whose libraries Cortázar pejoratively locates structuralism and systems of scientific classification.

While it may appear that *Prosa* juxtaposes the seas and skies with the urban, in fact Cortázar uses urban space to elide European scientific scholarship with Indian astronomy and mathematics:

> puede ocurrir que entremos en los parques de Jaipur o de Delhi, o que en el corazón de Saint-Germain-des-Près alcancemos a rozar

> otro posible perfil del hombre; pueden pasarnos cosas irrisorias o terribles, acceder a ciclos que comienzan en la puerta de un café y desembocan en una horca sobre la plaza mayor de Bagdad, o pisar una anguila en la rue du Dragon. (54–55).
>
> (it just might happen that we walk into the parks of Jaipur or Delhi, or that in the heart of Saint-Germain-des-Près we manage to brush against another profile of a man; terrible or laughable things might happen to us, like accessing cycles that begin in the doorway of a café and end up on the gallows in the main square of Bagdad, or we might step on an eel on the Rue du Dragon.)

The essay offers entrance into other possibilities or "cycles," access to alternative realities, and encounters with other species as experiences as plausible as the eels' incredible migration. The photographs in *Prosa* have the reader/spectator pass through Jai Singh's arches and ascend his ramps toward a vision–literally–not of the stars themselves (not observable in his photos) but of alternative systems or matrices for reading reality.

Science and writing for Cortázar cannot be disassociated. As mechanisms of urban semiotics, they are compromised by the same political structures and limited by similar institutional designs. As Sara Castro-Klarén mentions, for Cortázar

> la creación del científico de la realidad no difiere del compromiso del escritor de explorar y ampliar la noción de la realidad, pues ambos se hallan empeñados en inventar o fabular al mundo y al mismo hombre. La invención para Cortázar se produce dentro del desideratum de lo desconocido (*lo otro*) . . . (20)
>
> (what the scientist creates from observing reality is no different from the writer's commitment to explore and expand the notion of reality, since both find themselves involved in inventing or "fabling" the world and man himself. Invention for Cortázar comes out of the desideratum of the unknown [*the other*] . . .)

Architecture, astronomy, ichthyology, photography itself (which Freund reminds us grows out of scientific experimentation [36]) rely not only on material industrial development (tools, laboratories, technology) but also on urban modes of thinking, urban infrastructures, on the very physical mappings of space. Jai Singh created his own semiotic system linking the urban with the celestial, and Cortázar attempts to migrate among the elements of light, water, air. His narration through words and photographs departs from and winds back to the urban; he questions urban structures while at the same time he exploits them for their "revolutionary" possibilities. In stead of an urban revolution that takes to the streets, Cortázar proposes a revolutionary metamorphosis against the city.

Just as Cortázar's fiction relies on the structures of jazz and the symbols of Asian mandalas, his passionate interest in other media continually incorporates visual expression into his writing. His metadiscursive maneuvers ensnare the visual into his language of representation beyond critiquing or introducing art. I concur with Dávila who aptly differentiates art criticism, where "los textos se proponen como una narrativa 'sobre,' 'para,' 'por' y 'desde' las imágenes que los acompañen" (182) (the verbal text offers a narrative "about," "for," "through" and "from" the images that it accompanies), from Cortázar's interartistic engagement with visual expression. Cortázar's aim is not to talk "about" images but rather to embrace visual expression as a corollary or partner in dialogue with verbal expression. The essay in *Prosa* even addresses the limitations of words:

> que nuevas palabras tranquilizadoras acompañan el asalto de la serpiente a los arrecifes, el avance a los estuarios, la incontenible invasión de los ríos; todo eso que no tiene nombre se llama ya de tantas maneras . . . (23)
>
> (may new tranquilizing words accompany the serpent's assault on the reefs, the advancing of the estuaries, the uncontainable invasion of the rivers; all that which does not have a name but ends up being called by so many names anyway.)

Aronne-Amestoy identifies "palabras" (words) as one of the three semantic components of the essay, along with eels and stars (60). Words themselves become fictionalized metaphors for photography in this elaborate critique of urban discourse. Rather than tools of expression, words are compromised entities, suspicious collaborators in the repressive structures of scientific lexicon and classificatory taxonomies. A parenthetical comment after a passage that blends the sky and the sea in *Prosa* justifies a distrust of words in favor of light: "y decirse una vez más que la casualidad, esa palabra tranquilizadora, ese otro umbral de la apertura. . . ." (49) (and declaring once again that coincidence, that calming word, that other threshold of the aperture). Wary of language's discursive gestures, Cortázar assigns photography its own powers of discourse. In *Prosa* in particular, where he narratively accompanies his own reproduced images, the visual and the verbal together undercut any orderly, conventional correspondence between the words and the photographs. The two must be read as curving stairways around a web of constellations, as fluid as his prose of long poetic sentences but as fragmented as the angular shadows of the photographs. The coinciding visual and verbal media offer this threshold onto a new city, built between the sea and the sky, where language, coming up against the elements of water and air, is either muffled or inadequate before their vast expanse.

Notes

1. Gisèle Freund traces photography back to European aristocratic portraiture and documents the transition from painted portraits through various methods of mechanical reproduction that coincide with an emergent bourgeoisie. See her chapter "Précurseurs de la photographie" (*Photographie et société* 11–19). Freund's work, like John Berger's, reveals a debt to Walter Benjamin.

2. See chapter two of my *Writing Paris* for a discussion of the relationship between Cortázar's short fiction and Paris. See Franco and Jones for discussions of the urban phenomenon of *Rayuela*.

3. See Juan-Navarro's chapter 4 for an effective analysis of collage in this novel.

4. See Russek's "Verbal/Visual Braids" for a welcome contribution on Cortázar's reliance on journalistic tropes and travel writing in *Ultimo round* and *La vuelta al día*.

5. See my contribution to Castillo and Paz-Soldán's volume for a discussion of these collaborations.

6. Essays that specifically incorporate dialogue to introduce the books' visual images include *Territorios* and *Alto el Perú*. The introduction to *Territorios* borrows fictional characters from *62: Modelo para armar* who banter with the narrator over the value or futility of writing about art. Cortázar frames his essay in *Alto el Perú* with a fictionalized conversation with the photographer, Manja Offerhaus. See also Alazraki (1982) on dialogue in Cortázar's essay style.

7. "*Prosa* es, pues, simultáneamente discurso científico, discurso poético y discurso crítico en el sentido más cabal" (Aronne-Amestoy 57).

8. Alazraki considers *Prosa* a sort of culmination of Cortázar's collage/catalogue projects:

> De esos libros-collage, en que los diferentes géneros alternaban como camaradas de camino a un libro en el que un género se funde camaleónicamente con otro había muy poca distancia. *Prosa del observatorio* es ese libro: prosa por su factura, poema por su ritmo e imaginería, narración por su voluntad de contar la saga de Jai Singh y la odisea de las anguilas, ensayo por su empeño reflexivo y otra vez poema–desde la prosa, desde la narración, desde la meditación–por la visión, más próxima a las iluminaciones de la poesía que al discurrir razonadamente articulado de la prosa, ensayística o narrativa. (108)
>
> (From those collage-books, in which the different genres alternate like traveling companions, to a book where one genre melts chameleon-like into another, is a very short distance. *Prosa del observatorio* is that book: prose for its facts, poem for its rhythm and imagination, narration for its desire to tell the saga of Jai Singh and the odyssey of the eels, essay for its reflexive tendency, and again poem—via prose, via narration, via meditation—for its vision, closer to poetic illumination than to the reasoned, articulated discourse of essayistic or narrative prose.)

9. See my "Cortázar under Exposure" for a discussion of distance in *Alto el Perú*.

10. "Carta del viajero" pertains more closely to the genre of art essay. While my analysis differentiates *Prosa* from the art historical or cataloguing endeavor of *Territorios* and some of Cortázar's other collaborations, the insistence on travel as a metanarrational trope alongside photographs so anchored in space (in this case, Fréderic Barzilay's photographs of the human body) make this example relevant to *Prosa*. See also Russek's "Verbal/Visual Braids" for his comments on travel writing in Cortázar.

11. See my discussion of this story, its presentation of other species, and the urban implications of colonial science, in *Writing Paris* 35–39.

12. Davies considers Jaipur "a unique fusion of Western and Eastern ideas of town planning" (371–72).

13. Physical images of connection abound in Cortázar's work. They are frequently architecturally configured, such as the plank between two buildings in chapter 41 of *Rayuela* and the bridge between Buda and Pest in "La lejana." See chapter 2 of my *Writing Paris* for a discussion of architectural structures in his short fiction related to Paris. These figures—bridges, arcades, windows, subterranean passages—always serve the fantastic conciliations and convergences of time and space in his fiction.

14. The latter resonates with the very beginning of the essay in *Prosa*:

> [e]sa hora que puede llegar alguna vez fuera de toda hora, agujero en la red del tiempo. . . . esa hora orificio a la que se accede al socaire de las otras horas, de la incontable vida con sus horas de frente y de lado, su tiempo para cada cosa, sus cosas en el preciso tiempo . . . (9)
>
> (that hour that can come up some time outside of any hour, hole in the net of time. . . . that orificial hour through which one accesses the shelter of the other hours, of uncountable life with its hours in front and to the side, its time for all things, its things at the precise time . . .)

References

Alazraki, Jaime. "Tema y sistema de *Prosa del observatorio* de Julio Cortázar." *La Torre* 1.1 (1987): 92–110.

______. "Tres formas del ensayo contemporaneo: Borges, Paz, Cortázar." *Revista de la Universidad de México* 17 (1982): 19–23.

Arrone-Amestoy, Lida. "Identidad y diferencia: discursos de la imagen en *Prosa del observatorio*." In *Los ochenta mundos de Cortázar: ensayos*. Ed. Fernando Burgos. Madrid: Edi-6, 1987, 55–66.

Bush, Andrew. "Supposing Morelli Had Meant to Go to Jaipur." In *Julio Cortázar: New Readings*. Ed. Carlos J. Alonso. Cambridge: Cambridge University Press, 1998, 130–54.

Cadava, Eduardo. *Words of Light. Theses on the Photography of History*. Princeton: Princeton University Press, 1997.

Castro-Klarén, Sara. "Fabulación ontológica: hacia una teoría de la literatura de Cortázar." *Escritura, transgresión y sujeto en la literatura latinoamericana*. Puebla, Mexico: La Red de Jonás, 1989, 15–29.

Cortázar, Julio. *Alto el Perú*. Photographs by Manja Offerhaus. Mexico City: Nueva Imagen, 1984.

______. *Buenos Aires, Buenos Aires*. Photographs by Sara Facio and Alicia d'Amico. Buenos Aires: Sudamericana, 1968.

______. *Cuentos completos*. 2 vols. Madrid: Alfaguara, 1994.

______. *Libro de Manuel*. 1973. Barcelona: Bruguera, 1983.

______. *París: ritmos de una ciudad.* Photographs by Alecio d'Andrade. Barcelona: Edhasa, 1981.
______. *Prosa del observatorio.* 1972. Barcelona: Lumen, 1974.
______. *Rayuela.* Buenos Aires: Sudamericana, 1963.
______. *62: Modelo para armar.* Buenos Aires: Sudamericana, 1968.
______. *Territorios.* 1978. Mexico City: Siglo XXI, 1992.
______. *Ultimo round.* 2 vols. 1969. Mexico City: Siglo XXI, 2001.
Cortázar, Julio, and Julio Silva. *Silvalandia.* Mexico City: Cultural GDA, 1975.
Davies, Philip. *The Penguin Guide to the Monuments of India.* Vol. 2. London: Viking, 1989.
Dávila, María de Lourdes. *Desembarcos en el papel: la imagen en la literatura de Julio Cortázar.* Rosario, Argentina: Beatriz Viterbo, 2001.
Ferré, Rosario. *El romántico en su observatorio.* San Juan, Puerto Rico: Literal, 1990.
Franco, Jean. "París, ciudad fabulosa." In *Novelistas hispanoamericanos de hoy.* John Loveluck, ed. Madrid: Taurus, 1976.
Freund, Gisèle. *Photographie et société.* Paris: Seuil, 1974.
García Canclini, Néstor. "Estética e imagen fotográfica." *Casa de las Américas* 25.149 (1985): 7–14.
Garfield, Evelyn Picón. "Julio Cortázar's Redheaded Night: Or Notes on Ordering the Universe in *Prosa del observatorio.*" *Review of Contemporary Fiction* 3.3 (1983): 71–77.
Goloboff, Mario. *Julio Cortázar, la biografía.* Barcelona: Seix Barral, 1998.
Jones, Julie. *A Common Place: The Representation of Paris in Spanish American Fiction* 1963–1982. Lewisburg, PA: Bucknell University Press, 1998.
Juan-Navarro, Santiago. *Archival Reflections: Postmodern Fiction of the Americas (Self- Reflexivity, Historical Revisionism, Utopia).* Lewisburg, PA: Bucknell University Press, 1999.
Kramholtz, Jonathan. "Literature and Photography: The Captioned Vision vs. the Firm, Mechanical Impression." *Centennial Review* 24.4 ((1980): 385–402.
Livingston, Morna. *Steps to Water: The Ancient Stepwells of India.* Foreword, Milo Beach. New York: Princeton Architectural Press, 2002.
Mitchell, W. J. T. *Iconology: Image, Text, Ideology.* Chicago: University of Chicago Press, 1986.
______. *Picture Theory.* Chicago: University of Chicago Press, 1994.
Nath, Aman. *Jaipur: The Last Destination.* Bombay: India Bookhouse, 1993.
Rama, Angel. *La ciudad letrada.* Hanover, NH: Norte, 1984.
Russek, Daniel. "Fixing Images: On the Photographic Model in Julio Cortázar's Short Fiction." Paper delivered at the American Comparative Literature Association conference, San Juan, Puerto Rico, April 2002.
______. "Verbal/Visual Braids: The Photographic Medium in the Work of Julio Cortázar." *Mosaic* 37.4 (2004): 71–86.
Schwartz, Marcy. "Cortázar under Exposure: Photography and Fiction in the City." In *Beyond the Lettered City: Latin American Literature and Mass Media.* Eds. Debra Castillo and José Edmundo Paz-Soldán. New York: Garland, 2000, 117–38.
______. *Writing Paris: Urban Topographies of Desire in Contemporary Latin American Fiction.* Albany, NY: State University of New York Press, 1999.
Sontag, Susan. *On Photography.* 1973. New York: Doubleday, 1990.

Chapter Six

Recycled Photographs

Moving Still Images of Mexico City, 1950–2000

Esther Gabara

French filmmaker Agnes Varda's 2000 *Les Glaneurs et la Glaneuse (The Gleaners and I)* follows the lives of modern-day scavengers in the city and the country, the people who survive on the trash of contemporary consumer society and who themselves are considered disposable. Her documentary gathers images of gleaners from the archives of art history and contemporary art, oral traditions, legal codes, religious beliefs, and urban lore. The overwhelming number of examples that she encounters reveals both the centrality of gleaning—and its concomitant scarcity—to these discourses, as well as the insistent repression of it from the social consciousness of the developed world. Varda portrays her own documentary practice as the attempt to glean forms of knowledge, as well as these images, from different places and times in France, salvaging their meaning and value. This film and Varda's 2002 return to the topic, *Les Glaneurs et la Glaneuse: deux ans après* (*The Gleaners and I: Two Years Later*), are entirely central to the present chapter, even as they are geographically and culturally foreign to it. These documentaries constantly return to a preoccupation with the waste of first-world societies and the creative strategies of those who subsist on their margins. Varda's films actually accomplish much of what I hope to do here: they move between elite and popular practices of gleaning, offer a poetic and concise criticism of a society of excess that leaves many hungry, and show the practice of documentary as a kind of "gleaning" of marginalized knowledge. Varda makes explicit her own move from film to video, her entry into digital technology, and its impact both on the process of film production and the journey she undertakes in *Les Glaneurs et la Glaneuse*. Finally, Varda presents a theory of gleaning as complete as any critical text on globalization and subalternity, and it is for this reason that I begin with her film as a crucial text in my bibliography.

◆ ◆ ◆

As much as Varda's brilliant documentary ranges expansively among many practices of gleaning, still photography has its own particular history of this practice, which I will call "recycling." Throughout the history of this technology of representation in Latin America, we see the same photograph circulate in time and space, between historical document and formal experiment, from mass media to curated exhibition. The same image works as state identification card and mug shot, as well as the document that insists on the visibility of those disappeared by the state. The liberatory potential of an oppositional photograph can easily be turned into a tool of an oppressive state, and vice versa. This mutability of the meaning and function of photography has had a tremendous impact on photography in Mexico. Canonical modernist photographer Manuel Álvarez Bravo's images from the 1920s on were printed in political magazines such as *Frente a Frente* and hung in New York's Museum of Modern Art. The movement of photographs from journalistic to art locations is a material form of recycling: they literally are reused in different spheres, to different ends.

The medium's so-called "indexical function," its seemingly inescapable reference to an object in the world, contributes to photography's habit of recycling. An emphasis on this material referentiality is very strong in the Latin American tradition in general, and particularly so in Mexico. In his wide-ranging history of photography, Olivier Debroise stresses the important connections between the tradition of art photography in Mexico and its use in anthropology (111). This historical link with the social sciences, in addition to the constant crossover between press and art photography, leads to a stress on the documentary function of the medium even within the artistic sphere. Rather than employ this tradition to argue about the "truth value" of any photograph, Alejandro Castellanos very productively suggests that in its motivation of the documentary impulse, photography is like the fetish; it is an "objeto en sí que siempre refiere a otro" (*Nacho López* n.p.) (an object in itself that always refers to another).[1] I will add to Castellanos's formulation: for photographic fetishes do not just refer to the lost objects they picture, but also to previous photographs. The images of other images that they contain, then, are recaptured and lost in the same fashion that the fetish sacralizes and obscures the desired object. The unique materiality of this relationship among photographs—objects and not the object themselves—leads to a theory of photographic recycling in time.

The recycling of photographic images in time presents a fascinating and complex historical narrative. In what follows, I trace such "recycled images" of Mexico City appearing at two crucial moments in the past century—the late 1950s and the 1990s—and show how this photographic practice underwrites recent critical theory from the region. In recent studies of massive urbanization and postmodernity, these two moments are frequently identified as the modern, cosmopolitan space and the postmodern, chaotic megacity, respectively. In comparisons of these two moments, the modern city often is viewed with a certain degree of nostalgia: the flâneur could still walk through its streets, and the intellectual could still recognize its order and his place in it. The postmodern city, in contrast, suffers an indescribable and overwhelming explosion of population, of vehicles, and of media; it is "invivible" (unlivable).[2] Despite the evident differences between the cities of these two periods, their representations—both photographic and theoretical—reflect important continuities by actively participating in a practice of recycling. Related to Varda's fascination with gleaning, this might seem a strange concept to be employed in the study of photography, a medium so frequently associated with the instantaneous, the ephemeral, the obsolete. Even if a specific photograph circulates between different spaces of exhibition, it would seem that its image must always remain fixed on the paper. However, I argue that photographic images work free of the paper on which they are printed, are recycled and reappear to allow the visualization of contemporary Mexico City and its (historical) modern counterpart of the 1950s. By tracing the relationship between photographic recycling and such recent Latin American theory, a vision of history emerges in the overwhelming sprawl of the Distrito Federal.

There is a concrete, everyday referent for this particular theoretical vocabulary: the process of recycling that converts a used, worthless object into something of value, a process of valorization that is most literally and painfully experienced by the poor in large urban centers such as Mexico City. The extraordinary currency of the issue of recycling in Latin America has been made even more evident by the crisis in Argentina since 2002. In Buenos Aires, thousands of people from very different (precrisis) backgrounds survive by scavenging paper and cardboard to be recycled.[3] The *pepenadores* in Mexico City live and work in garbage dumps, converting the materials they find into products to sell in markets. I propose that tracing "recycled images" of Mexico City reveals important, even urgent intellectual structures for understanding urban spaces at the end of the twentieth century. The word's resonance with real-world economic and ecological emergencies emphasizes the inseparability of photographic representation—especially the documentary tradition—from problems of inequality and poverty.[4] Its suggestion of a change of value, however, rejects the idea of a stable or objectified photographic representation of these troubled spaces. Recycling photographs, therefore, alters the effect of the fetishization associated with the medium, disturbing the pleasure of the viewer upon witnessing the repetition of these urban dramas. The same kind of recycling of theories about the city, when placed alongside their photographic counterparts, can lead us to perform the same operation of revaluation.[5]

Picturing Mexico City: 1950s, 1990s

Two series of photographs of Mexico City clearly articulate recycling as a critical practice: Nacho López's *Yo, el ciudadano* (I, Citizen 1984), a collection composed of photographs from the late 1950s and early 1960s, and Pablo Ortiz Monasterio's *La última ciudad* (The Last City 1996), a book of photographs taken during the mid 1980s and early 1990s. López is revered as the chronicler of Mexico City, practicing the photographic equivalent of the tradition of essayistic and journalistic writings exemplified by Salvador Novo, and more recently, Carlos Monsiváis. López occupied a shifting ground between photojournalism and art photography, having studied with famed modernist photographer Manuel Álvarez Bravo and taught fine art photography at several universities, while the majority of his images were published as photoessays for popular weekly journals such as *Siempre*, *Hoy*, and *Mañana* (Mraz "From Positivism to Populism" 10). Most of the images included in *Yo, el ciudadano* also appeared in a photoessay entitled "La ciudad de México," published in 1962 in *Artes de México*, an elite art journal quite different from the weeklies mentioned by Mraz.[6] The images in *Artes de México* were introduced by essays and stories by novelist Agustín Yañez, poet and chronicler Salvador Novo, and architect Manuel Larrosa; the photoessay's format was designed by Vicente Rojo. As Mraz notes, many of the photographs included, however, had been published previously in a variety of photoessays, including "Prisión de sueños," which appeared in *Mañana* in 1952. Here we see no less than three instances of recycling: from the 1952 popular weekly publication into the art magazine, and again in the 1984 tribute to López's impact on Mexican photography.

The 1984 book *Yo, el ciudadano* was published in a series entitled "Río de Luz," which has contributed greatly to documenting the history of photography in Latin America. Ortiz Monasterio was part of the committee that compiled and selected the photographs included in the 1984 collection, a role that had a great impact on his 1996 book, *La última ciudad*. Indeed, he draws parallels between his extensive editorial and archival research, and his work as a photographer, especially with regard to the act of selection involved in both. Ortiz Monasterio goes so far as to state that the "originality" of his photographs does not matter to him, that he is not attached to claims of authorship. Rather, he sees the work of other photographers reappearing in his own (personal interview). Indeed, throughout *La última ciudad*, Ortiz Monasterio quotes López's photographs from *Yo, el ciudadano*, reconsidering his take on the city and addressing key assumptions about the transition from the modern to the postmodern. A comparison of these two collections of photographs of Mexico City shows Ortiz Monasterio over and over again practicing a recycling of figures in his re-vision of López's Mexico City. This reuse not only reflects important changes in representing the city from the modern to its most current incarnation, but also insists upon the currency of the past in this "new" city. By tracing these recycled figures, I argue that Ortiz Monasterio offers a means of theorizing contemporary Latin America as pictured in cities.

Critical Recycling

The "help" that the concept of recycling provides for working with critical theory located in the city is not new to Latin American criticism. Angel Rama's 1984 landmark book *La ciudad letrada* begins in Mexico City just when it began to exist as such:

> Desde la remodelación de Tenochtitlan, luego de su destrucción por Hernán Cortés en 1521, hasta la inauguración en 1960 del más fabuloso sueño de urbe de que han sido capaces los americanos, la Brasilia de Lucio Costa y Oscar Niemeyer, la ciudad latinoamericana ha venido siendo básicamente un parto de la inteligencia, pues quedó inscripta en un ciclo de la cultura universal en que la ciudad pasó a ser el sueño de un orden y encontró en las tierras del Nuevo Continente, el único sitio propicio para encarnar. (1)
>
> (From the remodeling of Tenochtitlan after its destruction by Hernán Cortés in 1521, to the 1960 inauguration of that most fabulous dream city of the Americas, Lucio Costa's and Oscar Niemeyer's Brasília, Latin American cities have ever been creations of the human mind. The ideal of the city as the embodiment of social order corresponded to a moment in the development of Western civilization as a whole, but only the lands of the new continent afforded a propitious place for the dream of an ordered city to become a reality.)[7]

The crucial role of the intellectual since the conquest has been to dream up the city; the question of how to write critical theory from and about Latin America is inextricably linked to understanding its experience of urbanism. Rama presents this process as a cycle of destruction and building, of imagination and incarnation, of urban planning and the already existing ground upon which cities take shape.

Since Rama's major contribution, this relationship between theory and city has become so central that the shape of the city has become the shape of the text. From his adopted home in Mexico City, Néstor García Canclini prefaces *Culturas híbridas* with the proposal that, "Quizá puede usarse este texto como una ciudad" (16) ("Maybe this text can be used like a city" *Hybrid Cultures* 2). This city-text offers new paths to track the developments of modern and postmodern culture in Latin America, and is—especially, but certainly not exclusively, in the Mexican tradition—intimately tied to the history of photography. Since canonical photographers such as Eugene Atget and Manuel Álvarez Bravo, the form of the modern city has been composed in images taken by flâneurs bearing cameras.[8]

García Canclini himself has written extensively on photography since the seventies, and his 1996 collaboration *La ciudad de los viajeros* (The City of Travelers) presents a photographic view of "cómo se organiza y desorganiza la vida urbana" (11) (how urban life is organized and disorganized). In it he proposes that photography perfectly encapsulates the postmodern experience of the city:

> Las fotografías, con su captación de instantes aislados, con los enormes espacios virtuales que dejan entre una imagen y otra, parecen representar mejor que el cine las percepciones y los saberes fragmentados que se obtienen de una gran ciudad. Hay una correspondencia entre las operaciones de recorte y encuadre que hacen las fotos y el conjunto de experiencias desarticuladas que se obtienen en una megaciudad. A diferencia de las narraciones cinematográficas que ayudan a imaginar ciudades más o menos integradas, la fotografía ofrece escenas o instantes discontinuos que pueden aspirar a una representatividad más extensa pero siempre separan una experiencia del contexto. (García Canclini et al. 109)
>
> (Photographs, with their capture of isolated instants, with the enormous virtual spaces that they leave between one image and another, seem to represent even better than film the perceptions and fragmentary knowledge that one obtains in a great city. There is a correspondence between the operations of cutting and framing that make photographs and the collection of fragmented experiences that one obtains in a megacity. In contrast to cinematic narratives that help one to imagine more or less integrated cities, photography offers scenes or discontinuous instants that can aspire to a more extensive representation but always separate an experience from its context.)

Yet here the act of photography in the city appears undifferentiated from the photographic print representing that city, so that every photograph in the end always only signifies a *rupture* in time and space. The image of the postmodern city as such a photographic rupture is quite widespread among theories of Latin American postmodernity and has faced accusations of stemming from a nostalgic vision of the modern city.[9] Indeed, this claim for photography as the experience of the contemporary megacity echoes similar proclamations of photography's function in the modern city of the fifties and even the avant-garde city of the twenties. The very concept of the photo-text as the best embodiment of contemporary Latin America recycles theory from these early periods. Rather than picture the photographic postmodern city as such a rupture, I find that Ortiz Monasterio's photo-text creates a kind of cultural archive of images, or figures, which also inhabit and embody López's. His practice of recycling includes the past city in the present, but alters the value of crucial figures that inhabit both.

The organization of urban life that García Canclini sees in photography takes place through the recycling of certain tropes in these city-texts.[10] Even as they repeat familiar refrains, these tropes are also employed to mark each city's difference from its predecessor. I find that many of the most interesting and insightful critics of the contemporary Latin American city participate in this practice of recycling, never reproducing the same texts as before, nor simply citing them as historical references, but rather recycling certain images in a new context to produce a different meaning and add new value to them. These critics rarely acknowledge their recycling; they are not as explicit about it as Ortiz Monasterio's *La última ciudad*. To better understand the mechanism of recycling in theory, I look to his photographic practice, focusing on four repeated figures: the shape of the city itself, youth, public women, and urban *indios*.[11]

The Shape of the City

The opening image of *La última ciudad* mirrors that of *Yo, el ciudadano*, greeting the viewer with a broad cityscape (figs. 6.1 and 6.2). Ortiz Monasterio's contemporary cityscape is peculiarly uncluttered; López's earlier city is more overwhelmingly blocked by the vertical lines of telephone poles and television antennas than Ortiz Monasterio's recent one. In fact, López's photo is just one of a large series that captures the labyrinth of rooftop antennas cluttering the city's sky. Even so, Fernando Benítez states, in his introduction to *Yo, el ciudadano*: "Ya existía, [in the 1950s] desafiante, la Torre Latinoamericana y cuatro o cinco modestos paquidermos de concreto, *pero la ciudad se conservaba horizontal y no pretendía escalar la región más transparente del aire*" (emphasis added, 8) (Already [in the 1950s], the Torre Latinoamericana existed, along with four or five modest, concrete pachyderms, *but the city was still horizontal, and didn't pretend to ascend to "where the air is clear"*).[12] This misreading of López's photograph is part of the common imagination of a 1950s Mexico City that was less vertical, imposing, and insurmountable than today's. The contemporary city is supposed to be more overwhelming, harder to see than the modern city. The defining image of this urban space is continually presented from the perspective of the end of the ordered city, the passage to a city that defies representation. From the rim of this abyss we hear the proclaimed "end" of the modern city and the transition to something else, often termed postmodern. Jesús Martín-Barbero writes that:

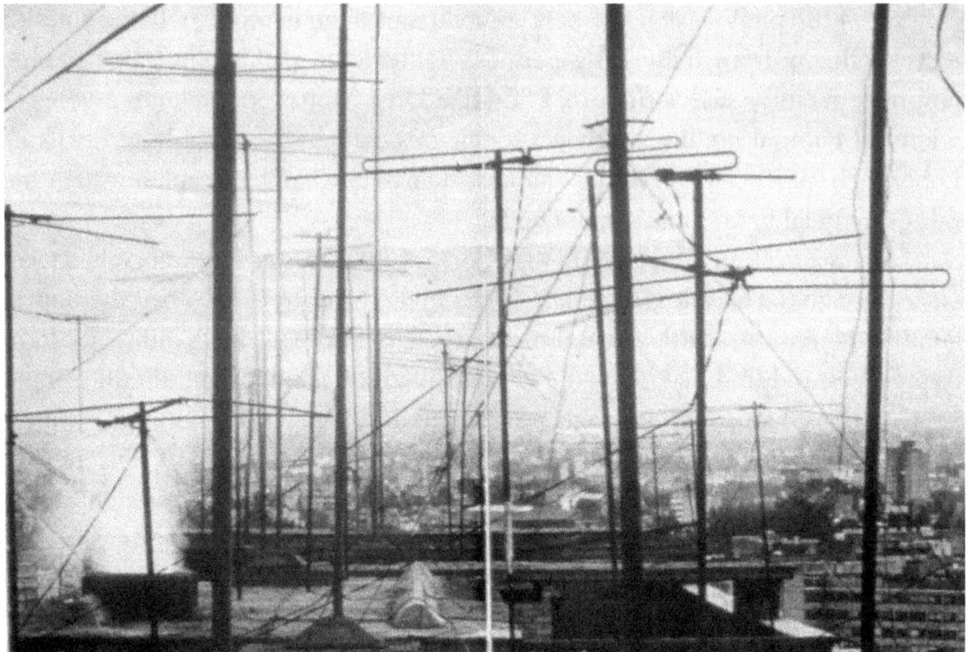

Fig. 6.1. Nacho López, "Antenas para televisión colocadas sobre azoteas" (Television Antennas Placed on Top of Roofs) circa 1957. © 382721 SINAFO-Fototeca Nacional de México.

> Nuestras ciudades son hoy el opaco y ambiguo escenario de algo no representable, ni desde la diferencia excluyente y excluida de lo autóctono ni desde la inclusión uniformante y disolvente de lo moderno. . . . cuya expresión más cierta está en los cambios que atraviesan los modos de experimentar la pertenencia al territorio y las formas de vivir la identidad. (36)
>
> (Our cities today are the opaque and ambiguous scene of something that is not representable, neither from the excluding and excluded difference of the authochthonous nor from the uniform and dissolving inclusion of the modern . . . whose most accurate expression is in the changes that traverse the modes of experiencing belonging to a territory and the forms of living an identity.)

Yet Ortiz Monasterio's postmodern cityscape is actually more literally horizontal than that of López, and his photographic eye is not as lost in his city as myths of the megacity suggest. This first photograph in the book defies assumptions about the modern and postmodern city and sets the reader off into the pictured city with the demand that she look anew at the relationship between the two.

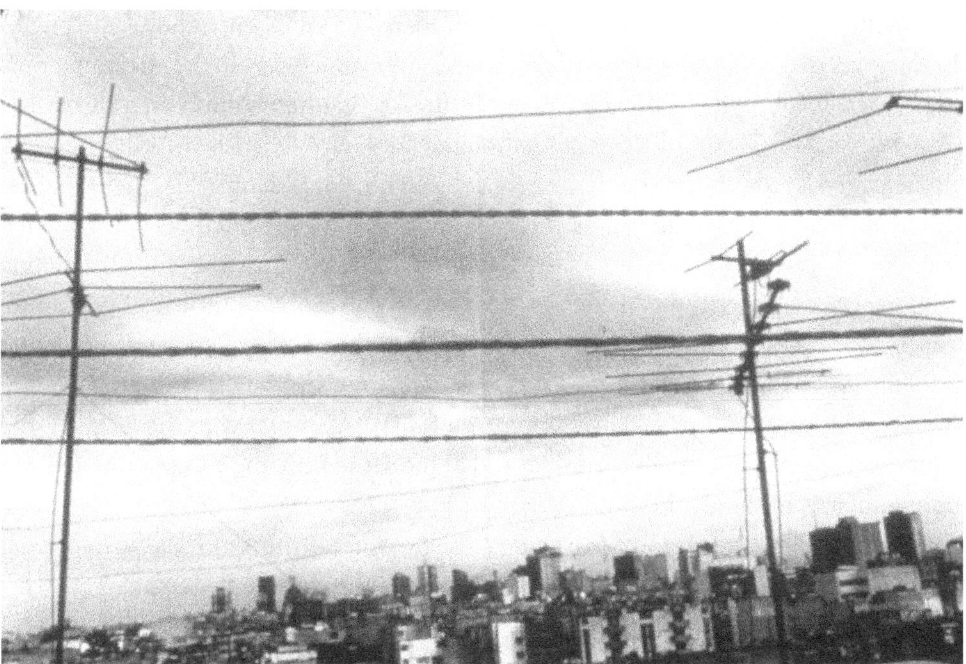

Fig. 6.2. Pablo Ortiz Monasterio, "Ciudad de México" (Mexico City) in *La última ciudad*, 1996. Courtesy of the artist.

The broader implications of the visual horizon of the city appear in the introduction to García Canclini's *Culturas híbridas*, where he states that he hopes to write a "city-text" that is *horizontally* rather than *vertically* oriented. He argues that the horizontal city permits a more democratic "flattening out" of concepts and participants than does the vertical one, and that in this city-text, "[a]dentro todo se mezcla, cada capítulo remite a los otros, y entonces *ya no importa saber por qué acceso se llegó*" (emphasis added, 16) ("[o]n the inside, everything gets mixed together; every chapter refers to all the others *and thus it is not important to know the approach by which one arrived*," emphasis added, *Hybrid Cultures* 2). He reads the inequities of the contemporary city in its vertical horizon, and like Benítez, hopes for a transition to a horizontal city.

García Canclini seeks to ensure the democratic nature of the city as text through the erasure of the path by which the critic-traveler arrives. Even so, he himself "arrives" in the contemporary photo-text of Mexico City via a certain theoretical path. He narrates the journeys through Mexico City that make up *La ciudad de los viajeros* in strikingly similar terms to those that appear in Octavio Paz's *El laberinto de la soledad* (*The Labyrinth of Solitude*). Both structure their narratives of "modern Mexico" beginning from the outside; both revisit the late nineteenth- to early-twentieth-century figure of the flâneur; both focus on the occupation of the city by indigenous people and by women. Paz begins his classic essay on Mexican national identity by locating the "Mexican" scent in the air that he breathed in a trip to Los Angeles, and his vision of this national character is embodied first in the figure of the *pachuco*.[13] As much as he demeans pachuco outsider identity, it is here that his discussion of Mexican solitariness begins. Similarly, García Canclini's point of entry into the city is from the position of the foreigner; his text begins with the explanation that "viajar a la ciudad de México es *para muchos extranjeros* buscar el encuentro con la mayor ciudad latinoamericana de origen prehispánico, y a la vez con la más poblada y contaminada del mundo" (*La ciudad*, 11, emphasis added) (traveling to Mexico City is *for many foreigners* the search for an encounter with the largest Latin American city of pre-Hispanic origins, and at the same time the most populated and contaminated in the world).

Much as the structure of *La ciudad de los viajeros* mirrors *El laberinto de la soledad*, García Canclini's titular subject in *Hybrid Cultures* also appears in Paz's canonical text:

> La irritación del norteamericano procede, a mi juicio, de que ve en el pachuco un ser mítico y por lo tanto virtualmente peligroso. Su peligrosidad brota de su singularidad. Todos coinciden en ver en él algo *híbrido*. Perturbador y fascinante. (*El laberinto* 15)
>
> (I believe that the North American's irritation results from his seeing the *pachuco* as a mythical figure and therefore, in effect, a danger. His dangerousness lies in his singularity. Everyone agrees in finding something *hybrid* about him, something perturbing and fascinating). (*The Labyrinth* 16)

It is this hybrid figure that provides Paz with his definition of "soledad" that configures Mexican identity: "Desprendido de su cultura tradicional, el pachuco se afirma un instante como soleded y reto" (Paz 16) (Taken out of his traditional culture, the pachuco at the same instant presents himself as solitariness and as a challenge [my translation]). García Canclini's hybridity is a similar mixture of the traditional and the modern in Latin America, the "'reconversión' económica y simbólica con que los migrantes campesinos adaptan sus saberes para vivir en la ciudad, y sus artesanías para interesar a consumidores urbanos . . . sin abandonar creencias antiguas" (*Culturas híbridas* 14) ("economic and symbolic 'reconversion' with which migrant farm workers adapt their knowledge to live in the city, and their crafts to interest urban consumers . . . without abandoning old beliefs" *Hybrid Cultures* 2). This recycled version does not reproduce Paz's picture of a solitary and tragic *mestizo*

Mexican identity. Instead, it is a concept based on the structures of modernization and modernity as much as on representations of race. Tracing the recycled image of hybridity allows a critique of Paz's text and forces us to be wary of the potential misuses of the concept.

Despite García Canclini's characterization of Paz's text as no longer relevant to contemporary Mexico, he himself recycles key structures, proceeding via similar intellectual roads, of picturing the city.[14] The close relationship between these two major works about *mestizaje* in twentieth-century Mexico shows that the significance of the traveler-critic's "approach" is very important. As much as today we must reject Paz's characterization of Mexican-Americans as suffering a pathological psychic rupture, I worry about García Canclini's presentation of a "horizontal," hybrid, and democratic city that does not present any signs of suffering its traversal. Paz's *pachuco* certainly suffers this journey more than García Canclini's inhabitant of the postmodern city: "el hibridismo de su lenguaje y de su porte me parecen indudable reflejo de una ocilación psíquica entre *dos mundos irreductibles*" (emphasis added, *El laberinto* 16, n.3) ("the hybridity of his language and manner seem to me an unquestionable reflection of a psychic oscillation between *two irreducible worlds*," emphasis added, *The Labyrinth* 18), which the pachuco is always trying to "conciliar y superar" ("reconcile and conquer"). García Canclini's postmodern city, as much as he finds it encapsulated in the rupture of the photographic moment, appears more navigable than Paz's Mexican Los Angeles.

Ortiz Monasterio capitalizes on his similar practice of recycling by refusing our expectations about the relationship between modern and postmodern city. He reverses the presumed move from horizontal to vertical city, insisting upon tracing the steps by which one enters, moves through, and creates the horizontal city-text. He presents us with tools for picturing a different kind of historical relationship created by (photographic) recycling. These recycled steps structure the image of the city and present a reconfigured vision of contemporary Mexico.

El joven: Adolescent Leaps through History

Martín Hopenhayn proposes a radically different methodology for mapping such a path through contemporary urban spaces in Latin America and for organizing their relationship to their past. His city-text proceeds via a series of paradoxes, by leaps in which, "El impulso centrífugo y la apertura a lo exógono se anuncia como promesa de nueva identidad . . . *La promesa de una nueva identidad no es acumulativa*" (63) (The centrifugal impulse and the opening toward the exogenous announces itself as the promise of a new identity . . . *This promise of a new identity is not cumulative*). This noncumulative identity would seem to reject my comparison of two moments in time, my suggestion of a recycling of representations of the city. Yet in this same essay, Hopenhayn calls the rejection of history "absurd" and describes the current condition of the region in which:

> [E]l impacto del consumo cultural industrial en la periferia latinoamericana exacerba un rasgo recurrente de la modernidad discontinua que desde siempre nos recorre, a saber, que ésta se vive como un *tiempo nuevo que contiene muchos tiempos*. (114)
>
> (The impact of industrial consumer culture in the Latin American periphery exacerbates a recurrent feature of the discontinuous modernity that always runs through us, that is, which is lived as *a new time that contains many times*.)

His vision of the contemporary resembles Jean-François Lyotard's picture of postmodernity as the use of "materiales combinables y desplazables a discreción" (117) (combinable materials that can be displaced at one's discretion). Hopenhayn explains that Latin America lives a version of this recycling of past (modern) styles and idiom in a recent context as a "desplazamiento de relatos" (displacement of tales). He insists, however, that the conditions of modernity and postmodernity on the periphery change the meaning of this movement, such that "[l]a diversidad se vive como fragmentación, la variedad como injusticia y la heterogeneidad como exclusión" (121) (diversity is lived as fragmentation, variety as injustice, and heterogeneity as exclusion). Here Hopenhayn brings the circulation of ideas back to the materiality of consumer culture and insists upon the importance of the path by which one moves through the city-text for the meaning of these key words.

In fact, Hopenhayn performs this vision of history in his own practice of recycling, for he asks, "¿Y por qué no [explorarla] con curiosidad infantil?" (68) (And why not [explore the city] with a childlike curiosity?). He proclaims this child to be an orphan, which he views as *the* figure of the contemporary city. This configuration of the revolutionary inhabitant of the city in a permanent state of infancy might seem to separate it radically from previous incarnations. However, Hopenhayn's orphan in its "revolutionary paradox" recycles a critical figure for visualizing the Latin American city. A dominant trope in the history of Mexico City (as well as Buenos Aires, Havana, Lima, and Santiago among others), "el joven," is born of the Mexican Revolution and meant to symbolize the new, modern Mexico.[15] The postrevolutionary projects of modernization and centralization included well-known educational programs that sought to convert the country's children into the "new men" of Mexico (Knight 395). Transforming this *hombre nuevo* into an orphan gives him a new set of challenges—those that Hopenhayn notes above—but the familiarity of the figure in national histories provides a continuity of categories in the reorganization of the city-text.

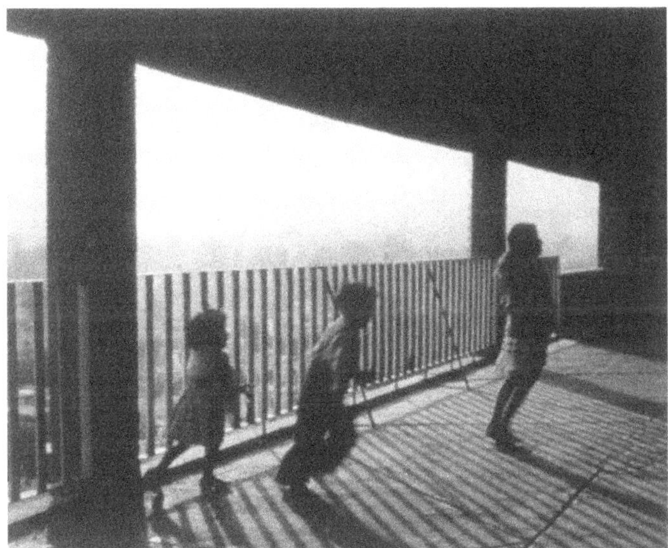

Fig. 6.3. Nacho López, "Niños y mujer en el corredor de un multifamiliar" (Children and Woman in the Corridor of a Housing Unit) circa 1960. © 381384 SINAFO-Fototeca Nacional de México.

"El joven" is a crucial figure in both López and Ortiz Monasterio's visions of Mexico City, and Ortiz Monasterio's recycling of it gestures toward the structure of history that Hopenhayn proposes for contemporary Latin America. In his poem "Yo, el ciudadano," which precedes both the 1962 photo-essay published in *Artes de México* and the 1984 book, López writes that:

> Los jóvenes hacen la historia del país
> y los viejos la escriben . . .
> 'Se solicitan hombres entre veinticinco y treinta y cinco años de edad, con personalidad optimista, para trabajo remunerativo en empresa de prestigio.'
> Pero muchos ya son demasiado viejos. (14)
> (Youths make the history of the country
> and the elderly write it . . .
> 'Wanted: men between twenty-five and thirty-five years of age, with an optimistic personality, for well-paid work in a prestigious business.'
> But many are already too old.)

The photograph by López selected by Ortiz Monasterio for inclusion in the 1984 tribute is taken from above, from the height of an adult looking down upon children (fig. 6.3). It repeats the sympathetic view with which López narrates the poem, sympathy for the generation left behind by a modern city made by and for the youth. While this generation of adults is excluded from the city of youth, they narrate its

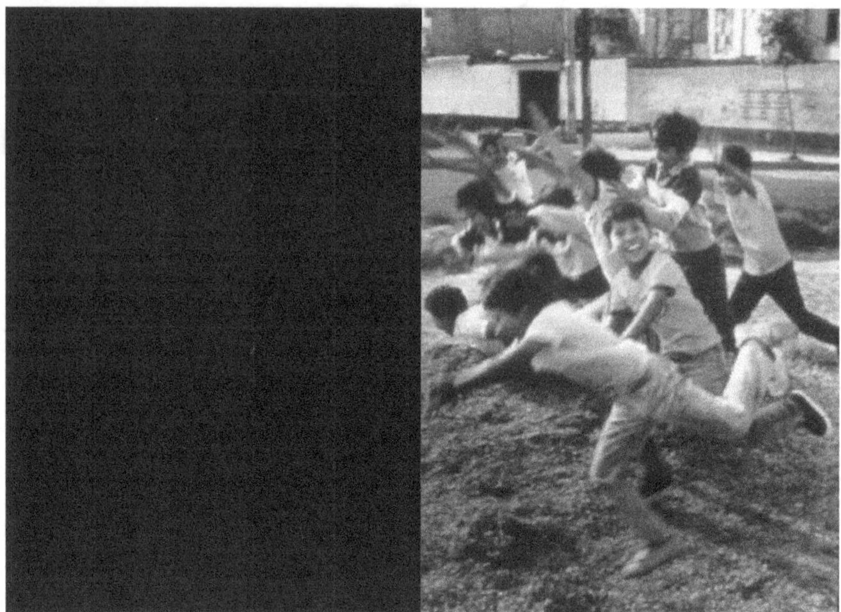

Fig. 6.4. Pablo Ortiz Monasterio, "Niños" (Children) in *La última ciudad*, 1996. Courtesy of the artist.

birth and are the guardians of its history. In this photograph, the children playing in the barred shadows of a balcony are inscribed by the projection of the railing that prevents them from falling into the abyss of the city below. While the blurred body of the boy breaks the imprisoning containment of the pattern of shadows, the direction of the children's movement is *away* from the drop into the bright expanse of the city. Thus while the modern city is visible in the figure of the *joven*, here we see that these youths obediently follow the forward direction of historical narrative, from left to right, led by the protective perspective of the adult-sized photographer-historian described in López's poem.

López works extensively with the narrativity of the photo-essay in "La ciudad de México", but it is important to note that this essay generally obeys a pattern of reading learned from written texts. He writes in the prologue to *Yo, el ciudadano* that:

> [L]a mayor parte de las fotos citadinas son resultado de intensa labor periodística que realicé en las revistas: *Hoy, Siempre!* y especialmente en *Mañana,* donde se me dió libertad absoluta en los temas de mi predilección y en el formato de mis reportajes, en conjunción con mi viejo amigo Esteban Cajiga, hasta meter mi nariz supervisando negativos e impresión del offset. (11)
>
> ([T]he majority of the urban photographs are the result of intensive journalistic work that I carried out in the journals *Hoy,*

> *Siempre!* and especially *Mañana,* where I was given absolute freedom in my selection of themes and in the format of my reports, in conjunction with my old friend Esteban Cajiga, up to the point of sticking my nose into the supervision of negatives and the offset printing.)

López clearly saw this participation in the graphic design as an essential part of his photographic process. The original printing of "La ciudad de México" begins with photographs of the landscape surrounding the city, gradually approaching it from the outside. Once the camera enters the city itself, it proceeds via a series of themes: children, love, death, religion, power, nightlife, and so on. These themes read progressively and cumulatively from left to right, not leaping from nightlife to the church, or power to love. While photo-essays certainly require a kind of reading that is not identical to the reading of texts, López does not force the reader's eye to break its habit of moving left to right, nor the "logic" of a kind of accumulation of ideas that follows that order. In their organization and composition, the images included in "La ciudad de México" remain under the custodianship of the older generation in charge of writing the city's history.

In Ortiz Monasterio's version of this picture (fig. 6.4), the children have multiplied and yet become more individual, as the frozen smile of the central boy is caught amid the blur of the other bodies. Unlike López's game of tag that leads the movement of the picture away from the drop off the balcony into the city, these children rush headlong into the darkness of the previous page. Ortiz Monasterio stresses that from its inception, he conceived of this project as a book rather than as an exhibition of photographs, and in working with the press was given complete control over its design (personal interview). The careful treatment of the photographs as they appear on the page, in relation to those that come before and after, is particularly evident in this layout. Not only is the dangerous world of the city made explicit, but the reversal of the direction of reading moves the reader-viewer's eye from right to left rather than left to right and creates a split between past and future. Ortiz Monasterio's recycled figure of the joven creates instead a vision of Mexico City and its history as "postapocalyptic," as José Emilio Pacheco terms it in his essay included in the book. The apocalyptic is a prediction of the future, generally of an ending: "de *apo*, lejos de, y *kalyptô*, velar, cubrir, ocultar: como quien dice *descubrimiento*, revelación, quitar el velo" (Monlau 335) (from *apo*, far from, and *kalyptô*, to veil, to cover, to hide: as one says discovery, revelation, remove the veil). Monasterio's text is, however, *post*apocalyptic; it takes place at a time *after* the act of unveiling or predicting, in a time that does not obey the rules of diachronic narrative, but rather refers to a past moment of future prediction. The figure of *el joven* pictured by Ortiz

Monasterio shows the postapocalyptic leap both backwards and forwards. This joven, therefore, jumps between Hopenhayn's historical paradoxes—what he calls "ni apocalípticos ni integrados" (neither apocalyptic nor integrated)—and still manages to carry with him certain key figures. In this postapocalyptic recycling of figures, the contemporary city-text is reinvented, and while it is still horizontal in orientation, it also exhibits the traces of its traversal. This process of recycling figures contributes a form of historicism that maintains a sense of responsibility and agency for subjects, without necessarily controlling the direction of the movement of history.

Gendered Photographic Subjects

Feminist scholar Nelly Richard articulates a related critique of a linear representation of history, arguing that photography is a privileged medium for the goal of replacing this linearity with a representation of history that includes the past in the present. Richard rejects the view of history as "una secuencia lineal y progresiva . . . hacia un solo y mismo resultado" (a linear and progressive sequence . . . toward one single result), but proposes instead "el pasado [como] un campo de citas atravesado tanto por la continuidad (las formas de suponer o imponer una idea de sucesión) como por las discontinuidades" (13–14) (the past as a field of citations, characterized as much by continuity [forms of supposing or imposing an idea of succession] as by discontinuities). The photographic can include:

> [un] gran retrato colectivo con muchas piezas de identidad desensambladas: un retrato genealógico [que incluye] lo *no sincrónico* (distintas temporalidades sociales e históricas separadas por abismos de distancia), lo *descalificado* (lo menor, lo subalterno) y lo *heterogéneo* (lo no idéntico, lo desuniforme). (14)
>
> ([a] great collective portrait with many disassembled pieces of identity: a genealogical portrait including the *asynchronic* [distinct social temporalities and histories separated by abysses of distance], the *unauthorized* [the minor, the subaltern], and the *heterogeneous* [the nonidentical, the nonuniform].)

Richard specifically connects photography's citationality with narrative experiments with *testimonio*, as well as with other documentary attempts to represent unique and painful experiences specifically related to gender. She refers to photography and testimonio as documents that change the idea of "truth," which disfigure and "hyperfictionalize" it: "hiperficcionalizaron la 'verdad' representacional del testimonio, mediante torsiones y contorsiones genérico-sexuales" (30) (they hyperfictionalized the representational 'truth' of testimonio, through gendered twists and contortions).

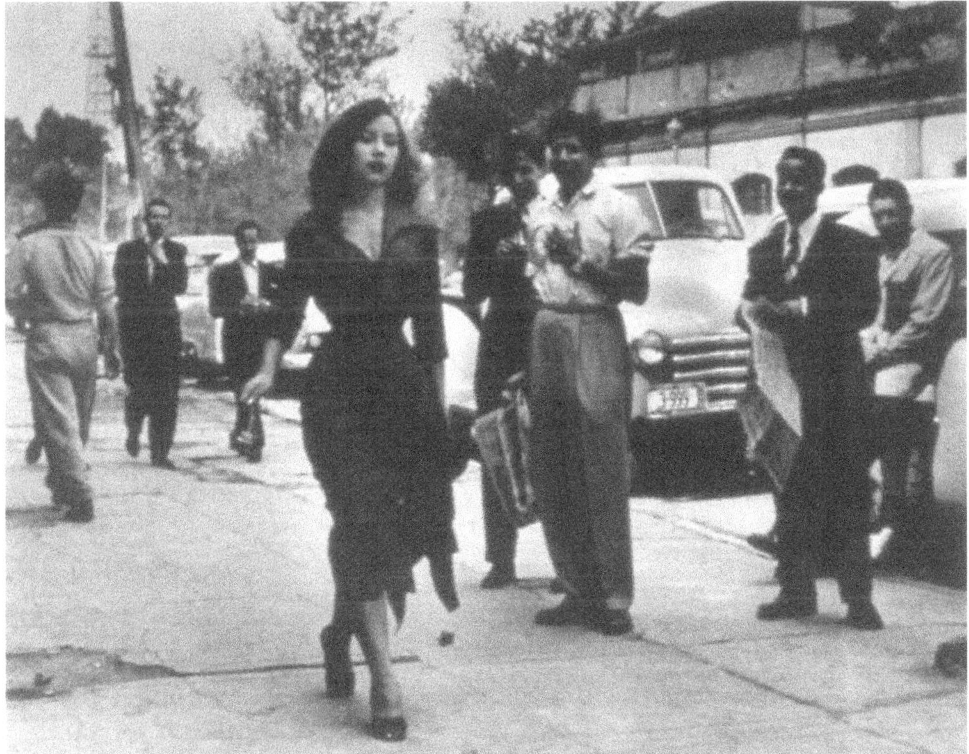

Fig. 6.5. Nacho López, "Hombres expectantes ante mujer" (Expectant Men before a Woman) circa 1950. © 405648 SINAFO-Fototeca Nacional de México, and courtesy of the actress Maty Huitrón.

The productive paradox produced by photographic and testimonial hyperfictions is made possible by their engagement with *género* as both gender and genre; the dual meaning of the word in Spanish captures the double meaning of photographs, their indexicality and invention, their past and future postapocalyptic time.

Both López and Ortiz Monasterio's photographic narratives recycle the image of the circulation of women in the city, focusing on the particular difference of their passage through city streets (figs. 6.5 and 6.6). Space limitations do not permit an in-depth review of the figure of the woman in the public sphere at different moments in Mexican history. However, Carlos Monsiváis's play on words sums it up quite well: he points out that the feminine linguistic equivalent of an *hombre público,* a man who works in the governmental sphere, would be a *mujer pública,* which in fact means a prostitute.[16] This photograph is one of López's most famous: a young woman walking down a city street, past three pairs of leering men.[17] She is the center of all the desiring gazes, including, of course, our own. They converge on her figure, her step forward causing a twisting motion, the wrinkles of her dress providing the few diagonal lines in the image, so that her body serves as a revolving locus of the

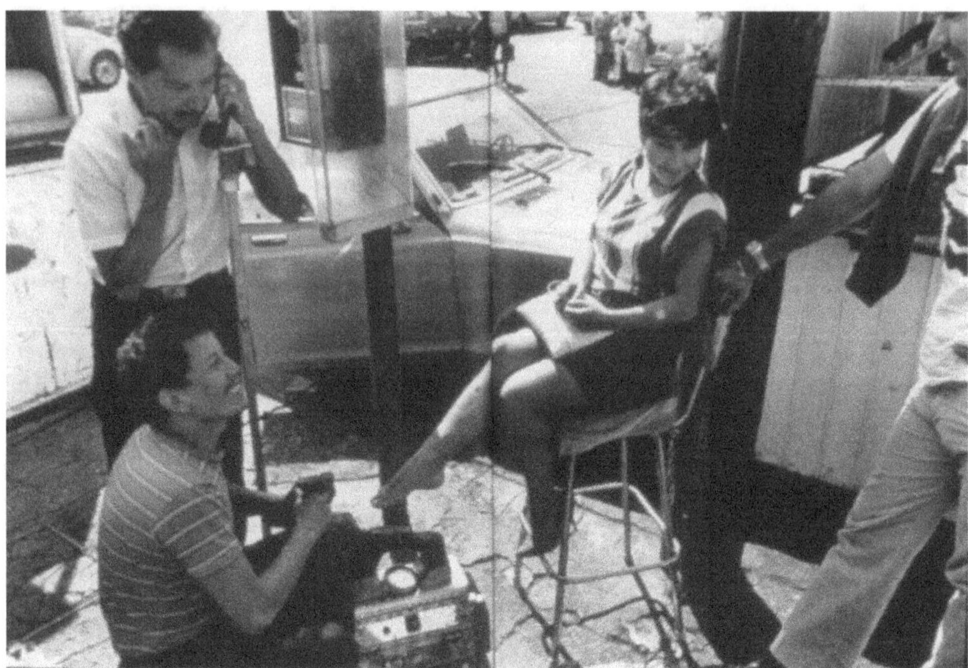

Fig. 6.6. Pablo Ortiz Monasterio, "San Angel" in *La última ciudad*, 1996. Courtesy of the artist.

picture. The diagonal movement of her figure focuses our attention on two points of her body, her hands and her feet, while her own gaze falls uncertainly downward toward an indeterminate point just beyond the frame of the photograph.

Ortiz Monasterio's revision of López's figure of woman as object of male sexual desire represents a fundamental change in the force of this figure in the narrative of Mexico City. Three male gazes are reproduced here, but they focus on her face rather than her torso. Once again, the woman's hands and feet are prominent points of focus, but her gaze meets the viewer's with a slightly mocking smile. This engaging look forces the viewer into an active participation in the scene and a conscious affiliation with the photographer's presence. In López's photograph, the camera is "erased" from the scene on the street; it is assumed to be neutral, invisible, and subtly complicit in the capture of the feminine. In Ortiz Monasterio's image, the presentation of the woman's body as a desired object is acknowledged, while its composition insists upon her ability to confront this photographic construction of male desire. The same components that configure desire in López's image are reproduced in Ortiz Monasterio's composition, but in his recycling he explodes the earlier formulation of gender and power. As in Richard's photographic citationality and documentary hyperfictionalization, these recycled images of the feminine theorize changes in the city-text grounded in gender. The recycling of López's image makes visible Richard's concept of photographic "hyperfiction," for it is one of his posed "journalistic" shots. John Mraz writes that, due to his interest in cinema, López hired little-known actress Maty Huitrón to parade down Balderas Street, while he photographed the reactions of the men watching her (Mraz, "Los dilemas"). The power of the male gaze on the female body is no fiction, but rather a hyperfiction that the medium of photography has a long tradition of producing. Returning, now, to Ortiz Monasterio's recycled image of this gaze, it becomes evident that if the city is mapped by its *transeuntes*, its passersby, the revelation of a place for the return of the masculine gaze *in its very streets* is a powerful intervention into its (photographic and theoretical) topography.

Monumental Problems

Ortiz Monasterio nevertheless remains more suspicious than Richard of the potential of his medium. As much as he employs the transfer of power of the desiring gaze to the young woman (see fig. 6.6), this revalorization also brings up a problem in photographic representation. The effect of photography that has cleared a space for a return feminine gaze becomes a recurring preoccupation in Ortiz Monasterio's book, in its reliance upon the seemingly inescapable, automatic monumentalization of the photographed subject. García Canclini refers to this effect of photography as he explains his own attempt to make visible

> el *patrimonio cultural no visible* (no monumental) de la ciudad. Dicho de otro modo: qué es lo fotografiable, entiendo la fotografía—una de sus funciones—como *un modo de solemnizar, fijar las conductas socialmente aprobadas o valiosas, para una comunidad.* (*La ciudad de los viajeros* 111)
>
> (the *invisible* [not monumental] *cultural patrimony* of the city. In other words: what is photographable, I understand photography—one of its functions—as a means of *making solemn, of fixing socially approved or valued conduct for a community.*)

This idea of monumentalization imagines a photography that, if handled correctly, could properly represent all of the excluded members of society. Alejandro Castellanos aptly summarizes the ongoing history of photographs to which García Canclini refers: "tomar fotografías a los sectores pobres de la población sigue siendo, para muchos, la manera más efectiva de ahondar en la identidad del mexicano"[18] ("Las herencias del mito" 652) (taking photographs of poor segments of the population continues to be, for many, the most effective manner of penetrating Mexican identity). Debroise traces the history of this line of Mexican photography as the practice of urban photographers who set out to picture rural, read "traditional" and

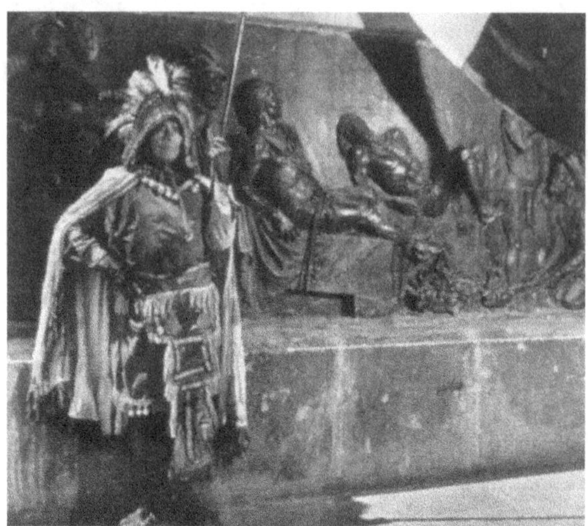

Fig. 6.7. Nacho López, "Danzantes montan guardia ante un monumento" (Dancers Stand Guard before a Monument) 1962. © 383106 SINAFO-Fototeca Nacional de México.

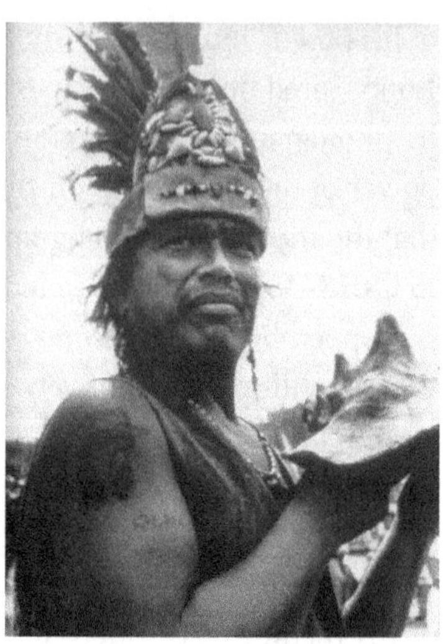

Fig. 6.8. Pablo Ortiz Monasterio, "La Raza" (Race) in *La última ciudad*, 1996. Courtesy of the artist.

"indigenous," Mexico. Typical of the historiography of this tradition, John Mraz's analysis of López's photographs of indigenous Mexicans—taken from a paternalistic perspective, from above—critiques the vision of the poor and the indigenous as helpless victims, but does not address how monumentalizing images of the same people might similarly place them outside of history.

Ortiz Monasterio states that one of the major goals of *La última ciudad* was to accurately represent the large presence and ongoing contributions of indigenous peoples to contemporary Mexico City (personal interview). In fact, he profoundly reconfigures López's image of an indigenous man in Mexico City in his ambivalent photograph of a young man with a tattoo (figs. 6.7 and 6.8). López's photograph, included in *Yo, el ciudadano*, shows an elderly *indio*, dressed entirely in non-Western clothing and posed in front of the monument to Cuauhtemoc, the conquered Aztec ruler. He resembles Paz's saddened figure of Mexico, a kind of living monument to something always already gone, temporally foreign to the modern city, bearing the Mexican flag only as a symbol of a foundational indigenous past. This is one of the few images printed in Ortiz Monasterio's 1984 homage to López that has no clear parallel image in the 1962 *Artes de México* essay, although it is from the same period in his career. Not only does Ortiz Monasterio's inclusion of this photograph reference the large number of photographs that López took of indigenous Mexicans, mostly in rural areas rather than the city, but it also demonstrates the centrality of this

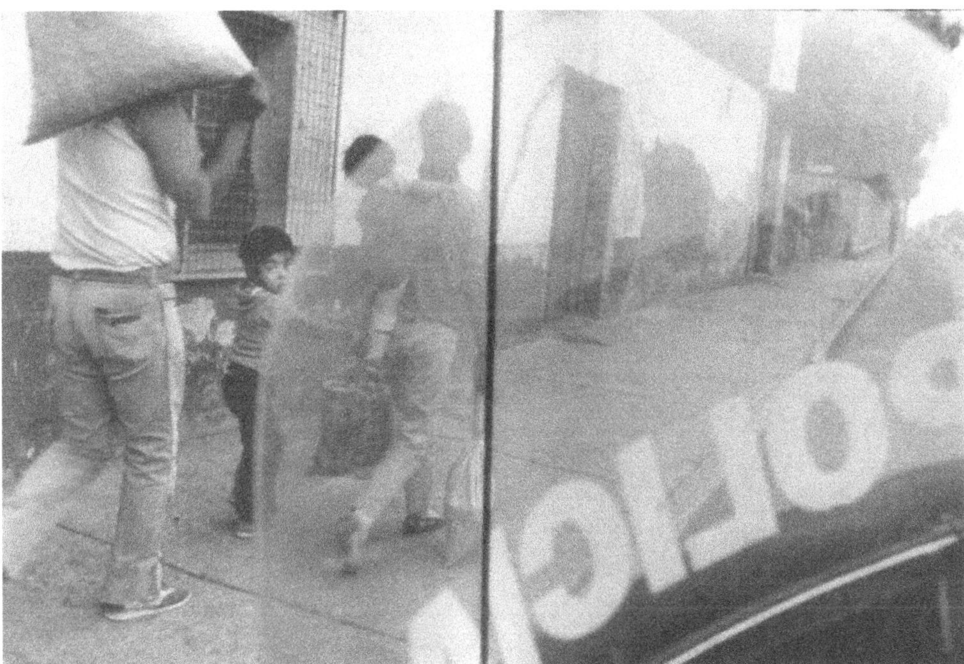

Fig. 6.9. Pablo Ortiz Monasterio, "Policía" (Police) in *La última ciudad*, 1996. Courtesy of the artist.

issue for Ortiz Monasterio in his role as the coordinator of *Yo, el ciudadano*.

In his version of this photograph in *La última ciudad*, Ortiz Monasterio detaches the figure from the backdrop of the monument to the past. Now he is dressed in a mixture of indigenous and Western clothing, and his tattoo covers a young, strong arm. Nonetheless, Ortiz Monasterio repeats López's act of monumentalization in his own figure of the indigenous. This photo, shot from below, frames Monasterio's subject against a bright sky, and, like López's photograph, captures him staring pensively off toward the horizon. While Ortiz Monasterio is clearly worried about this question as a central one for Mexican photography, the young man's gaze does not become the challenging confrontation of the young woman having her shoes shined. In the end, this particular act of recycling does not fundamentally change the representation of the presence of indigenous people in Mexico City.

The absence of the returned gaze we saw in the earlier photograph of the woman marks Ortiz Monasterio's recognition of the limits of his ability to represent those groups that Richard terms marginal or subaltern. Throughout *La última ciudad*, as much as he pictures these sectors of society, Ortiz Monasterio also builds obstacles that block the viewer's access to their image. The photographs often align us with a gaze that forces the recognition that this view may be used just as easily to control the people pictured as to demand their rights. Ortiz Monasterio goes so far as to take a photograph through the clear fairing of a police motorcycle, so that it doubles

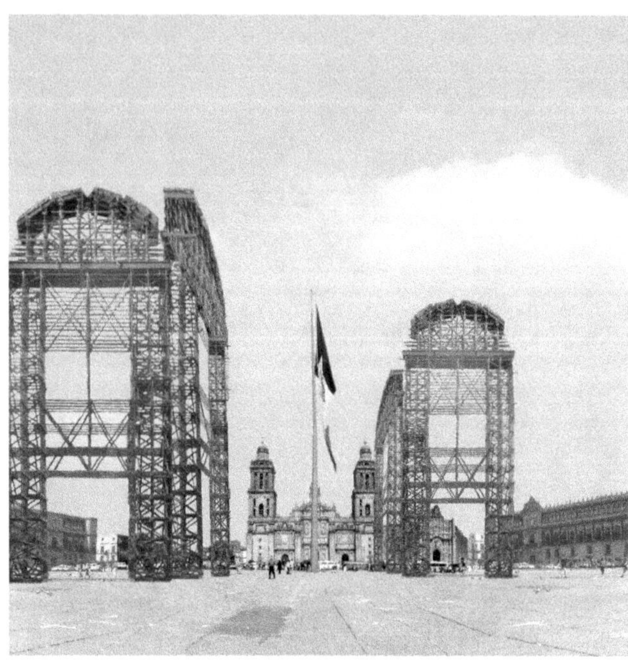

Fig. 6.10. Peter Lasch Thaler, "Una propuesta escultórica para el Zócalo" (A Sculptural Proposal for the Zócalo), simulation, 1999. Courtesy of the artist.

the divide of the camera lens, and the viewer must read the image through the letters in the lower third of the frame that spell out P-O-L-I-C-I-A (fig. 6.9). We also come face-to-face, or eye-to-eye, with a pistol pointed at us by one of the urban "youths," plainly portraying the relationship between photographer and subject as a violently conflictive one. While this book participates in the tradition of Mexican documentary photography of the disenfranchised inhabitants of the capital city, it ultimately presents itself as a doomed project—the *last city*.

Monumentalizing images of an undifferentiated indigenous population have existed in Mexico for decades as the proclaimed basis for a national identity, but they have not achieved any lasting social, political, or economic gains for these groups. Instead, as many scholars of Mexico have noted, they freeze the indigenous communities in an inactive past, denying them political representation, human rights, or any economic benefits of citizenship. The very contemporary nature of this problem of the monumentalizing nature of photography, and the difficulty that this tradition in Mexican photography has with representing the presence of indigenous peoples in the capital city, is clear from the impact of the Zapatista march in February and March of 2001. Members of the Zapatista army marched from Chiapas to the seat of government in Mexico City, a demonstration that culminated in an address to the Mexican senate by Comandante Esther.[19] Unlike monumentalizing photographs, this march transformed the presence of indigenous and mestizo Mexicans in the capital city from a clichéd contrast of traditional and modern—which disengages the

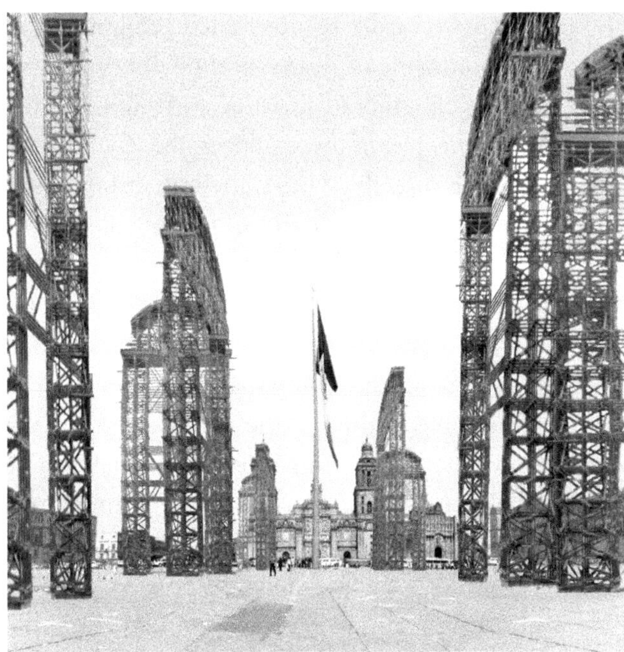

Fig. 6.11. Peter Lasch Thaler, "Una propuesta escultórica para el Zócalo" (A Sculptural Proposal for the Zócalo), simulation, 1999. Courtesy of the artist.

historical impulse—into a demand for the rights of citizenship, a demand to be part of the ongoing history of the nation.

Digital Photography, or: "Oficialmente, el Zócalo no existe"

The recycling of the image of otherness presents a profound question for contemporary photography: is there a way to imagine such a city-text without reinscribing the ahistorical monumentality of the "Other"? I see a potential answer in the history of the medium, with innovations in the relatively new field of digital photography from the end of the last century.[20]

"Una propuesta escultórica para el Zócalo, Ciudad de México" ("A Sculptural Proposal for the Zócalo, Mexico City"), by Mexican artist Peter Lasch Thaler, was accepted in 1999 by the Comisión de Arte en Espacios Públicos and published with accompanying digital photographs in the arts journal *Curare*.[21] The Zócalo, the vast square in the historical center of the city, is bordered by the Catedral Metropolitana and the Palacio Nacional (the site of Comandante Esther's address), and is empty of permanent structures, with the exception of a pole flying an immense Mexican flag. Lasch writes that this space creates "una imponente experiencia física y espiritual: la del monumental vacío" (89) (an imposing physical and spiritual experience: that of monumental emptiness).[22] For over eight years, the inside of the cathedral that borders the Zócalo was filled with scaffolding during massive structural renovations. Lasch calls his proposal "agresivamente simple": upon the conclusion of renovations, the scaffolding from inside the Cathedral would be reconstructed temporarily in the center of the Zócalo. The digital photographs in the essay show the imagined construction and deconstruction of this ephemeral structure surrounding the Mexican flag (figs. 6.10 and 6.11).[23] The perspective of these images, the Zócalo seen from the Avenida del 20 de Noviembre, leads directly to the cathedral; it shows how the revolutionary avenue leads the *transeunte* directly into the religious center rather than to the seat of government, the Palacio Nacional. The empty plaza pictured here mirrors the cathedral with its own negative image, creating what Lasch calls "un andamio para la construcción de una réplica invisible de la Catedral, una catedral secular, tal vez, envestida de sus propias actividades, emblemas y rituales" (95) (a scaffolding for the construction of an invisible replica of the cathedral, a secular cathedral perhaps, adorned with its own activities, emblems, and rituals). The cathedral turned inside out forms the skeleton of a strange national monument: one that reflects the ongoing imbrications of the Catholic Church in national politics and that also is imagined as a potential space for the expression of alternative national identities. The scaffolding would serve the same purpose it does in other parts of the city, offering an opportunity for advertising, political slogans, graffiti, and the other formal and informal messages that fill the streets.

Lasch insists upon the importance of reusing the scaffolding in the proposal, so that none of the materials for this project are new, but simply reassembled. Rather than attempt to "'crear' nuevos significados" (create new meanings), he describes his relationship to the tradition of the ready-made: "el ejercicio artístico de apropiarse de objetos de uso diario, sacándolos de su contexto" (90) (the artistic exercise of appropriating objects of daily use, taking them out of their context). Yet the process of de- and re-construction of the scaffolding with the Mexican flag at its center carries this project one step further than the idea of the ready-made. Lasch writes that the cathedral would have been under scaffolding during the two hundred years of its construction, and Renato González Mello, who introduces the published proposal, refers to the importance of the image of the scaffold in utopian avant-garde projects such as Diego Rivera's murals and Vladimir Tatlin's metallic monuments. This particular scaffolding, unlike Rivera's, does not simply support the plaza's traditional function as the space for the "edificación de nuestra cultura e identidad nacional" (92) (construction of our culture and national identity). The proposal creates an antimonument through an act of historical recycling that is both material and symbolic. Lasch creates what he calls "una escultura temporal, aunque monumental . . . una especie de 'Monumento a la *Restauración*'" (92) (a temporary sculpture, although monumental . . . a type of "Monument to *Restoration*").[24] This monument insists on the process of recycling itself; as much as it recycles materials it also makes a new structure, one that does not just support renovations but that stands on its own. Lasch explains that while architectural photography is traditionally about the completed building, these digital images go against that idea of photography and of urban architecture. Instead, they present the two as always already in a process of construction and destruction, documentation and invention.

While called a sculptural proposal, Lasch's relationship to the actual building of the monument is ambivalent, for he places it within a long history of never-completed projects for the Zócalo. The most recent of these proposals was the *convocatoria* announced in July 1998 by the then new mayor of Mexico City, Cuauhtemoc Cárdenas, which called for proposals to renovate the plaza that it describes as, "fundamental en la identidad de los mexicanos; sede de los poderes de la República, plena de simbolismo y de significación histórica, [y que] ha merecido ser considerada en el inventario del patrimonio cultural de la humanidad" (Convocatoria n.p.) (fundamental to the identity of Mexicans, seat of the powers of the Republic, full of symbolism and historical significance, [and that] has deserved consideration in the inventory of the cultural patrimony of all humanity). While a winner was chosen (the architectural group led by Celia Cortés), any hope for it being completed ended when Cárdenas stepped down from the governorship in September 1999. The oldest of the "proposals" for this central square is the competition announced in 1843 by the Academia de Bellas Artes, which gave the plaza its colloquial name: el Zócalo. The winning proposal by architect Lorenzo de la Hidalga for a monument to memorialize independence-era General Santa Ana was never constructed, leaving only "el zócalo," literally the base upon which a sculpture or monument rests (Monsiváis "Sobre los monumentos" 110). As José Joaquín Blanco wrote in 1963 in *La Jornada*: "El Zócalo oficialmente no existe . . . el Zócalo no tiene ningún zócalo, ningún 'cuerpo inferior de pedestal,' ninguna 'basa de columna'" (23) (officially the Zócalo does not exist . . . the Zócalo has no 'zócalo,' no 'lower part of a pedestal,' no 'base of a column'). The name of the square is still "Plaza de la Constitución" on all official maps of the city, despite the spread of the word *zócalo* to mean "central plaza" throughout the Americas. Lasch explains that in his original conception, the project itself existed *as* a proposal: as the digitized photographs and a written, conceptual response to the problems of representation at hand.

In this tradition, Lasch's proposal functions as a (virtual) image and embodies the in-between status of digital photographs. While it may create fictional pictures of events that never happened, digital photography frequently, though not always, manipulates traditional, analog photographs.[25] The relationship between digital and darkroom photography is not necessarily conflictive:

> Any number of critics have pointed out that there is much more continuity than discontinuity in the shift from darkroom to digital.

> The notion that photographic truth was based on a pure, unmediated representation of a 'real' referent was shattered . . . since the use of multiple exposures, multiple negatives and alterations of the plate in blatant reworking of the metaphysically endowed-with-truth 'light' let in by the lens, as well as careful manipulation of the exposure and print, were all tools of the photographer's trade almost from its origin in the early nineteenth century. (Drucker 142)

While Drucker is certainly correct about this history of photographic manipulation, it is also impossible to ignore what has been called its indexicality, or the effect of the real in photography, with which this article began. Digital photographs therefore might most productively be seen as containing the trace of the real of photography twice removed, or even recycled. Lasch's digitalized photographs insist on such a reading, for they present the material space of the Zócalo *as always already a virtual project of national identity*. The digitized images of this ephemeral structure draw attention to the *lack* of monument that the Zócalo—this empty pedestal—represents.

These digital images—necessarily recycled and invented—bring us to a new place from which to look upon the familiar debate about photography's documentary function and its relation to historical narrative. They show the impossibility of disentangling documentary and fiction in Mexican photography and letters, yet do not erase the concrete issues raised by "recycling": poverty, necessity, and social exclusion. I conclude where Lasch's photoessay leaves us, between critical essay and digital photo-essay, in order to gesture toward an important critical sphere mapped out by photographic recycling at the junction between the twentieth and the twenty-first centuries.

Disciplines, Conclusions, and Returns

Lurking behind this concept of recycling is its relationship to the established art-historical practice of citing earlier influences: of always showing two slides, one beside the other, in presentations and classes, thereby pointing out formal similarities. My methodology of a comparative reading of images on a diachronic model seems to resemble (recycle) a tradition of art-historical narratives that ask from this comparison, "how did *we* get to where we are *now*?" (Nelson 35). Robert Nelson sees a problem in these art-historical narratives:

> In a linear narrative, marginalization is accomplished by shifting a civilization out of direct chronological sequence. These temporal anomalies, these deliberate denials of coevalness, these devices for manipulating time and societies are what Johannes Fabian call

> allochronism and are important clues to the larger intentions of the narrative. (36)

The reference to Fabian is particularly appropriate to the history of photography in Latin America, because of the history of its employment in anthropology and ethnography.

In contrast, the semantic and formal changes that Ortiz Monasterio makes in his recycling of López's images avoid what Nelson points out to be the important "shifters" in this traditional art-historical approach: an assumed "we" and an understood "now." The "we" of the viewer-historian is forced into question when it comes face-to-face with the youth's gun in Mexico City. Each recycled image conjures up its predecessor, changing its value and creating the postapocalyptic historical movement, so that the "now" to which it refers is multiple: the moment of the new photograph as well as that of the old, the time of reading that links the two, and the time that has passed between them. This practice of recycling permits a vision of history, while sidestepping both the allochronism that Fabian encounters and the linear progress of history rejected by Richard and Hopenhayn.

Analyzing these photographs as participants in a practice of recycling also alters their status as objects of study. Not only does the history of (art) photography in Latin America require knowledge of ethnographic and journalistic photography, the idea of recycling makes the photograph both itself and something more. Nelson warns that traditional practices of art history create a similar effect to the approach that Bourdieu terms objectivism, both of which constitute:

> the social world as a spectacle presented to an observer who takes up a point of view on the action, who stands back so as to observe it and, transferring into the object the principles of his relation to the object, conceives of it as a totality intended for cognition alone, in which all interactions are reduced to symbolic exchanges. (cited in Nelson 36)

Even García Canclini's reading and writing of the city as text does not resolve this problem of the constitution of object and social world, for it instead flattens out the differences between city and text and contributes to what I have described as the erasure of difference between kinds of arrival and travel through the city. The practice of "objectivism" also depends upon what Craig Owens identifies as a problem in contemporary criticism: a strict division of labor between artist-producer and critic-historian, in which the artist's production of the object is considered outside theory. He rejects academic writers' control of theory, which depends upon the reduction of even highly theorized and critical artwork to a symptom of the artistic unconscious (Stephanson 63). The structure of the present chapter—reading photographs *as* a theory of recycling—seeks to avoid this trap, for the practices of these artists precisely engage with the "objectness" *and* the theoretical argument of the photographs. By reading photographic recycling as referring simultaneously to the material and symbolic circulation of images in time, we can maintain what Castellanos has called the fetishistic (non)object status of the photograph and permit it entry into a theoretical bibliography.[26]

The proposal that these photographs of Mexico City be viewed as "recycled figures" is therefore also a disciplinary proposal, a question of writing "visual culture" in conversation with art history. W. J. T. Mitchell calls "visual culture" "an 'interdiscipline,' a site of convergence and conversation across disciplinary lines . . . [that] names a problematic rather than a well-defined theoretical object" (540, 542). The freer definition of theory in visual culture allows precisely the kind of dialogue between photograph and text that has taken place throughout this essay.[27] Hopenhayn's paradoxical method of writing history leads him to similar conclusions regarding the necessary interdisciplinarity of contemporary studies of Latin America: "No es casualidad que la investigación exija cada vez más la compenetración de disciplinas, la intrusión en campos ajenos para la reinterpretación de lo del campo propio" (118) (It is not a coincidence that research requires ever more co-penetration of disciplines, the intrusion in foreign fields for the reinterpretation of one's own). Therefore this practice of photographic recycling that pictures the city becomes a map for such an "interdiscipline" in Latin American studies: a formulation of the relationship between two picture moments, which participates in the dialogues of recent Latin American theory.[28]

The practice of interdisciplinarity returns us once again to the photograph's peculiar status as a type of fetish, as both object and non-object. Ortiz Monasterio calls photography the "materialización presente de todos los tiempos" (1992, 20) (present materialization of all times), and Lasch's proposal formulates the digitized images as "un simple *deseo* de materialización" (emphasis added, Lasch 94) (a simple *desire* for materialization). The first image of materiality imagines history in the present instance of the photograph; the second projects this materiality into the future. The same formal elements that allow these photographs to function as art objects—their composition, use of light, graphic design, and engagement with a history of iconography—must also be read (interdisciplinarily) as the *material* of an explicit historical critique. These photographic (non)objects contain the theory for their own analysis, a theory that imagines a process of materialization.

Framed by these recent works—Varda's documentary and Lasch's virtual project for restoration—Ortiz Monasterio's recycling of López's photographs gains a broader scope in both time and place. By focusing on the act of recycling inherent in photography, digital or analog, documentary or faked, these photographers reveal the real urgency of the process by which history and the present are constituted. They offer a material projection of the postapocalyptic city: a theory and practice of images that are both the past and that predict a city to come. The implications are important. If we imagine an absolute rupture of the kind that has been mistakenly called "photographic," we learn less from the past and our responsibility toward future cities is erased.

Notes

1. Unless otherwise indicated, all translations are my own.

2. This is how Carlos Monsiváis summarizes contemporary, apocalyptic visions of Mexico City, in contrast to that of Salvador Novo in his 1946 essay, *Nueva grandeza mexicana* ("Prólogo," 9).

3. This phenomenon is so widespread it has even been reported on National Public Radio. See National Public Radio (NPR), "All Things Considered," August 14, 2002.

4. Recycling is clearly related to Robert Stam's analysis of the "aesthetics of garbage" (see his "Tropical Detritus"). While I find his analysis important and suggestive, my emphasis here is on the recycling of photographic images in the construction of contemporary history, and therefore falls less on the materiality of trash and more on the simultaneous object-nonobject operation of the recycled photographic image. What is more, while the ethical and political power of recycling trash is certainly part of my argument, I examine recycling not only of garbage but also of the most cherished components of culture, in order to alter their symbolic value.

5. In contemporary art there is a clear trend toward a similar reuse of materials. In fact, it might be easier to write about "recycling" in the twentieth-century tradition of the ready-made, from Marcel Duchamp to Cindy Sherman. Brazilian artist Cildo Meireles has produced a powerful series of works based on the circulation of objects and values. In his 1970 *Inserções em circuitos ideológicos: projeto Coca-Cola* (Insertions in Ideological Circuits: The Coca-Cola Project), Meireles stenciled "Yankee go home" on Coke bottles in white paint matching the script of the soda company that is the icon of U.S. cultural and economic dominance in the region. Meireles's work depends on the actual recycling of bottles that happens throughout Latin America (unlike in the United States); the bottles are washed, filled, and reused. In fact, it is impossible to see Meireles's work before the bottle is filled with the popular brown drink, for the white writing on the clear glass is practically invisible. In this practice of recycling, Meireles's oppositional political messages piggyback on the very objects whose social and economic value they critique. Despite the fascinating examples of the importance of recycling in contemporary art practice, it is because of this material reference that I am particularly concerned with the simultaneously material and ephemeral recycling of photographic images. I do not wish to be too literal about the idea of recycling, however, for as he would undoubtedly explain, no forest will be saved and no family fed from Mereiles's recycling of Coca-Cola bottles. I take up the relationship of recycling to the ready-made at the end of this chapter, in my discussion of Peter Lasch's work.

6. Nacho López frequently took a large number of photographs of the same event in order to select one image later, much as news photographers still do today. Several of the photographs in *Yo, el ciudadano* that were not included in the 1962 "La ciudad de México" belong to the same series of images that were reproduced in the new volume.

7. *The Lettered City* 1. The published translation cited here departs substantively from the Spanish, substituting "Western civilization" for Rama's "cultura universal," losing the important word "inscripta" (inscribed), and diminishing the carnal imagery of the original.

8. On *flaneando*, an invented verb in Spanish describing the practice of the flâneur, versus "traveling," see García Canclini, *Hybrid Cultures*, 33.

9. Beatriz Sarlo defends herself from such accusations in the response "Retomar el debate" that appeared in a series of short articles in *Punto de vista*.

10. My use of *figures*, or historical tropes, is clearly indebted to Hayden White's work.

11. Ortiz Monasterio retakes many more images from López's essay, but space limitations here do not permit analysis of all of them. Some further examples are the series of images of religious processions and icons, the masses (large street demonstrations), and portraits of poverty.

12. This quote references Carlos Fuentes's classic 1959 novel, *La región más transparente*.

13. *Pachuco* is a term used to refer to Mexican Americans, especially urban youth who were purported to be active in gangs following the Second World War. Pachucos were also characterized by their use of stylized suits and large hats.

14. Public lecture, Stanford University, spring 1998.

15. See also Mario Margulis, *La vida nocturna de los jóvenes en Buenos Aires*.

16. See Debra Castillo, *Easy Women: Sex and Gender in Modern Mexican Fiction*.

17. The version of the this photograph printed in *Yo, el ciudadano* is slightly different from the one in "La ciudad de México." It clearly comes, however, from the same series of shots.

18. I would like to thank Alejandro Castellanos for his helpful conversation about this article and his suggestions regarding *La última ciudad*.

19. All Zapatistas, including Subcomandante Marcos, avoid using their last names.

20. It should be clear, given the present argument about photographic recycling, that this avenue for representation is not governed by any technological determinism. The "invention" of digital photography did not produce a new mode of representation, but artists' experiments with this new technology have created a new series of representational strategies.

21. I would like to thank Peter Lasch Thaler for sharing with me his remarkable research into the history of the Zócalo. Much of what follows comes from his investigations.

22. There are however, ephemeral markets, tents, and stages constantly appearing and disappearing in the plaza. These structures were of more interest to Lasch than any kind of permanent monument.

23. Lasch created the digital images for the proposal by photographing the scaffolding inside the cathedral, and then measuring the same number of steps from the flag as he took from the *crucero* to take the picture.

24. Here Lasch is playing on the similarity of *Monumento a la Restauración* to the Monumento de la Revolución in Mexico City.

25. There are digital photographs that store mathematical equations or computer programs, with no connection to the traditional darkroom photograph. See Drucker, "Digital Ontologies." Her point regarding the flexibility of the "truth" of traditional photography is especially relevant to the case of López, who posed many of his "journalistic" photographs.

26. This is why I referred to Varda's documentary film as crucial to my "bibliography."

27. Since the conceptual art of the 1960s and 1970s has gained greater presence in art history classrooms and scholarship, a similar interdisciplinarity of theory and practice, or written text and artwork, can be observed. In the many heated debates about the formulation of "Visual Culture" or "Visual Studies" and their relationship to art history and to cultural studies, the interdiscipline is often characterized by its resistance to a hierarchy of popular and elite culture. Because the recycling of photographs between these realms and the interdisciplinarity of theory itself are so much at the center of this essay, I believe it resides more comfortably in visual

culture. However, it must also engage, and even borrow from the methodologies of art history in order to allow the transvaluation of images to take place. For more on these disciplinary and methodological discussions, see Holly and Moxey, eds., *Art History, Aesthetics, Visual Studies*, the famous "Visual Culture Questionnaire," published in *October* 77; and Mirzoeff, ed. *The Visual Culture Reader 2.0*.

28. This idea of recycling has been influenced by the lively debate about the relevance to Latin American critical thought of Raymond Williams's concepts of a "structure of feeling" and dominant, emergent, and residual components of culture. As Sarlo writes, "En la estructura de sentimiento, la dimensión simbólica de lo social muestra precisamente ese carácter huidizo que está en el origen del prolongado debate sobre la inscripción de lo social en lo estético . . . Pero no solamente es eso: en la medida en que ella capta los tonos de una época, permite ver qué hay en común entre discursos y prácticas cuyos materiales son diferentes" ("Raymond Williams" 14) (In the structure of feeling, the symbolic dimension of the social shows precisely that fleeting character that is at the origin of the prolonged debate about the inscription of the social in the aesthetic . . . But it is not only that: in the sense that it captures the tone of an epoch, it permits us to see what there is in common between discourses and practices whose materials are different). Sarlo explains that Williams's vision works better for a theory of cultural transformation than for one of rupture.

References

Blanco, José Joaquín. "El Zócalo (primera de cuatro partes)." *La Jornada* (1963), reprinted March 2, 1990: 23.

Castellanos, Alejandro. "Las herencias del mito: fotografía e identidad en México, 1920–1940." *Arte, historia e identidad en América: visiones comparativas*. Vol. 2. Eds. Gustavo Curiel, Renato González Mello, and Juana Gutiérrez Haces. Mexico City: UNAM/IIE, 1994, 647–54.

______. *Nacho López: antología de fetiches*. Xalapa, Veracruz: Galería del Estado-IVEC/ Ediciones Mar y Tierra, 1996.

Castillo, Debra. *Easy Women: Sex and Gender in Modern Mexican Fiction*. Minneapolis: University of Minnesota Press, 1998.

Convocatoria. www.df.gob.mx.

Debroise, Olivier. *Fuga mexicana: un recorrido por la fotografía en México*. Mexico City: Consejo Nacional para la Cultura y las Artes, 1994.

Drucker, Johanna. "Digital Ontologies: The Ideality of Form in/and Code Storage—or—Can Graphesis Challenge Mathesis?" *Leonardo* 34.2 (2001): 141–45.

García Canclini, Nestor. *Culturas híbridas: estrategias para entrar y salir de la modernidad*. Mexico City: Grijalbo/Consejo Nacional para la Cultura y las Artes, 1989.

______. *Hybrid Cultures: Strategies for Entering and Leaving Modernity*. Trans. Christopher L. Chiappari and Silvia L. López. Minneapolis: University of Minnesota Press, 1995.

García Canclini, Nestor, Alejandro Castellanos, and Ana Rosas Mantecón. *La ciudad de los viajeros. Travesías e imaginarios urbanos: México, 1940–2000*. Mexico City: Editorial Grijalbo, 1996.

Holly, Michael Ann, and Keith Moxey, eds. *Art History, Aesthetics, Visual Studies*. Williamstown, MA: Clark Studies in the Visual Arts, 2002.

Hopenhayn, Martín. *Ni apocalípticos ni integrados: aventuras de la modernidad en América Latina*. Santiago, Chile: Fondo de Cultura Económica, 1994.

Knight, Alan. "Popular Culture and the Revolutionary State in Mexico, 1910–1940." *Hispanic American Historical Review* 74.3 (1994): 393–444.

Lasch Thaler, Peter. "Una propuesta escultórica para el Zócalo, Ciudad de México." *Curare* 15 (1999): 88–95.
López, Nacho. "La ciudad de México." *Artes de México* 12.58/59 (1964). Special number.
______. *Yo, el ciudadano*. Comp. Fernando Benítez and Pablo Ortiz Monasterio. Mexico City: Fondo de Cultura Económica, 1984.
Margulis, Mario. *La vida nocturna de los jóvenes en Buenos Aires*. Buenos Aires: Espas, 1994.
Martín-Barbero, Jesús. *Pre-textos: conversaciones sobre la comunicación y sus contextos*. Santiago de Calí, Colombia: Editorial Universidad del Valle, 1996.
Mirzoeff, Nicholas, ed. *The Visual Culture Reader* 2.0. New York: Routledge, 2002.
Mitchell, W. J. T. "Interdisciplinarity and Visual Culture." *Art Bulletin* 77.4 (1995): 540–44.
Monlau, Pedro Felipe. *Diccionario etimológico de la lengua castellana: precedido de unos rudimentos de etimología*. Buenos Aires: Librería "El Ateneo," 1946.
Monsiváis, Carlos. "Prólogo." In *Nueva grandeza mexicana*. Salvador Novo. Mexico City: Cien de México/Consejo Nacional para la Cultura y las Artes, 1992, 9–17.
______. "Sobre los monumentos cívicos y sus espectadores." *Monumentos mexicanos: de las estatuas de sal y de piedra*. Coord. Helen Escobedo. Mexico City: CONACULTA/Camera Lucida/Grijalbo, 1989.
Mraz, John. "From Positivism to Populism: Toward a History of Photojournalism in Mexico." *Afterimage* 18.6 (1991): 8–11.
______. "Los dilemas del realismo." *La Jornada*. August 7, 1999. http://www.jornada.unam.mx/1999/sep99/990905/texto15.html.
______. *Nacho López y el fotoperiodismo mexicano en los años cincuenta*. Mexico: Editorial Océano de México/Instituto Nacional de Antropología e Historia, 1999.
Nelson, Robert S. "The Map of Art History." *Art Bulletin* 79.1 (1997): 28–40.
Novo, Salvador. *La nueva grandeza mexicana*. Mexico City: Editorial Hermes, 1946.
Ortiz Monasterio, Pablo. "Artists statements." *Center Quarterly* 14.1 (1992): 18–22.
______. Personal interview. August 7, 2003, Mexico City.
______. *La última ciudad*. Text, José Emilio Pacheco. Mexico City: Casa de las Imágenes, 1996.
Paz, Octavio. *El laberinto de la soledad*. 1950. Mexico: Fondo de Cultura Económica, 1986.
______. *The Labyrinth of Solitude and Other Writings*. 1962. Trans. Lysander Kemp, Yara Milos, and Rachel Phillips Belash. New York: Grove Press, 1985.
Rama, Angel. *La ciudad letrada*. Hanover, NH: Ediciones del Norte, 1984.
______. *The Lettered City*. Trans. John Charles Chasteen. Durham, NC: Duke University Press, 1996.
Richard, Nelly. "Roturas, memorial y discontinuidades. (En homenaje a W. Benjamin)." *La insubordinación de los signos (cambio político, transformaciones culturales y poéticas de la crisis)*. Santiago, Chile: Editorial Cuarto Propio, 1994, 13–36.
Sarlo, Beatriz. "Raymond Williams: una relectura." *Punto de Vista* 45 (1993): 12–15.
______. "Retomar el debate." *Punto de Vista* 55 (1996): 38–42.
Stam, Robert. "Tropical Detritus: *Terra Em Transe*, Tropicalia and the Aesthetics of Garbage." *Studies in Latin American Popular Culture* 19 (2000): 83–93.
Stephanson, Anders. "Interview with Craig Owens." *Social Text* 27 (1990): 55–71.
Varda, Agnes, dir. *Les Glaneurs et la Glaneuse*. Ciné-tamaris and Scréren/C.N.D.P. DVD. New York: Zeitgeist Video, 2000.
______. *Les Glaneurs et la Glaneuse: deux ans après*. Ciné-tamaris and Scréren/C.N.D.P. DVD. New York: Zeitgeist Video, 2002.
"Visual Cultural Questionnaire." *October* 77 (1996): 25–70.

Part III

Photographic and Narrative Confrontations

Chapter Seven

Ekphrasis and the Contest of Representations in Tomás Eloy Martínez's *La novela de Perón*

Dan Russek

Photography has been a constant motif in modern Latin American fictional narratives, becoming a foremost medium to express the literary possibilities and limitations of the fixed image. In this essay I argue that *La novela de Perón* (1985) is a paradigmatic text in the way it incorporates some of the classic themes regarding the uses of photography. Throughout the novel, Tomás Eloy Martínez explores the nature of this visual medium as public sign and as vehicle for personal recollection, as testimony of historical truth and as rhetorical weapon, as melancholic substitute for the absent and as magical medium through which the dead are resurrected. Photographs become vicarious presences that shelter the needy, evoke the joys of the past, monumentalize an icon, or rob someone else's soul. The novel constantly probes the abiding human need to produce the "image that will stick" in the mind of individuals as well as in the collective memory. To fix a meaningful pose—one of photography's classic roles—becomes of paramount importance in an environment in which messages vie for attention.

Photography constantly mediates in the plot between past and present, memory and perception, the contingent and the ideal. More importantly, it becomes the model for the variety of visual signs deployed in the narrative. It is no coincidence that *ekphrasis*, the description of photographic representations, is one of Martínez's recurring textual strategies. Photographic images are awarded a privileged place in the general economy of representations the novel deploys.

In the text, photographs play a paradoxical role: they are fictions within a fiction, but they also purport to certify the authenticity of events. They provide a range of *effets du réel* (effects of the actual) that anchor discourse in referential illusions. The ekphrastic moments show the power of photography to fictionalize

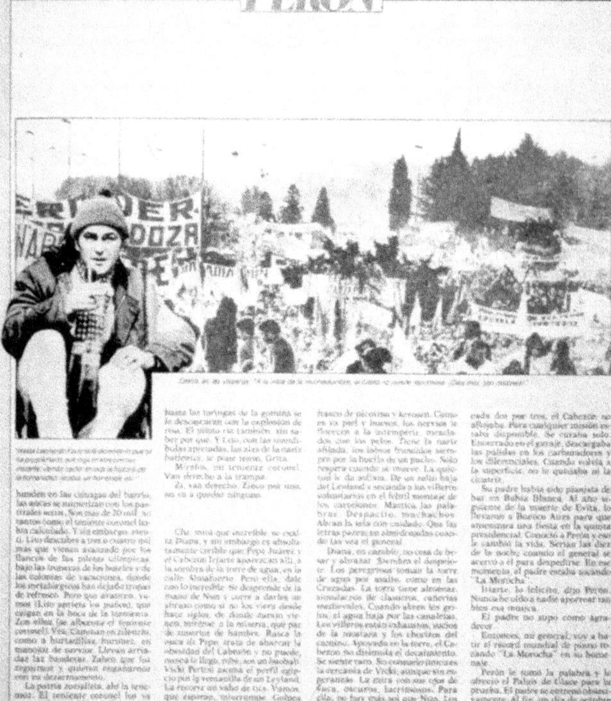

Fig. 7.1. “Peronist groups on their way to Ezeiza. The actor and filmmaker Leonardo Favio addressing the crowd.” *El Periodista*, 28 (March 22–28, 1985), 27. From newpaper serial publication of *La novela de Péron.*

the diegetic reality of the novel. In other words, both the reader and the characters in the text take for granted the “analogical plenitude” of the photographs, but these same photographs shape, edit, distort, magnify, or idealize the purported reality that generates them as signs.

La novela de Perón also stages a contest among media of communication. It can be read as a semiotic spectacle, an arena where competing versions of events clash and the tensions of verbal and visual representations come to the surface. In this sense, the novel is about a political figure, and also about how a political figure is constructed. On the level of production, circulation, and reception of representations, words and images interact in pursuit of the “truth” of the main character.

The book has mainly been interpreted as a fictionalization of historical events or as a novelistic version of Argentine politics during the twentieth century. It is also an exploration of the links between historical truth, literary fiction, and journalism. It falls into what Linda Hutcheon calls “historiographic metafiction,” a category in which fictional texts “foreground the productive, constructing aspects of their acts of representing” (22). Though underpinned by biographical information, it is not a biography of Perón, but a cross-section of his personal and social background, his ideas, his ascent to power, and his exile and fateful return to Argentina in 1973.[1]

Published in 1985, in the aftermath of the Dirty War that plagued Argentina from 1976 to 1983, *La novela de Perón* can be read as a reflection on the immediate past. It is certainly not a commentary on the political and social plight of Argentines in those years, but it provides useful historical background.[2] The novel avoids references to the core of Perón's political career—his two presidential terms from 1946 to 1955—but it constantly alludes to the military institution from which he rose to prominence and which dominated Argentine politics from the 1930s. While portraying the last days of Perón, who is unable to tame the social tensions and political struggles after his long exile, the text can be read as an indictment of sorts. Perón's pathetic legacy—represented by the short-lived government headed by the inept Isabel Martínez, Perón's third wife, and the Machiavellian José López Rega, his personal secretary—contained the seeds of the imminent social anarchy and the subsequent military regime that seized power in 1976. In this sense, *La novela de Perón* traces the long historical shadow of his leadership and the effects of his crumbling authority.

The point of departure of the story is June 20, 1973. Millions of Argentines gather for the long-awaited return of Perón from exile. The narrative skillfully interweaves the lives of the protagonists, all converging in the multitudinous welcome at Ezeiza airport, which by the end of the novel culminates in the murderous rampage against leftist Peronist groups by police and paramilitary forces (fig. 7.1).

Between the Billboard and TV

It is telling that *La novela de Perón* begins and ends with images. The first one is a billboard featuring Isabelita, under which Arcángelo Gobbi, a thug working for Perón's personal secretary, the infamous López Rega, awaits the leader's arrival. The final one is a television image featuring the body of Juan Domingo Perón, broadcast during his wake. From the outset, billboard and television screen provide the grounds for an ironic interplay between sign and referent: the meaningless, ineffectual Isabelita acquires monumental proportions, and the larger-than-life Perón ends up trapped in a plastic box beaming a bluish light. These images signal one of the salient features of the novel: its wide range of interactions between realms of meaning and representation.

Both images express the pictorial wish to fix and preserve the semblance of the absent, while circulating it in the public domain. There is a photographic component in both images. On the one hand, portraits on billboards, which rely on realistic codes, are drawn from carefully selected photographs.[3] On the other, Peron's last television image points toward photographic representation in two ways: first, he remains paralyzed in death, and second, the camera shot does not change. Both in billboard and television image, the medium magnifies, multiplies, and ends up freezing a countenance.

Bracketing the proliferation that the novel displays, billboard and television image point toward the variety of roles visual artifacts play in the novel. Images acquire a life of their own, brought to light by ekphrastic strategies. The persistent life of the dead has been a constant topic in Martínez's work. He has devoted some essays to the "necrophiliac" aspects of Argentine culture, and his own *Santa Evita* (1995) can be read as an extended parable on the power of the dead over the living, the passive image over the active mind.[4] As André Bazin might have said, Evita the mummy is suggestive of photography, insofar as she is fixed in a pose for eternity.[5] The practice and theory of photography have always been linked to the memorializing of the dead and a mournful/melancholic outlook on life, and the ways photography gives shape to this imaginary but poignant link to death also pervade *La novela de Perón*.

The photographic motif plays a central role in the development of two main topics: the rituals of the image, and the quest for the truth about Perón. As I show in the next section, it also appears in incidental but meaningful instances in many chapters.

A Collection of Photographs

La novela de Perón is a veritable album of ekphrastic moments. Few Latin American novels contain so many explicit allusions to photography, from mere snapshots to doctored images, from postcards to family albums to posters. This wealth of references highlights the variety and force of the interactions between human beings and photographic signs. In this verbal texture teeming with visual allusions, the author exploits what W. J. T. Mitchell calls the "ekphrastic hope" of a literary text, which is at work

> when the impossibility of ekphrasis is overcome in imagination or metaphor, when we discover a "sense" in which language can do what so many writers have wanted it to do: "to make us see." (152)

Indeed, the reader is constantly referred to photographs scattered throughout the story. Isabel, who Perón says "tenía la virtud de ver sólo la superficie de las personas" (12) ("had the virtue of seeing only the surface of people" 4) kills time looking at a picture magazine in the plane that brings the Peróns back to Argentina.[6] In Madrid, some weeks before, while the tensions of the imminent trip have been building up, Perón takes a melancholic stroll around his house and, on the balcony, fancies himself in front of a cheering crowd waving "photographs and placards" (6) from the Plaza de Mayo. Photographs of the first Peronist regime adorn the dining room of the home

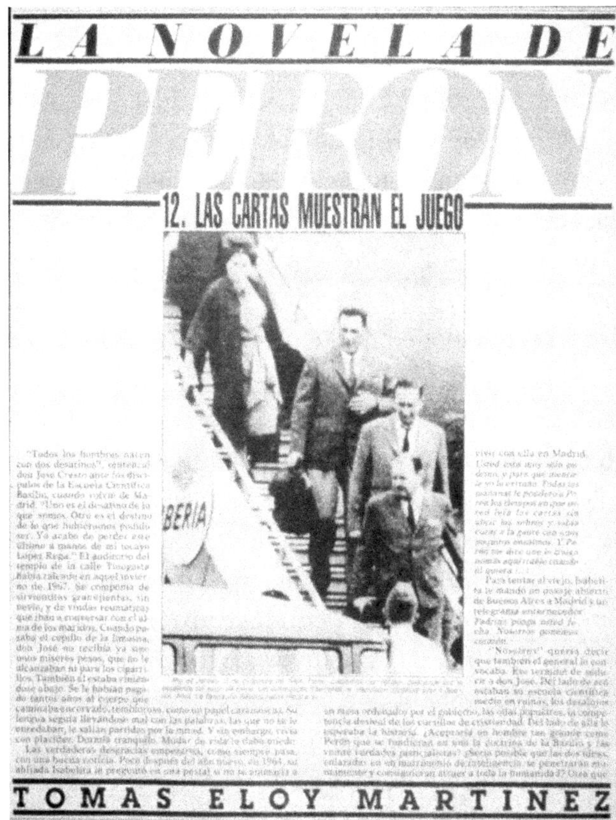
LA NOVELA DE PERON

12. LAS CARTAS MUESTRAN EL JUEGO

TOMAS ELOY MARTINEZ

Fig. 7.2. "Campora and Perón in Madrid." *El Periodista*, 9 (Nov. 10–16, 1984), 25. From newpaper serial publication of *La novela de Péron.*

(93). Cámpora, elected president as Perón's deputy, pays a visit to the leader in Madrid (fig. 7.2). He looks at the photographs and thinks, with nostalgia, that "todo era más claro en aquel pasado" (98) ("everything was clearer in those days" 93), as if glimpsing the turmoil that the failure of Perón's upcoming regime will bring about.

As the plot unfolds, photography chronicles both achievements and disgraces. Examples abound: the young Perón receives a photographic album the day he graduates from the military academy, as a token of triumph after the harsh training. On his way to the desolate fields of Patagonia, where his father had decided to pursue a living, Perón looks in awe at the photographs of the failed expedition to the South Pole by Scott, thinking that one day Argentines will accomplish the feat.

Photography plays a crucial role in the capture of general Lonardi, who was caught spying on the Chilean army in 1938. Lonardi, who would head the military coup to unseat Perón in 1955, was then a newly appointed military attaché at the Argentine embassy, replacing Perón. Zamora, the journalist who is covering Perón's life for a special issue of the magazine *Horizonte*, learns the details of the case from Lonardi's embittered widow. Chapter 12 opens with the journalist visiting the woman: "Zamora la ha imaginado como ya no es. Ha esperado encontrarse con el rostro frágil e imperial que asomaba en las fotografías de 1955" (225) ("Zamora had imagined her as she no longer is. He had anticipated the same fragile, imperious features of the 1955 photographs" 221). According to the widow, who shares her notes and diaries with Zamora, Perón left the plot ready to unfold, only to see it explode in Lonardi's hands when he was discovered in flagrante by the Chilean intelligence service, photographing secret documents.

The day Perón is scheduled to return from Madrid, some of his relatives, mostly elders who have not seen him for decades, have been invited to receive him at the airport. Their testimonies have been included in the special issue of *Horizonte* entitled "La vida entera de Perón/El Hombre/El Líder/Documentos y relatos de cien testigos" ("Perón: His Entire Life/Documents and Photos of 100 Witnesses"). Bored and frustrated, they pass time reading the magazine, discovering their own stories in its pages. Sometimes cheerily, but most often with awe, nostalgia, or disgust, they look at their personal photographs displayed in a public medium. Powerless to control the images already printed in the magazine, they are also powerless in the hallways of the airport. Mistreated by the security personnel anxiously awaiting Peron's arrival, the relatives board a bus that takes them away, to the outskirts of the airport. During the short trip, Benita, wife of one of Peron's cousins, discovers a photograph of herself as a teenager on a torn page of the magazine lying on the floor of the bus. For this group of ailing, unwilling, unsuspecting witnesses of Peron's life, photography is almost all that is left of life. It emblematizes a graphic register of decadence, a visible inscription of the tragic flow of time. This impression is reinforced by the sheer indifference with which the "distinguished guests" are treated—first by the staff of the magazine, then by the police forces—as if they have already vanished and been forgotten, very much like old images in a discarded publication.

Another classic theme of photographic representation—the vicarious presence of the absent, the iconic sign that substitutes for the living—is exploited by the dubious sorcery of López Rega (nicknamed "el brujo," the sorceror) and José Cresto, Isabelita's godfather. For these characters, plainly convinced of the powers of magic and espousing a hodgepodge of spiritualist beliefs and superstitions, photography is a medium in the esoteric sense, a channel that eerily communicates between the worlds of bodies and spirits. Photographs are galleries of ghosts waiting to become incarnate. Cresto, Isabelita's pathetic counselor, is also the director of the Escuela Científica Basilio, a spiritual center where candles illuminate "las fotos de los espíritus que hacían penitencia en la casa" (27) ("the photographs of spirits that were doing penance in the house" 18).

López Rega makes use of photographs as a means of magical influence and possession. He used to court luck by printing postcards of Perón and Isabelita, which he would send all over the world (129). When he arrives in Madrid in 1966, he spares no effort to gain influence over the gullible Isabelita. After settling in Spain's capital, he engages in a quest to eliminate the obscure Cresto. Both he and the spiritual counselor vie for Perón's favors, embarking on a contest of sorcerers' tricks. López Rega manages to set a trap into which Cresto finally falls, by cunningly employing a photograph that pits the lame godfather against the general. López Rega learns that Perón hated a man named Marcelino Canosa, a peasant with whom his widowed mother once had an affair. The secretary manages to get a photograph where Canosa and Perón's mother pose together and retouches the image in such a way that the features of the man resemble those of Cresto. Then he puts the doctored image in Perón's hands, suggesting, as the narrator puts it, that Cresto "había tomado posesión del espíritu de Canosa" (139) ("had taken possession of Canosa's spirit" 133). After this successful case of "magic antipathy," Perón conflates both men and gets rid of Cresto.

References to spiritual possession and soul transfusion point to a worldview espoused by López Rega and satirized by the narrator. These spiritist references are also a symbol of political power. The novel shows López Rega surrounding himself by images in his quest to capture his victims' essence (253). This is manifest in the delirious project of grafting Evita's soul from her mummy to Isabel's body, in the attic of the house in Madrid. The eternally frozen corpse of Perón's second wife—very much like a photograph—is a visual sign at the mercy of whomever wants to endow it with words, fantasies, or "spiritual" power.

Many more references to photography can be found.[7] This wealth of allusions emphasizes—to use the title of David Freedberg's book—"the power of images" in the unfolding of the plot. To understand the complexity of the links between individuals and visual signs, Freedberg embarks on a criticism based not on art-historical concepts, but in terms of the actual responses of people to images as determined by psychology, cognition, and culture. Images are created, circulate in society, and produce a sphere of influence of their own. Freedberg is less interested in analyzing their symbolic or iconological content than in the way they affect people and the way people behave toward them. One of the privileged arenas in which images assert their power is the realm of ritual.

Photography and the Rituals of the Image

The ritual use of photography in the novel takes the form of uncanny doubles, monumentalized icons, and idealized effigies. The billboard under which Arcangelo Gobbi stands guard—a sign that is being built as the plot unfolds—has a primarily scenographic function. It sets the political stage and establishes, in the best (or worst) tradition of personality cults, the figures of authority. It can be seen as the last stage of magnification of a portrait. If, as John Barnicoat points out, "an element of fantasy is introduced at the sight of a perfectly normal image that has become giant"

(157), billboards convey a sense of unreality, making a myth out of the features of a public figure.

Isabel's portrait emblematizes the power of secular deities, a charged zone to which the attention of the crowd is directed. In Gobbi's case, the image also connotes protection and familiarity. During his childhood as an orphan, he was obsessed with Isabelita's visage, which he confused in dreams with the Virgin Mary's. Gobbi is both sheltering and being sheltered by the image of his patron saint, whom he faithfully serves as soldier. From his vantage point, Gobbi looks at a photograph of Perón on a stage that the narrator explicitly calls an "altar" (17). Later in the day, when the Montoneros attack the box where Perón is expected to speak to the masses, the narrator endows the billboard with religious powers. Thus, "la foto jubilosa de Isabel" ("Isabel's jubilant photograph") will pour forth "el diluvio de su protección" (288) ("the flood of her protection" 285) onto Arcángelo.[8]

I have pointed out the ritual use of photographs in Jose Cresto's spiritual institution. By striving to invoke and appease souls through magical practices that capitalize on contemporary technology, photography links popular faith—esoteric and premodern—with the material changes introduced by modernization.[9] As is well known, the rhetoric of magic has accompanied conceptions of photography since its inception.[10]

Besides trying to transform Isabelita into a new Eva Perón, López Rega also engages in an operation of soul snatching, through his rewriting of Perón's memoirs, by adding, dropping, and correcting experiences he never had.[11] Before meeting Perón in Madrid, López Rega learned his books by heart (129); after becoming the general's secretary, his increasing familiarity and immediacy pushes him to fuse his voice with his master's. His schemes are graphically exposed in one of the last passages of the novel. In a press conference broadcast on television just after Perón's arrival, the Argentine leader appears on screen, but the viewers perceive something strange, as if his lips were out of sync with the voice they hear. The audience notices that Perón speaks, but only after López Rega's whispered words. Insofar as a living subject speaks in place of a lifeless effigy, ventriloquism becomes a master metaphor in this and other scenes. This strategy affects not only the development of the characters (Perón ventriloquizing Prussian military strategists, the group of Montoneros adopting the voice of "Che" Guevara and other revolutionary heroes), but this same operation applies to the author, who endows his characters–both imaginary and those based on real-life individuals—with a voice.

Another fixed image on television also serves to set up a ritual. In a tiny home in a shantytown, ironically called Villa Insuperable, the neighbor women ("comadres") have placed a television set on top of some boxes and a blanket as a makeshift altar (they do this after hearing that the weavers of Pergamino have decided to hold a wake over a poster of Perón in the local union). Neighbors pass by to pay their respects to the general. At Perón's funeral, the TV camera captures his visage, as if it were a photographic portrait, before he and the image on the screen fade away completely. The novel ends when a poor woman climbs on top of the improvised altar and embraces the television set. She implores the general to rise from the dead, in an uncanny blend of sentimentality, popular faith, and technological imagery.

One could speculate about the shift from billboard to television—that is, from a painted sign in public space to the electronic proliferation of information in primarily private venues, or to use another perspective, from monumental and scenographic imagery to the neatly boxed, bounded, and increasingly private consumption of images—as one token of a historical shift in the way public figures are represented. Nonetheless, this divide is not so clear-cut in the novel, insofar as the billboard of Isabelita has a deep personal meaning to Arcángelo Gobbi. At the same time, television, though an essentially domestic appliance, functions as a gathering place, a magnet for public assembly.

Photography and the Search for Truth

The second realm where photography plays a major role is that of the search for the truth about Perón. The novel shows how words and images compete on the semiotic level to pin down Perón's character and history. The struggle is deployed in two main stages: first, the "memories" Perón fashions with the insidious help of López Rega, and second, Zamora's journalistic quest to get to the bottom of Perón's life.

Photography, as an artifact that strives to transcend forgetfulness, to master time, and to control history, is very much present in Perón's old age. Sensing the proximity of death, Perón tries to channel his energies into writing his memoir, and López Rega constantly triggers Perón's recollections with the help of photographs. Ironically, these pictures feature events the general attended but does not always recall (172).

In this respect, photography participates in a series of narrative folds that exploit the fuzzy limits between literary writing, journalistic research, and historical knowledge. The best example of the conjunction between novelistic fiction and factual information is provided by the appearance of Tomás Eloy Martínez as a character in his own novel. The very day of Perón's arrival, Zamora interviews him. Zamora, who is a colleague of Martínez in the story, can be interpreted also as an alter ego of the author, as they are both engaged in writing Perón's story. In the chapter entitled "Primera persona" ("First Person"), the character Tomás Eloy Martínez decides to speak his mind. Even though his words pretend to be a confession, they really mask and deflect his own motivations regarding his pursuit of truth. Nonetheless, his first move is straightforward: he shows Zamora some snapshots as a confirmation of the truthfulness of his account (256). The referential illusion is stressed grammatically by the use of the imperative mood—"Vea estas fotografías" ("Take a long look at these snapshots")—as well as by the sharp, brief, general description of the images—"Somos Perón y yo, un día de primavera, en Madrid, conversando" (259) ("Perón and me, one spring day in Madrid, chatting" 256).

Before becoming a novelist, Tomás Eloy Martínez worked as a journalist for the weekly *Primera Plana* in Buenos Aires. He has been engaged in journalism since then, contributing regularly to newspapers such as *La Nación*, in Argentina, and *El País*, in Spain. For instance, *La novela de Perón* was first published as a newspaper serial between August of 1984 and June of 1985.[12] Each week a new chapter was published, illustrated with photographs and political cartoons (See figs. 7.1, 7.2, and 7.3). Scenes of the life of Perón and other Argentine public figures are the content of most of the photographs, some of which Martínez himself found in public archives in the cities of Comodoro, Rivadavia, and Camarones, in the province of Chubut, and some of which he received from Benita Escudero, married to a cousin of Perón and included as a character in chapter three, "Las fotos de los testigos" (40).[13]

As is common practice in journalism, the author had no say about the text that introduced the serialized novel, the graphic material, or the layout. *El periodista de Buenos Aires* was an independent weekly that began circulation in 1984, in the aftermath of the military regime and the reestablishment of democratic rule in Argentina, under the elected president, Raúl Alfonsín. The publication, which was critical of the military dictatorship, had popular appeal and benefited from the newly acquired freedom of the press. Publishing the text in serial form signals an implicit authorial intention. Martínez's portrait of one of Argentina's foremost historical figures echoes one of the nation's foundational texts, *Facundo*, by Domingo Sarmiento, which was also published in serial form in 1845, in Santiago, Chile.[14] Bridging their many differences, both texts aim to inscribe in the national imagination an unofficial version of a political leader through literary fiction. Both texts, merging biography and history, also intend to provide a critical assessment of the political practices and institutions of their age through the portrait of a "caudillo," or strong man, a figure who has dominated the political culture of Argentina, and Latin America in general, since its independence.[15]

Martínez interviewed Perón in March of 1970 for *Panorama*, another Argentine weekly. The material of their encounters, later incorporated in the novel as Peron's (fictitious) memoirs, was published as *Las memorias del General*. As a character in the text, Eloy Martínez recalls that interview and reflects on his mixed feelings regarding the consistency of Perón's profile.[16] Though Perón is the momentous incarnation of twenty years of Argentine history, he appears to Eloy Martínez mostly as a skillful political actor, an expert in the art of manipulation, and also as a mere mortal. Even in this context, photography functions as a weapon, a critical wedge, since it provides proof against a dubious claim. This is the case with one of Martínez's images, where Perón appears with a triumphant smile, on the footrest of the car of general Uriburu during the coup d'état in 1930, a compromising document that Perón, and López Rega, strive to deny or reinterpret.

The possibility of representing "what it is" and of capturing the truth of a given scene has been a central concern in the theory of photography. From the realism of the photographic image espoused by theorists such as the early Barthes, to the extreme fictionality of photography practiced by postmodern photographers such as Joan Fontcuberta or Cindy Sherman, photography has been inextricably implicated in the debate about the truthfulness of representations.[17] The linkage between the narration that mixes fact and fiction and the constant allusions in the plot to photography as a primary source of information functions primarily as a strategy for establishing verisimilitude. Those references also point to our abiding need to seek and find evidence in visual signs, even if they are illusory constructions.[18]

In the novel, journalism is the foremost example of the interaction of word and image. In particular, the issue of the illustrated magazine *Horizonte* epitomizes the collaborative tensions between diverse media. Zamora assembles a collage that aspires to show Perón's entire life. Mirroring the novel in which it is embedded, the magazine presents the psychological, familial, and social backgrounds that can serve to explain the causes of Perón's behavior, ideas, and political career.[19] Zamora distrusts the whole project, which was imposed on him by the editor of the magazine. What his boss calls the "truth about Perón" seems to Zamora nothing more than a flashy title and a ploy to lure readers. Zamora, less an enterprising reporter than a man caught between his moral scruples and the cogs of a news organization, manages to assemble a story but one that he finally disavows. He sometimes looks more like a victim of circumstances, doubtful of his own skills and the trade he has chosen, an attitude underscored by the fact that he misses the chance to witness firsthand the bloody events at Ezeiza. Humiliatingly, he learns about the debacle later in the day, as reported on television (350).

The issue of *Horizonte* is a narrative construction in a competing arena of narrative constructions. Perón's "entire life"—which we and the characters of the novel read in bits and pieces—is a compilation of a variety of verbal and visual sources. Perón's memoirs also show this fragmented structure. Both the magazine and the memoirs try to recapture the complexity and uncertainty of the past, but they do so from contrasting perspectives regarding its reception. While the totalizing effort of the biographical scrutiny of *Horizonte* is targeted to a mass audience, Perón and López Rega are busy fashioning in the intimate space of their retreat a version whose virtual audience is none other than "History." Whereas the witnesses who were interviewed for the issue complain about the distortions and half-truths they find in the magazine,

López Rega is eager to sculpt a heroic, monolithic portrait in the wishful belief that it will outlast the revisions of historical writing. Disillusioned with Perón's recollections and his seeming lack of concern, he strives to magnify and glorify the general's portrait through editing, reinterpretation, and outright distortion of the material. Perón says, in a gesture that is meant to stress his authoritarianism, that men, with their senseless passion for truth, will ultimately adopt his version of affairs. That has to do, as the novel paints him, with his elusive ideological stance and his adept embracing of contradictory political positions, a strategy located at the very core of Peronism.

Although journalism is regarded as a privileged site for producing meaning, the novel is also highly critical of that medium. To the pretentious story in *Horizonte*, the witnesses oppose their own intimate memories. The group of Montoneros put forward their own "antimemoirs." Nun Antezana, the guerrilla cell leader who pinpoints the ideological distortions of the publication, considers the portrait of the too-human Perón, "porquerías mercenarias" (69) ("commercial crap" 63), a pack of lies about the patriarch and leader. Even Zamora sees the project as "la glorificación cloacal del periodismo argentino" (39) ("the apotheosis of Argentine cesspool journalism" 32). The widow of Lonardi, after reading the old press reports from *Horizonte* regarding her husband's espionage episode in Chile, complains to Zamora: "¿Así, con esta clase de harapos, escriben la historia ustedes: los periodistas?" (234) ("Is this the kind of drivel you newspapermen pass off as history?" 231). Finally, Eloy Martínez, himself a journalist in the novel, declares that "el periodismo es una profesión maldita" (260) ("the profession of journalism is fiendish" 257). The remark, as is true of so many other passages, drips with dark humor. After all, precisely because of his trade, the author was forced to flee Argentina in 1975, threatened by the Triple A paramilitary group, run by none other than López Rega. It must be added that thanks to his contacts in the world of journalism, the author in fact managed to escape and earn a livelihood abroad.[20]

The proliferation of points of view all in search of the "truth" finds a symbol in the fly. The insect embodies a kind of super-vision with its hundreds of eyes, but its elusive flight also points toward the difficulty of getting ahold of truth. There is no better symbol than the fly to connote expiration and decomposition (even more so in a novel dealing with personal and social decadence). If the eyes of the fly index a multitude of perspectives, flies themselves are figures of unbounded, bothersome multiplication. In chapter 10, "Los ojos de la mosca" ("The Eyes of the Fly"), disconnected events are linked by the sudden appearance of a fly in each scene. In one of those passages, Zamora is driving his car to Buenos Aires from Ezeiza and passes some groups of faithful Peronistas marching to the airport. He notices a fly on the side mirror, and says to himself:

> Bajo la mosca, en el espejo del Renault, cabe la entera postal del peronismo: las vinchas, los blue-jeans de ruedo acampanado, las remeras cantando que Perón Vuelve y Vence. (192)
>
> [T]he entire postcard of Peronism fits on the mirror underneath the fly; the headbands, bell-bottom jeans, T-shirts singing 'Perón Comes Back and Conquers.' (188)

Again, Martínez resorts to photography as a metaphor to capture the typical traits of a given situation. The postcard of Peronism that Zamora reads into the mirror points less to its historical roots in the '40s than to the galvanizing power of the old leader to breathe life into a political movement in Argentina in the early '70s. The scene just cited can also be read as an allegorical snapshot of an individual trying to make sense of the entanglements of history. Only the rearview of a mirror allows Zamora—traveling away from the day's historical event—to see a future ambiguously modeled on past conquests.

If the fly—with its fragmentary, proliferating vision—is living proof of the impossibility of reaching the "truth," perhaps an image, carefully composed, can substitute for the unmanageable multiplication of perspectives. That explains the "portrait" of Perón in his memoirs. In the writing process, López Rega advises Perón: "Sea más histórico, mi general, ¿Lo ve?, ponga un poco de mármol en el retrato" (107) ("Be more historic, General. Do you know what I mean? Try to make the image look a little more like marble" 102). The "stuff" Perón's portrait is made of functions as a metaphor of majesty and firmness, but also connotes fixity and coldness. To add marble to the portrait also points towards the three-dimensional nature of sculpture and architecture, and more specifically, to national monuments and funerary statues.[21]

In his interview with Zamora, the character Eloy Martínez also mentions a raw material that he employs to describe Perón: "Es un hombre de mercurio" (259) ("He is a man of mercury" 257), referring to his lack of substance and feelings, his malleability, and the impossibility of getting ahold of him (mercury, it should be added, is also a poisonous substance). In the same passage, the visual arts provide yet another metaphor: Perón, Eloy Martínez points out, "carece de dibujo" ("has no contours"), an ironic statement from the author of a novel devoted to painting, profiling, or x-raying Argentina's foremost leader.[22]

The reference to portraiture in the above quotation is particularly meaningful. Even though López Rega fashions a written portrait, the thrust of the novel is to produce and assemble a set of images that could encode the life of the general. In the variety of interactions in which they are engaged, words and images both collaborate with and compete against each other. Ekphrastic strategies pit the visual against the verbal, as in the passage where Eloy Martínez uses a photograph as a piece of evidence contradicting a statement by Perón. In other cases, they point toward the same goal: where words describe a destiny, images try to sketch it.

One of the basic assumptions of the novel is that the truth about a character is found in visual artifacts that picture–or try to picture—his or her essence.[23] There is no better example of this use of imagery than the poster of Perón included in *Horizonte*. It is also the best example of the fictionalization of a fiction that is turned on its head and stands as an undisputed truth.

Nun Antezana, on his way to the command center, picks up a copy of the magazine at a newsstand. Again the whole title is mentioned—"Perón: His Entire Life/Documents and Photos of 100 Witnesses"—so as to reinforce the magnificent, almost epic achievement of Argentine journalism in the wake of Perón's return. At this point we learn that the issue contains "un poster gigante del susodicho, sonriente como una águila guerrera" (68) ("a giant poster of the man himself smiling, looking like a fierce eagle" 63). It is ironic that precisely Antezana, the leader of the guerrilla cell, would be the character to present the reader with the poster: the smile of Perón and his majestic gesture can be read as a bad omen. In the light of the upcoming massacre of leftist groups at Ezeiza, Perón's pose is indeed sarcastic.

The poster is both portable and imposing, combining features of the conventional, standard-size photograph and the public billboard. If its reference in the plot is a fold in the narrative, opening up the possibility of new story lines, the poster as such is literally folded into the magazine. Presumably stapled at the very center of the verbal-visual artifact in which it is embedded, thus signaling its crucial role, this single image aspires to synthesize the life and myth of Perón in one graphic stroke, in the same way as the readers of the magazine will consider the poster as a visual summary of the verbal description of events, memories, and anecdotes. The poster is a gift or supplement that happens to function as the ultimate emblem of the subject it features.

The reference to the eagle endows the image with mythic power. From the passage, it is not clear if the phrase "sonriente como una águila guerrera" is a caption written on the poster, a remark or thought by Antezana, or a statement by the omniscient narrator. The ambiguity seems to enhance the scope of Perón's stature, as if the description were a matter of course, not anyone's individual opinion. The "águila guerrera" points to the tradition of war posters dating from the First World War (Barnicoat 22), as well as to the symbols and iconography of twentieth-century authoritarian regimes.[24]

The hyperbolic reference to the gigantic size of the poster also reinforces the impression of a larger-than-life personality. The big-format reproduction resonates with the banners and spectacular images that have been placed in the streets in preparation for the president's arrival. Moreover, it is probable that the poster included in the magazine is the very one the weavers of Pergamino hang and venerate when

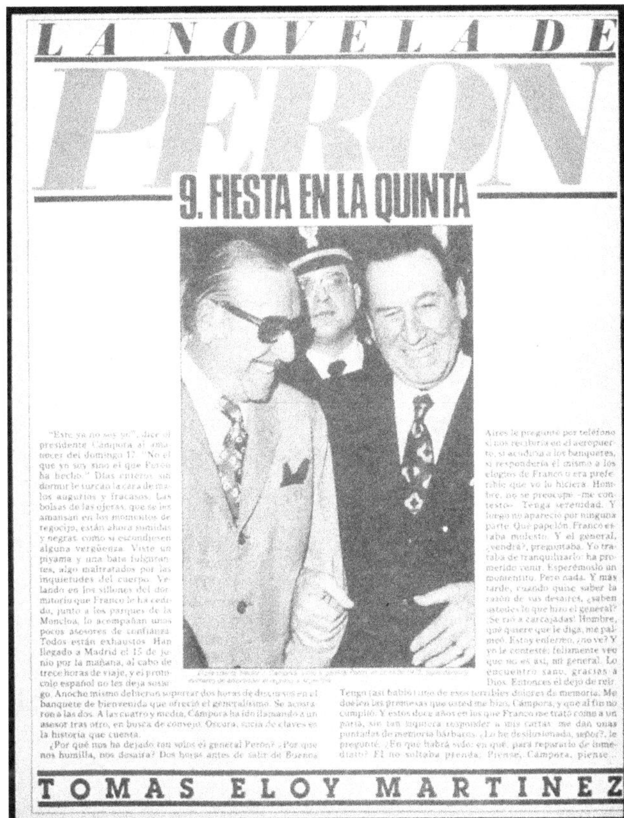

LA NOVELA DE PERON

9. FIESTA EN LA QUINTA

TOMAS ELOY MARTINEZ

Fig.7.3. "Perón arriving from Madrid." *El Periodista*, 12, (Dec. 1–6, 1984), 25. From newpaper serial publication of *La novela de Péron*.

Perón dies (though no explicit link is made). The image of the warrior eagle also parallels the fact that Perón, in the present of the narration, is flying on his way to Argentina. In light of the events and the profile of the aging Perón, the poster of a victorious effigy produces both irony and sadness.

In conclusion, the ekphrastic strategies in the novel manage to endow the photographic image with a prominent role in the production of meaning. Even though words and images are mutually implicated in the representation of the world and are both prone to distortion and manipulation, images tend to function as "the last word" of a person or event. They are like seals that give permanence and consistency to fleeting events and personal decay, as well as provide an anchor for the unbounded proliferation of representations. Michel Frizot refers to the evidentiary power of photographs as "the authenticity of a typological model" (371). Both in the fictitious space of the novel and in the general economy of representations, photographic images serve as visual epigrams through which a person's essence is emblematized and will be remembered.[25]

A final point can be made about the pertinence of not including actual photographic images in the book. The authorial and editorial decision of excluding pictures of the protagonists–especially the widely photographed Perón and Evita—enhances rather than weakens the fictional impact of the work (as opposed to its testimonial and reportorial dimensions). While constantly creating in the reader the illusion of looking–and looking at people looking—at visual signs charged with meaning, the text forces the reader to fill in the spaces and picture by himself or herself the array of photographic allusions.

As this essay has strived to show, Martínez's ekphrastic strategy is not incidental, but rather is a fundamental aspect of the novel. The frequency, density, and scope of the descriptions of photographic images foreground the increasing importance of the interactions among heterogeneous means of representation. Beyond the formalist commonplace that literary texts always allude to other literary texts, *La novela de Perón* points to an emerging visual culture and media environment that traditional literary studies, with their emphasis on linguistic analysis, have overlooked (Mitchell 6). By setting a stage on which word and image constantly cooperate with, compete against, and contradict each other, the novel exemplifies how, in an age where the mechanically reproduced image has pervaded all aspects of culture, the construction of historical figures, the unfolding of political struggles, and the mediation between personal experience and social context, are inextricably bound to the realm of visual communication.

Notes

1. See Colás, Halperín Donghi, and Martin. Menton, following Anderson Imbert, excludes *La novela de Perón* from the category of the new historical novel in Latin American, on the grounds that, despite its "significant historical dimension," the novel encompasses, "at least partially, the author's own time frame" (14).

2. Diana Taylor points out the differences between Perón's authoritarian practices in the 1940s and the terror unleashed by the military regime in the 1970s (93).

3. In chapter 2, the portrait of Isabel is referred to explicitly as a "foto de ocho metros" (36) ("a twenty-five-foot portrait" *The Perón Novel* 28).

4. See, for example, "Necrofilias argentinas," in his first book of essays, *El sueño argentino*. In his latest collection of writings, *Réquiem por un país perdido* (2003), a book that expands and updates his previous volume of essays, Martínez exploits, almost with dark delight, the links between social and political decadence and his personal sense of melancholia.

5. For the French critic, photography "embalms time" (14).

6. English translations from *The Perón Novel*. Whenever quotes occur, they are given first in the original Spanish edition, with the corresponding page numbers, and then from the English translation, also with page numbers. In nonquoted references, page numbers are those of the Spanish edition.

7. Photographs in *Horizonte* of Evita as a young girl (325); Perón and Evita photographed in the radio station where she worked (295); Evita photographed with Franco's ministers (299); Evita on the cover of *Time* magazine (299); the photograph of Isabel's deceased father (21); the melancholic postcards young Isabelita sends from Chile and Colombia to the Crestos (23); a picture of an overweight Isabelita with Perón in Caracas (24); the supposed photograph of López

Rega posing as singer in the magazine *Sintonía* (28); Cipriano Tizón, Potota's father, owner of a photography shop (172); Aurelia Tizón, Perón's first wife, weeping with a photograph of her mother in her hand (215); the editor of *Horizonte* showing Zamora photographs of Perón's exile (31); chapter 3, entitled "Photographs of the witnesses"; a swarm of photographers in Madrid shooting Perón just before his return to Argentina (317); reporters at Ezeiza (335); the prohibition against taking photographs in a press conference at the airport after the massacre (343); and the flash of photographic cameras when Perón exits the airplane in Morón (349).

8. A reference to the rituals of the image is found in Parodi (40).

9. See the introduction of Sarlo's book on the impact of new technologies on the collective imaginary at the beginning of the twentieth century in Argentina.

10. See, as a sample, Bazin (239), Newhall (18), Snyder (364), and Sontag (*On Photography* 155). For Barthes, writing in the late 1970s, photography is still an "emanation of *past reality*: a *magic*, not an art" (*Camera Lucida* 88).

11. See Martínez's *Las memorias del General* (11).

12. The novel was not yet finished when it began appearing in serial form. This may explain some of the changes in structure and style from its weekly publication to its final book form. There is no indication in the book that the text first appeared in the newspaper.

13. Information provided by Tomás Eloy Martínez in a written communication (March 22, 2004). I thank him and Professor Marcy Schwartz for their support in my research.

14. See Elizabeth Garrels, "El *Facundo* como folletín."

15. Martínez strives to do retroactively, or melancholically, what Doris Sommer identifies as the goal of nineteenth-century Latin American writers: "In the epistemological gaps that the non-science of history leaves open, narrators could project an ideal future" (7). By reinterpreting history, Sommer continues, Martínez is also guided by the belief that "literature has the capacity to intervene in history, to help construct it" (10).

16. Eloy Martínez refers to the fictional character while Martínez refers to the real life author.

17. Fontcuberta claims that "[t]oda fotografía es una ficción que se presenta como verdadera" (15) (all photographs are fictions that present themselves as true). Critics such as Rosalind Krauss (17) and Amelie Jones (33) have pointed out Cindy Sherman's deep investment in the culture of simulation that characterizes postmodernity.

18. Hutcheon points out that "[t]he photo ratifies what was there, what it represents, and does so in a way that language can never do. It is not odd that the historiographic metafictionist, grappling with the same issue of representation of the past, might want to turn, for analogies and inspiration, to this other medium, this 'certificate of presence' (Barthes 1981: 87), this paradoxically undermining yet authentifying representation of the past real" (91).

19. Insofar as the reader of the novel has to assemble the narrative pieces that compose each chapter, research journalism can be regarded as a principle of organization of the plot as well.

20. See Streitfeld's article on the last hours of Martínez in Argentina.

21. Santiago Colás remarks that Tomás Eloy Martínez's basic literary operation consisted in rewriting history and demythologizing Perón: "Martínez's novel . . . attempts to renegotiate the course of history, of society. . . . it does so by *respiración artificial*: resuscitating not the dead General but the petrified image that the General carefully left behind" (157). Marble, indeed, seals a destiny in death. In the text, Perón chats with Cámpora and refers to his advisor Figuerola: "[C]ierta vez me advirtió Figuerola que los argentinos somos adictos a la muerte. Empleó una palabra extraña: tanatófilos" (318) ("Figuerola once called to my attention that the Argentines are death-oriented. He used a strange word: 'thanatophiles'" 316). As I have suggested before, this is an opinion the author also subscribes to.

22. The character Eloy Martínez could agree with Baudrillard that simulacra have taken over the real Perón, and no original can be found to sustain the proliferation of replicas. After

interviewing him, Eloy Martínez ends up believing that the general is an empty form: "Tantos rostros le ví que me decepcioné. De repente, dejó de ser un mito. Finalmente me dije: él es nadie. Apenas es Perón" (261) ("I saw so many of his semblances that I became disillusioned. He was no longer a myth. At last, I said to myself, he's nobody. He's hardly even Perón" 259). It is less likely that this reflects the position of the author, who after all traces the decadence of an all-too-real historical figure.

23. Martin points out that the novel provides not a "portrait" but a "picture" of Perón, by which he presumably means that the novel does not specifically intend to depict the man's life, but rather to contextualize it (342).

24. Max Gallo points out that

> [C]rowds were organized to acclaim these men [Hitler, Mussolini, and Stalin,] whose pictures appeared in increasing numbers on walls. . . . On posters showing these leaders, words had all but disappeared. At most the posters bore a few words—"Heil Hitler" or "Sì" (the latter when inviting people to vote yes in a plebiscite). Otherwise, the image was enough. In public Hitler and Mussolini always wore the military trappings of their offices. Until early in the 1930s, Mussolini often appeared in civilian clothes, like the chiefs of foreign states he was meeting. But after the Ethiopian war and the triumph of German Nazism, he appeared only in uniform. Posters after 1935 show him helmeted, with his jaws clamped shut and his face set in what he believed to be a heroic expression. (246–49)

Gallo includes an illustration of one of these posters in which Mussolini dons a black helmet adorned with a silver eagle (247).

25. The point is made by Sontag in *Regarding the Pain of Others*: "In an era of information overload, the photograph provides a quick way of apprehending something and a compact form for memorizing it" (22).

References

Barnicoat, John. *A Concise History of Posters: 1870–1970*. New York: Harry N. Abrams, 1972.

Barthes, Roland. *Image Music Text*. Trans. Stephen Heath. New York: Farrar, Strauss and Giroux, 1977.

______. *Camera Lucida: Reflections on Photography*. Trans. Richard Howard. New York: Farrar, Strauss and Giroux, 1981.

Baudrillard, Jean. *Simulacra and Simulation*. Trans. Sheila Glaser. Ann Arbor: University of Michigan Press, 1995.

Bazin, André. "The Ontology of the Photographic Image." In *What is Cinema?* Vol. 1. Trans. Hugh Gray. Berkeley and Los Angeles: University of California Press, 1967, 9–16.

Colás, Santiago. *Postmodernity in Latin America: The Argentine Paradigm*. Durham, NC: Duke University Press, 1994.

Fontcuberta, Joan. *El beso de Judas: fotografía y verdad*. Barcelona: Gustavo Gili, 1998.

Freedberg, David. *The Power of Images: Studies in the History and Theory of Response*. Chicago: University of Chicago Press, 1989.

Frizot, Michel, ed. *A New History of Photography*. Köln: Konemann, 1998.

Gallo, Max. *The Poster in History*. New York and London: W.W. Norton, 2001.

Garrels, Elizabeth. "El *Facundo* como folletín." *Revista Iberoamericana* 44:143 (1988): 419–47.

Halperin Donghi, Tulio. "El presente transforma el pasado: el impacto del reciente terror en

la imagen de la historia argentina." In *Ficción y política: la narrativa argentina durante el proceso militar*. Ed. Daniel Balderston et al. Buenos Aires: Alianza; Minneapolis: Institute for the Study of Ideologies & Literature, University of Minnesota, 1987, 71–95.
Hunter, Jefferson. *Image and Word: The Interaction of Twentieth-Century Photographs and Texts.* Cambridge, MA, and London: Harvard University Press, 1987.
Hutcheon, Linda. *The Politics of Postmodernism*. London and New York: Routledge, 1989.
Jones, Amelie. "Tracing the Subject with Cindy Sherman." *Cindy Sherman Retrospective*. New York: Thames & Hudson, 1997, 33–53.
Krauss, Rosalind. *Cindy Sherman 1975–1993*. New York: Rizzoli, 1993.
Krieger, Murray. *Ekphrasis: the Illusion of the Natural Sign*. Baltimore: Johns Hopkins University Press, 1992.
Martin, Gerald. *Journeys through the Labyrinth*. London: Verso, 1989.
Martínez, Tomás Eloy. "Ficción e historia en *La novela de Perón*." *Hispamérica: Revista de Literatura* 17.49 (1988): 41–49.
______. *Las memorias del General*. Buenos Aires: Editorial Planeta, 1996.
______. *La novela de Perón*. 1985. Buenos Aires: Planeta, 1991.
______. *The Perón Novel*. Trans. Asa Zatz. New York: Pantheon, 1988.
______. "Prólogo." In *Ficciones verdaderas: hechos reales que inspiraron grandes obras literarias*. Buenos Aires: Editorial Planeta, 2000.
______. *Réquiem por un país perdido*. Buenos Aires: Aguilar, 2003.
______. *Santa Evita*. Buenos Aires: Editorial Planeta, 1995.
______. *El sueño argentino*. Ed. Carmen Perilli. Buenos Aires: Planeta, 1999.
Menton, Seymour. *Latin America's New Historical Novel*. Austin: University of Texas Press, 1993.
Mitchell, W. J. T. *Picture Theory: Essays on Verbal and Visual Representation*. Chicago: University of Chicago Press, 1994.
Newhall, Beaumont. *The History of Photography: From 1839 to the Present Day*. New York: Museum of Modern Art, 1997.
Parodi, Cristina. "Ficción y realidad en *La novela de Perón* de Tomás Eloy Martínez." *Nuevo Texto Critico* 4.8 (1991): 39–43.
Rabb, Jane M., ed. *Literature and Photography/Interactions 1840–1990. A Critical Anthology*. Albuquerque: University of New Mexico Press, 1995.
Rock, David. *Argentina 1516–1982: From Spanish Colonization to the Falklands War*. Berkeley: University of California Press, 1985.
Rosenblum, Naomi. *A World History of Photography*. New York: Abbeville, 1997.
Sarlo, Beatriz. *La imaginación técnica: sueños modernos de la cultura argentina*. Buenos Aires: Nueva Visión, 1992.
Sarmiento, Domingo. *Facundo, o civilización y barbarie*. 1845. Caracas: Ayacucho, 1977.
Snyder, Joel. "What Happens by Itself in Photography?" In *Pursuits of Reason: Essays in Honor of Stanley Cavel*. Eds. Ted Cohen, Paul Guyer, and Hilary Putnam. Lubbock: Texas Tech University Press, 1993, 361–74.
Sommer, Doris. *Foundational Fictions: The National Romances of Latin America*. Berkeley and Los Angeles: University of California Press, 1991.
Sontag, Susan. *On Photography*. New York: Doubleday, 1990.
______. *Regarding the Pain of Others*. New York: Farrar, Strauss and Giroux, 2003.
Streitfeld, David. "Evita: The Body of a Novelist's Work." *Washington Post*, December 24, 1996.
Taylor, Diana. *Disappearing Acts*. Durham and London: Duke University Press, 2000.
White, Hayden. *Tropics of Discourse: Essays in Cultural Criticism*. Baltimore and London: Johns Hopkins University Press, 1985.

Chapter Eight

Hidden Camera

The Photographic Theatre of Edgardo Rodríguez Juliá

Leo Cabranes-Grant

Among Puerto Rican authors writing either in the Caribbean or in the United States today, Edgardo Rodríguez Juliá remains unique in his dedication to the analysis of pictures. The ekphrasis of drawings and paintings plays an important role in at least two of his novels: *La renuncia del héroe Baltasar* (*The Renunciation*, 1974) and *La noche oscura del niño Avilés* (*Niño Avilés's Dark Night*, 1984). In *Campeche o los diablejos de la melancolía* (*Campeche or the Demons of Melancholy*, 1986), Rodríguez Juliá studies various works by Puerto Rican painter José Campeche (1751–1809) in order to reconstruct the formation of the island's creole consciousness. In *Puertorriqueños* (*Puerto Ricans*, 1988), the format of a photographic album enables him to retrace the slow emergence of a modernized Puerto Rican middle class after the American invasion of 1898. In all four books, the use of images allows Rodríguez Juliá to conceptualize the past as a confrontation between the archive—official records, photographs, or paintings—and the untold stories that tend to lurk behind visual or written documents. For Rodríguez Juliá, the task of the writer is to reenact the hidden desires that inspired a photograph in the first place, finding out or even inventing characters and events that facilitate an imaginary rescue of those occluded narratives.

When dealing with photographic materials, Rodríguez Juliá frames each photograph with a speculative account of how, when, or why that photograph has been taken. Pierre Bourdieu argues that the semantic content of a photograph is the result of "the meanings which it *proclaims*, that is, to a certain extent, the explicit intentions of the photographer . . . the surplus of meaning which it *betrays* by being part of the symbolism of an age, a class or an artistic group" (7). What the photograph betrays is always more relevant for Rodríguez Juliá than what the photograph proclaims; as a result, he is less interested in photography itself than in the *reception* of certain photographs. He shows a marginal interest in explaining the technical aspects of photography, but his main objective is the careful analysis of the images themselves, a quest for the semiotic unconscious that grounds the production of all iconocity.

Rodríguez Juliá does not share Roland Barthes's distrust of ekphrasis. Barthes claims that, due to the fact that a photograph is an "analogon" of reality, its relationship to the external world should be self-evident. To describe a photograph implies that its visual content needs to be translated into another discourse; therefore, in Barthes's opinion, the practice of ekphrasis implicitly declares the photograph to be insufficient (Barthes 15–31). Rodríguez Juliá's work improves upon this argument by suggesting that photographs are supplemented with verbal descriptions precisely because they are just an "analogon" of reality, not the experience of reality itself. A photograph never provides the whole picture, only certain "facts" that remain elusive unless they are linguistically re-encoded. To disclose their meaning, visual "facts" have to be "fictionalized," reinserted into cultural discourse through an active process that transforms them into stories or anecdotes.

In a study of the impact of photography in Marcel Proust's style, Mieke Bal proposes that the French novelist reacts to the unidimensional world of photography through a process of *figuration*, by which the text "forms or deforms itself into what we can think of as properly visual writing" (4). Proust's attention to tangible details treats reality as a frozen image that can be meticulously observed. His descriptions aspire to mimic the fixed accuracy of pictures. Instead of replicating the texture of a photograph, as Proust does, Rodríguez Juliá develops a fictional critique of the visible, a figuration of the potential narratives enclosed within a picture. He seems to be particularly invested in proving that photographs and story telling are interdependent. In *Cámara secreta* (Hidden Camera), this method of fictional criticism is applied to the understanding of pornographic images. In its beginnings, "pornographos" defined a literary practice: the biographies of prostitutes or courtesans. In ancient times, books describing sexual techniques or practices formed a separate genre: manuals known as "an-ainshkunto-graphoi," or writings on shameful subjects (Parker 90–111). *Cámara secreta* conflates both genres by offering both the erotic biography of a male's subjectivity and a detailed catalogue of sexual scenes.

Rodríguez Juliá opens the book with a quote from Gustave Flaubert. The accusations of obscenity thrown at Flaubert in 1857 as a result of the publication of *Madame Bovary* are an inevitable point of reference for all later discussions on the presumed immorality of art. Nonetheless, the quote used by Rodríguez Juliá comes from Flaubert's historical novel *Salambó*: "[e]se día, en efecto, el impulso hembra invadía y confundía todo; una lascivia mística se dilataba en la opresiva pesadez de la tarde" (that day, no doubt, the female impulse was invading and confusing everything; a mystical voluptuousness expanded itself through the opressive mood of

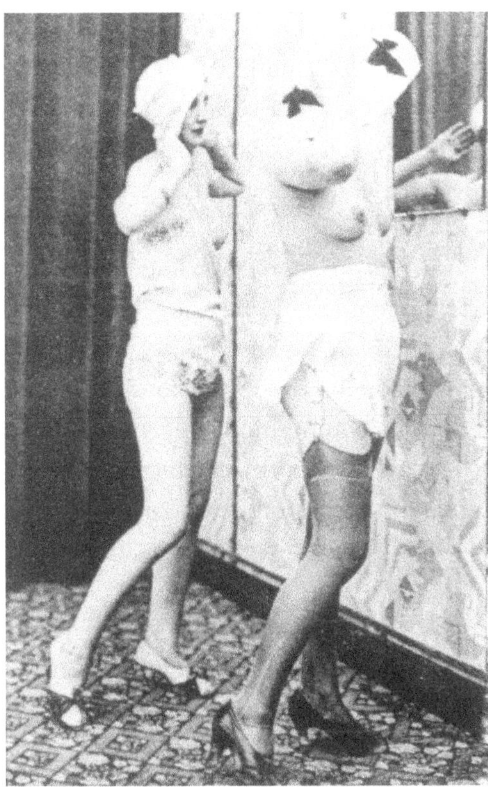

Fig. 8.1. Unknown photographer, untitled. From *Cámara secreta.* Courtesy of Monte Avila Editores Latinoamericana.

the afternoon [my translation]). In Flaubert's passage, nature has been transformed into a feminine body that is both sensual and religious. On the title page of the book, Flaubert's quote is juxtaposed with a photograph of two women facing a mirror (fig. 8.1), which gives us a partial glimpse of the armpit of one of the models. A persistent dismemberment of the female body permeates the visual presentation of the entire book; a series of small photographs, added at the bottom of every page, presents a fetishistic inventory of eyes, mouths, breasts, buttocks, and feet. Since these are fragmented copies of the same photographs that illustrate the text, this phantasmagoric gallery of isolated body parts works also as a sequence of self-referential quotes. Floating at the margins of the written, the small photographs act as the book's unconscious, promoting an alternative reading. *Cámara secreta* simultaneously creates a primary text and its memory, a subliminal meta-discourse in which those images are allowed to circulate out of context, acting oneirically or hallucinogenically. The book "dreams" itself, celebrating and fantasizing its own textuality, acting out the same desires it attempts to describe.

Structurally, then, *Cámara secreta* performs an onanistic ritual. The book is divided into seven sections: 1. "Zola y amante" (Zola and lover); 2."La azotea"

(The roof-top terrace); 3. "Café Luxemburgo, Café Paradiso" (Luxemburg Café, Paradise Café); 4. "Arabia" (Araby); 5. "La amortajada" (The shrouded woman); 6. "México, 1930. Relato" (Mexico, 1930. Story); and 7. "Cámara secreta. Ensayo-relato" (Hidden camera. essay-story). Topics discussed in the first five sections are presented as fiction in section six, while section seven serves as a recapitulation of the entire work. This progression is far from accidental. The subtitle of *Cámara secreta* is "Ensayos apócrifos y relatos verosímiles de la fotografía erótica" (Apocryphal essays and verisimilar stories about erotic photography). The essays have been fictionalized and the stories could, after all, be true. The organization of the book is eminently musical: names, bodies, and previously discussed allusions are constantly being recalled, giving shape to a contrapuntal composition, elegantly elaborated, a piece of chamber music, "música de cámara." In Spanish, *cámara* means both "room," or "chamber," and "camera"; profiting from this pun, Rodríguez Juliá discloses for us a mental museum, providing an anatomy—in more than one sense—of his tricks as a chronicler and writer.

To Celebrate and to Cerebrate: The Writer Behind the Lens

Cámara secreta begins with "Zola y amante" (Zola and lover), a discussion of the French novelist's photographic experiments. But this is not just another variant of the jaded equation between realism and photography. Rodríguez Juliá intentionally undoes that cliché by stating that Zola's real aim is to reproduce desire, not appearance. Zola

> entendió la fotografía no sólo como un medio para documentar el contorno más cercano, sino también como una manera de adentramiento a su más íntima autoimagen . . . El mejor arte fotográfico no es una mera revelación de superficies; los grandes fotógrafos han adivinado ese lugar insinuado desde la piel . . . el espacio del deseo. (*Cámara secreta* 7)
>
> *(Zola understood the photograph not only as a medium for documenting immediate reality, but also as a means of penetrating into his most intimate self-image . . . The best photographic art is more than a mere revelation of surfaces; the great photographers have captured what the skin only insinuates . . . the space of Desire)*[1]

This analysis rejects a purely descriptive assessment of Zola's photographs, authorizing a hermeneutics of his images. For Rodríguez Juliá, a photograph is a surface that hides its meaning from plain sight; the beholder needs to fix (or fixate on) what each photograph really signifies by finding a story that frames it. To reveal the *unseen* aspects of some of Zola's images, Rodríguez Juliá has to tell the story of how the young laundress Jeanne Rozerot became Zola's lover.

Zola photographs himself as he is planning to photograph Jeanne: "El artista se contempla en el acto de contemplar el deseo como algo propio y también ajeno a él" (*Cámara secreta* 11) (The artist observes himself in the act of contemplating Desire both as something of his own and also foreign to him). Zola, behind one camera, is getting ready to take a photograph of Jeanne's profile; but Zola is actually staging this scene in front of another camera, which in turn photographs both the writer and the model. As he photographs himself looking at Jeanne, Zola has transformed himself into a voyeur who also shares his fantasies with others. Zola has joined two self-portraits into a single photograph; his image merges, in one complex shot, invisibility with visibility, the objective and the subjective. Zola's double exposure is proposing both a "celebration" and a "cerebration" of his lover. In Puerto Rico, the colloquial expression "hacer cerebrito" ("to cerebrate") describes a person who looks at another body lustily, celebrating its sex appeal. Rodríguez Juliá explains the conceptual link between "celebration" and "cerebration" by analyzing Gustave Courbet's painting "The Origin of the World." Courbet's famous canvas presents a detailed image of a woman's naked body, but her face is not included in the picture, turning her depersonalized body into a paradigmatic icon of the "female impulse." The almost excessive verisimilitude of the painting simultaneously expresses a *celebration* of female flesh and the meticulous skill or *cerebration* process that lies behind Courbet's realistic technique.

In Zola's photograph, the frisson arising from the contrast between celebration (a portrait of his lover) and cerebration (Zola, using two cameras in order to take two pictures instead of one) posits a tension between desire and art. More than photographing the desired object, Zola has managed to take a photograph of Desire itself. For Rodríguez Juliá, a photograph becomes an image only if it comes to insinuate something that is not explicit or evident. If this potential is not fulfilled, the photograph remains a superficial photocopy. This axiom is exemplified in the second section of *Cámara secreta*, "La azotea" (The roof-top terrace). Rodríguez Juliá introduces the differences between "naked" and "nude" bodies in terms of an acute contrast between the voyeur who celebrates and the artist who cerebrates. Rodríguez Juliá relies here on former discussions about the nude body by Kenneth Clark (23–54) and John Berger (45–64). While the nude body is usually the result of deliberate posing, the naked body can be the result of an improvised picture, and, as such, sometimes it can be the outcome of an intrusion into a person's privacy. As photographed by Edward Weston, lying on a roof in a series of now canonized images, Tina Modotti's body is slowly transformed by the artist into a depersonalized shape, "la concepción fotográfica del desnudo femenino" (*Cámara secreta* 25) (the photographic conceptualization of the feminine naked body). Decentering her face or even avoiding it, Weston's photograph emphasizes Modotti's body. Weston is not only trying to capture Modotti's features; he is actually abstracting her subjectivity from the photograph in order to show her body as pure form, line, geometry. Celebration is being superseded by cerebration; the concrete person is being transformed into a ghost. Susan Sontag has called attention to the illusory character of photographs: "first of all a photograph is not only an image (as a painting is an image), an interpretation of the real; it is also a trace, something directly stenciled off the real, like a footprint or a death mask . . . A photograph is never less than the registering of an emanation (light waves reflected by objects)—a material vestige of the subject" (54).

Rodríguez Juliá compares the ghostly condition of some of Weston's nudes with the altered states of consciousness induced by hashish. The hallucinatory power of the drug to create liminal spaces serves here as a metaphor for the erotic photograph. Weston's move from the nude-as-portrait to the nude-as-design leaves Tina Modotti's body in a conceptual limbo, where her emanation is neither a purely aesthetic object nor a psychological portrait. Once a body inhabits this ambivalence, the meaning of its nakedness is not defined by the photographer's eye any longer, but by the beholder's desire. The trace of Modotti's naked body will signify either art or pornography (or both) depending on the kind of story it incites in the person that views the photograph. The pornographic hinges on this conflict between the naked body as the vestige of an actual person and its depersonalized reduction to mere form. Pornography is not in the image itself, but in the stories the beholder develops in order to create a connection between art and experience, between the object presented by the photograph (Modotti's naked body) and his or her subjectivity (the observer). The remainder of *Cámara secreta* focuses on the search for this enigmatic and evasive fissure through which the visual meets the verbal. To explain how the exposure of a naked body becomes a narrative of our desire for it, Rodríguez Juliá moves into an analysis of voyeurism.

Theorizing the Voyeur: The Body and the Eye

In "Café Luxemburgo, Café Paradiso," Rodríguez Juliá reacts to a photograph by Cheryl Koralic that is, in turn, based on another photograph by Brassai (fig. 8.2). The image consists of three women, standing in front of a mirror in a bar. One of them is turning her head, "looking back" at us. Her gesture represents to Rodríguez Juliá a traumatic episode, in which the photograph ceases to be impersonal. Since the woman is staring at him, the photograph becomes the sign of a reciprocal relation. Laura Mulvey claims that women's bodies are exposed in order to "connote to-be-looked-at-ness." The active gaze of the male (or female) observer is thus contrasted with the passive display of female flesh: "The presence of woman is an indispensable

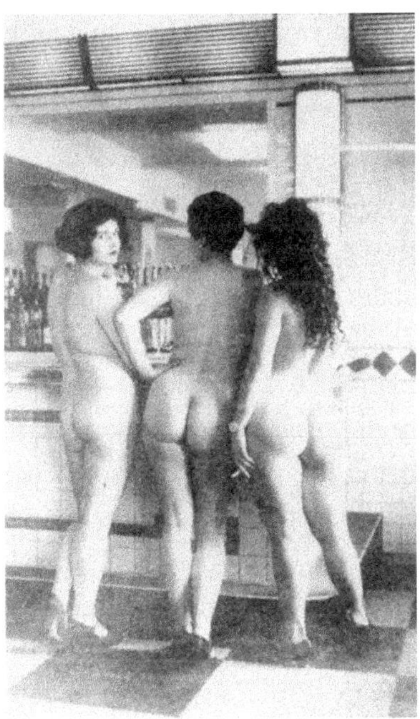

Fig. 8.2. Cheryl Koralic, "Café Luxemburg," published in *Interview*. From *Cámara secreta*. Courtesy of Monte Avila Editores Latinoamericana.

element of spectacle in normal narrative film, yet her visual presence tends to work against the development of a story-line, to freeze the flow of action in moments of erotic contemplation" (188). Voyeurism is not dialogical; by looking back at him, the woman in Koralic's photograph challenges Rodríguez Juliá's scopophilia, his pleasure in looking at her. To regain his position as a voyeur, Rodríguez Juliá decides to reconceptualize Koralic's photograph as a striptease. The high heels, the earrings, and the wristwatch that one of the women wears would suggest a nude-in-progress, an unfinished uncovering, a theatrical scene in front of which the beholder becomes a voyeur again, an audience. Voyeurism can be reestablished if the photograph is reencoded as theatre, as spectacle; only the illusion of a plot line can restore to these naked bodies part of their original mystery, their "to-be-looked-at-ness."

While explaining the interaction between observer and painting during the Enlightenment, Michael Fried remarked that our reaction to a painting depends on how the figures *within* relate to the spectator *without* (1–30). According to him, figures that seem to be self-absorbed or whose attention is otherwise engaged exclude the onlooker. However, those figures that glance at us or seem to be conscious of our gaze provoke an effect of theatricality. "Café Luxemburgo, Café Paradiso" explores a similar set of distinctions with an emphasis bordering on the obsessive. When an erotic photograph does not include the beholder directly, it allows the spectator to act as a voyeur. But if the erotic image engages our gaze directly, it makes us all accomplices; in that case, *voyeurism* veers into *exhibitionism*. The voyeur becomes either an actor or a writer; the photograph becomes a scene. The emergence of this theatrical effect is seen by Rodríguez Juliá as an expulsion from paradise, "ese lugar donde la ensoñación erótica del otro cuerpo es posible sin el auxilio de la fantasía" (*Cámara secreta* 43) (that location where erotic dreamings about another body are possible without the aid of fantasizing). To a certain extent, voyeurism resembles a state of innocence, a place where language (fantasy) is not needed yet, "la fuerte añoranza histérica por conocer el momento en que fui deseo, sólo deseo" (*Cámara secreta* 39) (the strong and hysterical nostalgia for recognizing the moment when I was Desire, only Desire). To talk about Koralic's photograph is to recognize that the original paradise of pure "erotic contemplation" has been lost.

Rodríguez Juliá associates the failure of voyeurism to preserve the paradise of "pure desire" with the experience of leaving the womb: "Al asomarnos al mundo perdimos el Paraíso, entre tantos pujos, viscosidades y pliegues" (*Cámara secreta* 39) (As we come into the world we lose paradise among all the urges, viscosities, and folds). Erotic fantasy—either through theatre or narrative—enacts an effort to regain "la memoria histérica . . . adivinar la cualidad del deseo anterior a nuestro nacimiento" (*Cámara secreta* 43) (the hysterical memory . . . to divine the quality of Desire preceding our birth). Two story lines are suggested in order to recapture the photograph's capacity to entice its observer. If we look again at the three women and take into consideration their vulnerability, their *mortality*, we will effect "un encuentro no del todo imposible con su propia sombra, el cuerpo que permanece desnudo a pesar de la tumba; el cuerpo aún deseado, el espejismo, esa momificación que es la fotografía" (*Cámara secreta* 43) (a not completely impossible encounter with its own shadow, the body that still remains naked in spite of the grave, the body still desired, a mirage, that mummification that is the photograph). Rodríguez Juliá also includes in this section the voices of three female characters, three fictionalized versions of the women seen in Koralic's picture: Teresa, Mónica, and Carmen.

For Rodríguez Juliá, erotic story telling remains a lesser form of voyeurism; once a naked body is inserted into a scene, the potential for sexual satisfaction unmediated by language has already been dismantled. Between the partially disempowered voyeur and Koralic's photograph, fantasy deploys now a Lacanian breach, a broken suture. The voyeur's subjectivity is permanently split by a disparity between "pure" Desire and its representation. In order to look again at Koralic's image, the use of extraphotographic means such as analogy, description, and narration is almost inevitable, but these verbal practices never substitute or completely communicate the "pure desire" of watching without being watched: "la fotografía de esas tres mujeres es una metáfora de algo imposible" (*Cámara secreta* 43) (the photograph of those three women is a metaphor for something impossible). Paradise is never regained once the voyeur is expelled from it: the rest is literature.

After the Fall: The Narratives of Seeing

Up to this point, Rodríguez Juliá has explored the connections between erotic pictures and story telling by emphasizing how desire disturbs the boundaries between the objective representation of the female body (its "cerebration" into an artistic form, the "nude") and our subjective enjoyment of it (its "celebration" as part of an erotic narrative). In their photographs, Emile Zola and Edward Weston wrestle with this tension. Jeanne Rozerot and Tina Modotti are both objectified into art, depersonalized by the camera. Nonetheless, what the observer of those photographs wants to understand and share is the attraction that made those bodies desirable; to reenact that original moment at which the images need to be transformed into stories. Once reduced to its photographic trace, the female body becomes a ghostly presence that, like a drug, deploys a liminal space where imagination and reality are inextricably entangled. Pornography thrives in that liminal location, and so does literature. For the voyeur, this translation from the realm of the flesh into the realm of language conveys a sense of loss, an eviction from the paradise of "pure" desire. Fantasy is the outcome of that frustration. Language vainly tries to reproduce the allure of unmediated desire by falling into narrative, relocating the naked body within a theatrical scene or inventing a story that reactivates its original attraction.

Starting in section four, *Cámara secreta* explores some of the potential plots or scenes through which "erotic contemplation" can be transferred into a textual "fantasy." The true structural function of "Café Luxemburgo, Café Paradiso" is, in a way, to naturalize a *collage* of different genres: essay, fiction, and literary criticism. Through sections three, four, and five of *Cámara secreta*, a deliberate mingling of discourses juxtaposes references to D. H. Lawrence, James Joyce, Luis Palés Matos, and Stendhal with photographs by Álvarez Bravo and Edward Weston and a number of photographs of Frida Kahlo. In sections four and five ("Arabia," "La amortajada"), the text continues reevaluating the relationship between photographs and words. Fiction is able to compensate for "la pérdida súbita del deseo entendido como aura, como nimbo fantasmático" (*Cámara secreta* 54) (the sudden loss of Desire understood as aura, as phantasmic nimbus). Photographs reproduce an external reality, freezing it in space and time; but only language is capable of reenacting the state of desire that motivated the photograph in the first place. The flat surface of the photograph discloses the fundamental failure of the world to satisfy fantasies: "En ese empobrecimiento la realidad social ocupa toda la imagen" (*Cámara secreta* 54) (In that impoverishment, social reality takes over the whole image). If it fails to provoke our desire, a photograph ends up being a mere documentation of reality. Only the incentive of a "nombre mágico" (magic noun) can turn perception into a *personal* experience: "Surge la ansiedad de recuperar el sitio perdido, aquel *Paradiso*: así asistimos al comienzo de la literatura, de cualquier arte" (*Cámara secreta* 54) (The anxious need arises to regain the lost place, that *Paradise*: thus we are present at the beginning of literature, of every art). Literature replaces the photograph when Benjamin's aura fails, when the image posits an excess of reality:

> Convertir una imagen en realidad social es arriesgarnos a degradarla, pervertirla, empobrecerla. Y ¿no sería la fotografía—con su inescapable verosimilitud—el arte más peligroso para cualquier imagen del deseo? (*Cámara secreta* 55)
>
> (To convert an image into social reality is to run the risk of degrading it, perverting it, impoverishing it. And might not photography—with its inescapable verisimilitude—be the most dangerous art when it comes to any image of desire whatsoever?)

In section six—the short story "Mexico, 1930"—the dualities already exposed by *Cámara secreta* (naked and nude, voyeurism and reciprocity, image and word) are all reconceptualized once more in terms of a debate on copulation versus fornication. In this new variation, it is an excess of matrimonial reality that provokes the need to fantasize. Matrimony, like the photograph, is unable to produce the magic word, the sense of incantation that imagined pleasures are able to evoke. In "México, 1930," a man trying to overcome a hangover masturbates as he recalls the three most important women of his erotic life. The bedroom where the male character spends the worst stage of this hangover is akin to a "camera oscura." He treasures in his briefcase "dos libros de fotos y postales pornográficas de la *belle époque*—o sea, pornografía hasta los años veinte, treinta y cuarenta, los de su *hysteria*—y todos los adminículos de su afición secreta a la marihuana y la madre cocaína" (*Cámara secreta* 98) (two photo albums and postcards from the *belle époque*—that is, pornography from the '20s, '30s and '40s, the years of his *hysteria*—plus all the paraphernalia related to his secret attachment to marihuana and mother cocaine). The unstoppable urge that compels the character to verbalize these photographs reintroduces the issue of pornographic literature. The photographs in the briefcase are pornographic not only for their content but also for their capacity to generate their own stories in the character's imagination. One photograph in particular, apparently taken in Mexico in the 1930s, shows two women together. This image provokes a series of sexual fantasies that include a ménage à trois and even homosexuality: The character symbolically licks himself through a vanilla popsicle, and imagines himself to be sodomized because his prostate hurts as he ejaculates.

In the "Mexican" photograph described by the character, one woman lies on a bed while another woman provides her oral stimulation. The face of the reclining female is visible, but that of the other female is not (fig. 8.3). The character's compulsion to

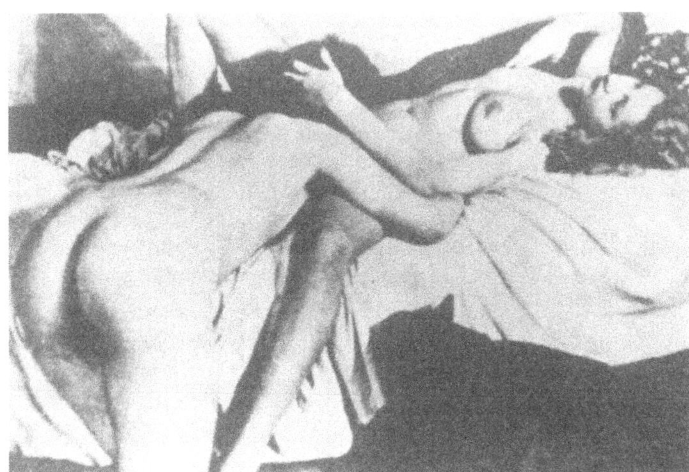

Fig. 8.3. Unknown photographer, untitled. From *Cámara secreta*. Courtesy of Monte Avila Editores Latinoamericana.

narrate this old picture shows that he considers it an insufficient image. At first, the naked bodies in the photograph are just two strangers, two depersonalized bodies. The photograph fails to excite him unless it is transformed into a story, *his* story; the "Mexican" picture thus becomes a *theatrum* where the character personalizes his desire, dramatizing his dual alienation from both his wife and his own lover. After looking for a while, the character covers his eyes with a mask. The important element here is not the picture (which, like a drug, only serves as a stimulant); what really matters is the fantasy it leads to in the character's mind. For Rodríguez Juliá, pornography is not a mood or an effect but a narrative device that mediates between a depersonalized *image* and a personalized *fantasy*. Rodríguez Juliá seems to propose that a pornographic picture—all pictures—lose their *aura* unless they are reconceptualized as dependent on fiction.

In her analysis of eighteenth-century French pornography, Lucienne Frappier-Mazur states that "[t]he truth of the obscene word . . . is that it manifests the dependence of eroticism on the imaginary" (218). To shape its own imaginary, *Cámara secreta* both constructs and deconstructs itself, laying bare its own strategies. The final essay, "Cámara secreta. Ensayo-relato" (Hidden camera. Essay-story), schematically re-enacts the itinerary of the book as a whole. There are three sections: "La desprevenida" (The unprepared woman), "El cuadro" (The painting), and "Cuba, 1930." The structure of each part is based on a series of polarizations. In this essay-story Rodríguez Juliá reviews the typology of the nude. We are shown the "desnudo desprevenido" (unprepared nakedness), the body surprised by a secret camera (or the candid camera), seen through "el ojo del ligón" (*Cámara secreta* 117) (the eyes of the Peeping Tom). The body surprised by the camera deploys "una condición radicalmente *temporal*, fragmentaria, fugaz e instantánea" (*Cámara secreta* 119) (a radically *temporary*, fragmented, fleeting, and instantaneous condition). In the

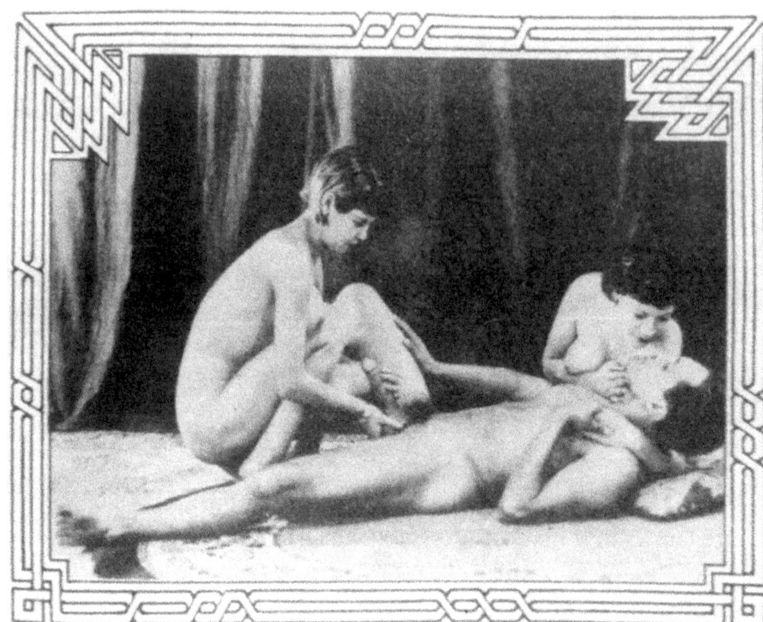

Fig. 8.4. Unknown photographer, "Cuba, 1930." From *Cámara secreta*. Courtesy of Monte Avila Editores Latinoamericana.

"desnudo posado" (posed nakedness, nude), on the contrary, everything is deliberate. The second part, "El cuadro," reintroduces the challenge of how to understand the pornographic. A photograph taken in "Cuba, 1930" shows two women who seductively caress a fully aroused mulatto (fig. 8.4). The composition formulates "un escenario, mejor dicho, es una escena donde la escenografía rehuye cualquier concreción histórica" (*Cámara secreta* 120) (a stage-set, or rather, it's a scene where the scenography avoids any historical specificity whatsoever).

"Cuba, 1930" allows for at least two alternative readings. In one potential reading of the picture, "[i]ntentamos conseguir que la foto nos hable, ella sola con toda su elocuencia. Trataríamos entonces de adivinar su justo valor dentro de una sintaxis mayor, de un discurso" (*Cámara secreta* 121) (we attempt to get the photograph to speak to us, the photograph alone, with all its eloquence. And then we could try to gauge its true value within a broader syntax, a discourse). The image can be seen for itself, without any links to its social background, or the image can be read *vis-à-vis* its history, as if it were an archival document. In both cases, something is still missing: the incantatory element that reinstalls the photograph's aura by restoring its "pura capacidad invocatoria" (*Cámara secreta* 121) (its pure capacity to invoke). Rodríguez Juliá finds a way out of this impasse by claiming that the photograph's title, "Cuba, 1930," is an invitation to create a story:

> El calce me obliga al relato, a la amplificación de la imagen hacia sus connotaciones históricas, míticas y anecdóticas. El calce funciona

> como una invocación que me obliga a tener un atisbo de la sintaxis mayor, de ese sitio donde ésta ha perdido su cualidad meramente formal para . . . lograr un efecto de encantación . . . alcanzando prontamente los linderos del relato. (*Cámara secreta* 120–21)
>
> (The photograph's title imposes storytelling, forces me to amplify the image toward its historical, mythical, and anecdotal connotations. The title functions as an invocation that obligates me to get a glimpse of the overall syntax, of that place where the photograph has lost its merely formal quality . . . in order to achieve an incantatory effect . . . rapidly reaching the edges of the story.)

The fluctuations between third and first person in the previous passage reflect a pendular motion from the personal to the depersonalized. The scenes in *Cámara secreta* devour themselves and replay their ideas constantly. The book is a self-consuming artifact. This is why the stories take place in a "recámara," or closed chamber, where the character is masturbating: "La masturbación es la recámara secreta por excelencia . . . la memoria de otros cuerpos" (*Cámara secreta* 120) (Masturbation is the secret chamber par excellence . . . the memory of other bodies). In this way, Rodríguez Juliá argues—as Walt Whitman did in *Song of Myself*—for a valid poetics of onanism, in which autoeroticism replicates the act of writing from, and about, the body.

Twice-Told Bodies: From Monologue to Dialogue

In one of his notes for the unfinished *Arcades Project*, Walter Benjamin points out how, during the 1800s,

> a series of lithographs . . . showed women reclining voluptuously on ottomans in a draperied, crepuscular boudoir, and these prints bore inscriptions: *On the Banks of the Tagus, On the Banks of the Neva, On the Banks of the Seine*, and so forth. The Guadalquivir, the Rhone, the Rhine, the Aar, the Tamis—all had their turn. That a national costume might have distinguished these female figures one from another may be safely doubted. It was up to the legénde, the caption inscribed beneath them, to conjure a fantasy landscape over the represented interiors. (213)

Like Flaubert's *Salambó*, these captions profited from an orientalist vein fostered by Western imperialism. In *Cámara secreta*, Rodríguez Juliá also unfolds his own theory of the caption; but in his case, instead of the exotic geographies of the East, it is literature that casts its shadow over the "represented interiors" of his photographs. An erotic picture conjures a fantasy landscape more effectively when its observer frames it with the incantatory spell of a "magic noun." The presence of a caption reveals that photographic representation is incapable, by itself, of reproducing the experience of desire. Without language, the naked body exposed in a photograph is merely a signifier that fails to signify its own erotic potential. Some of the "magic" captions suggested by Rodríguez Juliá are literary works: "Araby" (James Joyce, *Dubliners*); "Kalahari" (a poem by Puerto Rican author Luis Palés Matos), and "Cartagena" (the title of one of his own novels, published in 1997). The function of these captions is to reactivate the aura lost by the photographs; like drugs, these words have the power to "conjure" and create an effect of liminality, an ambiguous space where fantasies are perceived as "real."

For Rodríguez Juliá, pornography is the process of transforming an impersonal picture into a personalized narrative or theatrical scene, in which the observer "acts out" his or her own fantasies. The last section of *Cámara secreta* attempts to reduce the distance between the imaginary of fantasy and the actual performance of the sexual act. The narrator of the "essay-story" ventures to share his erotic briefcase with Teresa, one of the women whose voices were included in "Café Luxemburgo, Café Paradiso." Teresa initiates a dialogue with the narrator about the photographs that summarizes some of the book's allusions and themes: Zola, Tina Modotti, Koralic, the Freudian fixation with the mother, and the photograph named "Cuba, 1930." Teresa suggests extending an invitation to one of her friends, Ada, for a ménage à trois. This new fantasy includes photographing that shared moment and calling it "Paris, 1979." By creating its own photograph, *Cámara secreta* is finally able to cross the line that separates the personal from the depersonalized. It is possible to see the inclusion of Teresa's "voice" as a moment in which the active gaze of the voyeur accepts the intervention of an equally active female subject. On a few occasions, *Cámara secreta* seems to be doing exactly that. In "La azotea," Weston's photographs of Tina Modotti's naked body are juxtaposed with Modotti's "memoirs." By providing the women in Koralic's photograph with the voices of his own fictional characters (Teresa, Mónica, Carmen), Rodríguez Juliá also works against their objectification as simple consumer goods. The inclusion of these "voices" in the text is not entirely successful in its attempt to provide women with a less objectified position. Due to the fact that they are given a "voice" only through the fantasy of their male observer, women speak here only to the extent that they serve the beholder's quest for gratification, his desire to rescue the lost aura of the picture. Nonetheless, the fact that the book concludes with a dialogue indicates that the text is finally trying to deploy a libidinal field based on reciprocity: the aesthetics of the voyeur have been replaced by a shared fantasy. Solitary pleasure has found company—at least for the time being.

In *Cámara secreta*, pornography always draws attention to the uncertainties of sexual fulfillment. Rodríguez Juliá compares this uncertainty to the failure of the photograph to exist outside a narrative frame. Berger and Mohr suggest that the fragmentary quality of any photograph tends to give the impression that images are always somehow incomplete. The spectator responds to this ambiguity by reframing the photograph within a narrative process, converting it into part of an idea, a "plot" (119–29). As opposed to Berger and Mohr, Rodríguez Juliá claims that we *do not* verbalize a photograph in order to complete the partial information that it offers, but rather in order to reestablish its aura. According to *Cámara secreta*, the photograph encourages verbalization because it is only through language that we can recapture its phantasmatic mood, the "magic noun" that photographs have traumatized with their radical dose of concrete reality. The aura lies not in the photograph, nor in the text, but in between them. Photographs should provide an experience of the world, not merely a copy of it; their reality is more relevant than their realism. Rodríguez Juliá believes that only a dialogue between image and text provides a competent frame for a narratology of Desire. To look is already to narrate. Pornography is never found exclusively in the photograph, but in the process of verbalizing it, of dramatizing it. Rodríguez Juliá's thesis also shares an affinity with some postmodern evaluations of the photograph such as Douglas Crimp's. In Crimp's opinion, the postmodern photograph attempts to question the notion of aura as established by Walter Benjamin, underlining the fact that any image is also a copy, "always-already-seen" (172–79). In accepting the limitations of photography, we are left with a verbal construct derived from it. Through the photograph, Desire transforms its hysteria into history, into story telling.

When referring to *Puertorriqueños* (1988), Aurea María Sotomayor declares that "al organizar su mirada y por virtud de su interpretación, Rodríguez Juliá se convierte en el fotógrafo de una foto ya tomada: doble nostalgia de la selección y de la construcción de la imagen" (147) (by organizing his gaze and by virtue of his interpretation, Rodríguez Juliá becomes the photographer of a photo already taken: a dual nostalgia for the selection and construction of the image [my translation]). Nostalgia, also, for the aura and the original fascination that motivated the photograph in the first place, that solitary moment when the observer "was" pure Desire. Rodríguez Juliá wishes to fantasize the real, to achieve a state of continuous poetic trance in front of nakedness. That state of perpetual voyeurism is a chimera; to look *again* is already a performative gesture, a re-presentation, in and of itself. We cannot realize without fantasizing (or celebrate without cerebrating). "The visual is essentially pornographic," says Fredric Jameson, "which is to say that it has its end in rapt, mindless fascination . . . which asks us to stare at the world as though it were a naked body" (6). That is precisely what *Cámara secreta* invites us to do, but Rodríguez Juliá takes Jameson's dictum one step further. He wants us to see the world as if it were the photograph of a naked body, a world already mediated by our desire to *look again*, to re-cognize it.

Notes

1. All translations from *Cámara secreta* are my own.

References

Bal, Mieke. *The Mottled Screen: Reading Proust Visually*. Stanford, CA: Stanford University Press, 1997.

Barthes, Roland. "The Photographic Message." In *Image, Music, Text*. New York: Hill and Wang, 1977, 15–31.

Benjamin, Walter. *The Arcades Project*. Cambridge: Harvard University Press, 1999.

Berger, John. *Ways of Seeing*. New York: Penguin Books, 1977.

Berger, John, and Joan Mohr. *Another Way of Telling*. New York: Vintage International, 1982.

Bourdieu, Pierre, et al. *Photography. A Middle-Brow Art*. Stanford, CA: Stanford University Press, 1990.

Clark, Kenneth. *The Nude: A Study in Ideal Form*. New York: Doubleday Anchor Books, 1956.

Crimp, Douglas. "On the Photographic Activity of Post-Modernism." In *Post-Modernism. A Reader*. Ed. Thomas Docherty. New York: Columbia UP, 1993, 172–79.

Frappier-Mazur, Lucienne. "On Truth and the Obscene Word in Eighteenth Century French Pornography." In *The Invention of Pornography. Obscenity and the Origins of Modernity, 1500–1800*. Ed. Lynn Hunt. New York: Zone Books, 1993, 203–21.

Fried, Michael. *Absorption and Theatricality: Painting and the Beholder in the Age of Diderot*. Berkeley: University of California Press, 1980.

Jameson, Fredric. *Signatures of the Visible*. New York: Routledge, 1992.

Mulvey, Laura. "Visual Pleasure and Narrative Cinema." In *Performance Analysis*. Eds. Colin Counsell and Laurie Wolf. London: Routledge, 2001, 185–93.

Parker, Holt N. "Love's Body Anatomized: The Ancient Erotic Handbooks and the Rhetoric of Sexuality." In *Pornography and Representation in Greece and Rome*. Ed. Amy Richlin. London: Oxford University Press, 1992, 90–111.

Rodríguez Juliá, Edgardo. *Cámara secreta*. Caracas: Monte Avila Editores, 1994.

______. *Campeche o los diablejos de la melancolia*. San Juan, Puerto Rico: Instituto de Cultura Puertorriqueña, 1986.

______. *La noche oscura del niño Avilés*. Río Piedras, Puerto Rico: Huracán, 1984.

______. *Puertorriqueños*. Río Piedras, Puerto Rico: Plaza Mayor, 1988.

______. *La renuncia del héroe Baltasar*. Río Piedras, Puerto Rico: Cultural, 1974.

Sontag, Susan. *On Photography*. New York: Anchor Books, 1990.

Sotomayor, Aurea María. "Escribir la Mirada." In *Las tribulaciones de Juliá*. Ed. Juan Duchesne Winter. San Juan, Puerto Rico: Instituto de Cultura Puertorriqueña, 1992.

Chapter Nine

"Things Were Different Then"

Photographic and Narrative Construction of Loss in Eduardo Belgrano Rawson's *Fuegia*

Magdalena Perkowska-Álvarez

For my mother, Maria Perkowska, with love and hope

American critic William J. Mitchell uses the terms *pictorial turn* (11) and *culture of spectators* (3) to allude to the overwhelming presence of images—paintings, photographs, television, and cinema—in our daily encounters with reality.[1] This saturation by the visual has changed our perception of reality and deepened our understanding of representation, which is no longer conceived as a "homogeneous field or grid of relationships governed by a single principle, but as a multidimensional and heterogeneous terrain, a collage or patchwork quilt assembled over time out of fragments" (419). Since at the turn of the twentieth century reality has become less and less "real" and more textual and pictorial, representation is seen as a complex practice in which diverse strategies and techniques intervene: it is necessary to resort to both words and images, the verbal and the visual, in order to capture the ever-changing and more elusive face of our world. Responding to this cultural need, contemporary Latin American literature has produced a large panoply of hybrid texts, combining a variety of arts and media, that explore representational dialogue and/or tension created through this interaction and reflect on memory, history, identity, (post)modernity, and ideology. The texts that incorporate photographs and narrative are one instance of this interartistic approach to representation. They are not confined to the boundaries of one specific genre; urban chronicle, essay, and novel lend their formal shape to the interplay of images and words. Among them, the novel presents an especially interesting case, because photography and fiction seem to belong to different ontological orders, and their conjunction within fictional space challenges and transgresses previously accepted limits between reality and fiction.

Several contemporary Latin American authors have published novels that unite narrative and photographs in their fictional frames and, therefore, are engaged in both telling a story about the world (or, rather, a fragment of it), and showing images of it. *La llegada (Crónica con "ficción")* by José Luis González (Puerto Rico, 1980), *Fuegia* by Eduardo Belgrano Rawson (Argentina, 1991), *Tinísima* by Elena Poniatowska (Mexico, 1992), *La destrucción del reino* by Miguel Gutiérrez y Julio Olavarría (Peru, 1992), *La mujer de Strasser* by Héctor Tizón (Argentina, 1997), and *El daño* by Seatiel Alatriste (Mexico, 2000) are among the most significant of these novels. All of them belong to such subgenres as historiographic metafiction and historical or biographical novel, which merge documentary and fictional discourses and lay claim to historical personages and events. Barbara Foley calls this category of fictional writing "the documentary novel" (25). Located on the borderline between fictional and factual discourses, the documentary novel "invokes familiar novelistic conventions, but it requires the reader to accept certain textual elements—characters, incidents, or actual documents—as possessing referents in the world of the reader" (26). This explains a seemingly natural and neutral way in which the photographs are integrated into the text in these novels: they do not seem to be a disrupting element, but rather a complementary visual document, an element of both verisimilitude and veracity that corroborates facts enunciated through the narrative. This perception of the function of photographs in the novel is closely connected to some common and still persistent views on photography itself, signaled by Susan Sontag: "Photography has the unappealing reputation of being the most realistic . . . of the mimetic arts" (51). While Sontag calls photography an art, highlighting its creative and interpretative aspects in her book *On Photography*, such widely known theorists as André Bazin and Rudolf Arnheim have defined photography as a mechanical reproduction of reality: the former claims that "[t]he photographic image is the object itself" (14), and photography is a mechanical process "in the making of which man plays no part" (12); while the latter affirms that "the physical objects themselves print their image by means of the optical and chemical action of light" (155). From this point of view, photography is not representation but a faithful, objective, and authentic transcription of reality, perceived even as a fragment of it. This presumption, which stresses the ontological relation of the photograph to reality, explains the interest and significance attributed to photographs as documents that offer transparent evidence by registering and illustrating reality as it is.[2]

Although these conceptions of photography have been challenged, they prove to be a good starting point for a reflection on photographs in a novel, precisely because they conceive of a photograph as a fragment of reality.[3] If a photograph is a piece of reality, then its insertion into the fictional world of a novel may be compared with the inclusion of newspaper clips in a cubist painting. It can be argued, therefore, that photography enters the novelistic space through the techniques of *collage* and *montage*: as in a cubist painting, the simulacrum of a life-world breaks into the fictional reality of the narrative, the visual sign irrupts into the verbal. Collage transfers materials from one context to another; that is to say, it consists of lifting "un certain nombre d'éléments dans des œuvres, des objets, des messages déjà existant, et à les intégrer dans une création nouvelle pour produire une totalité originale où se manifestent des ruptures de types divers" (Groupe Mu 13) (a number of elements in existing works, objects and messages, and integrating them into a new creation in order to produce an original whole that exhibits a variety of ruptures).[4] Montage is the "dissemination" and "assemblage" of these materials into the new setting (Ulmer 84). Together, collage and montage dismantle the illusion of reality, or the "reality effect" (Barthes, "The Reality Effect" 148) that photographs—or rather certain traditional perceptions of photographs—might carry into the text. According to Walter Benjamin, in montage "the superimposed element disrupts the context in which it is inserted" ("The Author as Producer" 778); this disruptive, subversive mechanics is its most relevant feature, because it opens multiple textual breaches and allows for unsuspected meanings and discursive complications and complexities to unfold, revealing the heterogeneous nature of our conceptions and representations of reality.[5]

The purpose of the present study is to examine this disruptive interaction of photographs and narrative in relation to the perception of time and the concept of loss in *Fuegia*, the third novel by the Argentine writer and journalist Eduardo Belgrano Rawson.[6] *Fuegia* recovers the history and memory of a people condemned to disappear: the Ona and Yagán Indians of Tierra del Fuego, whose existence and culture were exterminated by white colonizers attracted to this "end of the world" at the end of the nineteenth century by gold, pastureland for sheep breeding, and whale and seal hunting. The novel incorporates thirteen photographs, one on the cover and one at the beginning of each of its twelve chapters.

The title of the novel is an oblique reference to the geographic setting in which its action takes place: Tierra del Fuego, or rather a fictional recreation of its geography and toponymy. The link between the two, the title and the place, is suggested by the similarity with the adjective *fueguino*, but the real connection is established through an association with the nickname of a real person who lived in that place and became one of the first victims of the exploration of the land by white scientists, missionaries, and adventurers,[7] Fuegia Basket, a nine-year-old Yagán girl, together with three other members of her ethnic group, was kidnapped and sent to London. There, all four of them were exhibited to the curious British public as a sort of "scientific sample" and underwent "civilizing" efforts on the part of their "hosts."[8] The title is, thus, symbolic, because besides pointing to a specific geographical region, it also raises the issues of abuse and victimization by making

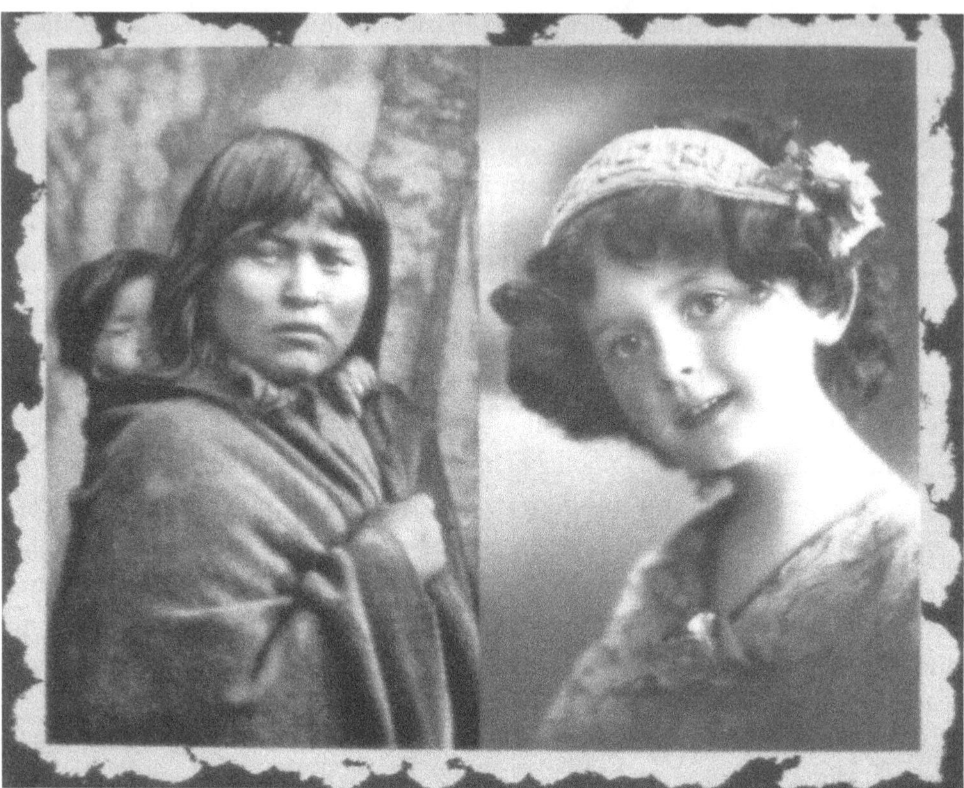

Fig. 9. 1."Camilena Kippa and Her Mother" in *Fuegia* (French Scientific Expedition, 1882, "A Woman and Her Baby"); "Federica" in *Fuegia*. Authorization Musée de l'Homme and Eduardo Belgrano Rawson.

reference to the native people as objectified victims of a colonial culture. Just like the setting of the novel's action, its characters are fictional or only slightly historical: Belgrano Rawson has insisted that *Fuegia* is not a historical novel ("Escribir del oído" 1). It is, however, certain that the novel fictionalizes episodes from the history of Tierra del Fuego mentioned in such texts as *La Patagonia trágica* by José María Borrero, or *La Australia argentina* by Roberto Payró. Both mention bounty hunting by ranchers, hunger, malnutrition, contagion of "white" diseases, destruction of the natural environment on which the survival of indigenous people depended, and the endless advance of the wire fences that marked the appropriated lands and hampered the natural migrational movement of the natives.

Another opening to the events recounted in the novel, besides its title, is a photograph reproduced on the book's cover (fig. 9.1). The image is a montage composed of two photographs from the series incorporated in the novel: the left half represents an indigenous woman with a baby, while the right half represents a white girl. The juxtaposition of these two figures anticipates the juxtaposition of the two cultures in the novel and also reveals some differences: the white girl wears a fine dress and a ribbon, while the Indian woman is wrapped in a coarse poncho; the girl smiles placidly, looking with confidence at the photographer and the reader, while the Indian woman looks to the side, as if she wished to avoid eye contact, or as if something had caught her attention. At first sight, this photograph does not suggest a clash but rather a convergence of differences, pointing out that *Fuegia* as text and Fuegia as territory might be a space of negotiation. After a closer examination, however, some disturbing details begin to stand out. The montage articulates the dichotomy between civilization and barbarism, from the viewpoint of Western prejudices. The smile and direct gaze of the girl inspire trust and associate her image with civilization, while the side glance and somber face of the woman recall stereotypical images of indigenous "barbarism." Seen from this perspective, the montage suggests a conflict reinforced by the formal characteristics of the image.[9] First, the boundary between the two halves is very sharp, implying a radical break between the two worlds, additionally underlined by the use of color: the photograph of the Indian woman is in silver or black–and–white, that of the girl, in sepia. This chromatic distinction functions as a code that conveys a double message. On the one hand, as Sarah Graham-Brown remarks, the color signifies the nature of the represented objects: "a soft sepia print can produce a calm aura of 'things past,' while a black-and-white image may 'convey a sense of harsh "reality"'" (quoted in Burke 22). The color of the cover photograph thus reinforces the dichotomy between "civilization" and "barbarism."

On the other hand, the cover's photomontage also highlights the fact that the two images belong to two different photographic genres: ethnographic photography and portraiture.[10] Both are products of Western culture and ideology, but their object and the perspective they use to define it differ radically, signaling a complex relationship between representation and ideology. The portrait is a celebration of sameness produced by a nostalgic gaze that immortalizes its object. Placed in a family album or living room, it participates in depicting and circumscribing the closed space of an "us," the symbolic reference of which can extend to a larger human community, such as a social class (bourgeoisie) or even a nation.[11] Ethnographic photography is a scrutiny of otherness realized by the scientific gaze of the colonizer, whose Western eye turns its object into a "study case"; in this instance, the photograph images the Other, taking part in the alliance of knowledge and domination and the interplay between representation and imperialism.[12] Another formal characteristic of the image is that reading it from left to right establishes a sequence: the indigenous woman appears first, the white girl second. This signals a chronology, a yesterday and a tomorrow, a past and a future, the indigenous world giving way to the white. The photograph encapsulates the events recounted in Belgrano Rawson's novel and foreshadows their outcome.[13]

One could say that the history narrated in *Fuegia* is a southern version of the Conquest of the Desert, the expansion of the Argentine national project to the far corners of its territory. The expression is an embodiment of silence and erasure to which civilization resorts in order to conceal its foundational violence. "Forgetting, I would even go so far as to say historical error, is a crucial factor in the creation of a nation," in the words of Ernest Renan (11), reminding us that all unity is reached through violence and brutality. Once created and consolidated, the nation must survive, prosper, and progress, and all these steps of the development of nation and civilization are also marked by barbarism, as observed by Walter Benjamin: "There is no document of culture which is not at the same time a document of barbarism" ("On the Concept of History" 392). The word *desierto* (desert) from the Argentine national project designates an empty and uninhabited space, a place of no-presence; it implies, therefore, that the "conquest" means to populate, organize, and cultivate a no-man's land. Through the use of this term, the act of creating it is erased from the discourse. The erasure is double, because the physical and cultural extermination coincides with the symbolic elimination from memory and history of the acts of violence and its victims. According to Ricardo Rey Beckford, silence is another form of violence: "Existen situaciones irreversibles, hechos definitivos, imposibles de enmendar. Pero por irreparable que sea un crimen, por terrible e inexorable que sea un destino, nada más cruel que el silencio, la mordaza" (5) (There are irreversible situations, definitive events, that are impossible to rectify. But as irreparable as a crime may be, as terrible and inexorable as a destiny may be, there is nothing more cruel than silence, the muzzle).

This double erasure of violence and silence is an overwhelming presence in *Fuegia*: the former, through extermination of native people embodied in the indigenous characters of the novel; the latter, through elimination of these events from memory by those responsible or by the authorities (both Argentine and Chilean) who benefited from the "progress" implemented on the islands by the colonizers. The narrator indicates this obliteration of memory (this "desmemoria") in the first chapter, a masterly prologue-epilogue entitled "Escenario" (Setting), which constitutes the frame for story-scenes narrated in the subsequent chapters:

> Cada tanto, algún forastero preguntaba por ellos [los parrikens asesinados]. Periodistas, profesores de historia, gente por el estilo. Querían averiguar la suerte de Camilena Kippa y de Tatesh Walaspaia, mientras tomaban toda clase de notas . . . Pero su principal objetivo era la matanza de Lackawana. Muchos los escuchaban incrédulamente, convencidos de que a las víctimas se las había llevado la gripe o sus propias desavenencias. Sostenían que

> Camilena Kippa sobrevivía en una caleta perdida junto a un hombre treinta años más joven. Pero todo era bastante difuso y los forasteros terminaban el día comiendo una fritada en Grisú, en compañía de algún comedido que los llevaría hasta Lackawana. (27)[14]
>
> (Every now and then, some outsider would ask about them [the assassinated Parrikens]. Journalists, history professors, these kinds of people. They wanted to find out what became of Camilena Kippa and Tatesh Walaspaia, taking notes all the while. . . . But they were most interested in finding out about the killing at Lackawana. Many listened to them incredulous, convinced that it was some flu or their own neglect that had done away with the victims. They claimed that Camilena Kippa was still living in a hidden cove with a man thirty years younger. But it was all rather vague, and the outsiders ended up eating a *fritada* in Grisú, accompanied by someone who would be taking them to Lackawana.)

The twelve chapters introduced by this prologue recount the episodes that led to the killing in Lackawana and evoke the massacre itself. They are a living memory that stands up against the willful forgetting (*desmemoria*); they recall the creation of a cultural and physical desert in order to counter the symbolic one, that of silence and oblivion.

The action of the novel takes place at the end of the nineteenth century; it lasts a little more than one year and concentrates on two moments related to two spaces on the island: an Anglican mission in the south, where the story begins, and a sheep ranch in the north, where everything comes to an end. An indigenous family, composed of the couple Camilena and Tatesh and their three children—the protagonists of the novel—constitutes the link between these two times and spaces. Camilena and Tatesh belong to two different ethnic groups: she represents the Yagán Indians, called *canaleses* in the novel, a tribe of canoeists who live in the south; he belongs to the Ona Indians, called *parrikens* in the novel, a tribe of hunters from the northern steppes. The family is, thus, a metaphorical microcosm that represents the island's ethnic composition. Further connecting geography and genealogy, the family travels from south to north, from the Anglican mission where we meet them for the first time, at the beginning of the novel, to the ranches in the north, where they disappear in the end. The journey—an escape from the harsh conditions that decimate the canaleses in the South—turns out to be a descent into hell, extermination in the north. The episodes from the three stories—the south, the journey, and the north—do not form a linear narrative, but rather a series of scenes arranged around certain groups of characters who provide the focus of narration.

In the south, the scenes are structured around the widow of an Anglican minister, a doctor, and his daughter, Federica. They span approximately one month, from the arrival of the doctor to the mission to the departure of the three characters. The mission, which according to the widow was prosperous in the past, has fallen into a decrepit state in the present. Very few canaleses remain there; most have been forced out by hunger, the shortage of seals, and the decreasing number of passengers arriving by ship to the port, with whom they used to trade goods. The final blow for the mission and the Indians is an outbreak of measles just at the time of the doctor's arrival. The departure of the doctor, his daughter, and the widow coincides with the death of the last Indian in the mission.

The migration of Camilena and Tatesh is motivated by worsening living conditions in the south: the shortage of ships and seals, which causes hunger, and violence by whites. In the second chapter, Camilena and two other native women are brutally raped by the crew of a sealer. The north, as recalled by Tatesh, seems to be a place of freedom and abundance. However, upon arrival, the Indians come up against wire fences that divide the pastures, blocking their way and separating them from the guanacos, their principal source of food. The fences force them to steal sheep; the theft of the livestock then becomes an easy pretext for their extermination. "No podemos seguir cruzados de brazos. . . . Tenemos derecho de defender lo nuestro" (160) (We can't just continue sitting on our hands. . . . We must defend what is ours), states the sinister character Thomas Jeremy Larch, a bounty hunter from England with fifty dogs to help him carry out the massacre of Lackawana. The episodes of the north are organized around this character and his assistants, the foreman and the workers from the Quartermaster Ranch. The story ends at Lackawana, where the Indians are trapped between the rising tide on one side and the guns and dogs on the other.

The organization of the narrative into scenes, and the constant change of narrative focus, textually recreate diverse aspects of the extermination of the Indians and present these events from different perspectives. The extermination is both cultural and physical. The cultural uprooting is evident in the imposition of European clothing by the missionary couple and in the names with which they baptize the Indians: "En [la carta de la viuda] costaba reconocer a los canaleses de Abigdon. ¿Karen Townsend? ¿George Beckenham? ¿Ann Mary Brown? La viuda parecía referirse más bien a colegiales ingleses y sus condiscípulas vírgenes" (114) (in [the widow's letter] it was difficult to recognize the Agibdon 'canalese.' Karen Townsend? George Beckenham? Ann Mary Brown? Rather the widow seemed to be referring to English school boys and their virgin companions). The physical extermination is carried out through personal and geographical violence: the destruction of the natural environment, land appropriation, kidnapping of women to work as maids in Buenos Aires, and organized killings, even of children, as exemplified in the chapter entitled "La madriguera" (The burrow). All these acts make up the politics of the creation of the desert, the results of which are described in the last two chapters of the novel. In the south, the mission is closed after the death of the last canalese, and the widow and doctor in their haste to catch the last ship leave without burying him. In the north, the Indians are massacred, and the only survivor is the youngest child of Camilena and Tatesh, who, retained as a servant and estranged from his culture, lives in the house of his parents' killer. The departure of the "well-meaning" whites and the death of the Indians leaves an empty space that can be conquered or colonized, extending the fences without boundaries.

The narrative develops the conflict foreshadowed in the photograph on the cover, the process that leads from the world of the Indian woman to that of the white girl, as if the figure of the former suddenly disappeared and that of the latter overtook the whole picture. At the same time, the text retrospectively amplifies the connotative readings of the photograph, adding new meanings or resignifying those already present in the image. The figure of the baby that the woman carries on her back becomes especially significant in this retrospective examination of the visual rendition of Fuegia's tragic fate. The child represents the future of the generation embodied in the woman, but, as the text suggests, this future will never materialize, because both adults and children are annihilated by the expansion of Western culture. In addition, the confrontation between the image and the text produces a drastic inversion of the values initially associated with the cultural loci represented by both figures on the montage, as it questions the innocence of the white world embodied in the girl and vindicates that of the indigenous people.

Both the photograph and the text stage a historical drama, a story of destruction and loss. In this sense, the ethnographic photograph of the Indian woman acquires another meaning: it fades as the image of the Other to become an index of her physical presence, a visual testimony that now rememorates that woman's existence, adopting the function of the white girl's portrait.[15] This revised perception of the photograph corroborates the claim that the account of the events in *Fuegia* is an act of recollection that opposes oblivion and contests the gag of silence.[16] In remembering the circumstances that create a physical, geographical, and cultural desert, the novel recovers the traces of the exterminated people and their ordeal. This remembrance metaphorically buries them in the sense suggested by Michel de Certeau, who establishes a link between historical writing and the social rite of burial: "writing plays the role of a burial rite . . . it exorcizes death by inserting it into discourse" (100). By means of writing, even in admittedly fictitious writing, the facts find their place in the discourse and from there the recovered traces resist oblivion.

Each recalled episode forms one chapter of the novel, which opens with a photograph representing a child, white (9) or indigenous (3). The captions identify

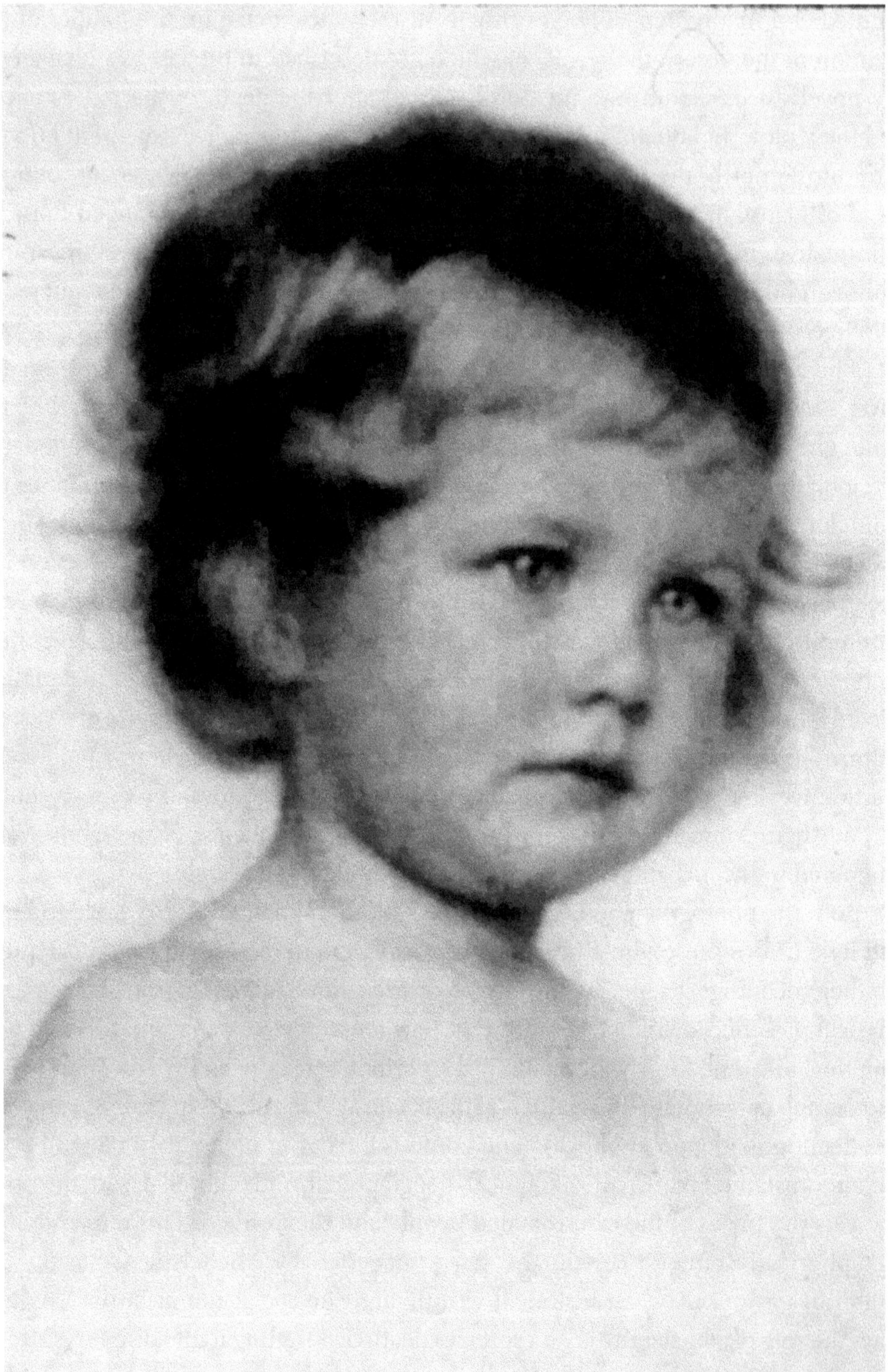

Fig. 9.2. "Thomas Jeremy Larch" in *Fuegia*. Authorization Eduardo Belgrano Rawson.

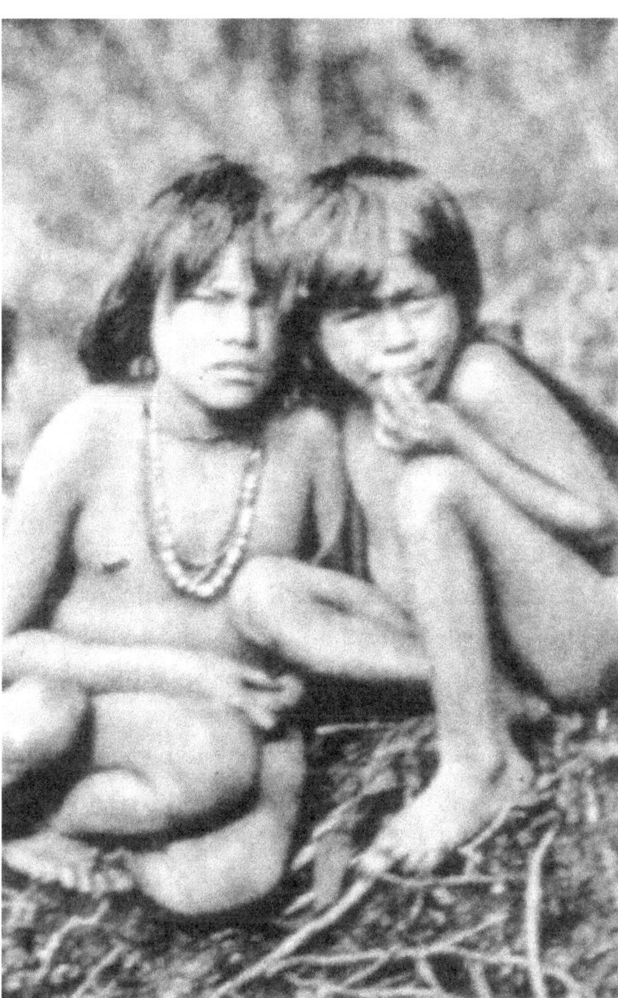

Fig. 9.3. "Tatesh Wulaspaia (on the right)" in *Fuegia* (French Scientific Expedition, 1882, "Two Boys and a Girl"). Authorization Musée de l'Homme and Eduardo Belgrano Rawson.

each represented person as one of the principal characters (figs. 9.2 and 9.3): Elizabeth Dobson, the widow; the doctor; Federica, the doctor's daughter; Thomas Jeremy Larch; Camilena, Tatesh, and their son, Lucca; etc.[17] Most discussion of the novel has ignored this visual element.[18] Márgara Averbach, who mentions photographs in her article, interprets their inclusion in the text as a technique of verisimilitude, a link between external reality and fiction, and as an element of realism: "El autor aumenta la verosimilitud con el uso de fotografías en las que aparecen niños de corta edad identificados mediante una corta explicación como personajes de la novela" (68) (the author augments the novel's verisimilitude with the use of photographs showing young children who are identified by a short explanation as characters in the novel). This interpretation raises certain problems that Averbach herself signals a little later in her article: "[Las] fotos de niños son reales pero las palabras que identifican a los fotografiados, son pura ficción, con lo cual estamos otra vez en el campo de la 'ficción de realidad'" (69) (the photos of children are real, but the words that identify them are pure fiction, which leaves us once again in the realm of "reality fiction"). If we assume, as does Florencia Garramuño in her analysis of photographs in *Fuegia*, that the characters of the novel are fictional, according to statements made by Belgrano Rawson, then the photograph, an image representing a real person, is associated with a fictional story. This means that instead of being indicative of verisimilitude, the photographs signal the process of fictionalization on which the novel is based: a history, a biography, a life, and a name are invented and attributed to a fragment of extratextual reality embodied in the photograph. The photographs do not illustrate or document the text, they do not evidence any real story. It is the text that creates a story for each of the photographs, and belief in the relationship between the narrative and the image requires a momentary suspension of disbelief.

On the other hand, while the photographs in *Fuegia* appear regularly at the beginning of each chapter and might, therefore, seem to constitute an element of cohesion of the novelistic universe, there is no immediate link between the content of the chapter and the person represented in the photograph accompanying it. In some cases, the character represented in the photograph and identified by the caption is the focal point of the chapter's content; in other cases, the relationship is barely perceptible, since the appearance of the photographed character in the story is so fleeting or insignificant that it does not seem to justify the presence of the image. This is why each chapter is introduced by a title that precedes the photograph and is a semantic indication signaling the core of its story. Chapter 9, for instance, opens with the title "La madriguera" (The burrow), followed by a photograph of a boy identified as Lucca, the youngest child of Camilena and Tatesh, and the only survivor of the massacre. The title describes the chapter's content: preparation of a hiding place for a group of forty children, one of whom is Lucca, who does not play any central role in the recounted events.

Indeed, the function of photographs in *Fuegia* is not to produce a "reality effect" (Barthes, "The Reality Effect" 148) or to organize the narrative content. Nor is it to be found on the level of denotation, but rather on that of connotation. Roland Barthes observed in his study of photographic expression that the selection of objects in photographs is one of the principal strategies of connotation, because the objects "constitute excellent elements of signification: on the one hand they are discontinuous and complete in themselves, a physical qualification for a sign, while on the other they refer to clear, familiar signifieds" ("The Photographic Message" 22–23). Another strategy consists of creating a sequence that combines these signifieds in an extended syntactical structure, in which "the signifier of connotation is . . . no longer to be found at the level of any one of the fragments of the sequence but at the level . . . of the concatenation" (24). As mentioned before, in *Fuegia* all photographs represent a child; the pose, the gaze, the setting, even the age, may vary, but the principal signifying element—childhood—remains unchanged throughout the series. The meaning of this "iconic text" (Lotman) relies on repetition in its units that draws attention to the connotative significance of the main component. The concept of "childhood" connotes, among other meanings, innocence, play, discovery, future, anticipation, and hope. The visual series thus produces a meaning that stands in radical opposition to the story articulated in the text, dominated by despair, hopelessness, fury, destruction, and a sensation of a world coming to an end, as if between the two, the visual and verbal texts, there were an abysmal gap. Such a gap does, in fact, exist, and is temporal. In the novel, the photographs do not represent arbitrary children or arbitrary childhood, but are, supposedly, the portraits of the characters when they were children. From this viewpoint, the series of twelve photographs with their captions introduces another temporal level, previous to that of the text; the photographs form the past of the present narrated in the text. In these portraits, as in memory, the presence of an absence emerges; they are image-memories of a previous world. This perception of the passage of time, of a past different from the present, reflects a similar opposition in the text, manifested through anachronies (analepses).[19] All of them refer to the same span of time in the past: the period when dreams, illusions, and hopes were still possible.

The events narrated in *Fuegia* constitute a narrative present, a "now" that leads irrevocably to a gloomy end. At the same time, this present is the future of past moments that the characters remember constantly through evocation. If one were to determine the frequency of word use in the novel, *recordar* (to remember) and *memorias* (memories) would be at the top of the list. All characters in *Fuegia* remember something from their past, or revive in dreams some happy past moment, one previous to the present of destruction and disillusion in which they are trapped. The widow remembers the happy days of her childhood in an English village, the name of which is also that of the mission; she constantly evokes the hopes of a perfect and efficient mission she shared with her late husband, just before their departure for Fuegia. The doctor remembers one special night, when he made love with his late wife, and peaceful days with Federica, who now lives far away. Father Lorenzo, a Salesian missionary, remembers his good intentions that came to almost nothing; Joaquín Palabra, a sealer mutilated by Camilena and Tatesh seeking vengeance for Camilena's rape, remembers his mother's house and her cooking. The *canaleses* and the *parrikens* remember a better time, when seals and whales abounded, when the little bays of the island overflowed with mussels, when guanacos used to descend to the shore from the mountains and the *parrikens* could hunt them, when work on ranches or begging was unnecessary, when people "sabía[n] encender un fuego como antes, golpeando dos piedras duras junto a unas briznas de musgo mezclado con nidos de arañas" (41) (knew how to light a fire like in the old times, banging hard rocks next to bits of moss mixed with spiders' nests). These are but a few examples of memories evoking a previous time, a better time, far away when things were different, and "todo parecía posible y el futuro aún estaba muy lejos" (128) (everything seemed possible and the future was still very far off). The future mentioned in this quote is the present in which characters suffer and die, the present from which they remember, knowing already that "todo había salido de mona" (165) (everything had turned out badly). Many memories flash back to the time alluded to in the photographs, the time of childhood, the world of innocence, when all possibilities were still open and all futures still possible.

The temporal structure of the narrative is divided into two zones, the past and the present of the recounted events. This structure is suggested, first, in the opening chapter, a prologue to and a summary of the whole story, composed entirely on the dichotomy between what was before and what is now.[20] The second clue is inscribed in the temporal tension between the photographs and the narrative. They are to the novel what the evocation of characters is to the story of the destruction of Fuegia's nature and culture, because the split temporality between the photographs and the text mirrors the temporal divide of the narrative. The photographs accentuate the difference between past hope, evoked constantly and idealized through evocation, and the present, which is the future of that past, in which idealization is no longer possible, and hope is lost forever. Susan Sontag affirms that: "Photographs state the innocence, the vulnerability of lives heading to their own destruction" (70). Few general statements about photography explain with as much insight as Sontag's the place and function of the photographic series in *Fuegia*. The childhood represented in the twelve portraits embodies that innocence and vulnerability, the future of which—to be victim or murderer, to perish or to survive, to hope or to despair, to realize a dream or to lose it—has not yet materialized. This future is articulated in the novel's text, which converts the soft abstract possibilities expressed in the photographs into a harsh and tragic reality: the recalled present, the time of destruction and disillusion, the time of loss.

Roland Barthes once observed that: "To ask whether a photograph is analogical or coded is not a good means of analysis. The important thing is that the photograph possesses an evidential force, and that its testimony bears not on the object but on time" (*Camera Lucida* 88–89). Photographs and narrative are two structural pivots for representing time and loss in *Fuegia*. The split construction of time, made visible by the juxtaposition of images and words and made intelligible through reminiscence within the narrative, creates a double image of loss—or an image of a double loss: that of the exterior world of historical and social reality, condemned to destruction and erased by the violence of "progress"; and that of the interior world, the subjective universe of hopes, desires, and dreams, lost to disillusion and desolation. The interplay between the photographs and the narrative does not transcribe that reality, but utters its unspeakable truths. In consequence, what matters are not the referential characteristics of the photographs, but their being within the text, as Barthes puts it, a "confusion of representation" (*S/Z* 216) that reveals a multidimensional textuality. The representational complexity produced by the inclusion of photographs goes beyond challenging the ontological distinction between reality and fiction. Their presence disrupts the apparently smooth surface of the text, as it breaks down temporality, unfolding its complexity and depth. The photographs are a visual clue; they do not hint, however, at some extratextual life-world, but critique representation itself, signaling that rather than reflecting reality, it constructs its multiple meanings.[21]

Notes

1. This work was supported in part by a grant from the City University of New York PSC–CUNY Research Award Program.

2. In Kendall L. Walton's theory, transparence is the principal characteristic of photography: "Photographs are transparent. We see the world through them" (251).

3. See studies by Barthes ("The Photographic Message," "Rhetoric of the Image," and *Camera Lucida)* and Sontag.

4. All translations are mine, unless published translations are cited with page references.

5. Another interesting interpretation of montage's effect is to see it, following Barthes, as a "confusion of representation," that is, a "moment of breakdown in the otherwise self-assured functioning of the economy of mimesis" (Prendergast 14).

6. Before *Fuegia*, Belgrano Rawson published *No se turbe vuestro corazón* (1974) and *El náufrago de las estrellas* (1979), for which he was awarded the prize Club de los Trece for the best novel. His last novel, *Noticias secretas de América*, appeared in 1998.

7. *Fueguino* is the Spanish term meaning of or from Tierra del Fuego.

8. The novel is dedicated to these four natives of Tierra del Fuego: Fuegia Basket, Jemmy Button, York Minster, and Boat Memory. Fuegia Basket, Jemmy Button, and York Minster managed to return to Tierra del Fuego, but Boat Memory died of smallpox in Plymouth. The historical episode to which the novel's title refers calls to mind the opening scene of Mario Vargas Llosa's novel *La casa verde*, which describes the kidnapping of two indigenous girls by two Catholic nuns accompanied by a detachment of Peruvian soldiers. After being brutally separated from their family, home, and culture, the girls are placed in a mission run by the nuns, where, according to the Mother Superior, they are given "un hogar, una familia, . . . un nombre . . . [y] un Dios" (38) (a home, a family, . . . a name . . . [and] a God). Most of the girls end up working as prostitutes or servants. The similarity between the historical and fictional episodes underlines the constant fusion of the two realms in Latin American literature.

9. According to Florencia Garramuño, the photographs in *Fuegia*—the montage on the cover as well as the sequence within the novel—participate in the novel's articulation of the cultural differences that united and divided the two cultural poles in specific instances (157). Although I share most of Garramuño's reading of the photographs, I believe that the montage on the cover connotes a more conflictive relationship than uniting or dividing cultural difference.

10. I am indebted to Esther Gabara of Duke University for pointing out this distinction. Florencia Garramuño remarks, in her study of *Fuegia*, that the distinction between these

two photographic "genres" is maintained in the photographic sequence within the novel: the photographs of indigenous characters belong always to the "documentary" or ethnographic format, while those of the white people are posed portraits. Garramuño interprets this distinction as an implicit comment on different mechanisms of representation (156).

11. The association between family (romance and marriage) and nation is an important aspect of nineteenth- and early-twentieth-century Latin American literature. See Doris Sommer, *Foundational Fictions: The National Romances of Latin America*. A recent example of this association (and its revision) is the essay by Edgardo Rodríguez Juliá, *Puertorriqueños: Album de la sagrada familia puertorriqueña a partir de 1898*.

12. "Photography grew up in the days of Empire and became an important adjunct of imperialism, for it returned to the Western spectator images of native people which frequently confirmed prevailing views of them as primitive, bizarre, barbaric or simply picturesque" (Price 68). For the relationship between representation and domination, see Edward Said, *Orientalism*; for the uses of photography within power relations, see John Tagg, *The Burden of Representation*; for the relationship between photography and imperialism, see James R. Ryan, *Picturing Empire*, and Jill Lloyd, "Old Photographs, Vanished People and Stolen Potatoes."

13. The analysis above is based on the Sudamericana edition of *Fuegia*. The photographic montage on the Seix Barral edition's cover is different, but it does not contradict my interpretation. It is composed of three photographs: that of the indigenous woman with a baby, that of a white girl, and another one representing a little white boy. The composition is triangular: the photograph of the girl is displaced towards the bottom, and its place to the right of the woman's image is taken by the portrait of the boy. This new arrangement maintains, and even reinforces, the chronological sequence present in the Sudamericana edition, since the photograph of the boy is associated in the text with the character of Thomas Jeremy Larch, a bounty hunter who is responsible for the massacre of the Indians.

14. This fragment in which the inhabitants erase the massacre from their memory is reminiscent of a similar situation in Gabriel García Márquez's *Cien años de soledad*, where the people of Macondo deny the massacre of plantation workers by the Banana Company.

15. A photographic image possesses both iconic and indexical properties. Susan Sontag stresses its indexical nature when she argues that, unlike a painting, which can be completely invented, a photograph is always a trace of a previous presence: "While a painting, even one that meets photographic standards of resemblance, is never more than stating of an interpretation, a photograph is never less than registering of an emanation . . .—a material vestige of its subject in a way that no painting can be" (Sontag 154).

16. "Recollection" and "evocation" (later in the text) are used here in the sense given to these concepts by Paul Ricœur in *La mémoire, l'histoire, l'oubli*. They refer to two aspects of memory, denominated *mnēmē* and *anamnēsis* by Plato and Aristotle. The former is a simple evocation, "la présence maintenant de l'absent antérieurement perçu, éprouvé, appris" (32) (the current presence of a previously perceived, felt, learned absence); the latter means memory as a sought-after object, an active way of recovering traces and fighting oblivion: " l''ana' d''anamn sis' signifie retour, reprise, recouvrement de ce qui a été auparavant vu, éprouvé ou appris . . . L'oubli est ainsi désigné obliquement comme cela contre quoi l'effort de rappel est dirigé. . . . On recherche ce qu'on craint d'avoir oublié provisoirement ou pour toujours" (6 and 33) (the "ana" of "anamnēsis" means return, reprise, recovery of that which previously has been seen, noticed or learned. . . . Oblivion is therefore obliquely designated as something against which the effort of remembering is directed. . . . One searches for that which one fears having forgotten, temporarily or forever). The translation of the second of these terms into Spanish as "rememoración" allows for a rich and evocative play of words and meanings, lost in English: oblivion or denial of memory is "DESmemoria" and the effort to recover the lost traces is then "REmemoración," where the prefix

"re" implies the "retour, reprise, recouvrement" (return, reprise, recovery) mentioned in Ricœur's text.

17. Camilena is represented in the photograph on the cover, which is reproduced in the text with a caption identifying her not as the woman, but as the baby on the woman's back.

18. See articles by Longhini, Mathieu, and Pérez Martín. The fact that these authors do not mention the photographs may indicate that they find their presence "normal" in this realist text.

19. I resort here to the concepts elaborated by Gérard Genette in *Narrative Discourse*. Genette defines *anachrony* as "all forms of discordance between the two temporal orders of story and narrative" (40). *Analepsis* is "any evocation after the fact of an event that took place earlier than the point in the story where we are at any given moment" (40).

20. This temporal divide is signaled by an almost obsessive repetition of expressions of time referring to what was before. Some examples are: "En tiempos del viejo Dobson" (16); "Era el mismo invitador escenario de los días del viejo Dobson, pero los barcos ya nunca se detenían" (17); "En otro tiempo estos sitios habían sido los mejores . . . pero ya casi no había lobos"(19); "En aquellos años había millones de lobos" (20); "Añoraban los días de buena cosecha"(22) (in the era of the old Dobson; It was the same inviting scenario of the days of Dobson, but the boats had already stopped coming by; In another era these places had been the best, but there were almost no sealions; In those years there were millions of sealions; They yearned for the days of good harvests).

21. I am grateful to Juan Carlos Álvarez for his help with the English version of this article and for his remarks on the photograph on *Fuegia's* cover, and to Marcy Schwartz for her insightful comments on an early version of this chapter.

References

Alatriste, Sealtiel. *El daño*. Madrid: Espasa, 2000.

Arnheim, Rudolf. "*On the Nature of Photography.*" *Critical Inquiry* 1 (September 1974): 149–61.

Averbach, Márgara. "Encuentro indio-blanco a principios de siglo: las dos puntas de América, *Fuegia* y *Mean Spirit*." *Primeras Jornadas Internacionales de la Literatura Argentina/ Comparatística. Actas*, n.s. Ed. Teresita Frugoni de Fritsche (1995): 61–72.

Barthes, Roland. *Camera Lucida*. London: Vintage, 1993.

______. "The Photographic Message." In *Image. Music. Text.* Trans. and ed. Stephen Heath. New York: Hill and Wang, 1977, 15–31.

______. "The Reality Effect." In *The Rustle of Language*. Trans. Richard Howard. New York: Hill and Wang, 1986, 141–48.

______. "Rhetoric of the Image." *Image. Music. Text.* Trans. and ed. Stephen Heath. New York: Hill and Wang, 1977, 32–51.

______. *S/Z*. Trans. Richard Miller. New York: Hill and Wang, 1974.

Bazin, André. "The Ontology of the Photographic Image." In *What is Cinema?*. Trans. Hugh Gray. Vol. 1. Berkeley and Los Angeles: University of California Press, 1967, 9–16.

Belgrano Rawson, Eduardo. "Escribir del oído." Interview. 15 September 2002, http://www.literama.net/e_belgrano.html.

______. *Fuegia*. Buenos Aires: Sudamericana, 1991.

______. *Fuegia*. Buenos Aires: Seix Barral, 1999.

______. *El náufrago de las estrellas*. Buenos Aires: Pomaire, 1979.

______. *No se turbe vuestro corazón*. 1974. Buenos Aires: Pomaire, 1981.

______. *Noticias secretas de América*. Buenos Aires: Planeta, 1998.

Benjamin, Walter. "The Author as Producer." In *Selected Writings*, vol. 2, 1927–1934. Trans. Rodney Livingstone et al. Ed. Michael W. Jennings, Howard Eiland, and Gary Smith. Cambridge, MA: Harvard University Press, 1999, 769–82.

______. "On the Concept of History." In *Selected Writings*. Vol. 4: 1938–1940. Trans. Edmund Jephcott et al. Eds. Howard Eiland and Michael W. Jennings. Cambridge, MA: Harvard University Press, 2003, 389–400.

Borrero, José María. *La Patagonia trágica*. Buenos Aires: Americana, 1957.

Burke, Peter. *Eyewitnessing: The Uses of Images as Historical Evidence*. Ithaca, NY: Cornell University Press, 2001.

Certeau, Michel de. *The Writing of History*. Trans. Tom Conley. New York: Columbia University Press, 1988.

Foley, Barbara. *Telling the Truth: The Theory and Practice of Documentary Fiction*. Ithaca, NY/London: Cornell University Press, 1986.

Garramuño, Florencia. *Genealogías culturales: Argentina, Brasil, Uruguay en la novela contemporánea (1981–1991)*. Rosario, Argentina: Beatriz Viterbo Editora, 1997.

Genette, Gérard. *Narrative Discourse: An Essay in Method*. Trans. Jane E. Lewin. Ithaca, NY: Cornell University Press, 1980.

González, José Luis. *La llegada. (Crónica con "ficción")*. 2nd ed. Río Piedras, Puerto Rico: Huracán, 1997.

Gutiérrez, Miguel, and Julio Olavarría. *La destrucción del reino*. Lima: Milla Batres, 1992.

Lloyd, Jill. "Old Photographs, Vanished Peoples and Stolen Potatoes." *Art Monthly* 83 (February 1985).

Longhini, Nora. "Las voces olvidadas en *Fuegia*, de Eduardo Belgrano Rawson." In *Primeras Jornadas Internacionales de la Literatura Argentina/Comparatística. Actas*, n.s. (Ed. Teresita Frugoni de Fritsche) (1995): 73–80.

Lotman, J. M. "The Discrete Text and the Iconic Text: Remarks on the Structure of Narrative." *New Literary History* 6 (1975): 333–38.

Mathieu, Corina S. "*Fuegia*: Crónica de una marginación." *Alba de América* 14.26–27 (July 1996): 147–54.

Mitchell, W. J. T. *Picture Theory*. Chicago/London: University of Chicago Press, 1994.

Payró, Roberto J. *La Australia argentina*. Buenos Aires: Centro Editor de América Latina, 1982.

Pérez Martín, Norma. "Dos novelas 'patagónicas' en la narrativa argentina actual: *Fuegia* y *El rey de Patagonia*." *Alba de América* 15. 28–29 (July 1997): 142–47.

Poniatowska, Elena. *Tinísima*. Mexico City: Era, 1992.

Prendergast, Christopher. *The Order of Mimesis: Balzac, Stendhal, Nerval, Flaubert*. Cambridge: Cambridge University Press, 1986.

Price, Derrick, "Surveyors and Surveyed: Photography out and about." In *Photography: A Critical Introduction*. Ed. Liz Wells. 2d ed. London/New York: Routledge, 2000, 67–115.

Renan, Ernest. "What is a Nation?" In *Nation and Narration*. Ed. Homi K. Bhabha. London: Routledge, 1990, 8–22.

Rey Beckford, Ricardo. "Palabras previas." In *La Patagonia trágica*. José María Borrero. Buenos Aires: Americana, 1957, 1–11.

Ricœur, Paul. *La mémoire, l'histoire, l'oubli*. Paris: Seuil, 2000.

Rodríguez Juliá, Edgardo. *Puertorriqueños: Album de la sagrada familia pueretorriqueña a partir de 1898*. Río Piedras, Puerto Rico: Plaza Mayor, 1988.

Ryan, James R. *Picturing Empire: Photography and the Visualisation of the British Empire*. London: Reaktion Books, 1997.

Said, Edward. *Orientalism*. New York: Vintage Books, 1978.

Sommer, Doris. *Foundational Fictions: The National Romances of Latin America*. Berkeley: University of California Press, 1991.

Sontag, Susan. *On Photography*. New York: Farrar, Strauss and Giroux, 1973.

Tagg, John. *The Burden of Representation: Essays on Photographies and Histories*. London: MacMillan, 1988.

Tizón, Héctor. *La mujer de Strasser*. Buenos Aires: Planeta, 1997.

Vargas Llosa, Mario. *La casa verde*. Bogotá: La Oveja Negra, 1984.

Walton, Kendall L. "Transparent Pictures: On the Nature of Photographic Realism." *Critical Inquiry* 11 (1984–85): 246–77.

Part IV

The Voice of the Image

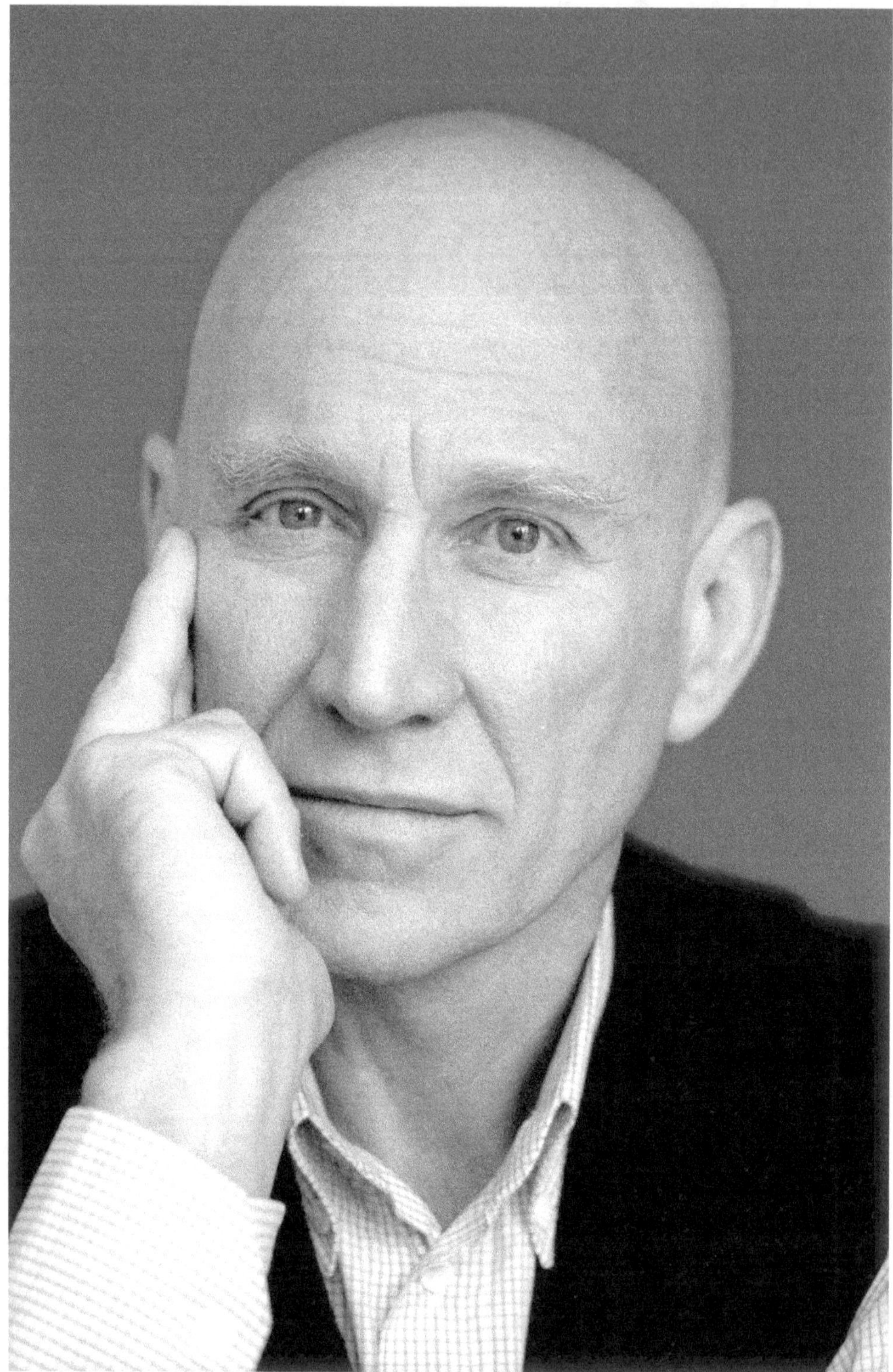

10.1. Portrait of Salgado by Nicole Toutounji, courtesy of UNICEF/HQ01–0123/Nicole Toutounji.

Chapter Ten

From Brazil, Abroad, and Back Again

Politics, Place, and Pictures—An Interview with Sebastião Salgado

Amanda Hopkinson

Sebastião Salgado is a global photographer. For thirty years, he has selected themes from all corners of the world, for a global audience. Most frequently he has sought to bring the faces of the "third" to the "first" world. All too often, the expressions on these faces show dispossession, even desperation. But at other times they show survival, inventiveness, even "an uncertain grace." This was the title of Salgado's first major touring exhibition (1990), following in the tracks of two earlier, regionally specific book projects (*Sahel: l'Homme en Detresse* [with Medecins sans Frontières] and *Other Americas*). In the subsequent thirteen years, he has produced such major shows as *Workers: An Archaeology of the Industrial Age*, *Exodus*, and *The Children*. Each has been created with photos in a large-scale black-and-white format, and in the postwar tradition of the "concerned photographer." Several of his projects have involved collaboration with writers such as the Brazilian poet and songwriter Chico Buarque and the Uruguayan writer Eduardo Galeano.

Funded by his photographic work, Salgado purchased family land in Brazil in 1991, where he started the Instituto Terra and began working on projects in conjunction with the Movimento Sem Terra (landless movement). The institute has initiated a reforestation project planting three hundred thousand trees, has founded a school, and collaborates with indigenous people who have been displaced from their land.

The following conversation has been edited from two interviews with Salgado. The first was conducted in Aimores, Brazil, and aired on the BBC radio network in February 2002. The second was a live interview held on March 22, 2003, at the Barbicon Gallery in London, during the showing of Salgado's exhibition *Exodus*.

Additional correspondence in late 2003 contributed new responses especially for this volume.

Amanda Hopkinson: Sebastião, to what do you owe your way of seeing, and from where does your sense of place and people derive?

Sebastião Salgado: New global information helps a new global way of looking: it has become easier to understand a different point of view and a different way to see. I try to understand people's own origins, their formation, even in the mass societies in which we now live. It's probably better for me to situate myself in this global context, to plan my work taking into account my life and where I come from. In fact this is the way in which I've always worked, but just the size of my projects seems to scare people. For *Workers* and for *Exodus*, I went to around forty countries for each. Every single person warned me that such projects were far, far too big.

But take a city like London, where we have a grandson, and he's in a school class with thirty or forty kids, all speaking different languages and coming from different cultures. I'm sure that all of them are far better placed to understand what I'm doing than those who were around twenty years ago, when the place was far more plain English. Young people today are in a position to understand cultural differences far better than the older generation, and they naturally make links across the world.

But if you go back to my own beginnings, I come from a country the size of a continent. From my home to Maranão, in the interior, it's 3000 km. That's about the same as from London to Moscow. I have seven sisters, all now married and living in different regions. To visit them is like traveling from London across the Mediterranean. When you grow up where I did, you have a different sense of space. Europe can fit two or three times over into Brazil. The size of the country and the needs of the people are so huge that you have to accept a different scale. You have to adapt, and so did I.

Like with Lelia, my wife. We met when she was sixteen and I was twenty years old, and we made a different kind of life together, always moving through the world. There's always that question when you are a photographer: what do you photograph? Whatever it is, you bring your own cultural heritage with you, it forms part of your own way of seeing.

My state in Brazil, Minas Gerais, is where the Brazilian Baroque was born. Our country's whole relationship with Christianity and with slavery was worked out there. That too is present in your pictures when you are taking them, all this you carry inside you, and it makes the way each of us works just that little bit different and individual. When you go into a small church here, you see how it is decorated to build a frame of mind. And when you go up the valley to see the sculptures by the dwarf-sized cripple O Aleijadinho, you get a sense of the tiny scale of man in the universe, or in this landscape. Everything here is very extreme, even his lifesized figures of the Passion at Ouro Preto, it is a very exaggerated style and you internalize that when you grow up with such an impressive and powerful art. That combines with our sugarloaf mountain ranges and the rest, so that the sense of natural scale and the power of the Baroque are, I believe, there in every photographic intervention I have ever made. And I'm often accused of exaggerating, of forging a strange kind of a universe, but I believe I come from a very special place.

AH: There's something fantastical about saying you're not exoticizing the exotic, because it already exists. It just looks so very exaggerated because of the gigantic scale of the surrounding environment. Were you aware of this in growing up, or did you take it all for granted, growing up in the small village of Conceicião do Capim, was it just what you became used to?

SS: No, I was always moved by it. That was why I came back. We were always linked by it and now, creating the school we have here, we are properly a part of this community again. I believe I have educated myself, my way of seeing, in the area where I was born and grew up. I believe my pictures have a lot of space, a lot of sky—from looking at the Brazilian skies, how heavy they are with clouds during the rainy season. They give the impression of being as heavy as lead, as if they could just fall on us, they're so weighed down. This metal sky lives inside me and forms my way of viewing and understanding the world. I know the people who live in the valleys going down to the sea and across to the neighbouring state of Spirito Santo, and they are very important to me. These things were always inside myself. The other day we went to the small nearby town of Coletina, and the German friend I was driving told me, "Sebastião, you have never left and will never leave this place. You have always carried it inside you, even during the last thirty-five years you have been living in France."

AH: Your description of your first portrait of Lelia—taken with her camera, *contre-jour*, already knowing how you wanted to portray her—is of "something exploding in my mind. It was like falling in love, like discovering a new language." Is becoming a photographer both to discover the world anew and to impose on it a new order of your own?

SS: For me, my discovery of photography was a real stroke of luck. I came to it very late. Lelia was doing her Ph. D. in architecture and I was working on mine in economics in Paris, where she bought a camera to take the necessary shots. It gave me my first opportunity to look through a camera lens, and it was fabulous. A real *coup de foudre*, a revelation of a new way to meet people, and to take their pictures. If Lelia had not bought the camera to do her architecture, I would have found no way into photography. For after this moment in time, I had other responsibilities, and would probably never have allowed myself to discover photography like this.

I worked as an economist for the International Coffee Organisation in London from 1971 to '73. This gave me the chance to travel to Africa with the World Bank. Whenever I got back home, the pictures gave me three times the pleasure of the economic reports I had to write. We went to the Photographers' Gallery to the first show I'd ever seen in my life, and we discovered photography, we seemed to see a new way. It gave me such a big, big pleasure.

When we returned to France, for me it was to discover this new life of photography. I had an invitation to go and work in Washington for the World Bank, or as an economist teaching in São Paulo University. Either was a fabulous job for a young economist. But Lelia and I were both active in the Leftist movement in Brazil, and things became very polarized while massive repression was introduced there [in 1964, when the military dictatorship seized power]. There was a time when it seemed highly likely we were both going to end up in prison. Staying in France made the life of a photographer possible, yet although it was possible, it was still very, very hard, freelancing for press agencies.

AH: Could you elaborate about that time when you feared imprisonment under the military regime?

SS: When you come from Brazil—or from anywhere with major social and political problems—you operate from day one within a system based on struggle. So, from an early age, I became a [Communist] Party member, then joined a still more radical movement called Catholic Action. This held similar views to those of the Cuban revolutionaries, advocating urban resistance against national repression and United States imperialism. Whereas you [in England] come from a tradition of political discussion and preparation, we arrived in France already politically formed in a Marxist tradition. We had a huge dictatorship in Brazil at the time, and a large number of Brazilians fled to France and became exiles. Many had been tortured and imprisoned at home, and it was impossible for them to return. Lots of them were in a very, very bad state.

Lelia and I helped to organize many, many actions, events, and projects with them across France, to help them and to raise money for food, doctors, dentists, and so on. And when you do something together, all this comes home to you, and Brazil seems very close. The military had seized our passports when we fled, and we were forbidden to return. We had to find a lawyer to fight for our right to go back, although by then France had made us French citizens and given us new passports.

AH: What has been happening recently in Brazil with the Movimento Sem Terra (MST, or the Landless Movement)? This is for you the project where your work, politics, and your homeland have all come together, in one of your books and exhibitions, called *Terra*.

SS: In 1979 Brazil offered exiles political amnesty, and Lelia and I landed there on September 15, after ten years out of the country, and I started shooting pictures of the land situation. That came naturally, because I am from the land, and a big majority of my pictures are taken in rural areas. I started a project on the landless before the MST was even formed in 1985. We had already had some experience of the Roman Catholic liberation theology movement. We already knew the Ligas Campanesas (rural unions) people. I was working so hard and taking so many pictures, that when my publisher told me: "I want to do a book on Brazil with you," I replied "The only book I can do is on the MST, the Landless Movement." *Terra* was published, and sold all across Europe, too.

Then, in 1991, my father left the farm where I grew up, and with Lelia I made the decision to buy the land and create a foundation and an institute, to replant the rainforest that used to be there. We decided to start an ecological school and to create a sustainable development project. It took us eleven years to fundraise and organize all of this: we have been around the world and raised $2.5 million, and we now have the biggest project of environmental regeneration in Brazil. You can see it's a full life!

So you can see that my photographs do not exist just because I made a decision to go to Africa, Asia, or Latin America, or to some unusual place in Europe. All those concerns, with the environment and my home country and everything, happen alongside the rest of this work. For example, I got into *Workers* because all across Europe the industrial age was coming to an end, and hundreds of thousands of workers, particularly in the steel and ship-building industries, were being fired at that time. For economic reasons, this world was being changed around us, and we made the decision to do something before it had disappeared altogether. That was our political response, because there was already a whole set of political decisions behind all those changes.

AH: *Terra*, which had a major impact, was distributed with a CD made by the pop singer Chico Buarque—who also came on board in another sense, since he's on your board of trustees here at the Instituto Terra.

SS: Chico Buarque composed his music simply because he was moved to do so. It seemed so normal working together because he was already visiting—not to sing but to play soccer, because he's a huge football enthusiast as well—these things are very mixed up together, culturally speaking.

I keep deliberately talking about "we" and "our," meaning Lelia and me, but there was also a small team of people, including my agent, involved as we put the project in place together. Each story always builds the next and the following story, and we build ourselves into them, these are pictures of us and our lives and of our society. They are a kind of mirror: they don't exist just because some smart photographer out there took them. It's about what's taking place on our planet, and I try like every photographer to link my life to the historic moment, doing what I feel motivated to do: take these pictures, provoke this discussion, and bring this debate into the open.

You have to get used to the fact that the whole world is your home. Wherever you are, wherever you sleep, that becomes your home, the place where you belong. There is a flow of things that become integrated into your life and you equally are a part of that flow.

AH: You have had your critics, who disbelieve what you do. It started over ten years ago with Ingrid Sischy in the *New Yorker*, who wrote: "To aestheticize tragedy is the fastest way to anaesthetize the viewer. Beauty is a call to admiration not to action." Yet you have been saying exactly the opposite: that your pictures are intended to raise consciousness, that "globalization," in the sense of planet-wide photography, can provoke local discussions everywhere.

SS: That argument you mounted is a very simplistic one. More recently, the *New Yorker* revisited my work with Susan Sontag, who said that what I do is "*real* documentary photography." The purpose of my work is to draw viewers to it, and that's generally what happens. Ingrid Sischy was an exception, although I didn't know that when she wrote this ten years ago. Then it hurt a great deal, and I talked about it with a great friend of ours, Warren Hope, who works on the *New York Times* magazine. And I asked him: "What do I do now, do I get a lawyer?" and he said: "No, do nothing. So few people in the United States get a thirteen-page spread on their work in the *New Yorker*." So I thanked him for his very interesting point of view and left it at that.

AH: Then, later, adverse criticism again worked well, thanks to *Le Monde*. Stacks of your books were sold under banner-sized reprints of a bad review.

SS: So what if I provoke a positive, or even sometimes a negative reaction? To me that's just a part of the dialectic which results from all this action. One or two years ago, I did an ad for an insurance company here; then an advertising campaign for Volvo; I shoot such things to pay the salaries of my staff. That's the only way I can do it; it's not that I was a rich man to begin with. I give the bigger part of my time to social photography. That's my choice about what I want to do. Aside from the ads, the big project I've just done is a "good news" story on polio for UNICEF.

AH: What—to you—is a good, proper, or "*real*" photograph?

SS: You start out as a photographer, already knowing all those 'good' and 'correct' pictures, and when you start out, you're like any other beginner. You don't really know if you're doing well or badly, if your pictures are correct or incorrect. I remember when I began in 1974 and was very quickly asked to join a press agency in Portugal. So I was simultaneously shooting for *Newsweek*, trying to calculate how to use flash and getting it wrong; then ending up with no images at all. Many times I went to do a report, and when I finished a shoot and got back to the agency, I found I'd forgotten to put film inside my camera. So you can have all these big conceptual discussions, but the really important point is to get the work published. For that you need film in the camera! Better still, when the critics start looking and finding something nasty to say about your work, that's when you know you've really arrived!

Question from audience: In the exhibition *Exodus*, the text wall ends with the words: "There is no answer." I want your opinion on what you really would like to happen as a result of your photographs, beyond having a whole lot of people look at them?

SS: I definitely *do* want to provoke a response. We have three thousand plus sets of images and posters. The exhibition being shown in London now is simultaneously being shown in China, the U.S. and Spain. Each show comes with eight sets of images and the accompanying educational programs attached. That's all evidence of my belief in a sense of social responsibility. But no, what I don't believe is that this will change the planet: this sort of photography, made with NGOs (non-governmental organizations), humanitarian care and aid agencies, and the debates around the rest of our programs, for which we supply facts and charts and background information, won't alter the way of the world. My work is a very small part of the global debate. I've made this television program with John Berger called, *The Spectre of Hope*. Globalization matters more than anything, because it affects all of us. That's why we have to put the people in these pictures inside the debate, make them a part of it.

Question from audience: I'm a youth worker—I work with young people—and your exhibition is very moving. But there's an issue about names, or the lack of them, on the picture captions. The news already just gives out about "Two Hundred Dead" or whatever, all of them nameless. What about all the children in your portraits?

SS: That's a decision I found I had to make. In some of my images, there are ten thousand people: my pictures can be very big. At one point we made the decision when I had shot, not just the kids in this show, but hundreds, it must be thousands, of them. It is at this stage that each kid comes to represent all of the others. I might add a name for myself—not for them—we live in a world where individuals are supposed to be made important, but that's not true. Individuals do not really have

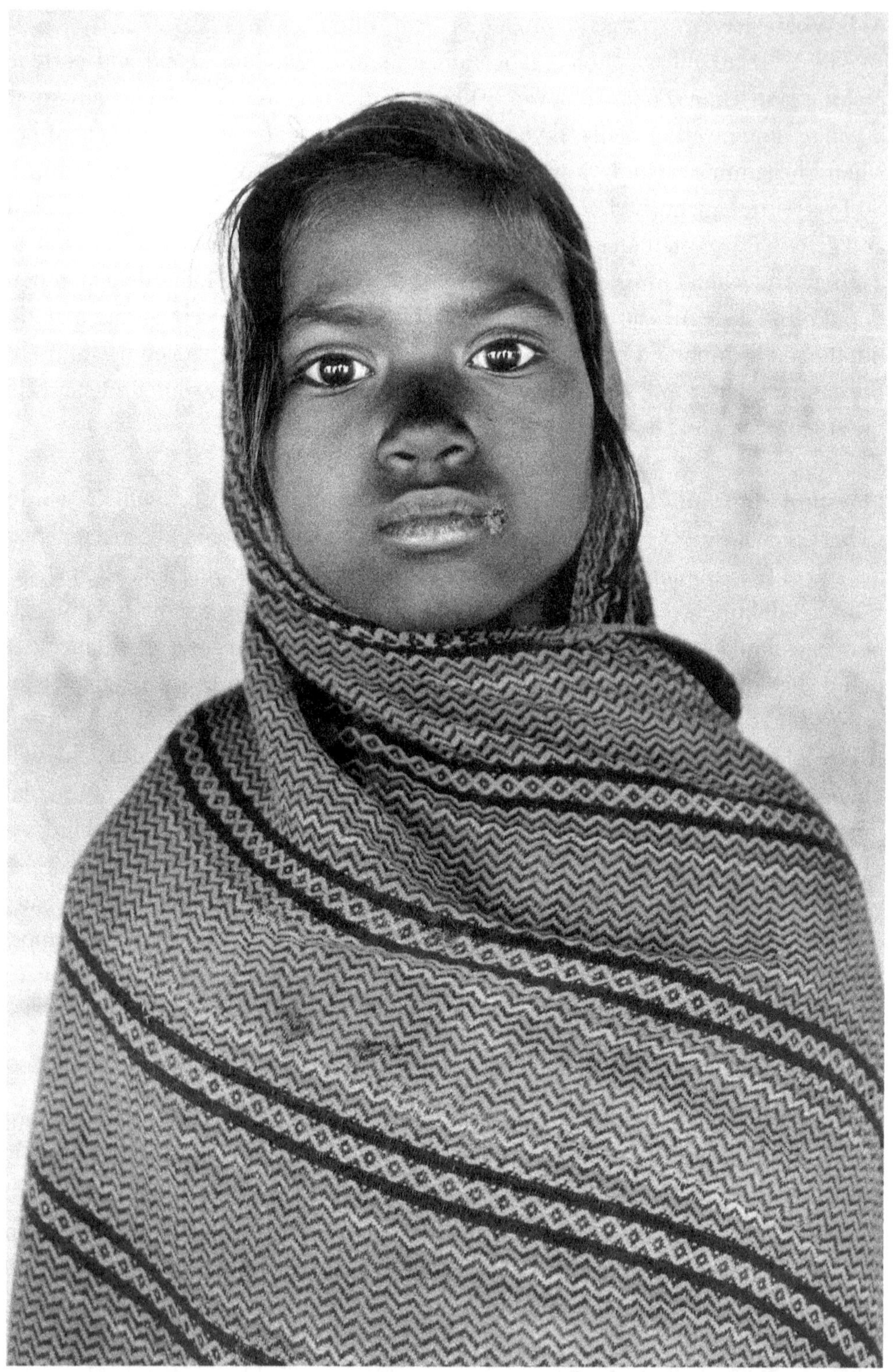

10.2. Sebastiao Salgado, "Center for Orphans from the Tribes of the Southern Bihar. Bihar State, India, 1997." © Sebastião Salgado/Amazonas/nbpictures.

impact, it's the community which counts. We live with the cult of the personality, as you see on TV, lonesome cowboys and heroes, violent and bad. I happen to believe the opposite: we don't need a name to characterize a kid, the one from Kosovo or Mozambique stands for all the others.

Exodus spent eight months hanging in Valencia, Spain, and was accompanied by a big educational outreach program. I met a teacher who told me she had had an exhibition of my work in her classroom. They had hung posters of my photographs, and all around them, the children had put all their own stuff. Their designs and writings were so fantastic, they created a whole debate around child portraiture: they didn't need to know a name to enter another child's world and make it all a part of their own discovery. If we involve this generation in a story like this, they will know it for the rest of their lives. This initiates them into a big discussion, and to me that's more important, if it turns them into activists for the future.

For myself, I don't believe that we should live without being activists. We live in such a strange way today, all isolated from one another, and from nature, and so on. For me the most important thing is to live your life as an activist, otherwise all too quickly you become a conformist.

AH: Is your photography, then, a way of making people aware, so that they may respond like you and hope and work for change? Was that behind the desire for raising consciousness?

SS: I believe it was, not that I went into photography in order to create a revolution and transform everything. I went into it because in the space of a month I discovered I had a tremendous passion for it, and I recognized its forms: I was born, as we were saying, with these forms living inside me, and I wanted them to be there in my photographs.

AH: But you didn't just take up photography for the sake of aesthetics?

SS: No, that's true. But I learned it as a language, and I learned that it was my language. And I live what I see and what is important to me, with passion. And I do believe that it is possible to work like this. To me all these activities hang together: there is no longer one box marked "social photography" and another marked "conceptual photography." To me photography is not an intellectual, rational, and Cartesian or postmodern act. It's not about producing objects for other people to stare at. No, it is the language of a whole life. It *is* my life.

AH: When you take an image, is it taken any differently if you think that you are shooting something in Central Africa to show in a village hall in Aimores or to mount a major exhibition in the Pompidou Centre in Paris?

SS: They are the same pictures that I show: I don't have one set of pictures to show here and another for somewhere else. None are "made for here" or "made for there." My viewer is absolutely assumed to be identical in every case. For me, the same picture is shown in the museum, in the newspaper, the NGO magazine, or wherever else. I don't have multiple sets for different outlets.

AH: Perhaps there aren't so many stories still to shoot around the world. You could do a book on Africa, on mining, or whatever, you still have so much existing material. Would you be happy to hang up your cameras and simply stay at home in Brazil in the future? Or do you still feel you are a full-on photographer?

SS: Yes, and a full-time one too! My God, yes, of course what I am is a photographer. Less than a month ago I was away shooting—next week I'm off on another story in Spain, about Real Madrid, the soccer team, because of course I'm Brazilian and I love soccer—at the same time I'm working on the polio book. And I was just now discussing with the World Bank in Washington about the funding—with Fred Ritchin, my editor in New York—and with *Vanity Fair,* who are going to run a big story just about the polio project, a thirty-two-page portfolio. So of course there's a lot of to-ing and fro-ing, but that's because I am a photographer, a 100 percent photographer. I'm not about to abandon it to become an ecologist here. At least until now, there's been no reason not to keep the two things going together for the last eleven years. On the contrary, far from being incompatible, photography and ecology complement one another.

Selected Works by Sebastião Salgado

The Children: Refugees and Migrants. New York: Aperture, 2000.
The End of Polio: A Global Effort to End a Disease. Forward Kofi A. Annan. Boston: Bulfinch, 2003.
Exodos. São Paulo: Companhia das Letras, 2000.
Exodus: Migrations against All Odds. New York: Aperture, 2001.
India, México: vientos paralelos. Photos Salgado, Graciela Iturbide, and Raghu Rai. Prologue Jean-Claude Carrière. Mexico City: Antiguo Colegio de San Ildefonso, DGE Ediciones, 2002.
Migrations: Humanity in Transition. New York: Aperture, 2000.
Other Americas. Intro. Alan Riding. New York: Pantheon, 1986.
Sahel: l'Homme en Detresse. Intro. Jean Lacouture. Text Xavier Emmanuelli. Paris: Prisma for Medecins sans Frontières, 1986.
Sebastião Salgado. Intro. Christian Caujolle. Paris: Centre National de la Photographie, 1993.
Terra: Struggle of the Landless. Preface José Saramago. Poetry Chico Buarque. London: Phaidon, 1997.
An Uncertain Grace. Text Eduardo Galeano and Fred Ritchin. New York: Aperture; San Francisco: San Francisco Museum of Modern Art, 1990.
Workers: An Archaeology of the Industrial Age. New York: Aperture; Philadelphia: Philadelphia Museum of Art, 1993.

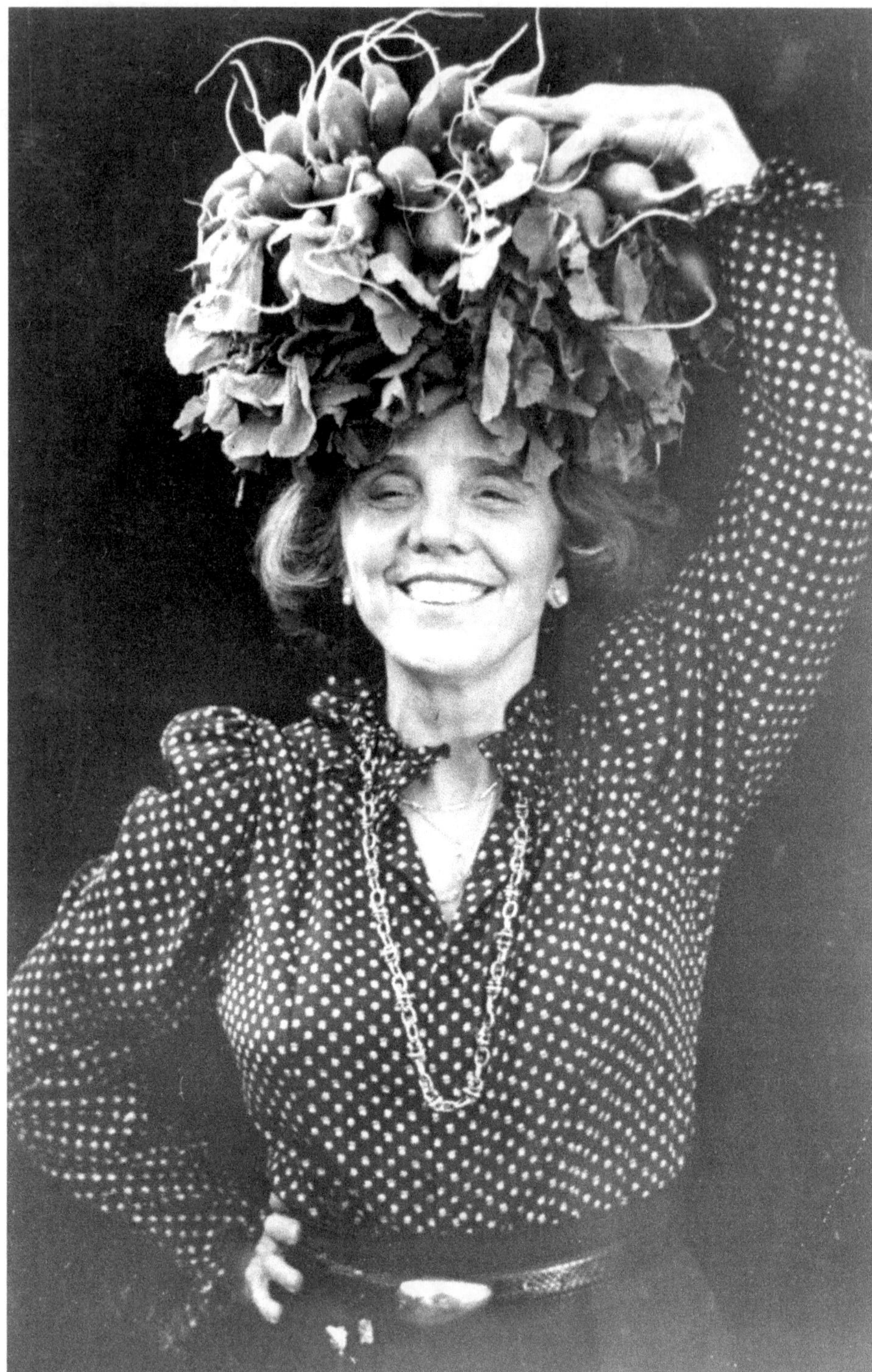

Fig. 11.1. Portrait of Elena Poniatowska in the market. From the author's personal archives.

Chapter Eleven

Literature and Photography

Parallel Crafts—An Interview with Elena Poniatowska

Dan Russek

Elena Poniatowska (1932) began her career as a journalist. She is one of the foremost chroniclers of Mexican culture and society of the second half of the twentieth century. Over the decades, her journalistic and fictional work has maintained an active relationship with photography. Photographs play a prominent role in works such as *La noche de Tlatelolco* (1971; *Massacre in México*, 1975), and *Nada, nadie* (1988), testimonies on the 1968 violence and the aftermath of the 1985 earthquake in Mexico City, respectively. Her works in collaboration include *Tlacotalpan* (with Mariana Yampolsky, 1987), *Juchitán de las mujeres* (with Graciela Iturbide, 1989), and *El Niño: Children of the Streets* (with Kent Klich, 1999). The novel *Tinísima* (1992) chronicles the life and times of the Italian photographer Tina Modotti. In this interview, Poniatowska talks about her friendship with photographers, her collaborative projects, the ideal relation between writer and photographer, and the challenges of the current landscape of visual culture.

Dan Russek: Photography is a thread running through your work as a chronicler and novelist. When and how did this relationship with photography get started?

Elena Poniatowska: I became interested in photography through journalism, and when I first started working as a journalist, in the early 1950s, sometimes I took pictures myself for my articles and interviews. Through the years I met many photographers. I started to work with a well-known photographer, Héctor García, and later on became friends with photographers Mariana Yampolsky and Graciela Iturbide, as well as Lola Álvarez Bravo and Pablo Ortiz Monasterio, the Chiapas photographer Raúl Ortega, and also Daniel Weinstock, who is very talented. I began to meet other artists, like Manuel Álvarez Bravo and Enrique Bostelmann, as well as the printmaker and photographer Alberto Beltrán, whose drawings illustrate the book of articles we did together, *Todo empezó el domingo*.

DR: Who are your favorite photographers?

EP: I've been interested in documentary photographers like Lewis Hine, whom I admire for denouncing child labor and for his images of immigrants to Ellis Island. I also really like Dorothea Lange, who documented the poverty and desperation during the Depression in the U.S. I could never forget that famous photo of the anguished mother's face who has nothing to feed her kids. I really admire Paul Strand, Ansel Adams, for his incredible landscapes, Cartier-Bresson and Robert Doisneau. Richard Avedon, Robert Capa, and Diane Arbus are also fine photographers. In Mexico, the Casasola brothers not only documented the Mexican Revolution but also the greater part of our modern national history. Other excellent photographers are Nacho López and Hugo Brehme, the German photographer who was in Mexico at the same time as Tina Modotti and Edward Weston. Right now, the best photographer in my mind is Kent Klich, who has published with Aperture. He's Swedish, although he lives in Denmark. We did a book together, published by Syracuse University Press, entitled *El Niño*, about street children. His images in this book are absolutely outstanding, and I've learned a lot from him. Forming a relationship with the street children was very difficult, and he managed to enter into their world so deftly, and after ten years of coming to Mexico to photograph them, he made friends with them. It was very complicated dealing with drug-addicted kids who reject well-intentioned outsiders. Many were ill, homeless, living under bridges and in pipes, in totally abominable conditions. They felt easily threatened, and it was a huge challenge to try to pull them out of these hellish surroundings.

DR: How has writing about photography and photographers affected your way of looking at literature?

EP: It's very important to me for a book or a newspaper to have illustrations. While it's a commonplace to say that a picture speaks a thousand words, certainly a photograph can have an enormous impact, just like the impact of a caricature or print.

DR: *La noche de Tlatelolco* would be without a doubt a very different book without the series of photographs that offer a visual prologue. Aside from the journalistic format, did you have in mind any literary precedent when you conceived of the design for this book?

EP: Experience dictated how I organized this book. The people that I interviewed said the same thing over and over, repeated that it was 5:19 p.m., that a green flare fell from a helicopter over the crowds in the Plaza of the Three Cultures, and that was the signal that unleashed the round of shooting on October 2 in Tlatelolco. I decided to do a montage, a collage, with people's versions of the massacre. I had no literary model. I've been told that the German essayist Enzensberger did something similar with a book on the anarchist Buenaventura Durruti. I was guided by intuition. I went to newspaper archives and chose the photographs. People also lent me photographs, as long as I assured them I would not reveal the names of those who gave them to me. At that time in Mexico we were under severe censorship, and people feared that I could be putting them in danger if I mentioned them. Those same photos were published later as if they were appearing for the first time, but they had been published in *La noche de Tlatelolco* first.

DR: Another book where the impact of photographic images is important is *Nada, nadie,* the book that gathers testimonies of the 1985 earthquake in Mexico. Did you choose the images and write the captions?

EP: In all my books I choose the photos and write the captions. The earthquake photos were given to me by Marco Antonio Cruz, an excellent photojournalist.

DR: When you wrote *Tinísima,* what most attracted you to Tina Modotti as a photographer?

EP: I was very intrigued by her interest in social themes, and of course the quality of her photographs: the roses, pelicans, the canvas of a circus tent, the huge straw hats viewed from above, the way she captures a washerwoman's hands. She had a great artistic sense, as well as great photographic intelligence, as revealed in her letters to Edward Weston, when he returned to Glendale, California.

DR: How would you compare your collaborations with Héctor García, Mariana Yampolsky, and Graciela Iturbide? What did you take with you, as far as creative energy, from your work with each of these artists?

EP: With Héctor García, the images were mainly to illustrate my reporting. He was rarely punctual, sometimes he brought along his wife, María, whom I taught to take pictures as we worked on these stories. She developed her husband's photos. My work with Héctor García was a brief project, immediate and temporary, of photojournalism. By contrast, Mariana and I went out sometimes for three days at a stretch, we stayed in little hotels or at houses of her friends, or even in rural huts. She liked to stop in every little village; she had a special sense for looking at things no one else bothered to see. In this way she was extraordinary. She made great discoveries—I consider her the Charles Darwin of photography. These trips made her very happy, and she transmitted that happiness. Sometimes I got exasperated with how slowly she drove her Volkswagen. It was hot as hell, and I was anxious to get there, so I'd complain, "Mariana, you're a terrible driver!" I'd be bored and impatient but suddenly she'd see something, she'd pull over onto a side road or into a ditch, and we'd discover extraordinary things. Sometimes we'd find ourselves in the middle of nowhere, at night, tired and hungry, but Mariana was totally seduced by what she was doing, and it was contagious.

My trips with Graciela Iturbide were also very gratifying. It's very revealing to observe what attracts each photographer and how she takes certain photos. For example, Graciela never hesitated to climb a fence or a tree, like Tina Modotti, to access a new angle. Graciela talks to people, laughs with them, "lives" with them before taking their picture. She's very sweet, accessible, and warm with others; watching her teaches you about life and about work. Another photographer I've worked with is Alicia Ahumada. She was Mariana's printer and she also worked with Graciela and with Víctor Flores Olea. She would emerge from the dark room with extraordinary prints. Another photographer who interests me is David Mahuad, who has documented miners dying of silicosis in the Pachuca mines.

DR: Did you establish any kind of artistic exchange with any of these photographers? For example, did you ever suggest that they take a particular photo?

EP: On the contrary, they were the ones who showed me things I hadn't seen. The only time I ever told a photographer what picture to take was with Héctor García, because in general he had a very specific task, which was to photograph whom I was interviewing. In this context he wasn't trying to take artistic pictures. I remember that he once took a picture of a child who was hiding in a wall, because my oldest son, Mane, had crawled in there. I told him to take that one. Another photo he took with me circulated all over the world. Through me he got permission to go into the Lecumberri prison. It's a picture of Siqueiros sticking his hand through the bars in protest. I don't think they would have let him in if I hadn't spoken to the prison director.

DR: In the book that you dedicated to Mariana Yampolsky—*Mariana Yampolsky y la buganvillia*—you mention that the pictures she took with you for the book on Tlacotalpan continue to affect you deeply. Beyond your friendship with her, can you comment on the emotional experience as a writer watching a photographer work?

EP: Mariana had the sensibility of a museum curator. She noticed how every object was placed, she plucked it out of the darkness and repositioned it into the light, she would see lace or embroidery on a blouse on an old woman in Tlacotalpan and she would stop to examine how it was unravelling. She had a great appreciation for detail. Once in Tlacotalpan she asked a woman if she could photograph her clothes, and the woman not only brought her the blouse but she washed it, starched it, ironed it, and made it look stunning, and then Mariana shot it. The same thing happened with embroidered sheets or mosquito nets or canopy beds. And of course this love of detail came into play when she photographed someone's face, even animals. She has a charming photo of a turkey looking at itself in the mirror—we consider turkeys very vain in Mexico—it's a marvelous photo. It was very special to witness the discovery of the world around us through Mariana. I will never be able to repay her for that; it was quite an apprenticeship.

DR: Could you talk about the creative process behind books like *Juchitán de las mujeres*, *Tlacotalpan*, or *Las soldaderas*? Did you generally see the photos before writing, basing your writing on them, or did you write first and then look for images related to the text?

EP: *Las soldaderas* was the only book where I saw the photos first. In my own books, I found the photos myself, after writing the text. That's how it worked in *La noche de Tlatelolco* and *Fuerte es el silencio*. In *Juchitán de las mujeres*, Graciela Iturbide and I went to Juchitán, where I met the women that Graciela photographed. Of course I saw the photos later on. In the case of artistic photos, like Graciela's and Mariana's, with whom I worked the most closely, I remembered the places we had visited together and the people with whom we'd talked. It's not like Mariana brought me her photos and asked me to write about them. On the contrary, we traveled together through those rural villages.

DR: What do you think is the ideal relationship between a writer and a photographer?

EP: The ideal relationship between a writer and a photographer emerges from our common projects, from the opportunity to travel together and share experiences, as occurred with Mariana. I'd like to do another book with Graciela Iturbide, one that we really work on in tandem, so that each evening we could discuss everything we had done during the day. Generally the photographer brings the images to the writer and says, "Now, you write." They leave you with the photographs, small prints or maybe contact sheets. The photographers recommend against describing the images. What I have to do is come to my own conclusions, rather than describe in words what they've already said with the photos. It's all about parallel crafts, as if we were the two rails of a train: the photographer is one rail and the writer is the other, although I consider the role of the writer as substantially less important than that of the photographer in a book with text and images. The photographs could be published without the text, but the text would not exist without the photos that came first.

DR: Which photos do you remember as having left a deep impression on you and why?

EP- A photo taken by a photographer named Ursula Bernath, a friend of Mathias Goeritz, affected me very deeply. I once went to a wedding with her. She was taking pictures of the bride and groom, the families and guests, you know, that very conventional kind of photography to satisfy the vanity of the customers. Suddenly, she turned and saw a poor little boy, a street kid who was watching the wedding, and the look on this boy's face is extraordinary. That face has stayed with me throughout my life. There are also those classic photos of the Jewish boy with his hands up in the Warsaw ghetto, the little naked girl running in the road in Viet Nam, Robert Capa's photographs of the Spanish Civil War.

More than their visual impression, they've stayed with me in my heart. I'm not very sophisticated, the photos that move me stir my feelings more than anything.

DR: Given your intellectual and professional trajectory, it seems only natural that your daughter, Paula, became a photographer. How do you view her career choice? Do you think that in some way she's following in your footsteps?

EP: My three children are good photographers, particularly Paula. One could say that photography runs in the family—it's a medium that we all respond to. More than following along their mother's path, my kids think writing is a drag. Since they were young they thought journalism was too much work, and that being in front of a typewriter all day is no way to live.

DR: Finally, what would you say are the challenges and opportunities that a writer faces today, given that we are living in such a visual culture?

EP: I sometimes feel a bit out of it, and that it's requiring more and more effort to adapt. When I see what visual culture produces, so immediate and fleeting, it's disappointing. It seems to me that if Flaubert, Dostoyevsky, and Tolstoy needed nothing more than paper and pen, that proves that it's the human mind that produces works of art, not technology. Although certainly technology facilitates things. I remember what was coming out fifty years ago. As journalists we wrote on recycled paper, beige, wrinkled, and cheap, that the newspapers gave us and that inevitably was destined for the garbage. I look at my articles from that time on that paper, as I've saved some of them, and I wonder what I was doing with my life, how I could be so passionately dedicated to something so fleeting and fragile. It's the feeling we get from these papers, yellowed and torn, where I look at them and say, "So this is what life amounts to!" And one comes to the inevitable conclusion: this is what's left of our work, our life.

Selected Works

By Elena Poniatowska:

Fuerte es el silencio. Mexico City: Era, 1981.

Hasta no verte Jesús mío. Mexico City: Era, 1969.

Massacre in Mexico. Trans. Helen Lane. New York: Viking, 1975.

Nada, nadie: las voces del temblor. Mexico City: Era, 1988.

La noche de Tlatelolco. Mexico City: Era, 1971.

Querido Diego, te abraza Quiela. Mexico City: Era, 1978.

"Some Women Photographers of Mexico." In *Compañeras de México: Women Photograph Women.* Ed. Amy Conger. Riverside, CA: University Art Gallery, Regents of the University of California, 1990, 43–55.

Tinísima. Mexico City: Era, 1992.

Visual collaborations:

Beltrán, Alberto. *Todo empezó el domingo.* Mexico City: Océano, 1997.

Iturbide, Graciela. *Luz y luna, las lunitas.* Mexico City: Era, 1994.

______. *Juchitán de las mujeres.* Mexico City: Toledo, 1989.

Klich, Kent. *El Niño: Children of the Streets.* Syracuse, NY: Syracuse University Press, 1999.

Yampolsky, Mariana. *La casa que canta.* Mexico City: SEP, 1982.

______. *Estancias del olvido.* Mexico City: Educación Gráfica, 1987.

______. *Mariana Yampolsky y la buganvillia.* Mexico City: Plaza y Janés, 2001.

______. *Mazahua.* Toluca, Mexico: Gobierno del Estado, 1993.

______. *Tlacotalpan.* Veracruz: Instituto Veracruzano de la Cultura, 1987.

Critical Sources:

Franco, Jean. *Plotting Women: Gender and Representation in Mexico.* New York: Columbia University Press, 1989.

Jorgensen, Beth. *The Writing of Elena Poniatowska: Engaging Dialogues.* Austin: University of Texas Press, 1994.

Schuessler, Michael K. *Elenísima: ingenio y figura de Elena Poniatowska.* Intro. Carlos Fuentes. Mexico City: Diana, 2003.

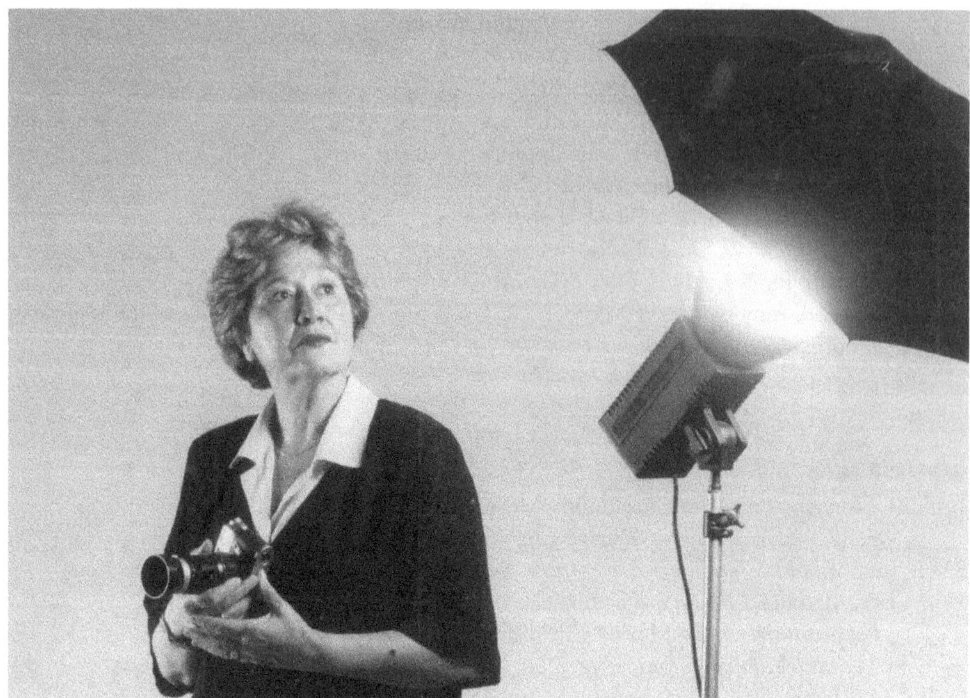

Fig. 12.1. Sara Facio. Autorretrato/Self-Portrait.

Chapter Twelve

Among Friends

Portraits of Writers—An Interview with Sara Facio

Jorge Schwartz

To say that Sara Facio changed the cultural landscape of photography in the second half of the twentieth century is no exaggeration. Her contribution to photography has been immense, not only in Argentina but throughout Latin America. Her artistic vision, together with her institutional ingenuity, erase the boundaries between advertising and art. I have followed her career since the late 1970s, when I first met her and her colleague, Alicia D'Amico, in their studio on Calle Juncal. I was invited along for a shoot of the huge papier-maché figure that was created in 1932 to promote Oliverio Girondo's book *Espantapájaros*. Over the years, their energy, conviction, and complete commitment to the profession have made their photographs, exhibits, and books real labors of love.

I would like to frame this interview by quoting some of the writers Sara Facio has featured in her outstanding collaborations between photography and literature. Their praise of her work reveals how honored they have felt to have been photographed by her, and the mutual respect and friendship inscribed in these projects. When Pablo Neruda saw Sara and Alicia's photographs, he wrote to them in a letter: "The two of you must be crazy, you come all the way to Chile but fail to visit your best friends: the penguins of Isla Negra. I rarely write letters, but I had to write to tell you how thrilled I am with your photographs." Julio Cortázar writes in *Territorios* about Facio and D'Amico's photographs of psychiatric patients: "Photographers from Buenos Aires, authors of admirable portraits, Sara and Alicia made the descent into the hell of a psychiatric hospital, and the testimony that they emerged with definitely merits its title, *Humanario*. I could not have written this text without their longstanding generosity and understanding. Avoiding sensationalism and horror, Sara and Alicia have broken through the barriers of hypocrisy, prejudice, and fear" (92) (editors' translation).

Since the nineteenth century, a falsely unified and idealized vision of Latin America persists. Now on the threshold of the twenty-first century, we are challenged to redefine that vision. Sara Facio's powerful lens illuminates the faces of Latin America's persistent attempts to forge a utopian vision. From her postcards to her books, Facio's sophisticated production is a legacy to artistic activism that is truly Latin American.

Jorge Schwartz: Severo Sarduy, who was voluntarily exiled in Paris, was criticized for saying that his *patria* was the page. Would you say your *patria* is the photographic image?

Sara Facio: Photography is my life. I cannot imagine myself doing anything else. By the same token, I am Argentine. There's nothing I deplore more than Argentines who want a double passport. I respect Sarduy's voluntary exile. He himself would tell anyone who would listen that as a homosexual, he couldn't live in Cuba.

JS: In your work, is there an alliance between aesthetics and ideology? Did you ever suffer any type of censorship as a portraitist of writers?

SF: I've never stopped myself from photographing something or from writing about someone for ideological reasons. It strikes me as small-minded, out of date, smacking of Stalinism or McCarthyism. Of course those kinds of restrictions are still being imposed, especially in journalism, but not against me.

I've been censored more for working with writers than for photographing them. The Argentine dictatorship in 1968 banned an exhibit of photographs from the book *Buenos Aires, Buenos Aires* at the Museum of Modern Art. Why? Because Julio Cortázar had written the text, and he had protested against the dictatorship in Paris. I've been censored several other times and there have been death threats, but I'd rather not look back.

JS: Among your books on writers or with writers, there are four that especially stand out for the intense interaction between the writers and your lens: Cortázar, Neruda, Miguel Ángel Asturias, and María Elena Walsh. These are such distinct worlds! Is there any writer who is missing in your repertoire, or any specific book photographing a writer that you would have liked to have done?

SF: There are two writers I admire enormously who are missing: Clarice Lispector and Manuel Puig. I once took color slides of Lispector, but the agency that hired me kept them. Whenever Puig and I ran into each other, we always talked about doing a project together, but it never came to pass. With the four writers you mention, I was able to really produce something special, because of the strong affinities between us that grew into real friendships. Working with them meant dialogue, shared ideas, and it was a pleasure to work together.

JS: What about writers who are associated with art and photography, for example, what do you think of Juan Rulfo's photography?

SF: I had a very enthusiastic response when I first saw it, and I exhibited his work in 1986 at the Teatro San Martín photo gallery. His work amazed the public because of its subject matter and because no one knew that Rulfo was such a good photographer.

JS: Your first books were produced in collaboration with the late Alicia D'Amico: *Buenos Aires, Buenos Aires* and *Humanario*, with texts by Cortázar, and *Geografía*, with text by Neruda. You've probably been asked this many times, but could you comment on these "four hands" productions, from the photographing to the book editing?

SF: Alicia and I met at the National School of Fine Arts when we were thirteen or fourteen years old. We studied together, graduated, and traveled to Paris in 1955, where we lived for over a year on scholarships from the French government. We traveled all over Europe and together became acquainted with German photography. So we had the same exact education and exposure. We were friends, we loved each other like sisters, and worked together for twenty-five years, starting in 1960. We never had any sense of competition. Everything we earned, and that was substantial, since we worked constantly, we shared. We were always each other's toughest critics. We only included the best in our books, photographs or text, regardless of which one of us had produced it. For example, in *Retratos y autorretratos*, there are writers that only one of us photographed. Alicia preferred to talk to Jorge Luis Borges rather than be distracted taking pictures. We never worried about the quantity of photographs that each of us contributed, although it might be hard to believe, since we were not in competition. In the darkroom, I was in charge of the printing, and we both worked on the grain. We would discuss endlessly over how dark or light a photo should be, but we always came to an agreement. In 1991 we had an exhibit at the Pompidou Center in Paris, and even though we each had our own studio at that time, we discussed the grain of each enlargement, and we redid them until we were both satisfied. We never had any serious disagreement over photography. Until the end, about photography and art in general, we were of a single mind.

JS: Some twenty-five years separate two of your best-known projects, *Retratos y autorretratos* (1973) and *Foto de escritor* (1998). How do you see the first of these from a distance? Could you comment on the differences between the two, as well as their authorship?

SF: *Retratos y autorretratos* is like a favorite child. It was my first book produced around a theme that affected every aspect: the photos, the texts, the editing, the production, everything. I felt like this project in its totality really belonged to me, without compromising for anything or anyone. The idea was to feature the photographed writer in his or her own surroundings, and the writer then wrote a self-portrait based on those photos. It was quite a task to contact twenty-five writers whom I didn't even know, who lived in different countries on several continents! Eventually only twenty-two were included in the book.

The adventure got underway in 1963, when there was no fax or email, and people didn't even use the phone much. Luckily there were two of us, and Alicia and I cosigned all our work without distinguishing which one of us took any given photo, although we knew which ones were taken by whom. We photographed the writers until 1973, but most intensively between 1969 and 1972. We traveled to Chile, Peru, Mexico, Spain, England, and Paris, since so many Latin Americans lived outside their own countries, (and so many still do). Gathering the written texts and the original signatures was another odyssey! But finally, without censorship, we managed to publish the book in an inexpensive newsprint edition, which we were very proud of, since only a good quality photo can be printed on poor quality paper.

Foto de escritor, from 1998, is a totally different concept. While this book still features Latin American writers (most of them appear in *Retratos y Autorretratos* of course, since they're the century's premier writers), there are a couple of important differences. This time more writers are included, and the text tells the story of how the photographs were taken as well as my impressions as the photographer in front of each of these figures. The book also includes a text chosen by each writer from his or her own work. The production was much more carefully done, on better quality paper that highlights the quality of the images.

JS: What is the role of the portrait today? Is it surviving as a genre?

SF: Portraiture is one of the origins of photography, and it will exist as long as the medium exists. That fusion between reality and subjectivity that the photographic gaze offers is a new and unique vision that no known medium up to the present can replace.

JS: Do you think there is such a thing as a "feminine gaze" in photography?

SF: Yes, I do, or at least I recognize it or sense it. It's not easy to explain, but I think there is a particular focus on events or a way of looking at objects that, like in plenty of other endeavors, distinguishes how women and men produce images.

JS: You have been involved with some significant institutions that have expanded the scope of photography in Argentina. Can you comment on your role in the Fotogalería del Teatro San Martín and the Museo Nacional de Bellas Artes?

SF: I opened the Fotogalería del Teatro San Martín in 1985, and it's become a very unique place in Buenos Aires, known for high quality. Our mission was to set the standard for how to exhibit photographic work and how to introduce a photographer, from biographical information to his or her aesthetic vision. The photographers felt respected and joined right in. This generated a certain self-esteem among the photographers that they had never before enjoyed.

My contribution to the Museo Nacional de Buenos Aires has been to establish the foundation for a National Photographic Collection. Since there are no funds for buying photographs, I started the collection by donating part of my private collection, works by well-known international artists like Alfred Stieglitz, Ralph Gibson, Annemarie Heinrich, Lucien Clergue, Sebastião Salgado, Graciela Iturbide, and Alejandro Witcomb. My publishing partner, María Cristina Orive, made a major donation of fundamental works by Manuel Álvarez Bravo, Luis González Palma, André Kertész, and so the collection grew.

Other friends in the artistic community continued to donate work, like María Elena Walsh, who gave some work by Franco Fontana and Henri Cartier Bresson. Eventually photographers themselves, Argentines as well as foreign artists, generously contributed some of their best work. It's so important for national culture for our main art museum to have a photography collection of this magnitude. The collection was finally exhibited to the public, with a corresponding catalogue, in 1998. I consider this exhibit to be the culmination of my efforts to integrate photography into the world of visual arts.

JS: How does La Azotea publishing house that you started with María Cristina Orive fit into your contribution to photography?

SF: María Cristina Orive and I founded La Azotea Photographic Publications in 1973. At first we worked out of my house, but once some projects got underway, we moved into the huge photography studio I shared with Alicia D'Amico, who also worked with us for a while. We published photography exclusively: books, posters, and postcards by the finest photographers in Latin America. We celebrated Azotea's thirtieth anniversary in 2003, and looking over three decades of work, we felt quite pleased with what we've accomplished, faithfully adhering to our initial goals. We've published real pioneers, like Martín Chambi from Peru, Yas-Noriega from Guatemala, Witcomb, Grete Stern, Annemarie Heinrich from Argentina. We were the first to publish reeditions of important historical and recent images. We generated an appreciation for the photographers who have come before us, awakening a historical consciousness that was lacking. We also highlighted the new generation of young talent: Marcos López, Adriana Lestido, and Oscar Pintor from Argentina, and Luis González Palma from Guatemala. La Azotea has had its own booth at international book fairs in Buenos Aires, Frankfurt, as well as at exhibits in France,

Mexico, and Venezuela. We've won national and international awards and prizes, sponsored photography events and exhibits throughout the Americas and Europe. All of these efforts impact the presence of photography on the cultural landscape.

JS: Let's talk a bit about the intellectual tradition behind your work that links writing and photography. Do you consider Gisèle Freund one of your inspirations?

SF: I saw Gisèle's photographs of writers long after I'd come to appreciate her as a theorist. I read her book *La fotografía y las clases medias* (Photography and the middle class), published in Buenos Aires, when I started my column *Tiempo de Fotografía* in *La Nación* around 1966 [see *Leyendo fotos*]. Her book raised a series of questions and opened up new horizons. Eventually I met her, and later I began to see her photos. I'm not sure I'd call her my inspiration, but I do consider her an important teacher. One of the things we had in common was a deep interest in Victoria Ocampo. I admired Victoria's talent and personality, and Gisèle was impressed with her humanitarianism, not just for helping her personally, but for all the help she lent European intellectuals during World War II.

JS: Are you working on any projects right now involving any writers?

SF: Yes, I'm currently editing two books on writers, Victoria Ocampo and Julio Cortázar. They are going to be almost entirely photographic, with very little text, very intimate, based on memories of conversations or letters. The letters, or at least the signatures, will be reproduced in facsimile.

JS: In Brazil, photographers such as Maureen Bissilliat and Ana Mariani are also connecting photography with literature, but in a different way; they are interested in trying to recreate a literary universe through photography, for example in their books on Guimarães Rosa and Jorge Amado, respectively. Would you say that your photographs of Asturia's Guatemala, of Neruda on Isla Negra, or of Borges in the National Library are the visual recreation of those literary universes? Do you think these correspondences are even possible? Or, in other words, what can the visual image give us that words can't, and what are the limits of images that words are able to overcome?

SF: For those of us who love literature, there's no doubt that language always offers a universe for interpretation. Photography is an immediate visual universe that, when it's most effective, integrates with language and produces a totality. I think this in evident in the case of Isla Negra. Neruda wrote beautiful poems and prose about his houses, things, friends, landscapes, but if you look at *Geografía*, we see all of this in its plenitude, it becomes embodied, it takes on a new identity, not that it's improved or diminished, but it simply completes the ideas.

On Guatemala, such a beautiful country, there are dozens of books and publications, but nevertheless, Miguel Ángel Asturias was very enthusiastic when he saw the proofs of *Actos de Fe*. Even though he was ill, he kept the images by his side, because he wanted to write about each and every one. Sadly, he died before he could finish. It was marvelous for María Cristina Orive and me to witness the passion with which Asturias devoured every image.

As far as the limits of words or images, I don't think there are any. The only limit is talent. A perfect poem by Neruda, Borges, or Asturias doesn't need visual images. A good photograph needs no words. But they certainly can be joined, they can complement one another, adding to the reader-spectator's experience.

Selected Works by Sara Facio

Actos de fe en Guatemala. Photos Sara Facio and María Cristina Orive. Text Miguel Ángel Asturias. Buenos Aires: Azotea, 1980.

Buenos Aires, Buenos Aires. Photos Sara Facio and Alicia D'Amico. Text Julio Cortázar. Buenos Aires: Sudamericana, 1968.

La colección fotográfica del Museo Nacional de Bellas Artes. Coord. Sara Facio and Jorge Glusberg. Buenos Aires: Azotea and Museo Nacional de Bellas Artes, 1998.

Foto de escritor. Photos by Sara Facio. Text various writers. Buenos Aires: Azotea, 1998.

La Fotogalería del Teatro San Martín. Comp. and text by Sara Facio. Buenos Aires: Azotea, 1990.

Geografía de Pablo Neruda. Photos Sara Facio and Alicia D'Amico. Text Pablo Neruda. Barcelona: Ayma, 1974.

Humanario. Photos Sara Facio and Alicia D'Amico. Text Julio Cortázar. Intro. Fernando Pagés Larraya. Buenos Aires: Azotea, 1976.

Leyendo fotos. Buenos Aires: Azotea, 2002.

María Elena Walsh: Retrato(s) de una artista libre. Photos Sara Facio. Buenos Aires: Azotea, 1999.

Pablo Neruda. Photos Sara Facio. Text Sara Facio, Pablo Neruda, and Diana Bellessi. Buenos Aires: Azotea, 1988.

Retratos y autorretratos. Photos Sara Facio and Alicia D'Amico. Text various writers. Buenos Aires: Crisis, 1973.

Sara Facio: Retratos (1960–1992). Photos Sara Facio. Text María Elena Walsh. Buenos Aires: Azotea, 1992.

References

Cortázar, Julio. *Territorios*. Mexico City: Siglo XXI, 1978.

Freund, Gisèle. *La fotografía y las clases medias*. Buenos Aires: Losada, 1946.

______. *Portraits d'écrivains et d'artistes*. Chirmer & Mosel, 1989.

Girondo, Oliverio. *Espantapájaros: al alcance de todos*. Buenos Aires: Proa, 1932.

Rulfo, Juan. *Juan Rulfo: México, fotógrafo*. Text Carlos Fuentes. Barcelona: Lunwerg, 2001.

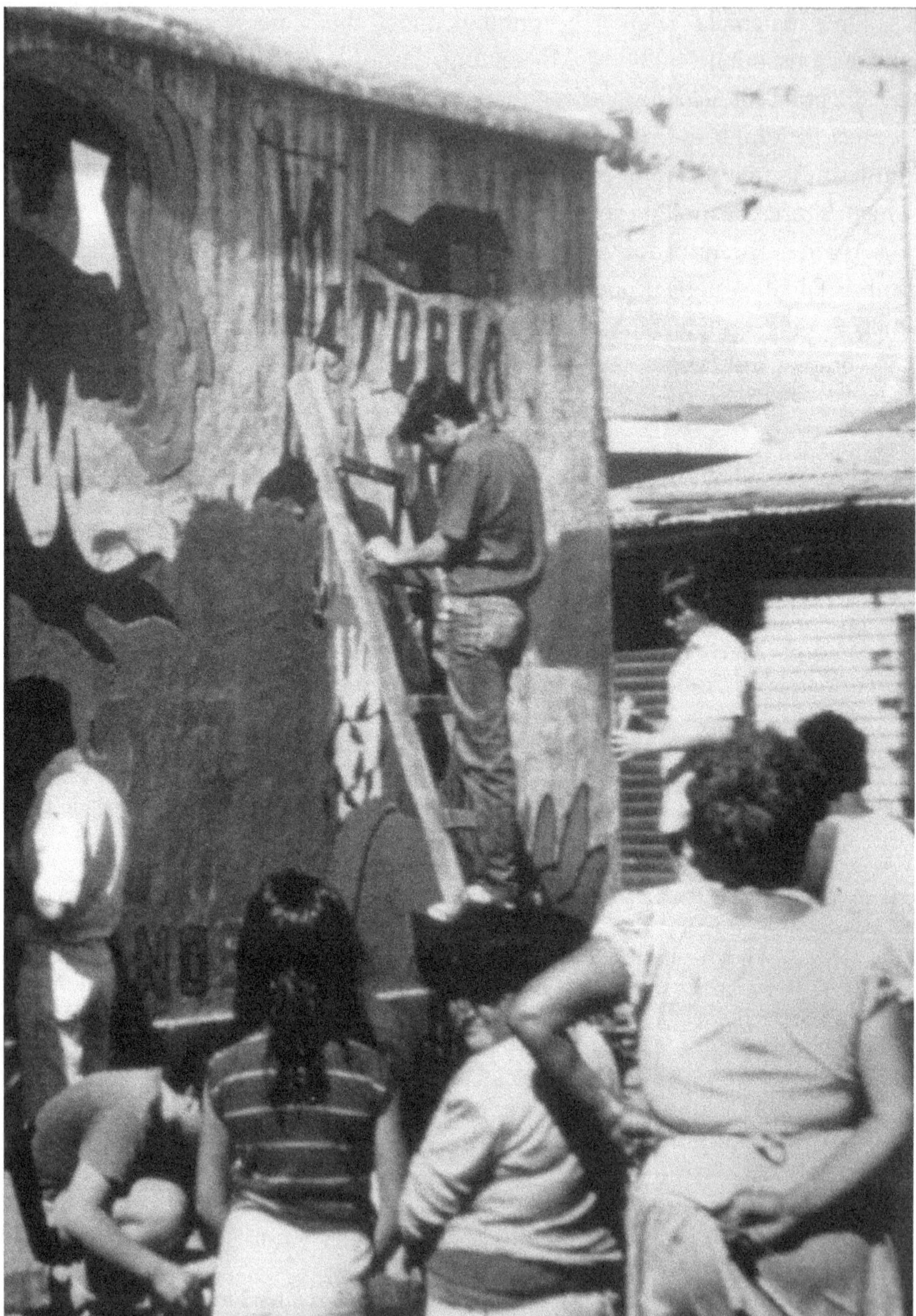

Fig. 13.1. APJ (Young Artist's Association), 1984, mural in the shantytown La Victoria, Santiago. From Nelly Richard, *Margins and Institutions*.

Chapter Thirteen

La Escena de Avanzada

Photography and Writing in Postcoup Chile —A Conversation with Nelly Richard

Idelber Avelar

Over the past twenty-five years, Nelly Richard has progressively become one of the foremost voices in Chilean and Latin American essayism. Since 1990, she has edited the influential *Revista de Crítica Cultural*, one of Latin America's main venues for cultural, literary, and artistic criticism. Her activity combines the insights of performance, experimental arts, and feminism, in order to stage disruptive interventions in the artistic world as well as in intellectual circles. Although her work is widely read in a number of academic circles, Nelly Richard is not herself an academic. Her trajectory includes active membership in and theorization of the avant-garde collectives known in the late 1970s as *escena de avanzada*, exhibit curating, and conference organizing. Her first book, entitled *Cuerpo correccional* (Correctional body), was published in 1980. The book was an in-depth analysis of the work of visual artist Carlos Leppe, while being at the same time an exercise in avant-garde writing in its own right. She later published *Margins and Institutions: Art in Chile since 1973* (1986), *Arte en Chile desde 1973: escena de avanzada y sociedad* (1987) (Art in Chile since 1973: The avant-garde scene and society), *La estratificación de los márgenes* (1989) (The stratification of the margins), *Masculino/ femenino: prácticas de la diferencia y cultura democrática* (1993) (*Masculine/Feminine: Practices of Difference and Democratic Culture*), *La insubordinación de los signos* (1994) (*The Insubordination of Signs*), and most recently *Residuos y metáforas* (1998) (Residues and metaphors). She was co-coordinator of the Rockefeller-sponsored seminar on postdictatorship, carried out by *Revista de Crítica Cultural* and ARCIS University (1999–2002). The following interview was carried out by email between March and September 2003.

Idelber Avelar: How would you contrast the role of photography in the activist art of *brigadismo* that dominated the artistic scene in precoup Chile with the role taken by photography subsequently, in the late 1970s, in the spectrum of avant-garde practices known as *escena de avanzada*?

Nelly Richard: Before answering your specific question on the role of photography in the *escena de avanzada*, I believe it is necessary to pinpoint the context of the debate that signaled the emergence of that scene, so one can understand the impact of its break with previous practices, such as muralism. Toward the late 1970s, under dictatorship in Chile, a number of artistic practices emerged and coalesced as a "scene," in the sense that they shared certain critical traces that produced a *collective effect*. It was the scene articulated theoretically as "*escena de avanzada*" in my *Margins and Institutions* (1986).

What endowed the *avanzada* with an explosive uniqueness in the context of the Chilean dictatorship was an odd mixture of a certain avant-garde experimentalism (the desire to transgress the institutional closure of the art system through practices that relied on the body and the city as social materials upon which creatively to intervene, so as to generate leaps and mutations in subjectivity) and the deconstructive will to radicalize a critique of representation that disassembled textual and visual signifying codes. The *avanzada* attempted to reconceptualize the link between art and politics outside the ideological codification of the traditional Left. This meant that the *avanzada* dwelled in a provocative and uncomfortable place on the map of anti-dictatorial culture in Chile. On the one hand, the *avanzada* situated itself in explicit opposition to the dictatorial paradigm, and therefore shared the experience of censorship and exclusion that affected, in those years, all activities of the resistance. At the same time, however, the *avanzada* maintained polemic relations with sectors of the traditional Left, whose activist culture privileged an aesthetic of testifying, denouncing, and protesting.

The activist art that expressed itself through circuits of alternative culture related to the social and political outside in linear referential modes. The Left that defended such art deemed the language of the *avanzada* cryptic and elitist, due to its semiotic-deconstructive turn that frustrated the pathos of a culture of martyrdom. The activist art of the orthodox Left, in its task of recuperating broken symbols of national memory and identity, defended an epic of a meta-meaning (Anti-Dictatorship, Resistance, the People, etc.), the historical rescuing of which served as an axis of community reintegration. Meanwhile, the *avanzada* art worked with fragments, *coupures*, sparks, and discontinuities, and remained skeptical of all totalization. A clash of languages and sensibilities thereby took place between, on the one hand, the heroic testimonialism of the aesthetic of denouncing, and on the other, the residual poetics of the *avanzada*, which resorted to the *margin* as a concept-metaphor to speak of residues and leftovers, of fractures and non-belonging, of liminal positions and political nomadism, of convulsive subjectivity and vocabulary in disarray. The *avanzada* thus privileged practices that were incompatible with the restitutive will of harmonizing meaning.

The recourse to photography granted the *avanzada* certain operative keys to break with the illusion of the organic totality of the form that used to sustain representational discourses. The photographic grammar of collage and montage (with techniques for cutting, fragmenting, juxtaposing, dissociating) emphasized fission and syntactic disconnection. This language allowed the *avanzada* to underscore the material violence of the fractures proper to a culture of fragments. The use of these techniques and supports questioned very strongly the academicism of painting as well as its contemplative rites, steeped in the aristocratic tradition of the fine arts. It is true that forerunners of this use of photography in the 1960s, such as Francisco Brugnoli, Virginia Errázuriz, and José Balmes, already linked art to the informative context of social and political news, for example, in the use of newspaper cutouts that intervened in the image. But it is only with the *avanzada* that photography undergoes the change from *technical recourse* to *theoretical figure*. This occurred thanks to works and texts that placed the question of photography at the center of the debate on history and memory, on trauma, drama, and experience.

IA: Is there a specific poetic organizing, in the *avanzada*, of the relationship between photography and writing (inscription of texts on the image, use of subtitles)? Who were the *avanzada* artists that resorted to photographic language in the most innovative way?

NR: First we would have to evoke the terms of a debate that opposed multiple and antagonistic positions in 1970s/'80s Chilean art between the partisans of photography and the defenders of painting. The most basic argument was that the camera was a visual instrument that was unmatched "when it came to show man in crisis," and that only photographic forms of documenting could depict real, social brutality, since the direct communicability of its language proved more effective to denounce the realities of dictatorial Chile than the imaginary recreation and stylistic transfiguration of painting.

As Adriana Valdés once pointed out, the advocates of photography resorted to it as a form of evidence and proof of accusation. They found that the pictorial exercise belonged to a subjective realm of individual expression that was ultimately selfish. The defense of the recourse to photography professed an ethical claim of social commitment to objective reality, against the aestheticizing subjectivism of painting. Seen from the angle of visual technologies of massive reproduction that were then changing artistic media, painting seemed relegated to a preindustrial image still trapped in the "cult value" of the artwork and in the metaphysics of creation (mystery, contemplation, retreat). The *avanzada* art attempted to refute such cult value of the canonized and sacralized art of museums, always complicitous with the academicism of the fine arts.

For Chilean artists and critics, the reading of Walter Benjamin's "The Work of Art in the Age of its Technological Reproducibility" was very important. It is interesting to note that in Chile, unlike in other places, Benjamin's thought was not circulated primarily by philosophy or literary studies, but by the visual arts and by the theoretical interpretations that were then being made of the art of the *avanzada*. On the one hand, Benjamin provided the idea of a "refractory art" that abandoned a number of inherited concepts and introduced others, which he defined as concepts that could not ever become useful for fascism. The notion of refractory art for us had to do with critical operations that produced conceptual breaks that could no longer be integrated or assimilated, either by the military regime's officialism or by the common sense of the traditional Left's ideological culture. The other intensive use of Benjamin arose out of the encounter between two key names: theoretician Ronald Kay and visual artist Eugenio Dittborn. In a remarkable piece entitled *Del espacio de acá* (1980), Kay elaborated a Benjaminian reflection on Dittborn's work. The cultural and theoretical resonance of that piece is still ineluctable.

Even though many important Chilean artists of that time should be remembered for the importance of their works and the role of photography in them (e.g. Carlos Leppe, Catalina Parra, Carlos Altamirano), it was Eugenio Dittborn who truly made his work a theoretical-visual investigation into the question of photography that stands out for its systematic character, rigor, and reflexive brilliance. Dittborn's work combines text and image; it combines photography, painting, and writing. It has consistently explored the social and technical mediations that stratify multiple forms of gazing in Latin America and thereby produce uneven leaps vis-à-vis the banner of linear progress coming from the metropolitan and modern centers. By juxtaposing distinct temporalities where the synchronic and the anachronistic coexist, Dittborn exposes the conflictive, residual heterogeneity of a Latin American social and cultural formation, where new visual technologies overlap and clash with buried pasts and untimely memories.

IA: Would you suggest that photography came to represent, in Pinochet's Chile, something beyond itself, that is to say, a particular relationship with the very memory of the nation? If so, what was the nature of that relationship?

NR: It is worth our while here to recall another particular feature of the *avanzada*'s relation to photography. I mentioned that their art attempted to mark itself off from the heroic-monumental cult of History and the epic of Memory. Through the art of intervention and urban performances, the *avanzada* played with a micro-poetics of precarious and fleeting events that refuted the solemnity proper to the eternalization of museums. The urban performances sought to produce marks of change in the images of the body and the city. The gesture was so ephemeral that the question of the "register" became obsessive. Video or photographic support to document performances and art happenings provided a supplement of duration that that fleeting creative practice needed in order to testify to its own existence. Rather than a "monument," the *avanzada* elected the "document" and envisioned a problematic connected to inscription, to remembrance, to tracing, to archiving. The *avanzada* thus intervened in the question of how to inscribe memory in an age when history has been progressively voided of referent.

Another interesting point is that various *avanzada* artists (mostly Dittborn, but also Carlos Leppe and Virginia Errázuriz) worked with *fotos carné*, the photos found on national ID cards. Dittborn carried out systematic work around the repressive grammar of the pose in this kind of photograph, one that displayed subjects captive of the legal procedures of control proper to the Law. Working with ID cards for the *avanzada* was a way of exposing the brutal *filing* as a common feature both of judicial photograph and of social-political repression. Under dictatorship, the procedures for capturing and detaining a self in the prison of ID cards were analogous to the daily violations of identity undergone by Chilean citizens. The photographic operations carried out by portraits and their framed, serializing poses–subject to numbering and classification—spoke visually about the "disciplinary society" as the sum of coercive techniques displayed by normative power. It is quite an impact retrospectively to read that work carried out by the *avanzada* with ID cards under dictatorship, if one puts it in perspective with what happened later. The families of detained and disappeared citizens, by reclaiming the theme of human rights, exhibited images of their loved ones, often taken from ID cards. It is as though the *avanzada* artifacts had anticipated, through the *fotos carné*, the language later brought to light by the device for suppressing identities: the language of anonymity, disappearance, and torture that went from *signs of identification* (the serial pose that files identities) to *the disidentification of signs* (the hiding of marks that individualize those who disappeared).

It is difficult to think of photography in postdictatorial Chile without letting oneself be traversed by the image of these photographic portraits displayed by the families of the detained and the disappeared in their marches. Maybe that is where the phantasmic and spectral character of photography–pointed out also by Derrida—becomes the most vibrant. It is linked with the temporal paradox of something real and unreal at the same time, present and past, alive and dead. The ambiguities of the *no longer* (disappearance) versus the *still present* (appearing), *consigning* and *not resigning*, inhabit these spectral photographs of the detained and the disappeared that have become the densest symbol of the crusade of memory.

IA: There is a photograph reproduced in your *Margins and Institutions*, before the chapter entitled "History and Memories," that I have always thought to be a powerful allegory (see fig. 13.1). It is a picture taken in the Victoria neighborhood. In a deep plane that includes several spectators, the image is centered on a young man standing on a rung of a ladder. The ladder leans against a wall on which one sees a grandiose activist painting with the word *Victoria* (Victory). The word stands in violent contrast with the image, since both the youth on the ladder and the one next to him (this one placed in a slightly lateral and marginal position) are looking down, melancholy and defeated. The image of their bodies forces us to read the word *victory* as an anachronism, an inadequate image that can only be taken ironically or sarcastically. I want to know if the inclusion of this image in the book had a specific meaning, or if it evokes a particular reflection for you.

NR: The truth is that I had not noticed this *punctum* that you point out in that photo, the unhinging between the glorious symbolism of the word *victoria* and the dejected gesture of retreat by the muralist who painted it on the wall. The choice for that photo in the book made reference to a kind of popular/working-class art—muralism—that was an active part of that culture of resistance being produced in circuits rather distant from the ones of the *avanzada*. That photo illustrates the last chapter of *Margins and Institutions*, which accounts for the "deflation" of the *avanzada*, that is, the ways in which through the 1980s you could see the predominance of the call to leave behind ciphered languages and make art in solidarity with political contingency, an echo of banners of democratic restoration. It is interesting to relate the photo you mention to another picture in the book (the one in the chapter "Social exteriority as a support in the production of art") that also shows an intervention upon a working class wall, this time by a spraying that says: NO + (No mas; no more).

The No + action is a work begun in 1983 and authored by the group CADA (Collective Actions of Art). *No +* was its primary matrix of political resistance and social denouncing, one that entered into a process of collective resignification as the sprayings multiplied with an array of added words all over the city: No + violence, No + dictatorship, No + disappeared, No + hunger, culminating with the No + Pinochet often seen around the 1989 plebiscite. It seems to me that the work of No + can be understood as one of the points of fracture in the debate on art and politics taking place among ourselves in those years.

While the CADA group is generally included within the *avanzada* scene, for it shared with them a neo-experimentalism in supports and techniques that displaced the official tradition of the art system in favor of a new and insurgent *politics of the gaze*, at the same time there was an area of considerable polemic between the *avanzada* and the members of CADA (Raul Zurita, Diamela Eltit, Lotty Rosenfeld, Juan Castillo, Fernando Balcells), one that by the way turned out to be highly productive.

Some of us reproached CADA for its historical grandiosity or the messianism of Zurita's prophetic tone, overcharged with grandiloquence. On the other hand, the CADA group always maintained a connection with the collective, with community processes. They tended to find that the works of artists such as Carlos Leppe and Eugenio Dittborn, however subversive and innovative, still operated within a self-referential and elitist closure of art, in a kind of surplus value of the signature.

Almost all of the members of CADA considered No + to be their most radical work, precisely because it dissolved the specificity of art in the collectivity of the social body by erasing the individualism of authorship. However, still today I have disagreements with Diamela Eltit in this regard. On the one hand, it seems to me that contemporary theoretical debates have offered good arguments for the need to revise the avant-garde banner of art/life that culminates in a work such as No + (where art blends with daily social experience). The reintegration of that work into the continuum of existence erases the system of semiotic-institutional inscriptions that operate as borders in the tension between the autonomy and the heteronomy of art, a tension that makes possible aesthetic debate as such.

Even supposing that the goal of No + was to inhabit the social totality as a creative support and to incorporate community participation in the ongoing changes of art, it seems to me that they operated with a production system that was still all too mechanical (the No + sprayed on walls) and that was only duplicating the instrumentality of the political banner, rather than twisting it or diverting it toward heightened symbolic density. If we compare the univocity of the sign of the cross in the No + sprayings with the plurivocity of the + sign in the work of Lotty Rosenfeld ("A thousand crosses on the pavement") to which they are contemporary. It stands out, at least to me, that the mechanical character of the + sign in the CADA spraying reproduces the operative logic of protest muralism, along the lines of art "at the service of political contingency." It is a step behind work such as Rosenfeld's, whose artistic-political subversion unsettles the signifying rhetoric of the art of social protest. To me, once one equates art and politics (once one erases the discontinuity and fractures between the two series in order to fuse art with social totality on the basis of the same, undifferentiating support), one loses the conflicts between form and representation that constitute the densest aesthetic gesture in its capacity to displace, with its own vocabulary, the political-referential and the ideological.

We have taken a turn around the question of photography, but I think the displacement helps recreate the tone of the discussions we had in those years, and which made the Chilean *avanzada* adventure so unique.

IA: You mentioned both the reading of Walter Benjamin done from the standpoint of the visual arts in Chile, as well as photography's critique of painting as an individualistic and egocentric medium. Those were debates that framed the question of the subject in two different ways. The photography of that time made extensive use of close-ups, of ID cards, of absolutely individualized images of a specific subject, but all of its context tends to encourage us to read it as an interruptive, desubjectifying space, where anonymity and multitudes are produced and the marks of the individual subject dissolve. This is a curious tension between the microscopic focalizations on a subject (the subjectifying function of photography) and the dissolutions to which those gestures of subjectification are submitted. The uses to which *fotos carné* are put in that Chilean art seem to me to have been extremely effective in producing the tension between facial singularity and anonymity in the multitude.

NR: The relevance of the use of ID card photos in Chilean art has to do precisely with having detected this instance of exchange and blackmail exercised by the Law (as noted by Ronald Kay) between the particular-individual subject and the multiple-collective trespassing of the series. The latter movement turns identity into sheer anonymity and stereotype for classification in an archive, by placing emphasis on the deindividualization. A photograph can be totally personal yet produce a deindividualizing effect of machines of serialization; those Chilean works of the 1980s connected with the disarrayed actuality of the portraits of the detained and the disappeared displayed on photo posters carried around the city.

In Chile, unlike Argentina, the reflection and debate on the theme of public art and commemorative monuments has been quite scant. There are two foremost "sites of memory": Villa Grimaldi, a former torture chamber, and the General Cemetery, with its memorial to those disappeared and those publicly executed. There is, however, one work that seems to me more meaningful in its conceptualization of memory. Two photographers, Claudio Pérez and Rodrigo Gómez, built a Wall of Memory at the Bulnes Bridge, where several workers and priests were murdered by the military dictatorship, with their bodies subsequently being thrown into the Mapocho River. Pérez and Gómez's Wall of Memory consists of a mural of ceramic tiles on which they imprinted the faces of 936 detained or disappeared persons. Around that surface there are also several tiles on which nothing is inscribed. Their empty spaces correspond to the number of bodies not found: 256. From the outset it seemed to me that this notion of incomplete memory in process was strategic: an unfinished memory of disappearance brings with it materially the sign of what is absent. Unlike other monuments, plaques, and memorials that seal historical remembrance in a definitive representation that ultimately aims at closure, this photographic mural displays a narrative of waiting. It is a partial and suspended story that sets memory to work in an exercise of *plural* construction.

But let us return to photography. There is another element that creates unsettling tension in the mural. Some of the photos of the disappeared are ID card pictures, some others are from family albums. This maximizes the counterpoint between the pose of those who had already come in contact with the Law—from their having been interpolated in the ID card photos by one of its identity-capturing machines–and those who were depicted, unprepared, in a daily scene by a photographic snapshot. The normalcy of a life that reveals the daily scene and the helpless pose of the album photos portrays a subject located in a time *before* the drama, a subject who believed him/herself to be safe. The album photographs of the disappeared point to the tension between the subject's unconcerned face in the past time of the photographic take and the present, in which we observe the picture of someone abruptly converted into a fatal victim of history. In addition to this point, there is the emotion of seeing how the photographs of family albums attempted to challenge the serialization of nonidentity reproduced by the ID card photos, and thus restore and restitute the affective signs proper to a singular biographical existence. The Bulnes Bridge Wall of Memory exposes to everyone's sight these two photographic signifiers, the ID card and the family album. They register, to be sure, a battle between individuality and disidentification. Instead of concentrating memory in a site of retreat (for instance, a cemetery) the Bulnes Bridge Wall of Memory inserts the figure of the multitude and disseminates particles of remembrance across the urban flows of thousands of passers-by that both *gaze* and *are gazed at* by these photographed faces.

IA: At some point in the trajectory of postcoup Chilean art the interest in spaces of enclosure and social exclusion such as asylums heightens. This is manifest, for example, in the work done by photographer Paz Errázuriz with writer Diamela Eltit in *El infarto del alma.* It seems to me that madness takes on a remarkable charge as a signifier to be photographed. It seems equally meaningful that women artists have been the ones most consistently to dedicate attention to these spaces.

NR: We could not have ended this conversation without touching on these aspects of Paz Errázuriz's work that you mention. As the dictatorial city was regimented by military control, and displayed its imposed facade of "order and peace," Paz Errázuriz trod the streets in order to expose, with her camera, the breaches of misery and madness that inhabited the system. Her aesthetic of the peripheral, the borders and the margins, uncovered the needs of several sectors of the underworld (the circus, boxers, paper collectors, etc.), at the same time as it highlighted the vagrancy and extravagance of those who escaped unidimensional existence through transvestism or madness. She was able to focus on subjectivities in ruins, disassembled bodies, and wandering minds, which manifest symptoms of social exclusion that displace all social normativity.

In the book you mention, *El infarto del alma*, done with Diamela Eltit, Paz Errázuriz breaks with expressionism and investigates one of the most enigmatic facets of madness, that of love between mad people, often depicted in the pose of a hug that orders the picture, granting some meaning to those meaningless, convulsive biographies of minds completely abandoned to the misery of the psychiatric institution.

In fact it is not an accident, that two women have taken charge of the question of madness. In the constant imbalance of belonging and not belonging to the social order that seals the legality of a socio-masculine pact, the feminine is a force that, by resorting to an aesthetic of eccentricity and borders, gathers the wandering margins of identity to highlight everything that cultural systems of official representation leave aside—the unassimilated, the excluded, the residual.

IA: Now on the twenty-fifth anniversary of the first sparks of the *avanzada* scene, do you see any dominant tendency, or any trend that is particularly noteworthy in contemporary Chilean photography? Could you make an assessment of what appears most relevant to you from the recent past?

NR: In the current field of Chilean visual arts, there are many practices and installations that continue to rely on photography, be it in its condition of a specific language, be it as documentary reference. I find this dominant landscape of installations in Chile to be saturated by a sort of deconstructive formalism, expert in intertextual citation but not sufficiently audacious to explore loose connections with social imaginaries that go beyond the specific repertoire proper to the art of international catalogues. This is why, within the current scenario of art that ultimately is rather predictable, the work of Juan Castillo [a former member of CADA now living in Sweden] has caught my attention, because it has managed to break with the self-enclosure of academicism proper to most recent trends in Chilean art. In 2001 Juan Castillo exhibited in Santiago an art project entitled "Geometry and Neighborhood Ministry." It incorporated a wide range of actions: 1) he interviewed and photographed some dwellers of a marginal neighborhood in Santiago to record a video with them relating their dreams; 2) he documented photographically both the inside and the outside of their houses, creating an archive of images that was later uploaded onto a web page; 3) he carried out a video installation in a neighborhood gallery named Galería Metropolitana, where, among other materials, he displayed lamp boxes that carried the inscription of serigraphic images of those subjects who had been interviewed; 4) he projected those faces at night, in an abandoned hospital located in an apartment complex in that neighborhood; 5) he later made serigraphs of those faces, along with fragments of their dream narratives, and reproduced them on walls.

It seems to me that this is a use of the photographic medium that makes it traverse multiple systems of referentiality, of tastes, and of cultural habits around the heterogeneous corpus of "popular" forms. I liked the way in which photography visited a wide range of daily aesthetics and urban poetics, from the family portraits kept at home (photographed and captured abruptly in its peripheral domestic intimacy and electronically displaced onto a web page) to the serigraphic image of those anonymous beings who, while being displayed on city walls (December 2001), shared the streets with political posters of candidates running for Santiago's municipal elections. On the one hand, Juan Castillo's "Geometry and Neighborhood Ministry" resorted to photography to recode the popular at the impure and uneven intersection of daily imaginaries and media communication. On the other hand, the multiple localities where the project was carried out (art gallery, neighborhood hospital, walls and pavement of the city, the Internet) functioned as a democratizing measure that displayed those faces in registers that the aristocratic tradition of the fine arts has attempted to maintain separate: technology and folklore, the local and the international, community art and critical-experimental art.

References

Benjamin, Walter. "The Work of Art in the Age of its Technological Reproducibility." In *Selected Writings*, vol. 3, 1935–1938. Cambridge, MA, and London: Harvard University Press, 2002, 101–33.

Errázuriz, Paz, and Diamela Eltit. *El infarto del alma*. Santiago, Chile: Francisco Zegers, 1994.

Kay, Ronald. *Del espacio de acá: señales para una mirada americana*. Santiago, Chile: Editores Asociados, 1990.

Richard, Nelly. *Cuerpo correccional*. Santiago, Chile: Visual, 1980.

______. *La estratificación de los márgenes*. Santiago, Chile, and Melbourne, Australia: Francisco Zegers and Art and Text, 1989.

______. *La insubordinación de los signos: cambio político, transformaciones culturales y poéticas de la crisis*. Santiago, Chile: Cuarto Propio, 1994.

______. *The Insubordination of Signs: Political Change, Cultural Transformation, and Poetics of the Crisis*. Trans. Alice A. Nelson and Silvia Tandeciarz. Durham, NC: Duke University Press, 2004.

______. *Margins and Institutions: Art in Chile Since 1973*. Bilingual edition. Melbourne, Australia: Art and Text, 1986.

______. *Masculino/femenino: prácticas de la diferencia*. Santiago, Chile: Francisco Zegers, 1993.

______. *Masculine/Feminine: Practices of Difference*. Trans. Alice A. Nelson and Silvia Tandeciarz. Durham, NC: Duke University Press, 2004.

______. *Residuos y metáforas: ensayos de crítica cultural sobre el Chile de la transición*. Santiago, Chile: Cuarto Propio, 1998.

______, ed. *Arte en Chile desde 1973: escena de avanzada y sociedad*. Santiago, Chile: FLACSO, 1987.

Valdés, Adriana. *Composición de lugar: escritos sobre cultura*. Santiago, Chile: Universitaria, 1995.

General Bibliography

Selected Theory and Criticism of Photography

Baer, Ulrich. *Spectral Evidence: The Photography of Trauma*. Cambridge, MA: MIT Press, 2002.

Banta, Melissa, and Curtis Hinsley. *From Site to Sight: Anthropology, Photography and the Power of Imagery*. Cambridge, MA: Peabody Museum of Archaeology and Ethnography, 1986.

Barthes, Roland. *Camera Lucida*. Trans. Richard Howard. 1980. New York: Hill and Wang, 1981.

______. *Image-Text-Music*. Trans. Stephen Heath. New York: Hill and Wang, 1977.

Bazin, André. "The Ontology of the Photographic Image." In *What Is Cinema?* Vol. 1. Trans. Hugh Gray. Berkeley and Los Angeles: University of California Press, 1967, 9–16.

Benjamin, Walter. *Illuminations*. Ed. Hannah Arendt. Trans. Harry Zohn. New York: Shocken, 1969.

______. *One Way Street and Other Writings*. Trans. Edmund Jephcott, Kingsley Shorter. London: NLB, 1979.

Berger, John. *Ways of Seeing*. 1972. New York: Viking, 1973.

Berger, John, and Jean Mohr. *Another Way of Telling*. 1982. New York: Vintage, 1995.

Bolton, Richard, ed. *The Contest of Meaning: Critical Histories of Photography*. Cambridge, MA: MIT Press, 1989.

Bourdieu, Pierre, et al. *Photography: A Middle-Brow Art*. Stanford: Stanford University Press, 1990.

Brassai. *Proust in the Power of Photography*. 1997. Trans. Richard Howard. Chicago: University of Chicago Press, 2001.

Burgin, Victor, ed. *Thinking Photography*. London: MacMillan, 1982.

Cadava, Eduardo. *Words of Light: Theses on the Photography of History*. Princeton, NJ: Princeton University Press, 1997.

Edwards, Elizabeth, ed. *Anthropology and Photography 1860–1920*. New Haven, CT: Yale University Press, 1992.

Freedberg, David. *The Power of Images: Studies in the History and Theory of Response*. Chicago: University of Chicago Press, 1989.

Freund, Gisèle. *Photographie et société*. Paris: Seuil, 1974.

Frizot, Michel, ed. *A New History of Photography*. Köln: Konemann, 1998.

Goldberg, Vicki, ed. *Photography in Print: Writings from 1816 to the Present*. Albuquerque: University of New Mexico Press, 1981.

Grojnowski, Daniel. *Photographie et language*. Paris: José Corti, 2002.

Hamon, Philippe. *Imageries*. Paris: José Corti, 2001.

Hirsch, Marianne. *Family Frames: Photography, Narrative and Postmemory*. Cambridge, MA: Harvard University Press, 1997.

______, ed. *The Familial Gaze*. Hanover, NH: Dartmouth University Press, 1999.

Hughes, Alex, and Andrea Noble, eds. *Phototextualities: Intersections of Photography and Narrative*. Albuquerque: University of New Mexico Press, 2003.

Hunter, Jefferson. *Image and Word: The Interaction of Twentieth-Century Photographs and Texts*. Cambridge, MA, and London: Harvard University Press, 1987.

Hutcheon, Linda. *The Politics of Postmodernism*. London and New York: Routledge, 1989.

Jameson, Fredric. *Signatures of the Visible*. New York: Routledge, 1992.

Jenks, Chris, ed. *Visual Culture*. New York: Routledge, 1995.

Kramholtz, Jonathan. "Literature and Photography: The Captioned Vision vs. the Firm, Mechanical Impression." *Centennial Review* 24.4 (1980): 385–402.

Krauss, Rosalind. *The Originality of the Avant Garde and Other Modernist Myths*. Cambridge, MA: MIT Press, 1985.

Maynard, Patrick. *The Engine of Visualization: Thinking through Photography*. Ithaca, NY: Cornell University Press, 1997.

Miller, Denise, ed. *Photography's Multiple Roles: Art, Document, Market, Science*. New York: Museum of Contemporary Photography, 1988.

Mitchell, W. J. T. *Iconology: Image, Text, Ideology*. Chicago: University of Chicago Press, 1986.

______. *Picture Theory*. Chicago: University of Chicago Press, 1994.

______, ed. *The Language of Images*. Chicago: University of Chicago Press, 1980.

Newhall, Beaumont. *The History of Photography: From 1839 to the Present Day*. 5th ed. New York: Museum of Modern Art, 1997.

Ortel, Philippe. *La littérature à l'ère de la photographie*. Paris: Jacqueline Chambon, 2002.

Parr, Martin, and Gerry Badger. *The Photobook: A History*., Vol. 1. London: Phaidon, 2004.

Phillips, Ruth B., and Christopher B. Steiner, eds. *Unpacking Culture: Art and Commodity in Colonial and Postcolonial Worlds*. Berkeley: University of California Press, 1999.

The Photograph. Special issue of *Mosaic* 37.4 (2004).

Pinney, Christopher, and Nicolas Peterson, eds. *Photography's Other Histories*. Durham, NC: Duke University Press, 2003.

Price, Mary. *The Photograph: A Strange, Confined Space*. Stanford, CA: Stanford University Press, 1994.

Pultz, John. *The Body and the Lens: Photography 1839 to the Present*. London: Harry N. Abrams, 1995.

Rabb, Jane M., ed. *Literature and Photography/Interactions 1840–1990: A Critical Anthology*. Albuquerque: University of New Mexico Press, 1995.

Rosenblum, Naomi. *A World History of Photography*. New York: Abbeville Press, 1997.

Sampson, Gary D., and Eleanor M. Hight, eds. *Colonialist Photography: Imagining Race and Place*. London: Routledge, 2002.

Sontag, Susan. *On Photography*. New York: Farrar, Strauss and Giroux, 1973.

______. *Regarding the Pain of Others*. New York: Farrar, Strauss and Giroux, 2003.

Tagg, John. *The Burden of Representation: Essays on Photographies and Histories*. London: MacMillan, 1988.

Thélot, Jérôme. *Les inventions littéraires de la photographie*. Paris: PUF, 2003.

Wells, Liz. *Photography: A Critical Introduction*. 3d ed. London: Routledge, 2004.

______. *The Photography Reader*. London: Routledge, 2002.

Selected Scholarship on Latin American Photography

Alvarado, Margarita, and Ilonka Csillag, eds. *Historia de la fotografía en Chile: rescate de huellas en la luz*. Santiago, Chile: Centro Nacional Patrimonio Fotográfico, 2000.

Álvarez Bravo, Manuel. *In Focus: Manuel Álvarez Bravo*. Photographs from the J. Paul Getty Museum. Los Angeles: J. Paul Getty Museum, 2001.

Cadernos de Fotografia Brasileira 2. São Paulo 450 Anos. São Paulo, Brazil: Instituto Moreira Salles, 2004.

Castellanos, Alejandro. *Nacho López: antología de fetiches*. Xalapa, Veracruz, Mexico: Galería del Estado-IVEC/Ediciones Mar y Tierra, 1996.

Conger, Amy, ed. *Compañeras de Mexico: Women Photograph Women*. Riverside, CA: Regents of the University of California, 1990.

______. *Edward Weston in Mexico, 1923–1926*. Albuquerque: University of New Mexico Press, 1983.

Coronil, Fernando, ed. *Can the Subaltern See? Photography as History*. Special issue of *Hispanic American Historical Review* 81.4 (2004).

Debroise, Olivier. *Fuga mexicana: un recorrido por la fotografía en México*. Mexico City: Consejo Nacional para la Cultura y las Artes, 1994.

______. *Mexican Suite: A History of Photography in Mexico*. Austin: University of Texas Press, 2001.

Facio, Sara. *Leyendo fotos*. Buenos Aires: La Azotea, 2002.

Gutiérrez, Ramón, Patrícia Mendea, and Solange Zúñif. *Bibliografia sobre história da fotografia na América Latina/Bibliografía sobre la historia de la fotografía en América Latina*. Rio de Janeiro: FUNARTE; Buenos Aires: CEDODAL, 1997.

Gutiérrez Ruvalcaba, Ignacio. "A Fresh Look at the Casasola Archive." *History of Photography*. Special issue on *Mexican Photography* 20.3 (1996): 191–95.

Hopkinson, Amanda, ed. and trans. *Desires and Disguises: Latin American Women Photographers. London: Serpent's Tail*, 1992.

Jiménez, Blanca, and Samuel Villela. *Los Salmerón: un siglo de fotografía en Guerrero*. Mexico City: INAH, 1998.

Kay, Ronald. *Del espacio de acá: señales para una mirada americana*. Santiago, Chile: Editores Asociados, 1990.

Lara Klahr, Flora, and Marco Antonio Hernández. *El poder de la imagen y la imagen del poder: fotografías de prensa del porfiriato a la época actual*. Chapingo, Mexico: Universidad Autónoma Chapingo, 1985.

Levine, Robert. *Images of History: Nineteenth and Early Twentieth Century Latin American Photographs as Documents*. Durham, NC, and London: Duke University Press, 1989.

Martínez-San Miguel, Yolanda. "Visualizaciones de la identidad nacional desde la migración. Las fotografías de Jack y Pablo Delano." In *Caribe Two Ways: cultura de la migración en el Caribe insular hispánico*. San Juan, Puerto Rico: Callejón, 2003, 51–102.

Mordinski, Daniel. *La ciudad de las palabras: retratos fotográficos con textos de Cortázar, Sarabia, Amado, et al.* Bogotá,: Norma, 1996.

Mraz, John. "De la fotografia histórica: particularidad y nostalgia." *Nexos* 91 (July 1985): 9–12.

______. *Imágenes ferrocarrileras: una visión poblana. Lecturas Históricas de Puebla*, vol. 59. Puebla, Mexico: Gobierno del Estado de Puebla, 1991.

______. "Mexican History in Photographs." In *The Mexico Reader: History, Culture, Politics*. Ed. Gilbert Joseph and Timothy Henderson. Durham, NC: Duke University Press, 2002, 116–57.

______. *Nacho López, Mexican Photographer*. Minneapolis: University of Minnesota Press, 2003.

______. "Photographing Mexico." *Mexican Studies/Estudios Mexicanos* 17.1 (2001): 193–211.

______."Sebastião Salgado: Ways of Seeing Latin America." Third Text 16.1 (2002): 15–30.

Mulligan, Therese. Introduction. *Modotti y Weston: mexicanidad*. La Coruña and Madrid: Fundación Pedro Barrié de la Maza, 1999.

Poniatowska, Elena. "Some Women Photographers of Mexico/Algunas fotógrafas de México." In Conger, *Compañeras de Mexico*, 43–55.

______. *Tina Modotti and the Mexican Renaissance*. Intro. Sam Stourdzé. Essays Patricia Albers and Karen Cordero Reinman. Paris: Jean-Michel Place, 2000.

Poniatowska, Elena, and Amy Conger. *Compañeras de Mexico: Women Photographing Women*. Riverside, CA: University Art Gallery, University of California-Riverside, 1990.

Poole, Deborah. "Figueroa Aznar and the Cusco *Indigenistas*: Photography and Modernism in Early-Twentieth-Century Peru." In *Photography's Other Histories*. Ed. Christopher Pinney and Nicolas Peterson. Durham, NC: Duke University Press, 2003, 173–201.

______. *Vision, Race, and Modernity: A Visual Economy of the Andean Image World*. Princeton, NJ: Princeton University Press, 1997.

Rodriguez Villegas, Hernan. *Historia de la fotografía: fotógrafos en Chile durante el siglo XIX*. Santiago, Chile: Centro Nacional del Patrimonio Fotográfico, 2001.

Zamora, Lois Parkinson, and Wendy Watriss, eds. *Image and Memory: Photography from Latin America 1866–1994*. Austin: University of Texas Press, 1998.

Selected Photography and Writing Collections from Latin America

Allen, Paula. *Flores en el desierto/Flowers in the Desert*. Santiago, Chile: Cuarto Propio, 1999.

Andrade, Yolanda, and Carlos Monsivais. *Yolanda Andrade: los velos transparentes, las transparencias veladas*. Villahermoso, Mexico: Gobierno del Estado de Tabasco, 1988.

Blanco, José Joaquín. *Ciudad de México: espejos del siglo XX. Mexico: Era, 1998.*

Brenner, Anita. *Idols behind Altars*. New York: Payson and Clarke, 1929.

______. *The Wind That Swept Mexico: The History of the Mexican Revolution 1910–1942*. New York: Harper & Brothers, 1943.

Carpentier, Alejo, and Paolo Gasparini. *La cuidad de las columnas*. Barcelona: Lumen, 1970.

Casasola, Agustín Víctor. *Albúm histórico gráfico: contiene los principales sucesos acaecidos durante las épocas de Díaz, de la Barra, Madero, Huerta y Obregón*. Mexico City: Agustín V. Casasola Editor, 1921.

Casasola, Gustavo. "Gustavo Casasola: todos nuestro ayeres." In Cristina Pacheco, *La luz de méxico: entrevistas con pintores y fotógrafos*. Mexico City: Fondo de Cultura Económica, 1988, 116–125.

______. *Historia gráfica de la Revolución Mexicana*, vol. 3. Mexico City: Trillas, 1973.

______. *Historia gráfica de la Revolución Mexicana*. Multiple editions.

______. *Seis siglos de historia gráfica de México*. Multiple editions.

Cortázar, Julio. Alto el Perú. Photos Manja Offerhaus. Mexico City: Nueva Imagen, 1984.

______. *Buenos Aires, Buenos Aires*. Photos Sara Facio and Alicia D'Amico. Buenos Aires: Sudamericana, 1968.

______. *París: ritmos de una ciudad*. Photos Alecio d'Andrade. Barcelona: Edhasa, 1981.

______. *Prosa del observatorio*. 1972. Barcelona: Lumen, 1974.

______. *Territorios*. 1978. Mexico City: Siglo XXI, 1992.

Errázuriz, Paz, and Claudia Donoso. *La manzana de Adán/Adam's Apple*. Santiago, Chile: Zona Editorial, 1990.

Errázuriz, Paz, and Diamela Eltit. *El infarto del alma*. Santiago, Chile: Francisco Zegers Editor, 1994.

Facio, Sara. *Foto de escritor: 1969–1993*. Buenos Aires: Azotea, 1998.

______. *Retratos y autorretratos: escritores de América Latina*. Buenos Aires: Crisis, 1973.

Facio, Sara, and Alicia D'Amico. *Humanario*. Buenos Aires: La Azotea, 1976.

Facio, Sara, and Cristina Oribe. *Actos de fe en Guatemala*. Buenos Aires: La Azotea, 1989.

Fuentes, Carlos, and Carlos Fuentes Lemus. *Retratos en el tiempo*. Mexico City: Alfaguara, 1998.

Fusco, Coco. "Essential Differences: Photographs of Mexican Women." In *Illuminations: Women Writing on Photography from the 1850s to the Present*. Ed. Liz Heron and Val Williams. Durham, NC: Duke University Press, 1996, 434–41.

Gálvez, José, and Luis Alberto Urrea. *Vatos*. El Paso, TX: Cinco Puntos, 2000.

García Márquez, Gabriel, text. Hannes Wallrafen, photos. *The World of Márquez: A Photographic Exploration of Macondo*. London: Ryan, 1992.

González, Reynaldo, Gabriel García Márquez, and Gianfranco Gorgoni (photos). *Cubano 100%*. 1998.

Gutiérrez, Miguel. *La destrucción del reino*. Photos: Julio Olavarría. Lima: Milla Batres Editorial, 1992.

______. *El mundo sin Xóchitl*. Photos: Julio Olavarría. Lima: Fondo de Cultura Económica, 2001.

Lawless, Cecilia. *Making Home in Havana*. Photos Pietropaolo Vincenzo. New Brunswick, NJ: Rutgers University Press, 2002.

López, Nacho. *Yo, el ciudadano*. Comp. Fernando Benítez and Pablo Ortíz Monasterio. Mexico City: Fondo de Cultura Económica, 1984.

Ortíz Monasterio, Pablo, ed. *Jefes, héroes y caudillos: Archivo Casasola*. Mexico City: Fondo de Cultura Económica, 1985.

______. *La última ciudad*. Text José Emilio Pacheco. Mexico City: Casa de las Imágenes, 1996.

Poniatowska, Elena. *Luz y luna: las lunitas*. Photos Graciela Iturbide. Mexico City: Era, 1994.

______. *El último guajolote: memoria y olvido; imágenes de México*. Mexico City: Secretaria de Educación Pública, 1982.

Poniatowska, Elena, and Graciela Iturbide. *Juchitán de las mujeres*. Mexico City: Ediciones Toledo, 1989.

Rulfo, Juan. *Arquitectura de México: fotografías de Juan Rulfo*. Mexico City: Consejo Nacional para la Cultura y las Artes, 1994.

______.*Mexico: Juan Rulfo: Fotógrafo*. Text Carlos Fuentes. Barcelona: Lunwerg, 2001.

______. *Juan Rulfo's Mexico*. Text Carlos Fuentes. Washington, D.C.: Smithsonian, 2002.

Salgado, Sebastião. *Other Americas*. New York: Pantheon, 1986.

______. *Terra: Struggle of the Landless*. Poetry Chico Buarque. Preface José Saramago. London: Phaidon, 1997.

Salgado, Sebastião, Eduardo Galeano, and Fred Ritchin. *An Uncertain Grace*. NY: Aperture; San Francisco: San Francisco Museum of Modern Art, 1990.

Zurita, Raúl. *Anteparaíso*. Santiago, Chile: Editores Asociados, 1982.

______. *La vida nueva*. Santiago, Chile: Universitaria, 1997.

Selected Articles on Photography and Writing in Latin America

García Canclini, Néstor. "Estética e imagen fotográfica." *Casa de las Américas* 25.149 (1985): 7–14.

______. "Fotografía e ideología: sus lugares comunes." *Hueso Húmero* 10 (1981): 116–24.

Mraz, John. "What's Documentary about Photography? From Directed to Digital Photojournalism." *Zonezero Magazine*, <www.zonezero.com>, 2002.

Pérez de Mendiola, Marina. "Mexican Contemporary Photography: Staging Ethnicity and Citizenship." *boundary 2* 31.3 (2004).

Richard, Nelly. *La estratificación de los márgenes*. Santiago, Chile: Francisco Zegers; Melbourne, Australia: Art and Text, 1989.

______. *Margins and Institutions: Art in Chile since 1973*. Bilingual edition. Melbourne: Art and Text, 1986.

______. *Residuos y metáforas: ensayos de crítica cultural sobre el Chile de la transición*. Santiago, Chile: Cuarto Propio, 1998.

______. "Roturas, memorial y discontinuidades. (En homenaje a W. Benjamin)." *La insubordinación de los signos: cambio político, transformaciones culturales y poéticas de la crisis*. Santiago: Cuarto Propio, 1994.

Russek, Dan. "Verbal/Visual Braids: The Photographic Medium in the Work of Julio Cortázar." *Mosaic* 37.4 (2004): 71–86.

Schwartz, Marcy. "Cortázar under Exposure: Photography and Fiction in the City." In *Beyond the Lettered City: Latin American Literature and Mass Media*, ed. Debra Castillo and José Edmundo Paz-Soldán. New York: Garland, 2000, 117–38.

Tierney-Tello, Mary Beth. "Testimony, Ethics, and the Aesthetic in Diamela Eltit." *PMLA* 114.1 (1999): 78–96.

Contributors

Idelber Avelar is associate professor and chair of the Department of Spanish and Portuguese at Tulane University. He is the author of *The Untimely Present: Postdictatorial Latin American Fiction and the Task of Mourning* (Duke, 1999) and *The Letter of Violence: Essays on Narrative and Theory* (Palgrave, 2004). He is at work on two manuscripts: *A Genealogy of Latin Americanism* and *Rhythm and Nationhood in Brazilian Youth Music (1970–2000)*.

Janis Breckenridge is assistant professor at Hiram College. Her Ph.D. (University of Chicago, 2002) dissertation work explored representations of violence and human rights violations in contemporary Argentine women's fiction. Janis's current research project involves commemorative efforts in public spaces—especially Buenos Aires, New York City, and Oklahoma City.

Leo Cabranes-Grant is associate professor in the departments of Spanish and Portuguese and Dramatic Art at the University of California, Santa Barbara. He teaches Spanish and Latin-American drama, with an emphasis on performance and intercultural relations. He is also a playwright and director.

Esther Gabara is assistant professor of Romance Studies and Art and Art History at Duke University. Her work considers the relationship between literature and the visual arts in twentieth-century Latin America. She is currently completing a manuscript entitled *The Ethos of Modernism: Photographic Aesthetics in Mexico and Brazil.*

Amanda Hopkinson is director of the British Centre for Literary Translation at the University of East Anglia and a senior research fellow at Cardiff University. Her recent publications include short monographs on the Peruvian photographer Martín Chambi (Phaidon, 2001) and the Mexican Manuel Álvarez Bravo (Phaidon, 2002) and a series of extended essays for the Routledge *Encyclopedia of Latin American and Caribbean Culture* (Routledge, 2003) and for the *Oxford Book of the Photograph* (Oxford).

John Mraz is a research professor at the Instituto de Ciencias Sociales y Humanidades, Universidad Autónoma de Puebla (Mexico). He has published widely on the uses of photography, cinema, and video in recounting the histories of Mexico and Cuba, directed award-winning documentary videotapes, and curated international exhibits of photography. He recently published *Nacho López, Mexican Photographer* (University of Minnesota Press, 2002).

Magdalena Perkowska-Álvarez is associate professor of Spanish at Hunter College (CUNY). She is currently completing a book manuscript entitled *Hybrid (Hi)stories: Challenging Postmodern Theories of History in the Latin American Historical Novel, 1985–2000*.

Elissa J. Rashkin is an independent scholar and writer. She is the author of *Women Filmmakers in Mexico: The Country of Which We Dream* (University of Texas Press, 2001). She is currently working on a project on the Estridentista movement in Mexico.

Dan Russek is lecturer of Spanish Literature at the University of Victoria, British Columbia. He has published essays on Cortázar, Valéry, David Lynch, and W. Eugene Smith, as well as poetry in Spanish. His current research revolves around the interactions between modern Latin American literature and photography.

Jorge Schwartz is professor emeritus of Spanish American Literature at the Universidade de São Paulo. His books include *Vanguardia y cosmopolitismo* (1993) and *Las vanguardias latinoamericanas* (2002). He has also curated *De la antropofagia a Brasilia* (2000) and edited *Borges no Brasil* (2001) and *Caixa Modernista* (2003).

Marcy Schwartz is associate professor of Spanish and acting director of Latin American Studies at Rutgers University–New Brunswick. She is the author of *Writing Paris: Urban Topographies of Desire in Contemporary Latin American Fiction* (SUNY, 1999) and coeditor with Daniel Balderston of *Voice-Overs: Translation and Latin American Literature* (SUNY, 2002).

Mary Beth Tierney-Tello is associate professor and chair of the Department of Hispanic and Italian Studies at Wheaton College in Massachusetts. She is the author of *Allegories of Transgression and Transformation: Latin American Women Writing under Dictatorship* (SUNY, 1996).

Index

English translations supplied by the authors are presented in brackets following the primary entry. Bilingual titles are in italics.

www.ingramcontent.com/pod-product-compliance
Lightning Source LLC
LaVergne TN
LVHW081258100826
845148LV00005B/903

* 9 7 8 0 8 2 6 3 3 8 0 8 2 *